Remaking the Chinese State

T0316018

After more than twenty years of economic and political reform, China is a vastly different country than the one left by Mao. Almost all of the characteristic policies, institutions, and practices of the Maoist era have been abandoned. The goals of the revolution in China's domestic and foreign policies have been replaced by emphasis on economic modernization. It has sustained a remarkably high rate of growth, allowed a private sector to re-emerge and gradually supplant the public sector, increased the level of foreign trade and investment, and joined a host of international organizations concerned with economic and military affairs. Many in Chinese society enjoy higher standards of living, migrate in search of better paying jobs, and enjoy opportunities for foreign and domestic travel and access to higher education and new sources of information. On almost any dimension, China today is a more vibrant, dynamic, and colorful place than it was at the end of the Maoist era.

Despite these dramatic changes, other fundamental features of domestic politics and foreign policy remain unchanged in China. The Communist Party remains the pre-eminent political authority and continues to prevent the formation of new organizations outside its control. Local officials promote economic growth but have not fully embraced the logic of the market economy. China remains wary of international pressures, whether economic, political, or military, and its ideological rhetoric often obscures its pragmatic behavior.

This book explores the strategies of reform in China and their implications for its domestic and foreign policies. Although these reforms have been cautious and incremental in nature, they have been radical in their cumulative impact. This book avoids simple generalizations about the nature of Chinese politics or China's future path. Instead it offers comparisons and contrasts between policy areas and regions within China to create a more complete picture of this complex and ever-changing country.

Chien-min Chao is Professor and Director of the Sun Yat-sen Graduate Institute of Social Sciences and Humanities at Chengchi University, Taiwan. He has published widely on Chinese politics. **Bruce J. Dickson** is Director of the Sigur Center for Asian Studies and the Asian Studies Program in the Elliott School of International Affairs, and Associate Professor in Political Science and International Affairs at the George Washington University. He is the author of *Democratization in China and Taiwan: The adaptability of Leninist parties* and *Communism in China: Institutional and comparative perspectives*.

Asia's Transformations

Edited by Mark Selden

Binghamton University and Cornell University, USA

The books in this series explore the political, social, economic, and cultural consequences of Asia's twentieth-century transformations. The series emphasizes the tumultuous interplay of local, national, regional, and global forces as Asia bids to become the hub of the world economy. While focusing on the contemporary, it also looks back to analyze the antecedents of Asia's contested rise.

This series comprises two strands: *Asia's Transformations* aims to address the needs of students and teachers, and the titles will be published in hardback and paperback. Titles include:

Debating Human Rights
Critical essays from the United States and Asia
Edited by Peter Van Ness

Hong Kong's History
State and society under colonial rule
Edited by Tak-Wing Ngo

Japan's Comfort Women
Yuki Tanaka

Opium, Empire and the Global Political Economy
Carl A. Trocki

Chinese Society
Change, conflict and resistance
Edited by Elizabeth J. Perry and Mark Selden

Mao's Children in the New China
Voices from the Red Guard generation
Yarong Jiang and David Ashley

Remaking the Chinese State
Strategies, society, and security
Edited by Chien-min Chao and Bruce J. Dickson

Routledge Studies in Asia's Transformations is a forum for innovative new research intended for a high-level specialist readership, and the titles will be available in hardback only. Titles include:

1 The American Occupation of Japan and Okinawa*
Literature and Memory
Michael Molasky

2 Koreans in Japan*
Critical voices from the margin
Edited by Sonia Ryang

3 Internationalizing the Pacific
The United States, Japan and the Institute of Pacific Relations, 1919–1945
Tomoko Akami

4 Imperialism in South East Asia
A fleeting, passing phase
Nicholas Tarling

*Now available in paperback

Remaking the Chinese State

Strategies, society, and security

Edited by Chien-min Chao and Bruce J. Dickson

Routledge
Taylor & Francis Group

LONDON AND NEW YORK

First published 2001
by Routledge
2 Park Square, Milton Park, Abingdon, Oxon OX14 4RN

Simultaneously published in the USA and Canada
by Routledge
711 Third Avenue, New York, NY 10017

Routledge is an imprint of the Taylor & Francis Group

Typeset in Baskerville by Taylor & Francis Books Ltd

British Library Cataloguing in Publication Data
A catalogue record for this book is available from the British
Library

Library of Congress Cataloging-in-Publication Data
Remaking the Chinese state: strategies, society, and security/edited by
Chien-min Chao and Bruce J. Dickson.
(Asia's transformations)
Includes bibliographical references and index.
1. China–Politics and government–1976–. 2. China–Economic
policy–1976–2000. I. Zhao, Jianmin, 1954– II. Dickson, Bruce J.
III. Series.
JQ1510 .R463 2001
320.951–dc21   2001019959

ISBN 0–415–26026–4

Contents

Illustrations

Figures

Tables

Contributors

Kenneth W. Allen focuses on China's foreign military relations and the PLA Air Force. He served in the US Air Force from 1971 to 1992, including assignments in Taipei and Beijing. He received a BA from the University of California at Davis, a BA from the University of Maryland in Asian Studies, and an MA from Boston University in International Relations.

Robert F. Ash holds the Chiang Ching-kuo Chair of Taiwan Studies at the School of Oriental and African Studies (SOAS) in the University of London. At SOAS, he is also Coordinator of the EU–China Academic Network (ECAN), and he was formerly Director of the Contemporary China Institute. He has published widely on agricultural development in China.

Chien-min Chao is Professor and Director of the Sun Yat-sen Graduate Institute of Social Sciences and Humanities at National Chengchi University in Taiwan. He has been a visiting distinguished professor at The George Washington University. His publications include *Taiwan and Mainland China: Relations and Foreign Competition* (1992), *Authoritarian Politics* (1994), *An Analysis of Contemporary Chinese Politics* (1997), and *Cross-Strait Relations and Taiwan's Foreign Policies* (2000). He is also co-editor of the book *The ROC on the Threshold of the 21st Century: A Paradigm Reexamined* (1999).

Jae Ho Chung is Associate Professor of International Relations at Seoul National University, Korea. He is the author of *Central Control and Local Discretion in China* (2000) and editor of *Cities in China* (1999) and *Provincial Strategies of Economic Reform in Post-Mao China* (1998). He is currently working on South Korea–China relations during 1949–99 and on China's civil aviation industry.

Bruce J. Dickson is Associate Professor of Political Science and International Affairs and Director of the Sigur Center for Asian Studies and the Asian Studies Program in the Elliott School of International Affairs at The George Washington University. He is the author of *Democratization in China and Taiwan: The Adaptability of Leninist Parties* (1997), and articles in *Asian Survey*, *China Quarterly*, *Comparative Political Studies*, *Political Science Quarterly*, and other publications. He is also Associate Editor of the journal *Problems of Post-Communism*.

Lowell Dittmer is Professor of Political Science and former Chair of the Center for Chinese Studies at the University of California at Berkeley. He is author (with Samuel Kim) of *China's Quest for National Identity* and four other books analyzing Chinese domestic and foreign policy, as well as many scholarly articles.

Bates Gill is Senior Fellow in Foreign Policy Studies and inaugural Director of the Center for Northeast Asian Policy Studies at the Brookings Institution in Washington, DC. A specialist in East Asian foreign policy and politics, his work focuses on security and military–technical issues, especially with regard to China. His next book, *Contrasting Visions: United States, China, and World Order*, will be published by the Brookings Institution Press in 2001.

David S. G. Goodman is Director of the Institute for International Studies, University of Technology, Sydney. His most recent publications include *Social and Political Change in Revolutionary China* and *Shanxi in Reform: Everyday Life in a North China Province*.

Teh-chang Lin is an Associate Professor in the Graduate Institute of Mainland China Studies, National Sun Yat-sen University, Kaohsiung, Taiwan. He has published many articles and books on the issues of foreign economic assistance, cross-Strait political and economic relations, and economic development in mainland China.

James Mulvenon is an Associate Political Scientist at the RAND Corporation in Washington, DC, specializing in Chinese military and security affairs. He has recently completed a book-length manuscript on the Chinese military's business empire, entitled *Soldiers of Fortune* (2000). His current research focuses on Chinese strategic weapons doctrines (information warfare and nuclear warfare), theater ballistic missile defenses (TBMD) in Asia, Chinese military commercial divestiture, and the military and civilian implications of the information revolution in China.

Chong-hai Shaw received his Ph.D. in history from St Louis University, USA. He is now a Professor at Sun Yat-sen Graduate Institute of Social Science and Humanities, National Chengchi University, Taiwan. His research fields are cross-Strait relations, Sino-American relations, the ROC government and constitution, nationalism, international politics, and studies on ethnic problems.

Dorothy J. Solinger is Professor of Political Science at the University of California, Irvine, and Adjunct Senior Research Scholar at the East Asian Institute, Columbia University. Her most recent book is *Contesting Citizenship in Urban California* (1999) and she is a co-editor of *States and Sovereignty in the Global Economy* (1999). Her current research is on unemployment in China.

Dali L. Yang is Associate Professor of Political Science and Director of the Committee on International Relations at the University of Chicago. His books include *Calamity and Reform in China* (1996), *Beyond Beijing* (1997), and a forthcoming volume on governance and state–business relations.

Acknowledgements

This book originated in an international conference in Taipei organized by the Sun Yat-sen Graduate Institute for Social Sciences and Humanities, National Chengchi University, in April 1999. Over twenty overseas scholars joined with a large number of Taiwan scholars, and participated in the event representing views from the United States, the United Kingdom, Hong Kong, Australia, the Republic of Korea, and Singapore. Thanks are due to all of those who presented their research papers at the conference and to all who served as formal as well as informal discussants. We would like to express our gratitude to Dr Ting-wong Cheng, President of National Chengchi University, and Dr Hsiao-hung Nancy Chen, Dean of the College of Social Sciences, National Chengchi University, for their support. Appreciation goes especially to Dr I. Yuan of the Institute of International Relations for his assistance in making this project possible. Thanks are due, too, to Hui-gen Cheng and Shi-gen Hsu for helping to organize the conference, and to Mark Selden, who as series editor of the *Asia's Transformations* book series at Routledge provided valuable advice to make the volume more presentable. We also want to thank Benita Wong for her careful copy-editing of the original manuscript.

Part of the financial support to bring scholars to the conference from abroad was provided by the Mainland Affairs Council of the Republic of China.

Finally, the editors gratefully acknowledge the assistance rendered by the Sun Yat-sen Graduate Institute and the Sigur Center for Asian Studies of the George Washington University.

Chien-min Chao
Bruce Dickson

Introduction
Remaking the Chinese state

Bruce J. Dickson and Chien-min Chao

The impact of more than two decades of reform in China has become a familiar story, so familiar in fact that it is easy to lose sight of how spectacular and sweeping the changes have been. Almost all of the characteristic policies, institutions, and practices of the Maoist era have been abandoned. The central planning system is being replaced by the use of the market to set prices and allocate most goods and services. The political campaigns and policies of class struggle used to divide society and allow the state's unchallenged hegemony over society, but no longer. State ownership in agriculture and industry has rapidly faded: the communes gave way to private farming, and the expanding private sector has gradually outstripped the state-owned enterprises in total production, rates of growth, and job creation. Policies of self-reliance have been replaced by the enthusiastic pursuit of foreign trade and investment. The registration system which bound people to residences in cities and the countryside has broken down, allowing large numbers of migrant workers to seek higher paying jobs elsewhere in the country. The frozen wages, work points, and rationing of food and other consumer goods are relics of the past. Today, most Chinese enjoy higher standards of living, including rising incomes, greater housing space, access to travel and sources of information, better education, and the availability of a growing diversity of consumer goods, most available through the market with little state interference. On almost any dimension, China today is a more vibrant, dynamic, and colorful place than it was at the end of the Maoist era.

The reforms in China had a variety of motivations, centered on the common theme of creating a more modern country with higher standards of living. State leaders and members of society alike had grown weary of the political campaigns that characterized the Maoist approach to policy implementation. The convulsive swings of policy, from "leftist" upheavals to periods of recovery, seemed arbitrary, even capricious, by the late Maoist era. Many of the leaders prominent in the post-Mao period had been victimized by one or more of Mao's ideological campaigns, beginning with the anti-rightist movement of 1957 and ending with the Cultural Revolution decade (1966–76). They experienced for themselves how Mao's emphasis on political propriety prevented economic development and damaged relations between state and society. While Mao and other party leaders led China into the disastrous policies of the Great Leap

Forward and the Cultural Revolution, the rest of the world, in particular China's East Asian neighbors, experienced phenomenal growth, leaving China economically, technologically, and culturally behind. The post-Mao reforms were designed to reduce the role of the state in the economy and the everyday lives of the Chinese people in order to catch up to international standards. The result has been dramatic.

Despite the many changes brought on by the reform era, one common link has been the continued role of the Chinese Communist Party (CCP). Although less intrusive than in the Maoist era, the state is none the less interested in preserving its power. Indeed, the various economic, political, and social reforms of the post-Mao era have been designed to enhance, not reduce, the state's power. The CCP hoped that it could increase its legitimacy and strengthen its authority by surrendering some of its control over the economy and society, allowing economic growth and a more lively cultural life to emerge. It has succeeded in part of this strategy: economic growth averaged almost 10 percent during the first twenty years of the reform era. A much greater array of consumer goods and services is available, and the market has steadily replaced the state's bureaucratic channels as the medium of distribution. The cultural realm has been reinvigorated, with renewed interest in Chinese traditions, as well as foreign (both Western and Asian) fashions, music, literature, movies, and other forms of artistic expression.

Despite these accomplishments, many question whether the CCP's primary goal – enhancing its own legitimacy – has been realized. In fact, the reform era has led to several negative and even unintended consequences that have detracted from this goal. The policies of reform and opening (*gaige kaifang*) have allowed rapid growth but also unchecked corruption by party and government officials. Privatization has led to greater growth and dynamism, but also greater insecurity among workers who no longer have their jobs and benefits guaranteed. The emphasis given to the industrial and commercial sectors has contributed to income gaps between the rural and urban areas. The withdrawal of the state from economic and social activity has limited its ability to monitor developments in enterprises and everyday life. The increased importance of market exchanges has reduced the state's role in the distribution of goods and services. The decentralization of decision-making authority to local governments has spurred growth-oriented policies, but may have also reduced Beijing's capacity to enforce its policies over local officials. In short, rather than rejuvenating the state, the consequence of the post-Mao reforms may be its gradual disintegration.[1] This "disintegration of the state" has little in common with Marx's prescription for the "withering away of the state," which he anticipated as leading to a communist utopia. The disintegration thesis, in contrast, anticipates the collapse of the communist system, but makes no predictions of what will come after.

Not all observers are persuaded by the argument that China is falling apart. Some argue that the loss of central control is exaggerated and ignores the variety of resources enjoyed by the center which allow it to remain influential.[2] Others, including several of the contributors to this volume, argue that the CCP has initiated a variety of political and administrative reforms that give the state more flexible control over the economy and society and also preserve central influence over local governments.[3] According to this argument, China has experienced much more political reform than most observers give it credit for, and these reforms may allow the CCP to adapt to the new economic and social environment. In addition, many outside of China are concerned that China's modernization will pose threats to its neighbors and other countries in the Asia–Pacific region. They tend to see a country unified by nationalism and strengthened by new military technology, but in the process ignore many of the internal trends in China.[4] Whether you are a scholar, journalist, businessperson, or government analyst, an understanding of the impact of economic reform on both the state and society is necessary to fully evaluate the course of reform and to anticipate what path China may follow in the immediate future.

Many in China are more concerned with the moral decay of the reform era than with the political consequences of the reforms. The reforms have set the stage for the disintegration of the state but have also destroyed the basic social fabric, leaving society with few shared values. The socialist value system of the Maoist era has been discredited and abandoned, but new values based on a market system have not yet fully taken hold. Some in China remain nostalgic for the Maoist era and committed to the communal ideals of that period. Many others do not seek a return to the policies of the past, which are associated with economic stagnation and political insecurity, but nevertheless mourn the loss of a shared belief system to bind the country together. This has been a familiar complaint since the attacks on the Confucian order that culminated in the May 4th movement and remains a cause of concern today. The success of economic reforms has only managed to aggravate the situation further. The biggest problem for "socialism with Chinese characteristics" may be that it has deprived the country of a moral basis.

To fill the void, nationalism has emerged as a prominent social trend and perhaps an influence on China's international behavior.[5] This has led to seemingly contradictory impulses. One the one hand, China needs Western technology and capital to continue its economic modernization, and many Chinese seek a Western education or a job with a Western company in China. On the other hand, China experiences periodic waves of anti-foreign sentiments when the pride of the Chinese people is damaged by real or perceived insults from the West (for instance, criticism of China's human rights record, the bombing of the Chinese embassy in Yugoslavia, and pressures to modify China's trade and military practices). The West's appeal as an alternative system of values is undermined by these sentiments, leaving many Chinese admiring the West for its promise and potential but also resentful of its treatment of China.[6]

The chapters in this volume do not answer the question "where is China going?" but they provide the information needed to address this important issue. In fact, the chapters point out that China's future is so uncertain because the trends of the recent past have been so ambiguous and even contradictory. The lessons we can draw about China's recent past vary by issue area and by region within China.

Incremental reforms, radical changes

One of the most important themes of the reform era, and of the chapters in this volume, is that although the reforms have been cautious and incremental in nature, they have been radical in their cumulative impact. As many have noted, China's post-Mao leaders had no blueprint for reform, and no model to follow. There was no way to predict in December 1978 that the initial reforms announced at the historic Third Plenum of the 11th Central Committee would ultimately lead to the state of affairs twenty years later, where virtually all prices are set by the market, where the private sector accounts for more than half of total production and will continue to grow even larger in the years to come, or where the transition from collectivized farming has led not only to the industrialization of the countryside but to the creation of large and growing numbers of migrant workers seeking jobs in the cities. Indeed, these were not the logical nor the inevitable outcomes of the initial reforms. Rather, they were the result of cumulative steps and often unintended consequences. The reform process generated its own momentum and its own constituency of supporters, as one set of changes created both new problems and new opportunities for more reform.

Many of the reform policies that have attracted so much attention in the post-Mao era had their origins in the early 1970s and even in the early 1960s when local officials experimented with various policies to recover from the economic disaster of the Great Leap Forward. Although the conventional dating of the start of reforms in 1978 is not totally precise, the Third Plenum of the 11th Central Committee in December 1978 does symbolize the fundamental shift in the policy preferences of China's central leaders that consequently led to a shift in officially sanctioned policies. The steady elimination of the beneficiaries of the Cultural Revolution at the central and local levels during the late 1970s and early 1980s created a coalition of officials in favor of continual reform and an end to the wild swings of policy that characterized the late Mao years. China's leaders continued to argue over the proper pace and extent of reform policies throughout the post-Mao period, but the general direction of reform was already apparent back in 1978.

Because China's reforms lacked a blueprint, many national policies were set only after extensive local experimentation. Local officials, farmers, entrepreneurs, and others took advantage of the ever-changing boundary between what was permissible and what was prohibited to try new policies and practices, often taking the reforms farther and faster than the divisive central elites were willing to go. Whether in the decollectivization of agriculture, the promotion of local industrialization, the adjustment of central–local relations, and more recently in the practice of village-level self-government, it was the localities that took the lead in innovating and experimenting with new economic, political, and social arrangements. Some of these experiments were later sanctioned by the center and implemented on a nationwide basis; others became the basis for competing models of local development. One consequence of this competition has been tremendous variation in both procedures and results, often depending on pre-existing conditions, such as natural resource endowments or the legacy of Maoist policies. One challenge facing scholars and other analysts is to find patterns in these local variations. Several authors in this volume attempt to show some of the patterns and the reasons for them.

Although the reforms have been described and defended by China's leaders in terms of theories and principles, they have been primarily pragmatic, especially in their implementation. This has been true in both foreign and domestic policies. Lowell Dittmer shows that China's foreign policy behavior in the post-Mao era has been reactive, with changes in fundamental policies a result of decisions made by other countries. For instance, the rising power of the United States beginning with the Reagan administration led China to adapt a more neutral stance toward the superpowers. Although China has given rhetorical support for Third World nations and causes, it has been reluctant to play a more active role as a leader of the Third World, preferring to engage in bilateral relations or to be active only when issues affecting its immediate interests arise (such as when military intervention may set a precedent for China's treatment of Tibet and Taiwan). Just as domestic reforms seem not to be guided by an explicit vision of a "good society" yet to come, so too its foreign policy seems to be guided by pragmatic rather than principled considerations.

The incremental and pragmatic nature of reform is best illustrated in the CCP's political reforms. The purpose of political reform was not to decrease or challenge the CCP's power, but to enhance it.[7] Any political reform must allow the CCP to maintain social and political stability in order to promote economic growth while at the same time strengthening the party's own legitimacy. There were no successful models of this balancing act from other countries, so China's reformers adopted a more incremental approach. In trying to enhance its political legitimization, the CCP emphasized various reform policies rather than specific theories or ideological goals. Local experiments with reform policies were later legitimated by the center.

One clear manifestation of these trends is that the control (or ownership) of resources matters less than who has discretion over their use. David Goodman notes the complexity of economic categories at a time when property rights have not been clearly defined by law. He finds that entrepreneurship exhibited by enterprise managers is more important than whether the enterprise is a state-owned, collective, or private enterprise. These categories do not have clear borders, either conceptually or empirically in China; what matters most is not the abstract and often vague issue of ownership but the quality of the individuals actually in charge of production and marketing. Some state-owned enterprise (SOE) managers have been more entrepreneurial in innovating and assuming risk. They may not own the property, but they have discretion over its use and in some cases make good use of it.

The contentious issue of central–local relations offers another example of discretion being more important than formal control. Jae Ho Chung is critical of many studies that analyze central–local relations solely in fiscal terms, especially those that track the percentage of taxes and profits controlled by the central and provincial governments. More important than the distribution of resources is the discretion in their use. Local governments have been given much more leeway in the post-Mao era than before. During the Maoist era, local governments retained a high share of revenues but had little discretion in how that money was put to use, due to ideological constraints, the planned economy, and Beijing's political dominance. In the reform era, local governments have become more entrepreneurial in their actions and have much greater discretion over the resources at their disposal. According to Chung, the center is willing to accept local deviations so long as they are growth oriented. However, it is not willing to tolerate deviations in political and organizational matters. This separation of economic and political change is a hallmark of the reform era, as will be discussed in more detail below.

These examples illustrate one of the overriding themes of the reform era, and of the findings of this volume: reform has been incremental and gradual, with national policies decided only after evaluating the results of local experiments. Nevertheless, the changes they have brought about have been staggering and inconceivable when China's leaders launched the reform process in the late 1970s.

Reform became the goal, not the means to an end

A second prominent theme, following from the first, is that the goals of reform have gradually and subtly changed. At the beginning of the reform era, the goal of reform was to strengthen socialism, and by extension the communist system in China and the CCP in particular. But in more recent years, the emphasis has changed. Rather than having the reforms strengthen socialism, more and more of the socialist system is being either transformed or abandoned in order to facilitate economic reform and opening and to sustain their momentum. Economic reform and opening are no longer just a means to an end, but the goal itself.[8]

This shift of goals is seen in both administrative and economic policies. Dali Yang's investigation of the political economy of government reforms shows how local initiative contributed to this change. As was true for economic reform, innovations in administrative and bureaucratic reforms were also at the initiative of local governments. He finds that the administrative reforms of the central government were cautious in their intent and limited in their results. Most significantly, the size of staffs actually grew despite the claims of bureaucratic streamlining. Local governments were more anxious to achieve real reductions in the number of both administrative organs and staff in order to facilitate marketizing reforms. Whereas Deng Xiaoping's goal in economic reform was to strengthen and rejuvenate the state, over time the goal of government, especially at the local level, changed to promote the reform process.

While tracing the dramatic improvements in agricultural production and rural consumption, Robert Ash cautions against characterizations of rural reform as unfettered marketization. He shows that an increasing share of agricultural goods came to be distributed through free markets during the reform era. But free markets were not the only channel for distribution: into the early 1990s, the vast majority of marketed grain and cotton was being sold through state commercial channels. He also notes the irony that despite the move to private farming, farmers still rely on the state more than the market for the supply and distribution of agricultural and consumer goods. Nor has the decollectivization of agriculture ended the state's exploitation of farmers. The practice of local officials issuing IOUs instead of paying cash for compulsory sales of grain and other agricultural goods to the state is an ongoing cause of friction and protest in the countryside, as are illegal extractions, such as excessive taxes and fees. Moreover, the end of collectivized agriculture has also been accompanied by the decline of communal projects, especially irrigation. Private farming has increased the incentives for greater production, and indeed the gross value of agriculture output has increased markedly throughout the reform era, but it has also made the introduction of technical improvements more difficult.

One exception to this trend of increased emphasis on marketization as a goal unto itself was the People's Liberation Army's experience with commercialism. Unlike other chapters which show a more linear process of ever greater commercialization, James Mulvenon's shows that the PLA's commercial activities have come full circle. The PLA had a long tradition of economic activities, even before the reform era. Beginning from the need to support the troops due to insufficient budgets, the PLA's economic operation gradually expanded to large-scale trade, investment, and commercial activities. The scope of these activities led to increasing dissatisfaction among the CCP's top leaders, who were concerned about reports of corruption and the potential for the military's commercial operations usurping its core mission of providing for the national defense. In 1998, Jiang Zemin ordered the PLA to dissolve its commercial empire. Whether the PLA complied in full with this order remains a point of contention, but in detailing the rise and fall of the PLA's entrepreneurial pursuits, Mulvenon shows how they provide a rare exception to the post-Mao revolution of commercialization.

Although China's leaders have developed a greater commitment to economic growth as their primary goal, there is less concern for what this growth should lead to. There has been little public debate over what a "good society" will look like, as is so common in the West. China's leaders do not seem to have a specific goal in mind for what rapid growth and modernization should lead to. This is generally a good thing, allowing policies to respond more flexibly to changing conditions. In sharp contrast to the Maoist era, there is no utopia against which to measure progress. Back in 1987, Zhao Ziyang remarked that he could not define socialism, and was not sure what it was. The message was that reform policies were not to be judged by how well they conformed to some notion of socialist orthodoxy, but how well they delivered the goods. Zhao was later castigated for making such statements, but in the post-Deng era it is even less clear what socialism is, even with Chinese characteristics.

Indeed, as many have noted, the tacit social contract of the reform era is a tradeoff of economic and political goals: so long as the state policies create growth and higher standards of living, society will not demand changes in the political institutions and distribution of political power. So far, this separation of politics and economics has worked, but will it continue to do so? Dali Yang argues in his chapter that the strategy of government reforms can allow the political system to adapt in minor ways without requiring fundamental change. In contrast, Teh-chang Lin offers a possible scenario that could lead to more widespread demands for political change. He argues that successful reform of SOEs may lead to important changes in state–society relations. As workers become less dependent on the state in favor of business associations and other intermediary organizations, they will also become more responsible for improving their own standards of living and quality of life. If this develops, they may begin to interact differently with the state, and be more willing to make new demands on it because they derive fewer benefits from it. The results of SOE reform are not yet known, and it may be several years before we can properly evaluate this intriguing scenario, but a more demanding society may be one of the unintended consequences of SOE reform.

One possible reason why this tradeoff of economic and political goals has worked so well up to now is suggested by David Goodman: there is a growing overlap of political and economic elites in China. In the Maoist era, there was a nearly perfect overlap of political and economic elites, especially after private businesses were eliminated in the 1950s. As the post-Mao reforms progressed and a private sector began to re-emerge, a separate but hardly autonomous realm of economic elites also began to take shape. Many enterprise owners and managers are the offspring of CCP members, and a good number belong to the party themselves. Others are being coopted into the party due to their rising economic influence. The beneficiaries of economic reform, in other words, have close ties to the existing political system and have little incentive to seek funda-mental change. This finding is consistent with the conclusions of previous scholarship: China's entrepreneurs are unlikely to be agents of political change. Instead, they seek to be partners with the state, not rivals or competitors.[9] Like China's leaders, China's entrepreneurs are concerned primarily with economic reform for its own sake.

Explaining regional variations

One of the important aspects of scholarship on the post-Mao period is the increasing attention paid to variations across regions and issue areas. Opportunities for extensive fieldwork and access to local histories and statistical data allow us to get a deeper appreciation for the complexities of contemporary China. This has led to a series of rich case studies, often of single locales, but also criticism that too much emphasis is given to the particular characteristics of individual cases and not enough to explaining regional variations with comparative studies. Several of the chapters in this volume provide generalizable explanations for these local variations.

Dorothy Solinger shows how the context of pre-existing political economy conditions shapes policy choices in different localities. In comparing how Guangzhou, Shenyang, and Wuhan have dealt with the problem of developing labor markets and re-employing laid-off workers from SOEs, she uses three independent variables: the health and wealth of a city's economy; the vitality of domestic markets; and the degree of international involvement. These key variables explain why Guangzhou, with its high values on these three variables, chose a "Thatcherite" strategy of relying on the market and non-state sector firms to boost employment and re-employment; why Shenyang, with its low values on the variables, used a more Keynesian approach by relying on state initiatives rather than the market; and why Wuhan – with a less dynamic market than Guangzhou but also less dominated by the state sector than Shenyang – used a mix of market and state initiatives. All three cities were able to experiment with different policies for creating labor markets, but the measures adopted were dependent on the existing structure of the local economies, as well as upon reform policies of the central government and the respective cities' geographical locations.

Jae Ho Chung's study of changing central–local relations also emphasizes how the context of reform policies helps explain policy results. He measures the degree of decentralization in nine issue areas where decision-making authority has been given to lower levels and where it has been retained by the center or even recentralized. Particularly useful in this regard is his treatment of non-economic issues, such as personnel control, administrative monitoring, local legislatures, and the potential for collusion by local civilian and military officials. He concludes that there is not a single trend in central–local relations, but that each issue area has its peculiar characteristics and that we should avoid inferring trends from one area to another. As noted above, the center has been more willing to tolerate local deviation and discretion so long as they promote aggregate economic growth. The center is also less likely to cede decision-making authority when national priorities are at stake, especially in those areas where it can accurately monitor local compliance. The result is a view of central–local relations that captures the complexity and ambiguity of their specific contexts, and that explains observed variations.

Dali Yang's analysis of government reforms also uses the environmental context as a key explanatory tool. He shows how the interplay of material conditions, ideas, leadership, and institutions explains why attempted governmental reforms produced so few results in the 1980s but proceeded at a more rapid pace after the mid-1990s. These changing environmental conditions may also be leading to the "rationalization" of the Chinese state: although the state played an important role in initiating the expansion of the market economy, the growth of market transactions and competitive forces has reduced the profitability of SOEs. As the non-state sectors contributed ever greater shares of economic production, job creation, new investments, and tax revenues, governments at all levels became less committed to the state sector. Whereas the state first promoted the expansion of the market, the expanding market may now be leading to the rationalization of the state.

Lowell Dittmer finds that variations in foreign policy views continue to exist, but with different patterns than in the Maoist era. The "informal networks" have shifted away from the field armies of old to other groupings. Moreover, it is hard to identify distinctive policy preferences of any individual loyalty group. In his view, bureaucratic bases offer better insights into competing views than do shifting factional alignments or tracing the personal ties of individual leaders.

Each of these approaches is fundamentally different from the elite perspective that is more common in analyzing the dynamics of reform. They show that policy is more context dependent, and – within certain limits – less personalistic than under Mao.

Contradictory goals

Reform goals have been partially contradictory, in both intent and implementation. In some cases, this is because the center and local governments have competing priorities. In other cases, it is because different reforms are inherently contradictory, so that measures to fulfill one policy come at the expense of another. Even when competing policies are not zero-sum in nature, decisions on policy implementation in one realm often have negative and sometimes unintended consequences for other policy goals.

One of the most prominent of these contradictory goals is the desire to promote growth and modernization, on the one hand, but also to protect local markets and workers, on the other. Dorothy Solinger finds a fundamental contradiction between the widely accepted goals of increasing competitiveness and protecting the job security of urban workers. At both the central and local levels, these goals are at odds with one another. Locally, in the cities, enterprises have a strong desire to hire cheap labor, usually rural and migrant workers, which reduces production costs and contributes to the creation of a labor market. At the same time, however, local governments have an equally strong commitment to protect the jobs of urban residents. In practice, this is done by setting limits on how many jobs – and what kinds of jobs – can be held by "outsiders" who are usually willing to work for much less than urban workers. Even Guangzhou, which exemplifies a market approach to economic reform among large cities, took steps to limit the share of outside workers.

The central government, which is very sensitive to potential unrest among unemployed urban workers, has also urged restricting the hiring of peasants in cities and the re-employment of laid-off city labor. But it is also concerned with promoting modernization, marketization, and competitiveness in the national economy and the construction of a genuine labor market. Local governments have a greater interest in protecting the interests of city workers who are rapidly losing their jobs due to SOE reform, competition from other enterprises, and especially to cheap migrant labor. In addition to difficulties arising from these conflicting goals, resources set aside for retraining workers are insufficient and new jobs are not being created rapidly enough to keep unemployment rates of urban residents from rising.

SOE reform is also bedeviled by contradictory goals, particularly the short- and long-term interests of the state. Teh-chang Lin analyzes the financial burdens on SOEs that hamper successful reform. Because unemployment and medical insurance and pensions are paid by the enterprise, not the state, workers risk losing these important benefits if they leave for new jobs in the private sector. This discourages labor mobility, an important factor in promoting the efficiencies and competitiveness needed for economic development. He suggests that successful economic reform will require simultaneous creation of a welfare system, not only for SOE workers but for all urban workers. However, the state is reluctant to do so because it does not want to bear the costs of expanded welfare benefits. The short-term financial constraints of the central government are obstacles to other, more long-term goals.

Perhaps the greatest contradiction is the state's desire to encourage domestic and foreign competitive pressures in the economy while preserving its unchallenged political authority. This has been a hallmark of the entire post-Mao era, exemplified by Deng's "Four Cardinal Principles" of 1979 and the continual refusal to tolerate any organized or even unorganized political behavior that is seen by party leaders to pose a challenge to the CCP's political monopoly. This point has been repeatedly made during the reform era: in the closing of Democracy Wall in 1979; the crackdown on student protests in 1986–7; the violent imposition of martial law to end the Tiananmen demonstrations in June 1989; the arrests and imprisonments of those attempting to form autonomous labor unions or organize branches of the Chinese Democratic Party; and the periodic harassment and suppression of religious groups, including both Christian "house churches" and spiritual groups such as Falun Gong. Many observers have wondered how long the discrepancy between economic liberalization and continued political authoritarianism can last. At some point, should not the level of freedom in politics and economics be in closer harmony?

This is one of the most important questions facing China's future, but those seeking answers have tended to equate "meaningful political reform" with democratization. To do so, however, misses important political changes that have been underway that are designed to implement more efficiently the state's goals, but not necessarily respond to societal demands. China has undertaken extensive political reforms, including streamlining the bureaucracy, upgrading the professional and technical qualifications of officials, bureaucrats, and enterprise managers, rationalizing the policy process, and so on. Even village elections have been justified by their ability to implement more easily unpopular policies such as family planning and tax collection, rather than their potential for creating grass-roots democracy.[10] If we look only for signs of increased democratization, we will overlook important changes that are making the political system more efficient, even if not more responsive.[11]

A reactive foreign policy

Understanding China's foreign relations requires different analytical tools than domestic policies, but the two have at least one thing in common: its pattern of behavior reflects not a principled adherence to a set of core beliefs and goals but pragmatic responses to changing circumstances. China's international behavior in the post-Mao era has been primarily reactive. Changes in its fundamental policies have been the result of decisions made abroad (the end of the Cold War, the foreign reaction to the 1989 Tiananmen tragedy, US-led military interventions in the Persian Gulf and the Balkans, etc.) rather than new strategic doctrines decided at home. China portrays itself as the object – even the victim – of international trends, rather than the agent of change. In the late 1970s, China abandoned its rhetorical commitment to global revolution and instead characterized the international environment as favoring "peace and development." By the late 1990s, many of China's foreign policy analysts began to reconsider whether this depiction of international trends still held true, or if China should become better prepared to defend itself against an increasingly hostile international environment. Throughout the 1990s, in fact, China shifted toward a greater emphasis on military modernization, which had been last on Deng's list of the four modernizations (the others being agriculture, industry, and science and technology). The need to maintain the loyalty of the PLA to the CCP's civilian leadership following the imposition of martial law in 1989, coupled with the need to respond to the revolution in military technology as exhibited in the Gulf War, required a greater commitment of resources to military modernization. However, political leaders reiterated that they saw peace and development as being the dominant trend, and that a change in their basic foreign policy orientation was not yet necessary.

China has been reluctant to be drawn too deeply into international organizations, even those for Asian or Third World countries. According to Lowell Dittmer, its support for the Third World has been largely rhetorical. It has stayed out of most Third World organizations, and when it did join it stayed out of functional committees and affiliated bodies where the most meaningful business is conducted. Instead, it prefers to develop a series of bilateral relations to keep the focus on itself, and not be just one actor among many in the larger international community. Under Jiang Zemin, China has revived Great Power diplomacy using "strategic partnerships" as the vehicle. It pursued a series of bilateral relations to try to put China at the center of the international system. Conversely, it has expected deference, not equality, when dealing with Asian countries. When it does not receive the deference it believes it is due, it cuts bilateral communications. China's relations with its Asian neighbors have been strongly influenced by Jiang's seeming preference for prestige and ceremonial ritual over substance and mutual benefit. This suggests a distinctly hierarchical perception of the international system, with the Great Powers (including China) occupying one tier and other lesser countries in a decidedly subordinate role.

China's integration into the international community has had two major goals. First, other countries have been eager to draw China into the international arena in order to change China's behavior. This has been particularly prominent in absorbing China into a variety of international arms control regimes, and most recently its agreement to join the World Trade Organization. Bates Gill provides a variety of examples of how international pressure has led China to sign non-proliferation treaties, such as the Chemical Weapons Convention, the Nuclear Non-Proliferation Treaty, and the Comprehensive Test Ban Treaty. The proliferation of agencies in the non-proliferation area has made China open to more voices, both at home and abroad, on this important issue. This is an important example of the positive impact of integration on China's behavior. Still, major concerns remain about China's non-compliance in a variety of areas, and with its continued involvement with nuclear development programs in Iran and Pakistan in particular. The change in China's behavior has been incremental, but still a clear break from the past. As is the case for many of its domestic policies, incremental changes in its foreign policy are also leading to a more substantial cumulative impact, even if the trend is not always straightforward.

The second goal of China's integration into the international community is not to influence behavior but to change perceptions. Kenneth Allen describes efforts to make other countries confident that China is not a threat to them and make China confident that the international environment – especially the military environment – is not threatening to China. He details a series of confidence-building measures (CBMs) between China and its neighbors, including members of the Association of Southeast Asian Nations, India, Russia, and the Central Asian Republics, as a way of reducing tensions along their borders.

On the sensitive issue of cross-strait relations with Taiwan, however, China's policy has not been primarily reactive, nor has it been willing to engage in CBMs as it has elsewhere. At least on this issue, China's behavior has been more "principled" than pragmatic. In other words, China's policies and behavior toward Taiwan are based on the familiar "one China" policy: that there is but one China and Taiwan is part of it. In its diplomacy, it has not wavered from this view, and has retaliated against other nations and international organizations that attempt to have more normalized, if not fully official, ties with Taiwan. But it has also shown some hints of flexibility toward Taiwan on the unification issue. For instance, some of China's top spokesmen on cross-straits relations, including Wang Daohan and Qian Qichen, have suggested that "one China" need not mean the PRC, implying that some other framework and name are conceivable. Even the most flexible of China's proposals have had little appeal in Taiwan, however. Taiwan already enjoys standards of living and high degrees of political and social freedoms that are still a long way off in China. Taiwan's leaders and the population at large seem to prefer to defer a final resolution of their relationship with the mainland until some unspecified time in the future. Although there is a growing economic integration between Taiwan and China as a result of rapidly expanding trade and Taiwanese investment on the mainland, these economic ties have not furthered the cause of political unification, as China's leaders have hoped. However, the patient approach adopted by Deng Xiaoping and Ye Jianying at the start of the reform era has been replaced by a more urgent desire on the part of Jiang Zemin and Qian Qichen to move expeditiously toward achieving Taiwan's unification with the mainland. This was made abundantly clear in a "White Paper" released in February 2000, which declared that Taiwan's indefinite refusal to negotiate substantive issues, although not necessarily reunification itself, could lead to China's use of force against it. China may be patient and flexible, but not infinitely so.

Cross-strait negotiations have a long and complicated history, and have led to changes in the atmosphere of relations between China and Taiwan more than their substance. In his analysis of cross-strait negotiations and the possibility of a future breakthrough, Chong-hai Shaw draws attention to the semantic and symbolic importance China gives to holding negotiations. In contrast, Taiwan is reluctant to admit it is engaging in negotiations, dialogs, or talks. It is wary of China's insistence that these negotiations focus on primary political questions – namely, Taiwan's relationship with the mainland – rather than procedural issues of fishing disputes, repatriation of criminals and illegal immigrants, protecting Taiwanese investment in China, and similar kinds of issues. He concludes that a resumption of negotiations in the short run is highly unlikely, and even in the middle to long term (past 2005) faces many obstacles. China must accept a looser concept of sovereignty to allow the two sides to negotiate as equal partners, and Taiwan must clarify its future direction by reiterating and abiding by the Guidelines for National Unification and resisting provocative moves, such as revising the constitution to allow the right to hold referenda, which some Democratic Progressive Party (DPP) leaders have said could be used to measure popular support for Taiwan's independence. Even if the likelihood of future cross-strait negotiations increases, the outcome of those negotiations is highly uncertain.

Short of a final resolution, Kenneth Allen proposes that China and Taiwan engage in CBMs to reduce tensions and the potential for miscalculation leading to hostilities. This would be one potential payoff from China's international integration: a willingness to apply the lessons from its general international relations and experiences to a specific, high-profile issue that is likely to lead to conflict. Although some tacit CBMs already exist, such as limits on the flight paths of fighter jets and hotlines for sea rescues, so far China has been unwilling to entertain the idea of formal CBMs in its relations with Taiwan. According to China, CBMs are only appropriate for relations between countries, and Taiwan is not an independent country but a part of China, therefore CBMs are not appropriate for cross-strait relations. This sophistic logic is one of many obstacles to breakthroughs in cross-strait relations. Even though China has unilaterally declared a "no first use" pledge regarding its nuclear weapons, has agreed not to target its nuclear weapons at the United States or Russia, and has agreed to "no first use of force" pledges with Russia, India, and countries of Central Asia, it has so far refused to renounce the use of force against Taiwan. The level of mistrust and misunderstanding is so high on both sides of the Taiwan Straits that agreements to engage in meaningful CBMs will be difficult, but they will be essential if the two sides want to develop a more cooperative relationship in the future.

Conclusion

The reform process in China is still unfolding, and the final outcome cannot be known with any degree of certainty. Scholars inside and outside of China debate whether the dominant trend is toward the disintegration of the political system followed by a period of instability, toward a more assertive China with the economic and military means to dominate the region and threaten Asian and US interests, or toward a more prosaic middle course. There is evidence to support each of these projections, but the evidence is ambiguous and a definitive answer is not possible. Nor is it necessary: the goal of the chapters in this volume is not to predict the future, but instead to explain how China has gotten to its current point. One of the main themes of this volume – namely, the complex patterns and variations across different parts of China and across different issue areas – points to the difficulty of making general predictions for the country as a whole when there is so much variation within the country.

Many observers of contemporary China are continually surprised by the frequent oscillations in the pace and direction of reform. A longer term perspective shows that this is in fact a defining feature of the reform process in China. Straight-line projections into the future are rarely accurate because of the incremental nature of the reforms. Despite the recurring reversals of direction, there is also an apparent secular trend toward broader and deeper reforms. Indeed, reform has become an end unto itself, requiring the socialist system to change to accommodate greater reform, rather than being a means to strengthen socialism in China. Parsimonious statements about the causes and consequences of reform can be overly simplistic, and even misleading, because of the complex variations within China. Policy outcomes vary according to local socio-economic factors, changing international environmental conditions, and the peculiarities of specific policy areas, not simply by the intentions of national leaders. The reform process is also beset by contradictory goals, both between levels of government and between competing policy objectives. In the foreign policy arena, many observers concentrate on China's often bellicose rhetoric, but fail to appreciate that its foreign policy behavior is generally reactive and accepting of many international norms.

These are the prevailing themes woven through the chapters of this volume. While these themes may be familiar to scholars actively following China, they are not so familiar to non-specialists. Before we can have confidence in what the future has in store, we need to have a better understanding of how China has gotten to its present position, and why. That still leaves plenty of room for further research and debate.

Notes

1   Andrew G. Walder, "The Quiet Revolution from Within: Economic Reform as a Source of Political Decline," in Andrew G. Walder (ed.), *The Waning of the Communist State: Economic Origins of Political Decline in China and Hungary* (Berkeley: University of California Press, 1995); Jack A. Goldstone, "The Coming Chinese Collapse," *Foreign Policy*, no. 99 (Summer 1995), pp. 35–52.

2 Yasheng Huang, *Inflation and Investment Controls in China: The Political Economy of Central–Local Relations during the Reform Era* (New York: Cambridge University Press, 1996); see also his "Why China Will Not Collapse," *Foreign Policy*, no. 99 (Summer 1995), pp. 54–68.

3 Jae Ho Chung, "Studies of Central–Provincial Relations in the People's Republic of China: A Mid-Term Appraisal," *China Quarterly*, no. 142 (June 1995), pp. 487–508; Pei Minxin, "Is China Democratizing?" *Foreign Affairs*, vol. 77, no. 1 (1998), pp. 68–82.

4 The "China threat" perspective is best represented by Richard Bernstein and Ross Munro, *The Coming Conflict with China* (New York: Knopf, 1991); the alternative viewpoint is presented in Andrew J. Nathan and Robert S. Ross, *The Great Wall and The Empty Fortress: China's Search for Security* (New York: Norton, 1997). An interesting contribution to this debate comes from a collection of essays by young Chinese scholars now teaching in US colleges and universities: Yong Deng and Fei-Ling Wang (eds.), *In the Eyes of the Dragon: China Views the World* (Lanham, MD: Rowman and Littlefield, 1999).

5 Suisheng Zhao, "Chinese Intellectuals' Quest for National Greatness and Nationalistic Writing in the 1990s," *China Quarterly*, no. 152 (December 1997), pp. 725–45; Yongnian Zheng, *Discovering Chinese Nationalism in China : Modernization, Identity, and International Relations* (New York: Cambridge University Press, 1999).

6 Geremie Barme, "To Screw Foreigners is Patriotic: China's Avant-Garde Nationalists," *The China Journal*, no. 34 (July 1995), pp. 209–34; Michael Dutton, "An All-Consuming Nationalism," *Current History* (1999), pp. 276–80.

7 Tony Saich, "Negotiating the State: The Development of Social Organizations in China," *China Quarterly*, no. 161 (March 2000), pp. 124–41; Bruce J. Dickson, "Cooptation and Corporatism in China: The Logic of Party Adaptation," *Political Science Quarterly*, vol. 115, no. 4 (Winter 2000–1), pp. 517–40.

8 Edward Steinfeld, "Beyond the Transition: China's Economy at Century's End," *Current History* (September 1999), pp. 271–5.

9 Margaret M. Pearson, *China's New Business Elite* (Berkeley: University of California Press, 1997); David L. Wank, "Private Business, Bureaucracy, and Political Alliance in a Chinese City," *Australian Journal of Chinese Affairs*, vol. 33 (January 1995), 63–5.

10 Daniel Kelliher, "The Chinese Debate over Village Self-Government," *China Journal*, no. 37 (January 1997), pp. 63–86; Lianjiang Li and Kevin J. O'Brien, "The Struggle over Village Elections," in Merle Goldman and Roderick MacFarquhar (eds.), *The Paradox of China's Post-Mao Reforms* (Cambridge, MA: Harvard University Press, 1999); Tianjian Shi, "Village Committee Elections in China: Institutionalist Tactics for Democracy," *World Politics*, vol. 51, no. 3 (April 1999), pp. 385–412.

11 Bruce J. Dickson, *Democratization in China and Taiwan: The Adaptability of Leninist Parties* (Oxford and New York: Oxford University Press, 1997); Pei, "Is China Democratizing?"

Part I

Political strategies in the reform era

1 Rationalizing the Chinese state

The political economy of government reform

Dali L. Yang

Though Mao sought to remedy the ills of bureaucratism through permanent revolution and new modes of organization, by the time of his death China had "one of the most bureaucratized social systems known to man."[1] Markets were suppressed and nearly all aspects of society and economy came under Leninist bureaucratic control. In contrast, the post-Mao reforms have provided much impetus for reorganizing the government itself and rationalizing the Chinese state. In this chapter, I seek to answer the following two questions. Despite repeated government attempts to reform the government itself, why did the attempted government reforms produce few results in the 1980s but have proceeded rapidly since the mid-1990s? To what extent are the recent reforms rationalizing the Chinese state?

In order to answer these questions, I shall examine the interplay among material conditions, ideas, leadership, and institutions. It is argued that while ideas for reform have floated around throughout this period, the incentives for reform have changed with time. Until the early 1990s, the state had tended to grow and become bloated. Buoyed by the tide of rapid economic growth, revenue expanded rapidly to sustain government expansion. Government expansion, in turn, offered a fertile soil for political patronage. As long as revenue rolled in, the political will to downsize was weak and all justifications to cut the government down to size remained on paper. In the meantime, it is expected that administrative reforms aimed at streamlining the government will be difficult to implement during the transition to market. Partial reforms and imperfections in the market invited government intervention.

As market transactions grow and competition erodes the profitability of state enterprises, the different levels of governments have reduced their "interests" in enterprises. It is expected that the rationalization of government will more likely be implemented in such circumstances because there are simply fewer "interests" for different government departments to fight over. While governmental reforms are ultimately political decisions,[2] the mechanisms identified here should nevertheless help account for the vicissitudes in China's efforts to reform government administration across time and space. In other words, I shall argue that while the Chinese state has played an important role in expanding the market, market expansion has, in turn, helped prepare the ground for the rationalization of the state.

Partial reforms and the pathologies of bureaucratic rationalization

As is well known in studies of China, it was the government (in different departments and at different levels) that eagerly pursued investment opportunities in the 1980s and sought to protect its interests in the companies in which it invested. The dual-track reforms not only entailed the continuation (albeit gradual shrinkage as a percentage of total economic activities) of the plan but also meant the persistence of bargaining relationships between state (as well as collective) enterprises and their bureaucratic superiors. These relationships were ones of mutual dependence that bordered on bilateral monopoly.[3] The enterprises counted on their superiors for supply and help with access to capital, protection from encroachment (including from other parts of government), and often preferential treatment (such as taxation and interest exemptions or steering projects their way). In return, the enterprises provided their bureaucratic superiors with revenue, employment (which often served as a patronage benefit), and products for the plan.

The strong state–enterprise bonds during the transitional period were thus manifestations of an administered economy. These bonds were firmly embedded in the Chinese bureaucratic hierarchy. Because Chinese decision making emphasized consensus, the proliferation of bureaucratic agencies and organizations required more time and effort for coordination. As a consequence, numerous *ad hoc* offices, such as for aircraft manufacturing, nuclear power, and electronics, were set up within the central government to act as coordinators and facilitators, only to engender conflicts with existing ministries and commissions. This phenomenon is also replicated within local governments. In one well-known example, the executive vice-governor of Hunan Province found himself the head of more than 200 *ad hoc* institutions and organizations.[4] Because these *ad hoc* institutions are staffed and funded by the government, their costs aggravated the fiscal burdens on all levels of government.

The expansion and proliferation of formal and informal bureaucratic organizations resulted in an exponential growth of decisions that were referred to higher levels for final decisions while the growth of social and intermediate organizations was retarded.[5] As a result, Chinese decision making was plagued by delays and inefficiency while the agenda of top leaders was overloaded with what would have been trivial matters in a market economy.[6] In the early 1980s, the city of Beijing had to seek the permission of the Communist Party's Political Bureau just to increase the price of a box of matches from two cents to three cents.[7] The growth of top-down interventions was exacerbated by cleavages along functional and territorial boundaries (*tiao-tiao* vs. *kuai-kuai*) and further complicated by the fault lines between party and administrative leaders within each organization and enterprise. Since each government department, such as the Ministry of Machine-building, had its own enterprises in the form of *zhishu qiye* (enterprises that were directly subordinate to it), it could not be counted on to regulate the entire industry impartially. Instead, that ministry was likely to parcel out funds and special treatment to its own enterprises first before it took care of similar enterprises that belonged to other ministries or local governments.[8] These other ministries and local governments had therefore to try hard to protect their own "children," leading to duplication of projects and often requiring the attention of national leaders.

The degeneration of bureaucratic expansion into proliferation of veto gates for economic actors and decision overloading for top leaders virtually guaranteed continuing demands for bureaucratic reform both from below and from above. While subordinates complained of lack of autonomy, and enterprise managers, who were asked to assume responsibility for enterprise performance, grumbled about too much intervention from government agencies, top leaders buried in detail worried about the lack of initiative and inefficiency. State ownership meant state involvement or intervention. The politicization of the economy thus begot more political intervention.

The tenacity of this system of mutual embeddedness of political and economic actors was revealed when large state enterprises were delegated to the care of local governments. The local authorities often had a hard time ensuring that the enterprises had adequate supplies of raw materials and energy and outlets for their products that were controlled through the now-defunct Ministry of Materials Supply. As a consequence, local governments sometimes begged central ministries to take these enterprises back.[9] In the command economy, an enterprise that lacked a super-ordinate government bureau was an orphan while a government agency that controlled no enterprises was a mere shell. Without alternatives to government allocation of resources, an enterprise that cut its ties to its controlling government bureau was like a ship without moorings.

As long as the bureaucracies played significant roles in providing for and protecting the enterprises under their jurisdiction in a partially reformed economy, efforts to rationalize the bureaucracy and state–business relations would meet with much resistance as they touch on vested interests. As the market expanded, the bureaucratic interests became major obstacles to a functioning market through various forms of interventions that were manifested in local protectionism, over-employment in state enterprises, and barriers to SOE bankruptcies. We thus expect no fundamental progress in the rationalization of the state until markets become a fact of life.[10]

In short, economic reform and administrative reform were caught in a classic chicken-and-egg situation. As long as the government supplanted the market, state enterprises would do well to seek a bureaucratic umbrella since each government agency or department possessed veto power over matters such as investment decisions that are normally the preserve of businesses.[11] Yet administrative reform stalled because state enterprises still relied on the state and demanded administrative protection.[12] From 1978 to 1995, Chinese state revenue rose by 5.1 times while administrative expenses in state expenditure grew by 17.8 times.[13] Most ominously, government administrative expenditure as a percentage of total government expenditure increased from about 5 percent in the mid-1970s to nearly 15 percent by the mid-1990s. These figures powerfully illustrate the deep problems of bureaucratism and inefficiency that Chinese reformers have repeatedly criticized.

Reforming the government at the dawn of market reform

The difficulties of government reforms in a partially reformed economy were evident throughout the 1980s in China. The death of Mao was followed by dramatic bureaucratic regeneration. Bureaucracies that had become skeletons during the Cultural Revolution were resurrected; deposed bureaucrats regained status and power following years of internal exile or imprisonment. In the meantime, greater reliance on the market required new institutions to support and regulate new activities. All four new institutions set up under the State Council within a year of Mao's death were concerned with the economy: The State Council Financial and Trade Group, the State Price Administration, the State Science and Technology Commission, and the People's Bank of China. Many more followed both in the central government and in the localities. Thus, following the end of the Cultural Revolution era, which had reduced the State Council bureaucratic setup to skeletal form, the early post-Mao era saw a dramatic growth in the number of State Council agencies. It rose swiftly from 52 in 1976 to reach a record 100 by the end of 1981. There was also a proliferation of vice-ministerial posts to accommodate the many cadres who suffered persecution during the Cultural Revolution; a number of ministries had more than a dozen vice-ministers.[14] Some of these elderly vice-ministers did little except to exercise the power of veto.

This proliferation of government agencies occurred during a period of fiscal stringency. Over the 1979–81 period, government revenue stagnated amid economic adjustment.[15] With the bureaucratic expansion and the growth of payroll and associated expenses, administrative expenditure as a percentage of total government expenditure rose from 4.9 percent in 1979 to 7.3 percent in 1981. The Chinese leadership centered round Deng Xiaoping concluded that the bureaucratic expansion was unsustainable and decided to rationalize the bureaucracy and, more broadly, the party–state.[16] Speaking at a Political Bureau meeting on bureaucratic streamlining in January 1982, Deng bluntly pointed to the ills of China's state apparatus. For Deng, the "overstaffed and overlapping Party and state organizations" were "without clearly defined duties and with many incompetent, irresponsible, lethargic, under-educated and inefficient staff members." This situation called for major reform in order to restore morale within the state and to win the people's support. Otherwise, Deng warned,

> If you don't carry out this revolution but let the old and ailing stand in the way of young people who are energetic and able, not only will the four modernizations fail but the Party and state will face a mortal trial and perhaps perish.[17]

The sense of peril on the part of the leadership provided a strong impetus for major reform. While calling for cutting staff by one-third, Deng displayed his steely resolve: "We can expect some trouble, including demonstrations. ... But come what may, we must stick to our guns in this revolution, standing staunch and unshakable."[18]

On the surface, Deng's call to arms resulted in immediate change. The number of bureaucratic agencies under the State Council was reduced from 100 in 1981 to sixty-one in 1982, a decrease of 39 percent. The number of ministers in thirty-eight commissions and ministries was reduced from 505 to 167.[19] Significant organizational streamlining and staffing cuts were also made in the lower levels of the government hierarchy in 1982. Moreover, major changes in norms such as retirement, age limits, and fixed terms of office were introduced and even enshrined in the revamped constitution of 1982. These changes not only resulted in an immediate decrease of the average age of officials but have had far-reaching consequences for elite mobility.[20] Meanwhile, a series of laws and regulations have been promulgated to regulate bureaucratic behavior and discipline bureaucrats.[21]

In reality, however, the bureaucratic rationalization of 1982 was only skin deep.[22] Most of the agency reductions were in the number of institutions or organizations directly subordinated to the State Council. In contrast, the number of government commissions and ministries saw a more modest reduction of nine from fifty-two in 1981. The situation was far more depressing when payroll was taken into account. At this time, even though some private businesses had begun to emerge, the government was virtually the only employer in urban China. Though the number of bureaucrats was reduced, the government payroll remained virtually the same whether the former bureaucrat had retired or moved to government-sponsored social organizations. Thus, Deng's strong commitment was helpful but not enough in effecting fundamental change at this time.

As long as the government remained heavily implicated in the economy by virtue of its ownership and investments, the pathologies described here persisted. Within the State Council, the number of government commissions and ministries immediately started to grow after the streamlining of 1982, increasing from sixty-one in 1982 to seventy-two in 1986. Yet the number of "temporary" institutions and organizations grew from thirty to seventy-seven.[23]

Thus, in spite of repeated attempts by the central government to streamline and rationalize the economic bureaucracy, Chinese administrative reforms through the early 1990s went through cycles of "streamlining – bloating – more streamlining – and more bloating." Some bureaucratic rationalization did occur, but overall, bureaucrats were simply too busy "helping" their enterprises and themselves. Instead, even while various central government documents were calling for simplifying administration in order to enliven enterprises, the proliferation of new economic entities and growing economic complexities were used to justify the establishment of government agencies and expansion of personnel because governance of the economy was heavily dependent on administrative intervention as long as the plan continued to exist.[24] As a consequence, Chinese efforts at bureaucratic rationalization became, in Winiecki's terms, "pseudo-reorganization" and Parkinsonian, like they did in the Soviet Union and East Europe.[25] Even when some bureaus were abolished, some other functional institutions or affiliated organizations (especially *shiye danwei*) were often added to or recreated to provide employment for bureaucrats.

From downsizing to rationalization: government reform in the middle of market reform

When briefed on the slowdown in China's economic growth for the first half of 1986, Deng commented that it was time that China pursued political reforms in order to re-energize the reforms. Disdainful of political systems with separation of powers, Deng's political reforms sought efficiency with order.[26] Harking back to the era of revolution, Deng stated that a major element of such reforms would be *jingbing jianzheng* or "better troops and simpler administration."[27] Top leaders such as Hu Qili, then a member of the Political Bureau, were aware, in the tradition of Marxian materialism, that economic changes in the direction of the market required appropriate changes in the state to ensure stability and speed up economic development.[28] Participants in the group drafting the political reform plan pointed out that the Chinese state had yet to transform itself from one devoted to making revolution to one for promoting economic construction. They were convinced that without political reform that rationalized the relationship between party and government and of the government itself, economic reforms would stall as well.[29] Economic and political reforms were interrelated.

These ideas for political reform were embodied in the report to the Thirteenth Party Congress held in the fall of 1987. The report called for building and nurturing a market system in which the government should refrain from the direct allocation of resources to enterprises and, with the exception of a very small number of key projects and special enterprises, shift to indirect means of macroeconomic control. While the enterprise is an administrative appendage of the state in the planned economy, the market economy calls for the government to transfer responsibility over production, sales, and pricing as well as decisions over investments, salaries, and hiring and promotions to the enterprise. This calls for reforming the political system to facilitate economic reforms: party and government should be separated, power should be further delegated to lower levels, the bureaucracy should be streamlined, a civil service was to be introduced, and efforts were to be made to strengthen the legal system.[30]

The designers of government reform envisioned a fundamental revamping of government functions rather than simple downsizing so that administrative streamlining would not be followed by renewed expansion. In the most ambitious version of their plan for governmental reform (Plan A), enterprises would sever their ties with administrative departments and become genuine business firms responsible for their own operations and survival. With the formation of a market economic system and sound legal system, the government would focus on the management of state assets and no longer allocate projects, investments, and materials by industry.[31] Yet the designers, drawing on limited experimentation in some cities, recognized that Plan A required far more complementary changes in China's economy and society than were possible at the time.[32] The Chinese economy was still wedded to the plan and suffering from shortages. Management skills and social psychology were as yet not ready for the big plunge. Indeed, the 1988 reform had called for the merger of the State Economic Commission with the State Planning Commission in order to overcome problems of coordination between economic planners and those overseeing economic operations and to strengthen macroeconomic oversight and policy implementation. Within months of the merger, however, the State Council had to establish a separate production committee to oversee plan implementation and industry regulation. This committee soon evolved into the powerful State Economic and Trade Commission.

The considerations about the broader socio-economic environment led the reformers to choose a middle road (Plan B) while keeping the goals of Plan A for the future.[33] On the one hand, specialized government departments (especially those along sectoral lines) and the internal departments of comprehensive government agencies were to be merged and reduced in order to give enterprises more autonomy and transform the government–enterprise relationship from direct to indirect management. On the other, certain agencies that had a comprehensive portfolio or were concerned with macroeconomic policy as well as those for supervision, auditing, and information were to be enhanced so that a smaller government could strengthen its capacity for macroeconomic control.[34] Among the latter are the Ministry of Supervision, the Ministry of Personnel, the Customs Administration, the Tax Bureau, the State Asset Administration, the People's Bank of China, and the Ministry of Finance.

Since it is far easier to establish new agencies than to cut existing ones, on balance the administrative reform of 1988 resulted in only modest streamlining – the number of State Council commissions and ministries was reduced from forty-five to forty-one.[35] By looking at staffing levels, however, the 1988 reform appears in a somewhat more favorable light. Staffing levels for line ministries saw substantial cuts, especially because all these departments employed more people than their staffing levels permitted. The Ministry of Commerce had a staffing level of 2,090 but actually employed 2,673; its new staffing level was set at 1,100. The staffing level of the Light Industry Ministry was cut to 627 from 936. The Machinery Commission and the Ministry of Electronics were authorized to employ 2,256 but actually had 2,840 people on the payroll; the staffing level for the newly constituted Ministry of Machinery and Electronics was set at 1,430. In the meantime, staffing levels at supervisory and macroeconomic institutions received a boost. The Ministry of Supervision and the Auditing Bureau were authorized to station 585 inspectors and 471 auditors respectively in other government departments. Staffing levels at the People's Bank of China and the Ministry of Finance were increased to 1,250 (from 581) and 1,240 (from 527) respectively. Altogether, staffing levels at thirty-two commissions, ministries, and State Council organizations were cut by 4,900 and actual payroll numbers by 9,700, whereas those for thirty others, including the People's Bank of China, were increased by 5,300.[36] Government officials vowed that the new staffing levels would be strictly enforced. In short, in spite of the reorganization, the overall staffing level increased rather than decreased.

All in all, the 1998 reforms marked a major step to slim down the agencies at the core of the planned economy. Moreover, as staffing levels were changed and agencies were streamlined, an effort was also made to codify the different responsibilities and coordination among the State Planning Commission, the Ministry of Finance, and the People's Bank of China. Governmental functions within some government departments, such as Light Industry and Environmental Protection, were also carefully delineated so as to prepare for the introduction of a civil service. In short, the government would not govern the economy with administrative means alone, but would have to combine administrative fiats with economic levers and legal means.

As the reformers chose a more moderate plan, they knew the 1988 reforms were transitional only. Seen from this perspective, the 1988 reform was surely limited in and by itself and, on the surface, bureaucrats used their survival strategies well to take care of themselves.[37] Yet the designers of government reforms also had a vision for the future. All the government reforms that were adopted needed to be deepened and refined later. In other words, government reforms would parallel the deepening of economic reforms. As economic reforms progressed, so would government reforms and vice versa. Fundamentally, as State Councilor Song Ping explained, a government could not and would not be able to assume responsibility for everything. Many of the functions currently being undertaken by the government would need to be taken over by corporations, associations, and other social organizations.[38] Essentially, the reformers had decided that the era of the totalist state was over for China. There needed to be a limited government. Thus the 1988 reform should be seen as the beginning of more reforms to come. It marked the arrival of the era of state rationalization. A leading participant later commented that the reforms of 1988 were probably too fast to be easily accepted and adopted.[39] Nevertheless, as I shall discuss later, the contours and long-range goals of these reforms have endured.

Small state, big society

The broad discussions about the role of government and government reforms at the center of power provided a stimulating context for reforms in some localities. As can be expected from our discussion about the pathologies of government reform, such innovation would first occur in areas that have relatively little historical baggage from the planned economy. The special economic zones led by Hainan and Shenzhen fulfilled such a role. Let me discuss the Hainan experiment first.

In spring 1988, when the central government formally announced its government reform plan, Hainan Island, formerly part of Guangdong Province, was made a separate province and China's largest special economic zone. A key member of the brains trust for the Hainan leadership was Liao Xun. Liao's father, Liao Gailong, was one of China's leading party historians and a major advocate of political reforms in the early 1980s. In 1987, Liao Gailong was also an important participant in the party center's discussions on political and especially government reforms. The younger Liao was thus keenly alert to the trends toward state rationalization. Intellectually, Liao had already started to expound on the virtues of a smaller state in 1986, drawing at first on Marx and Engels but later also making reference to contemporary Western social science theories.[40] In 1987, Liao, then based in the Chinese Academy of Social Sciences (CASS), became a member of a working group to develop a blueprint for Hainan in anticipation of its provincial status. In the pioneering environment of Hainan, Liao's argument for a "small state, big society" won a receptive audience.[41] Liao himself jumped ship from CASS, where he was a lowly assistant research fellow, to become deputy director of the Hainan provincial Research Center for Social and Economic Development in 1988.

Liao argued that the big government system in the planned economy was the biggest obstacle to China's opening. Because the government interfered in everything, individuals and enterprises were left with minimal autonomy. The suppression of economic freedom led to a paucity of economic information and a lack of initiative, making it difficult for China to take advantage of opportunities in world markets while causing administrative expenses to rise rapidly and economic efficiency to go down. As a special economic zone and a new province, Hainan was allowed to adopt a whole host of special policies to encourage economic liberties. Liao warned, however, that the special policies for social and economic freedom in a market economy ought to be guaranteed under a new system of "small government, big society." In other words, the government should reduce its scope and let society, including labor, youth, and women's organizations, play a bigger role. Instead, the government needed to focus on (1) protecting the external environment for social and economic operations; (2) setting and safeguarding the rules of the market; (3) carrying out economic forecasting and formulating development plans; (4) protecting public and private property; and (5) providing public projects and services, protecting the environment.[42] A repudiation of the paradigm of totalist state control, Liao's argument for "small government, big society" thus envisioned the rise of an autonomous sphere of economic and social activities that could serve as the basis for a civil society.

Following the doctrine of small government, which the central government supported, the Hainan leadership, led by Party Secretary Xu Shijie and Governor Liu Jianfeng, set up the provincial government in May 1988 with twenty-six bureau-level departments, far fewer than in other provincial-level governments.[43] They also removed an intermediate level of territorial government, the *zizhizhou* or autonomous prefecture, in order to simplify administration and enhance efficiency.[44] Doing away with departments focusing on specific industrial sectors, the Hainan government instead relied on comprehensive agencies including a Bureau of Trade and Industry. To facilitate investment from the outside and to simplify approval procedures, a Bureau of Economic Cooperation was also established.[45] Indeed, Hainan has become especially noted for its radical experiment to reduce government interference in the economy.[46] Companies simply register with the relevant government department rather than apply for permission to get started. Moreover, the province has adopted a series of policies promoting factor markets. Travelers may get a visa upon landing; employees can change jobs freely; and barriers and toll stations were removed from highways following reforms that converted various fees into a fuel tax. In short, the Hainan experience represented a major reorientation in the relationship between state and society as well as between state and economy.

Hainan, Shenzhen, and the other special economic zones were not the only local governments that tried to delimit the scope of government. Another example is Shandong's Weihai municipality, which was established in 1987 through a combination of three adjacent counties in eastern Shandong province. Weihai had no central-government-controlled state enterprise and very few provincial government enterprises. Being less beholden to the past, the Weihai government from the start made little effort to interfere in the operations of enterprises but focused its efforts on infrastructure. Enterprises had to survive on their own in the market. Such a philosophy meant that the government did not have to be large in size or scope. Indeed, municipal leaders made a deliberate decision to establish a compact government with only 800 staff members (compared with more than 2,000 in comparable cities).[47]

The political economy of rationalization post-Tiananmen

The Tiananmen crisis of 1989 not only was traumatic in itself but also affected the pace of economic and political reforms adversely. Confronted with the crisis of socialism both at home and abroad, central leaders naturally chose to focus on the political and economic problems of the day rather than difficult issues for the long haul. Amid the overall adjustment of the economy, the central leadership put a stop to local government reforms in 1989.[48] Put on the defensive, advocates for government reform placed their emphasis on consolidation rather than the launching of new initiatives in order to preserve the fruits of reforms.[49] As the most progressive experiment of its kind, Hainan's small government experiment and other policies came under much pressure from many directions. This pressure caused Hainan's leadership, which had undergone some reshuffle, to take a pause and indeed led to some backtracking in Hainan's government reform in 1991–2.[50]

Renewing the commitment to government reform

In spite of the political fallout from the 1989 crisis, reformers had by the end of 1990 begun to put government reform experimentation back on track. It was decided to conduct local reform trials in one provincial administration (Hebei), four municipalities (Harbin, Wuhan, Qingdao, and Shenzhen), and nine counties. Moreover, provincial-level governments were authorized to conduct their own experiments in one or two cities (or counties). The State Committee on Organizations and Staff Size (Guojia Jigou Bianzhi Weiyuanhui) emphasized that the experiments were to be comprehensive, involving both downsizing and a transformation in the role of government from micro-management to macro-economic supervision.[51]

Deng's southern tour in 1992 not only gave a boost to economic growth but also helped re-energize government reforms.[52] In various settings, top leaders renewed the commitment to government reform. Speaking at the 14th Party Congress on China's reform agenda in the 1990s, General Secretary Jiang Zemin stipulated that the transformation of government functions, especially the separation of government and enterprise, was indispensable to the building of a market economy. More specifically, Jiang stated that government agencies at different levels should not intercept the rights that belong to enterprises by law or by government regulation. The government should focus its attention on planning, policy formulation, information and guidance, coordination, service, and monitoring. For Jiang, without such a transformation of government functions, reform could not be deepened and a market economic system would not materialize.[53] In the meantime, reformers at the State Committee on Organizations and Staff Size and the State Economic System Reform Commission openly touted the model of "small government, big society" for government reforms in counties and urged provincial leaders to take initiatives.[54]

Incrementalism at the center

Because the 1987–8 reforms were closely associated with deposed General Secretary Zhao Ziyang, some designers of the 1993 reforms claimed they were making a breakthrough beyond mere organizational reform (*jigou gaige*).[55] In fact, while the 1993 government reforms were certainly more comprehensive than in 1988, they did not go beyond the vision of Zhao and his associates.[56] In a fundamental sense, the 1993 reforms were a revival and continuation of the 1988 reforms. The Chinese leadership's commitment to the market had become stronger, but the aims of the reforms, particularly the separation of government and enterprise, remained virtually the same and would in fact remain unfulfilled this time around.

Because of the unsettled political circumstances – including fallout from the Tiananmen crisis of 1989 and the fall of the Soviet Union – Chinese leaders emphasized prudence in carrying out the reforms so as to preserve political stability. General Secretary Jiang Zemin explicitly stated that government ministries that were the legacies of the planned economy could not be abolished yet, because the market economy was still in the process of formation in China. He conceded that the reforms in the State Council and the provincial governments were transitional. Instead, Jiang called for these agencies to transform their functions and trim internal organizations and staff.[57]

Starting from such a premise, government ministers could easily justify the continual existence of their ministries. In this context, Premier Li Peng should not be blamed for not drastically cutting the number of government commissions and ministries. Tactically, having just suffered the infamy of being the point-man during the 1989 crackdown, Li was careful not to stir up too much antagonism in the bureaucracy. He allowed the agencies to draft plans for their own reforms. This strategy of asking patients to prescribe their own remedies virtually ensured that the 1993 reforms would be incremental.[58] The State Council established various general corporations to replace certain ministries (such as Ordnance, Aerospace, and Aviation), but these so-called corporations still retained their regulatory functions in their tightly supervised industrial sectors. For many people involved, this reform smacked of a change in name only.

Variations in the fortunes of bureaucratic reform across civilian industrial ministries seem to confirm our earlier hypothesis about where government reforms are expected to happen first. In 1993, the Ministries of Textile Industry and Light Industry were converted into industry councils. The conversion was made relatively easily, with little political resistance, for two major reasons. First, though these industries were heavyweights in the overall economy in terms of employment and exports, they were relatively weak bureaucratically. The two industries were heavily fragmented across bureaucratic boundaries and regional administrations and the ministries never totally controlled the industries. In fact, low barriers to entry in textiles and light industry have meant that there are a huge number of non-state enterprises, including TVEs (Township and Village Enterprises) and private enterprises, in these sectors. These enterprises did not fall under the direct supervision of the two ministries. Though these ministries fought hard to gain regulatory control over the non-state enterprises, they were fighting a losing battle but had nevertheless gradually learned to become more market oriented. In this sense, the ministries were more ready for administrative rationalization. Second, the pains of adjustment were eased because the two councils were still allowed to retain certain government regulatory functions, such as licenses for spindle production, that were eventually to be transferred to comprehensive government departments, such as the State Economic and Trade Commission. Central leaders argued that, while government ministerial departmentalism suited the planned economy, industry oversight (*hangye guanli*) via industry councils and associations were suited to the market economy as the intermediate realm between macroeconomic management and enterprise management.[59]

Whereas the textile and light industry ministries quickly changed their names, change occurred far more slowly in the core of the planned economy. In 1995 then Premier Li Peng asked the Ministries of Electric Power, Electronics, and Metallurgical Industry to experiment with becoming holding corporations for managing state assets in their respective sectors. The government regulatory functions of these ministries were eventually to be transferred to the State Economic and Trade Commission, which oversees the day-to-day operations of the economy, and the State Planning Commission. Subsequently, only the Ministry of Electric Power (Li Peng's old turf) was able to form the State Power Corporation and prepare for transferring its regulatory functions to the commissions. This was partly because of Li Peng's clout with the Ministry of Electric Power. But equally important was the fact that, like Aviation and Aerospace, assets in the power industry, especially the power grid, were easily controlled. Bureaucrats at the Ministry of Electric Power not only would lose little authority by transforming itself into a corporation, but would also gain greater flexibility and more perks as corporate executives in charge of the national power grids.

In contrast, a similar attempt at reforming the Ministry of Metallurgical Industry was held up for political reasons. As the industry was in a slump and most firms were doing badly, the ministry began its reorganization initiative by trying to take control of better performing corporations such as the Shanghai-based Baoshan Iron and Steel Group as the cornerstone of its holding corporation. This was strongly resisted by the corporations. Baoshan secured the support of Vice-Premier Zhu Rongji to put an end to such an attempt. The ministerial leaders lost their appetite for the holding corporation initiative after they found out that they would not be able to gain control over profitable behemoths such as Baoshan.[60] The central holding corporation model thus fizzled out, albeit not without first sending shivers down the spines of numerous state enterprise managers, who feared the reform would reduce their power and autonomy.[61]

Just as rationalization stalled, the task of cutting the size of bureaucratic staff by 25 percent or about 2 million was mixed as well. In fact, the number of government, party, and social organization employees actually increased between 1993 and 1996. While staffing size was reduced in traditional planning bureaucracies, especially the industrial ministries, some government agencies, including the State Economic and Trade Commission, the State Commission for Restructuring the Economic System, and the Ministry of Labor enjoyed huge staff increases over this period.[62]

Another major disappointment was in the separation of government and enterprise. Jiang stated that government departments at all levels must not set up enterprises and the existing enterprises should sever their ties with the government departments.[63] This injunction had only a brief restraining effect. In fact, the large bureaucracy in a time of fiscal stringency not only reduced efficiency but also became a major source of corruption. Provided with meager budgets, bureaucratic departments were urged to generate supplementary revenue to cover budget shortfalls. Such institutionalized incentives for bureaucratic revenue generation turned into incentives for bureaucratic rent seeking. As is well known, virtually all elements of the Chinese state, from the military and armed police to judiciary departments and the party propaganda department, established and owned businesses to supplement their budgets amid the free-wheeling economic atmosphere of the early and mid-1990s. The revenue imperative, in turn,

resulted in growing burdens for citizens and businesses in the form of a proliferation of fees, levies, and surcharges and spawned many an opportunity for
corruption.

Incentives and emulation in local reforms

By the early 1990s, there was general recognition of the strong interrelationships
between political and economic reforms. When the central government promulgated a set of regulations in 1992 on transforming the operating mechanism of
state-owned industrial enterprises, the initial enthusiasm of state enterprise
managers was soon dampened by the realization that, as long as the state
bureaucracy remained top heavy and meddlesome, the regulations would not be
truly implemented. Some managers predicted that the aims of the regulations
would be an illusion without a transformation of the government itself.[64]

Whereas administrative reforms in the central government were timid in
action, General Secretary Jiang Zemin nevertheless left much room for local
initiatives. This was in accordance with Jiang's politics of prudence, in part
gleaned from China's earlier reform experiences. Even if one locality ended in
disaster by pursuing reforms, the central government could easily reclaim control
and learn lessons from the failure; in contrast, launching drastic reforms from the
top down might run the risk of systemic failure. It was thus reasonable for Jiang
to permit local authorities to adjust their institutional setup to suit local conditions. And reforms at the county level were encouraged to take "a bigger step."[65]
As a consequence, while reforms in the upper levels inched forward, major initiatives occurred in various localities. Since local governments tended to be in
closer touch with market forces compared with the upper levels of government,
they were expected to be more eager to pursue the reforms.

Whereas earlier government reforms were frustrated by an economy that was
dominated by the state and, indeed, was embedded in the state, changing
economic conditions at the turn of the 1990s had made local leaders much more
receptive to the idea of "small government, big society." By 1992–3, China had
not only just gone through a recession associated with the crisis of 1989, but also
begun to welcome in a buyer's market for many products. By 1994 local governments had come under the spell of the Budget Implementation Law, which
forbade local governments from running budget deficits. With corporate and
government revenue growth being constrained by increasing competition in the
marketplace and prohibitions on government borrowing, local governments still
had to take care of their staff as well as tens of thousands of money-losing state
enterprises. It gradually dawned on officials and managers alike that, even
though the national economy was growing at double-digit growth rates, most of
these state enterprises had no hope of being turned around. Ownership can
mean privileges as well as liabilities.

Meanwhile, with the arrival of a buyer's market and intense competition,
state enterprise managers began to find that, except in a small number of heavily
regulated industries such as telecommunications, the value of government

bureaucratic protection had depreciated sharply. After all, a firm could by now secure inputs and sell its products on the market. In many instances, an administrative affiliation with a government department had become a burden for an enterprise. While a state enterprise was required to remit profits and provide welfare and retirement benefits, it had to compete with private and rural enterprises that carried little or no such burden.

With encouragement from the central government, the incentives discussed here stimulated a flurry of experiments with the rationalization of state–business relations and of the government itself. Earlier I briefly discussed the case of Hainan, where government reforms were revived by 1993. Here I would like to turn my attention to Shanghai first.

As in Hainan, the Shanghai municipal government decided to adopt the philosophy of small government in the Pudong New Zone at the beginning of the 1990s. It moved the markets for property rights, real estate, securities, grain and oil, and ocean shipping to Pudong and opened up the secondary real estate market there as well. In the meantime, a court for intellectual property rights, a legal assistance center, and police reforms were set up or introduced in Pudong in order to gain experience for adoption in the rest of the city.[66]

With the 1993 reforms, the leaders of Shanghai began to push for coordinated reforms in the management of state assets, the transformation of government functions, and the promotion of enterprise reforms. In late 1993, the Shanghai authorities transformed the municipal Textile Bureau, the Instrument and Electronics Bureau, and a corporation into three state asset management corporations. The Textile Bureau, for example, became the Shanghai City Textile State Asset Operation and Management Corporation. By late 1996, Shanghai had abolished most industrial bureaus.[67]

Initially, the asset management corporations inherited various government functions. Gradually these bureaucratic functions were transferred to the Municipal Economic Committee to allow for industry monitoring and correspondence with industrial ministries (and councils) in the central government. Meanwhile, the holding corporations, as the owners of state enterprises, began to emphasize the management of state assets for preservation and appreciation. Unlike the industrial bureaus from which they emerged, the holding corporations were not limited to investments in specific sectors and have become a major force in enterprise mergers and reorganizations. There have also been mergers between holding corporations.[68]

It should be added that not all industrial bureaus in Shanghai became holding corporations. In June 1994, the Second Bureau of Commerce and the Bureau of Aquatic Products, with a total staff size of 330 people, were abolished and succeeded by two small management offices of about forty people. In the days of scarcity, these bureaus had overseen the production and supply of non-staple foods and aquatic products and between them handled over eighty types of rationing coupons at one time. As these products have become plentiful with market reforms, there was no longer the need for a large bureaucracy. Instead, the management offices are retained to monitor market developments, facilitate the production and supply of non-staple products, and ensure the supply of a small number of goods under the direction of the municipal government.[69] In short, the timing of the administrative rationalization in Shanghai evidently coincided with the liberalization of prices and changing market conditions. This seems to corroborate the hypothesis about the market conditions for state rationalization.

In addition to Shanghai, various other localities also quietly pushed through administrative reforms, including those on the central government's list of experimental sites. Here I want to describe two other cases, Shuozhou, in inland Shanxi, and Shunde, in coastal Guangdong.

Shanxi's Shuozhou municipality is rich in land and mineral (coal) resources. In 1992, the Shuozhou leadership undertook a series of reforms to restructure the relationship between government and economy. Under the rubric of government reforms, various government departments and organizations were streamlined, cut, or converted into non-government services. The reorganization reduced the number of party and government departments and organizations from about 300 to 108 and the number of staff from 4,937 to 2,426. Most importantly, with the reorganization, the Shuozhou government ceased to have government departments that directly controlled state enterprises. Instead, state enterprises were assessed on three dimensions (management, profit and tax performance, and state asset preservation) and converted into shareholding firms *en masse*. As a consequence of these reforms, Shuozhou leaders believed that they had gone a long way toward the model of "small government, big society."[70]

While the reforms in Shuozhou appeared to have been carried out to please reformist demands from above, the rationalizing reforms in Guangdong's Shunde, a spectacular story of industrial success in China and indeed globally,[71] seem to have stemmed more from local desires. In the early 1990s, local leaders in Shunde became worried about the growing liabilities that the local government took on to facilitate the expansion of local state enterprises. They characterized the situation as follows: "enterprises taking care of profits, governments taking care of losses, and banks taking care of loans." There was no clear system of accountability between enterprise management and government. For government officials, many managers of state and collective enterprises had become emperors unto themselves. They spent company funds on fancy buildings and luxury cars and sometimes even passed managerial control to family members. The city (and township governments) got little in return.[72] Concerned about the long-term competitiveness of the local economy, Shunde leaders launched a series of reforms to reshape government–business relations and rationalize government administration.

The essence of Shunde's reforms was to limit the scope of government. Local leaders had spent much time on state enterprises but had no way of adequately monitoring them. They realized that, given limited energy and financial resources, a government must not try to do everything but should refrain from doing certain things that were taken for granted, such as micromanaging enterprises.[73] Shunde officials decided to divest government investment out of state enterprises, reasoning that they could fetch a good price at a time when the businesses were doing well (the colloquial expression was to "marry off the daughters while they are still young and beautiful"). They introduced foreign capital as equity holders and adopted shareholding or leasing out, thus ensuring that new owners would do the monitoring job that officials had been unable to adequately perform. In spite of some resistance from managers, local officials pushed through the divestiture.[74] In 1992, the Shunde government had 1,001 SOEs on its books. By the end of 1997, the government was owner of only ninety-four SOEs and partial owner of about seventy others; many of these were in infrastructure and some in high-tech industries.[75]

With the divestiture, the Shunde government also reformed its management of state assets by establishing a three-tier public asset management system to separate government from public assets in 1992–4. The business divestment freed the government to broaden the coverage of the social security system and invest in education and infrastructure (such as a 130 kilometer highway that cost RMB 4 billion).[76] Equally important, the divestiture reduced the demand on government in traditional areas and prompted Shunde leaders to rationalize the government itself and reduce staff. The staff cuts were carried out relatively easily because the booming economy and reform euphoria in 1992–4 presented numerous new opportunities for cadres parachuting out of government. This, in turn, made it possible to strengthen government efficiency.[77] In the words of Shunde mayor Feng Runsheng, "we are going to build a genuine market economy, providing a fair, competitive and open market environment for all enterprises."[78]

By the mid-1990s, the experiences of rationalizing reforms in the special economic zones as well as in Shanghai, Shunde, Zhucheng, and other places were widely known in both internal and popular publications, thus widening the realm of the possible and opening up new vistas for officials elsewhere to emulate and experiment. In the meantime, the pressures or incentives for reform had become stronger. First, local government officials frustrated by the double whammy of soaring administrative expenses and declining state enterprise performance saw no quick relief in sight as the central government adopted macroeconomic austerity measures to stabilize the economy.[79] Second, as firms relied on markets, staff in government bureaus keenly felt their loss of power and realized that the bureaus were looking more and more like shells. Convinced that further administrative rationalization was inevitable, officials of the industrial bureaus hoped to find a landing for themselves rather than become irrelevant. The holding corporations allowed the bureaucrats to become asset managers. In other words, just as in the case of the Minister of Electric Power acting as Chairman of the State Power Corporation, industrial bureaucrats can gain access to real power and resources in the transition to holding corporations. These incentives ensured the gradual spread of government rationalization once local governments began to emulate the Shanghai, Shunde, and Zhucheng experiences with eagerness.

Pathologies again

In short, though reforms in the central government proceeded slowly between 1992 and 1997, there was much experimentation with government rationalization, particularly at the local level, in China. Moreover, these reforms were very important in preparing the ground for further reforms. When I conducted interviews in various government departments and agencies in 1994 and later years, I found a widespread acceptance or resignation on the part of government staff that further government reforms involving staff reductions would be inevitable. While few wanted to become the victim of such reforms, changes in the economy had created other opportunities and made it possible for government staff to conceive of employment outside of the government. Some younger staff members even saw the reforms as a good opportunity for trying out alternatives.

The local experimentation served to highlight the difficulties of localized reforms in the absence of corresponding changes in the central government. For local governments, not having bureaus or offices that corresponded with those that existed at upper levels, especially the central government, can be a frustrating experience. Local officials may not receive central documents and invitations to conferences if they do not directly belong to a chain of hierarchy. Thus, even though local governments could simply abolish various bureaus, they retained remnants of the bureaus often in the form of offices in order to remain a part of the official policy and benefits loop. For the same reason, local governments would allow one office or bureau to be known simultaneously under different guises. This partly accounts for the growth in the number of bureaus in Hainan.

The success of local experimentation with rationalization elicited more demands for reform at the central government level. During the annual NPC (National People's Congress) session in spring 1997, delegates complained that the government had promised much for state enterprise reforms but had not truly delivered. They complained that reform of the investment decision-making mechanism was lagging behind changes in the market. There were too many government departments overseeing state enterprises, resulting in regulatory "disorder."[80] More broadly, as the Asian financial crisis came knocking on China's doors in 1997, there were deep concerns about China's own prospects. The expansion of the state did not just produce a proliferation of fees, levies, and surcharges that added burdens on businesses and citizens alike. Businesses associated with various state agencies were rigging the regulatory landscape and creating corruption just as in some of the collapsed economies in Southeast Asia. Such state corruption threatened to undermine not only the basis for sustained economic growth but also the legitimacy of the Chinese leadership and of the reforms.

The rationalization of 1998

It was in this context that the Chinese leadership decided to launch another drive to rationalize the government. In his report to the 15th National Congress of the Communist Party held in fall 1997, General Secretary Jiang Zemin reiterated the need for a new round of administrative reform. He stated that "unwieldy organization, bloated personnel, failure to separate functions of government from those of enterprises, and serious bureaucratism directly hamper the deepening of reform and the development of the economy and affect the relationship between the party and the masses."[81] In March 1998, the NPC approved a sweeping plan by incoming premier Zhu Rongji to streamline the Chinese bureaucracy and reduce the bureaucratic staff size by as much as one-half.[82] In spite of press speculations of bureaucratic resistance, the plan passed with 97 percent of the NPC votes, an overwhelming endorsement by the increasingly independent legislature.

The 1998 government restructuring program reduced the number of government ministries from forty to twenty-nine, with staff size trimmed by nearly half.[83] The heaviest axe fell on the industrial ministries that were the bulwarks of planning. The Ministry of Electric Power surrendered its regulatory powers to the State Economic and Trade Commission and became the State Power Corporation. The Ministries of Coal Industry, Machine-building, Metallurgical Industry, Internal Trade, Forestry as well as the national councils of Light Industry and Textile Industry were streamlined and downgraded to become industry bureaus under the supervision of the State Economic and Trade Commission. In addition to these industry bureaus, the restructuring program created the State Petroleum and Chemical Industry Bureau, also put under the SETC, by merging the administrative functions of the Ministry of Chemical Industry, the China Petroleum and Natural Gas Corporation, and the China Petroleum and Chemical Industry Corporation. All these bureaus were absorbed into the SETC in early 2001. The SETC thus became a MITI-style super-ministerial government agency for overseeing and regulating industrial enterprises.

The major exception to this trend of subsuming industrial regulation under the SETC was the creation of the Ministry of Information Industry (MII). In an apparent attempt to break down administrative barriers and streamline regulatory functions, the MII was created out of a merger of the Ministry of Posts and Telecommunications and the Ministry of Electronics Industry to oversee the industrial sectors playing a key role in China's information revolution. The MII also assumed the government functions for information and network management that previously resided in the Ministry of Broadcast, Film and Television, the China Aerospace Industry Corporation, and the China Aviation Industry Corporation.

All in all, with the government restructuring of 1998, China reached the final stage for transforming a government designed for central planning and bureaucratic command to a regulatory state catering to the market. As most industrial ministries lost their separate identities, the bureaucratic lineup in China became very much like those that are found in other East Asian economies. The SETC, the Ministry of Finance, and the People's Bank of China are the central institutions of economic governance. Rather than the core of the central government, the State Planning Commission was renamed the State Development Planning Commission, shifting its main duty to that of forecasting medium- and long-range growth targets. These macroeconomic agencies are complemented by a list of newly organized ministries including Science and Technology, Education, Labor and Social Security,[84] Personnel,[85] Land and Resources, as well as the Commission of Science, Technology, and Industry for National Defense. The Ministries of Railways, Communications (transportation), Construction, Agriculture, Water Resources, and Foreign Trade and Economic Cooperation did not undergo major reorganization. Other agencies that did not undergo a reorganization include the State Family Planning Commission, the State Nationalities Affairs Commission, and the Ministries of Foreign Affairs, National Defense, Culture, Health, Justice, Public Security, State Security, Civil Affairs, and Supervision as well as the increasingly prominent Audit Administration.

The shakeup in the bureaucratic lineup was matched by the transformation in economic philosophy that State Councilor Luo Gan enunciated in his report to the NPC. For Luo, the main duties of government agencies such as the SETC, the State Development Planning Commission, and the People's Bank of China should be focused on maintaining an overall economic balance, curbing inflation, and optimizing economic structure so as to achieve a sustained, rapid, and sound development of the economy. To American readers familiar with the talk from the Chairman of the Federal Reserve Bank or the Treasury Secretary, the Chinese stance sounds remarkably familiar.

The government statement on state enterprise relations is equally remarkable. The industry bureaus are still charged with the formulation and implementation of sectoral policies and regulations and the maintenance of market order. However, they lost the right to directly supervise and intervene in enterprises and institutions such as universities and research institutes.[86] According to Luo, the economic departments "should all practice the separation of administration from business operation, effectively change their functions and they no longer directly administer enterprises." The government will supervise state enterprises, including the evaluation and appointment of management, only as far as owner's equity permits it. Even so, these enterprises will, according to law, manage enterprise operations on their own with a view toward enhancing shareholder's asset value, take responsibility for their own profits and losses, and pay taxes.[87]

The strong legislative mandate notwithstanding, the bold government restructuring plan was greeted with mixed feelings. Enthusiasts believe the restructuring will mark the final stage of China's market-oriented reforms. Once this restructuring is complete, the Chinese bureaucracy will finally have been transformed from an apparatus for old-style planning to a regulatory state. Skeptics, however, point out that the history of Chinese bureaucratic reforms is littered with aborted reform plans and thus expect little chance of success for the present effort at bureaucratic rationalization.[88] After all, the Chinese leadership already had enough socio-economic challenges on hand and would probably hesitate to alienate a large number of government employees.

In fact, while causing some short-term uncertainty, the streamlining at the central government confounded skeptics and proceeded well. The State Development and Planning Commission downsized from 1,119 to 590; the Ministry of Finance and the People's Bank of China went from 1,144 and 948 respectively to 610 and 500.[89] The government bureaus and ministries I visited in August through September 1998 had already decided on a slimmed-down staff and were operating with reduced staff levels. For example, the State Bureau of Textile Industry, which was under the supervision of the MITI-like SETC, retained a staff of just seventy people in Beijing. Other sectoral administrations also trimmed their staff size from more than 200–400 to fewer than 100. In the case of the Bureau of Internal Trade, staff size was cut from 842 to 160.[90] Staff members I interviewed recognized that even this arrangement would be temporary and would eventually be phased out, as was indeed the case in 2001.

A major weakness of previous government reforms was that bureaucrats who lost their bureaucratic posts were simply moved to other government organizations or institutions. As a consequence, there was no reduction in payroll size. According to one report, there were as of 1998 1.3 million government-affiliated organizations or institutions (*shiye danwei*), including research institutes and universities, with a total payroll of about 28 million people. The annual expenditures for the *shiye danwei* accounted for 17 percent of central government spending.[91]

In an important departure from past practices, the 1998 government restructuring program has included a program to wean most *shiye danwei* from government support over a three-year period. After 2000, most *shiye danwei* will receive no budgetary allocations from the government.[92] For some units, this will be a painful transition that the government may relent on later. For others, this transition to the market is relatively easy to make. The China Electric Power Association, for example, was transformed from a government-supported company into a non-governmental industry organization, to be supported by cash-rich members. Various technical institutes, especially those focusing on applied technology research, should also find it relatively easy to survive on their own in the marketplace.[93] Even those institutes that will likely continue receiving government largess, including the Institute of Mathematics at the Chinese Academy of Sciences, have undertaken reforms to reduce staff and improve efficiency.[94] All in all, the reduction in government spending on institutions and organizations will help achieve a genuine reduction in government payroll.

Compared with the rationalization of central government, downsizing at lower levels of government will be more arduous. Central government staff tend to have university degrees, technical skills, and extensive social capital and are thus easier to place outside the bureaucracy, whereas the far larger number of redundant local staff possess less human capital on average and will thus face more difficulties in securing alternative employment, especially amid an economic downturn. Nevertheless, the local government reform experiments mentioned earlier suggest that some localities will be more eager to restructure than others. My visits to various local governments suggest that many staff members already anticipate the inevitability of bureaucratic rationalizations to come.

In the middle of 1999, the central government began to formally launch local government reforms which seek to eventually match the extent of staff cuts at the central government, i.e., cutting staffing size for all local governments, which stood at 5.18 million (actual employment 5.48 million), by half. Following the restructuring, the number of government departments in most provincial-level governments will drop from around fifty-three to about forty, with provinces or autonomous regions that are underdeveloped and less populous having only about thirty. For centrally administrated municipalities (Beijing, Shanghai, Tianjin, and Chongqing), the number of bureaus or departments will be reduced to about forty-five, down from sixty-one. Smaller cuts will also be made in other cities and counties. Large cities will cut the number of bureaus from fifty-five to about forty, whereas medium-sized cities will keep only thirty and small ones only twenty-two, down from thirty-seven and thirty respectively. For counties, large ones will decrease the number of departments from thirty to twenty-two; medium-sized and small counties will have only between fourteen and eighteen, down from an average of twenty-four.[95] In short, even if these local reforms only partially meet the centrally enunciated goals, they will still likely yield substantial benefits for society and businesses.

Skeptics may question the extent to which the government's declared position on state enterprise relations will be realized. However, there can be little doubt that the reduction in the number of government ministries and reshuffling of departments in other ministries will mean a less meddlesome government administration. Though there is still a long way to go before the Chinese economy enjoys a genuinely fair, transparent, and efficient regulatory environment, the environment for businesses can only change in the direction of more relaxation for at least three reasons. First, the streamlining means that there are fewer government ministries and a smaller staff to shift the responsibility around or to make trouble.[96] Second, the Chinese bureaucracy is known for its grinding consensual decision-making process.[97] There is a saying that while one-third of the bureaucrats seek to push forward, another one-third are actually pulling backward. The reduction and streamlining means that fewer government departments will have overlapping functions that cause infighting and gridlock. Finally, the staff reductions have made bureaucratic positions more scarce and thus more valuable, making existing staff members work harder to retain their positions. During the streamlining in 1998, staff members voted on divisional and departmental directors who then chose those to be retained in their respective division or department. Such bilateral selection appears to have boosted morale in the bureaucracies.[98] Many local governments have also started to use public competition to recruit mid-level officials. In 1999, the Ministry of Personnel required governments at all levels to recruit civil servants for middle-ranking party and government posts through open and fair competition rather than by appointment in order to promote clean and efficient government and revitalize the civil service system. In addition, the system had adopted annual performance appraisals, exchange of posts, and dismissal of incompetent offi-cials in order to enhance performance and reduce corruption.[99] These measures plus others aimed at making government more transparent, including greater use of the Internet, have helped reshape the behavior of bureaucrats from those of gate-keepers to become more service oriented.

Conclusions

In China, as elsewhere, government reforms have not occurred simply because someone has good plans for doing so. In the early 1980s as well as in 1998, strong political commitment has helped produce more sweeping cuts than in the late 1980s and early 1990s. The importance of politics and even an element of contingency have been especially apparent in the push for government reform since 1997. It was the perceived crisis of the state against the background of the Asian financial crisis, manifested in dramatic revenue shortfalls and rampant corruption by state agents, that finally galvanized the Chinese leadership to implement a massive restructuring of the government.

While the rationalization of government administration is a political act, politicians need the right soil for their ideas to germinate into new formation. This is particularly the case for the transformation of the socialist state. The mutual dependence between bureaucratic agency and state enterprise has proven to be especially tenacious. Such mutual dependence, as Chinese leaders correctly noted, also implied a strong interrelationship between the reform of government and economy. Whereas administrative reforms launched in the early 1980s were quickly eroded, the growth and steady expansion of the market since then have provided a nourishing environment for the rationalization of the state in the 1990s. As an official from Liaoning's Haicheng put it, "it was the market that liberated the government" and enabled the latter to truly reform itself.[100] Viewed together with other major initiatives, the implementation of recent government reforms should put China well on its way toward rationalizing the Chinese state for a modern market economy.

Notes

1 Martin Whyte, "Who Hates Bureaucracy? A Chinese Puzzle," in Victor Nee and David Stark (eds.), *Remaking the Economic Institutions of Socialism: China and Eastern Europe* (Stanford: Stanford University Press, 1989), p. 252.
2 Bernard Silberman, *Cages of Reason: The Rise of the Rational State in France, Japan, the United States, and Great Britain* (Chicago: University of Chicago Press, 1993).
3 Barry Naughton, "Hierarchy and the Bargaining Economy: Government and Enterprise in the Reform Process," in Kenneth G. Lieberthal and David M. Lampton (eds.), *Bureaucracy, Politics, and Decision Making in Post-Mao China* (Berkeley: University of California Press, 1992), pp. 271–5.
4 *Guangzhou ribao* (Guangzhou Daily), 6 June 1999.
5 Kenneth Lieberthal and Michel Oksenberg, *Policy Making in China: Leaders, Structures, and Processes* (Princeton: Princeton University Press, 1988); Susan Shirk, *The Political Logic of Economic Reform in China* (Berkeley: University of California Press, 1993).

6 Wu Guoguang, *Zhao Ziyang yu zhengzhi gaige* (Political reform under Zhao Ziyang) (Taibei: Yuanjing chuban shiye gongsi, 1997), pp. 72–6.
7 Cited in Wu Guoguang, *Zhao Ziyang yu zhengzhi gaige*, p. 72.
8 Xue Muqiao, "Wending jingji, shenhua gaige, yi gaige zonglan quanju" (Stabilize the economy, deepen reforms, and use reforms to steer the overall situation), *Zhongguo jingji nianjian* (Almanac of China's economy) (Beijing: Jingji guanli chubanshe, 1988).
9 Interview with ministerial personnel, 1994.
10 Here we leave aside the issue of market formation.
11 On bureaucratic decision making in China, see Kenneth Lieberthal and Michel Oksenberg, *Policy Making in China: Leaders, Structures, and Processes* (Princeton: Princeton University Press, 1988). The following quote from Ren Zhongyi, former First Party Secretary of Guangdong, captures well the challenge facing businesses:

> Before a plan could be executed, it had to be stamped with scores of chops of approval. The collection of all the necessary chops could take months and sometimes the documents could be lost in the process. Besides, everyone along the line usually had the veto power. If he questioned the validity of a certain part of the plan, the whole plan would be shelved until his objection was resolved.

> (Quoted in John Burns, "Reforming China's Bureaucracy, 1979–82", *Asian Survey*, vol. 23, no. 6 (June 1983), p. 696)

12 Chen Ruisheng, Pang Yuanzheng, and Zhu Manliang (eds.), *Zhongguo gaige quanshu: zhengzhi tizhi gaige juan* (The complete Chinese reforms: political system reform volume) (Dalian: Dalian chubanshe, 1993), p. 28.
13 *Zhongguo jingji shibao* (Chinese Economic Times), 28 October 1997.
14 Chen Ruisheng, Pang Yuanzheng, and Zhu Manliang (eds.), *Zhongguo gaige quanshu*, p. 21.
15 The index of gross government revenue was, with the past year as 100, 98.4 (1979), 98.4 (1980), 100.4 (1981), and 103.2 (1982). State Statistical Bureau, *Statistical Yearbook of China 1990* (Beijing: China Statistical Publishing House, 1990), p. 229.
16 As part of the bureaucratic rationalization, lifetime tenure was abolished and a norm of retirement was initiated (Melanie Manion, *Retirement of Revolutionaries in China* (Princeton: Princeton University Press, 1993)). The rationalization of the party–state included a significant streamlining of party organizations and a major reduction in the size of the army. More broadly, China adopted a new constitution.
17 Deng Xiaoping, "Streamlining Organizations Constitutes a Revolution," in Deng Xiaoping, *Selected Works of Deng Xiaoping (1975–1982)* (Beijing: Foreign Languages Press, 1982), pp. 374–5.
18 Ibid., p. 376.
19 Chen Ruisheng, Pang Yuanzheng, and Zhu Manliang (eds.), *Zhongguo gaige quanshu*, p. 22.
20 Melanie Manion, *Retirement of Revolutionaries in China* (Princeton: Princeton University Press, 1993).
21 Stephen K. Ma, *Administrative Reform in Post-Mao China: Efficiency or Ethics* (Lanham, MD: University Press of America, 1996), pp. 122–9.
22 John Burns, "Reforming China's Bureaucracy, 1979–82," *Asian Survey*, vol., 23, no. 6 (June 1983), pp. 692–722.
23 Chen Ruisheng, Pang Yuanzheng, and Zhu Manliang (eds.), *Zhongguo gaige quanshu*, p. 27.
24 For documents on simplifying administration and enlivening enterprises, see, for example, the annual publication *Zhongguo jingji nianjian* (Almanac of China's economy).

25 Jan Winiecki, "Why Economic Reforms Fail in the Soviet System: A Property Rights-based Approach," *Economic Inquiry*, vol. 28 (April 1990).
26 See the quote in Wu Guoguang, *Zhao Ziyang yu zhengzhi gaige*, p. 422.
27 Deng Xiaoping, *Deng Xiaoping wenxuan* (Selected works of Deng Xiaoping) (Beijing: Renmin chubanshe, 1993), vol. 3, p.160.
28 Wu Guoguang, *Zhao Ziyang yu zhengzhi gaige*, p.31, provides a memo of Hu's remarks.
29 Wu Guoguang, *Zhao Ziyang yu zhengzhi gaige*, pp. 73, 87. For a review of the discussions in Chinese publications at this time, see Stephen K. Ma, *Administrative Reform in Post-Mao China*, esp. ch. 4. Many of the ideas were already adumbrated earlier.
30 Zhao Ziyang, "Yanzhe you Zhongguo tese de shehui zhuyi daolu qianjin" (Advance along the road of socialism with Chinese characteristics), *Zhongguo jingji nianjian* (1988), p. I-1–20. An earlier draft of the report for the 13th Party Congress stated that "bureaucratism had become unbearable" (Wu Guoguang, ibid., p. 462).
31 For an explication of this point, see Gu Jiaqi, *Cong jigou gaige dao xingzheng tizhi gaige de shijian ye sikao* (From organizational to administrative system reform: practice and reflections) (Beijing: Zhongguo fazhan chubanshe, 1997), p. 28.
32 For evidence of such local experimentation, see He Guanghui, *Yige gaigezhe de zuji* (Footsteps of a reformer) (Beijing: Gaige chubanshe, 1996), pp. 10, 34.
33 Plan C called for some streamlining without major changes in structure.
34 Zhao Ziyang, "Yanzhe you Zhongguo tese de shehui zhuyi daolu qianjin" (Advance along the road of socialism with Chinese characteristics).
35 For details, including the explanation given by State Councilor Song Ping at the first session of the 7th NPC, see Gu Jiaqi, *Cong jigou gaige dao xingzheng tizhi gaige de shijian ye sikao*, pp. 33–53.
36 Ibid., pp. 36–7, 83.
37 For some of these strategies of negative adjustment, see Stephen K. Ma, "Chinese Bureaucracy and Post-Mao Reforms: Negative Adjustment," *Asian Survey*, vol., 30, no. 11 (November 1990), pp. 1038–52.
38 Song Ping, "Guanyu Guowuyuan jigou gaige fang'an de shuoming" (Explanations of the State Council's organizational reforms), in Gu Jiaqi, ibid., p. 52. The Ministry of Light Industry was found to have 170 roles and functions. Of the 170, 9 belonged to local governments, 15 should be handled by enterprises and social organizations, 37 could be transferred to industry associations. Similar experimentation was also conducted in the Ministry of Communications, the State Environmental Protection Agency, and the Bureau of Construction Materials (Gu Jiaqi, ibid., p. 81).
39 He Guanghui, *Yige gaigezhe de zuji*, p. 7.
40 Liao Xun, *Kaifang de chengben* (The costs of opening up) (Haikou: Nanhai chuban gongsi, 1994), p. 78; *Xiao zhengfu, da shehui: Hainan xin tizhi de lilun yu shijian* (Small government, big society: The theory and practice of Hainan's new system) (Haikou: Sanhuan chubanshe, 1991); *Marx Engels "xiao zhengfu" sixiang yu dangdai jingji gaige* (The theory of "small state" in Marx and Engels and contemporary economic reform) (Kaikou: Hainan renmin chubanshe, 1988).
41 The Chinese characters Liao used were *xiao zhengfu, da shehui*. This can be literally translated as "small government, big society," though it is probably more appropriate to substitute "state" for "government."
42 Liao Xun, *Kaifang de chengben*, pp. 9–18. For an assessment of Liao's ideas, see also Kjeld Erik Brodsgaard, "State and Society in Hainan: Liao Xun's Ideas on 'Small Government, Big Society,'" in Kjeld Erik Brodsgaard and David Strand (eds.), *Reconstructing Twentieth-Century China: State Control, Civil Society, and National Identity* (Oxford: Clarendon Press, 1998).
43 In the notice on the establishment of Hainan Province, the party center and the State Council stipulated that the provincial government should have a small bureaucracy. Hainan should make a breakthrough in organizational setup and serve as an experiment in provincial-level government reforms. Quoted in Chinese Academy of Social

Sciences Project Group, *"Xiao zhengfu da shehui" de lilun yu shijian: Hainan zhengzhi tizhi yu shehui tizhi gaige yanjiu* (The theory and practice of "small government, big society": A study of political and social system reform in Hainan) (Beijing: Shehui kexue wenxian chubanshe, 1998), p. 7.

44 Xu Shijie Huainian, *Huainian Xu Shijie* (Remembering Xu Shijie) (Guangdong: Guangdong renmin chubanshe, 1992), pp. 316–17.

45 Liao Xun, *Kaifang de chengben*, p. 18.

46 For comprehensive studies of Hainan's administrative, economic, and social reforms, see Chinese Academy of Social Sciences Project Group, *"Xiao zhengfu da shehui" de lilun yu shijian: Hainan zhengzhi tizhi yu shehui tizhi gaige yanjiu*; Wang Luolin, (ed.), *Hainan jianli shehui zhuyi shichang jingji tizhi de shijian* (Hainan's practice in building a socialist market economic system) (Beijing: Shehui kexue wenxian chubanshe, 1997).

47 Jiang Bo, Yu Yong, and Li Benjun, "Shiji zhengfu gan shenmo" (What should municipal governments do?), *Jingji ribao* (Economic Daily), 28 October 1996.

48 Gu Jiaqi, *Cong jigou gaige dao xingzheng tizhi gaige de shijian ye sikao* (Beijing: Zhongguo fazhan chubanshe, 1997), p. 123.

49 Ibid., p. 108.

50 Chinese Academy of Social Sciences Project Group, *"Xiao zhengfu da shehui" de lilun yu shijian: Hainan zhengzhi tizhi yu shehui tizhi gaige yanjiu*, p. 8.

51 Gu Jiaqi, *Cong jigou gaige dao xingzheng tizhi gaige de shijian ye sikao*, p. 123.

52 Deng's push for growth was not an unalloyed success but had substantial negative consequences. Dali L. Yang, "Economic Crisis and Market Transition in the 1990s", in Edwin Winckler (ed.), *China's Transition from Leninism* (Boulder, CO: Lynne Rienner, 1999), pp. 151–77.

53 Zhonggong Zhongyang Wenxian Yanjiushi (ed.), *Shisida yilai zhongyao wenxian xuanbian: shang* (Selection of important documents since the Fourteenth CCP Party Congress: Part I) (Beijing: Renmin chubanshe, 1996), p. 22.

54 Gu Jiaqi, *Cong jigou gaige dao xingzheng tizhi gaige de shijian ye sikao*, p. 188.

55 Ibid., p. 236; Jiang Zemin's speech to the second plenary session of the 14th CCP Central Committee in March 1993, Zhonggong Zhongyang Wenxian Yanjiushi (ed.), *Shisida yilai zhongyao wenxian xuanbian: shang*, p.124.

56 Ironically, Gu himself participated in designing the 1988 government reforms.

57 Zhonggong Zhongyang Wenxian Yanjiushi (ed.), *Shisida yilai zhongyao wenxian xuanbian: shang*, p. 125.

58 This observation is based on various conversations and interviews with people knowledgeable about the government reforms.

59 *Jingji ribao* (Economic Daily), 19 November 1996.

60 Personal interviews.

61 Some local governments, especially Shanghai, have adopted the holding company model.

62 John Burns, "China's Leviathan," *Asian Wall Street Journal*, 17 March 1998.

63 Zhonggong Zhongyang Wenxian Yanjiushi (ed.), *Shisida yilai zhongyao wenxian xuanbian: shang*, p. 125.

64 *Jingji ribao* (Economic Daily), 13 September 1992.

65 Zhonggong Zhongyang Wenxian Yanjiushi (ed.), *Shisida yilai zhongyao wenxian xuanbian: shang*, p. 125.

66 *Renmin ribao* (People's Daily), overseas ed., 19 April 1997.

67 Shanghai, n.d. "Shanghai guoyou konggu gongsi guanli tixi yanjiu" (The management system of Shanghai's state holding corporations), Mimeo.

68 Shanghai State Asset Management Office, "Shenhua guoyou zichan guanli tizhi gaige, tui dong guoysu cunliang zichan de liudong he chongzu" (Deepen reforms of the state asset management system, promote the circulation and reorganization of existing state assets), Mimeo (21 May 1997).

69 *Jingji cankao bao* (Economic Reference Daily), 19 June 1994.

70 *Jingji ribao* (Economic Daily), 29 May 1994.
71 By the mid-1990s, Shunde, a lowly ranked county-level city, produced one-third of China's electric fans and microwave ovens, one-eighth of the refrigerators, and one-half of water heaters and rice cookers (Jianhong Zhu, "Kao gaige chuang xin youshi" (Rely on reform to create new advantages), *Renmin ribao* (People's Daily), 7 November 1997, p. 2).
72 Dow Jones Newswire, 14 March 1994.
73 Jianhong Zhu, "Kao gaige chuang xin youshi" (Rely on reform to create new advantages), *Renmin ribao* (People's Daily), 7 November 1997.
74 Dow Jones Newswire, 15 March 1994.
75 *China Daily Business Weekly*, 19 January 1998.
76 Ibid.
77 *Renmin ribao*, south China ed., 26 November 1997.
78 *China Daily Business Weekly*, 19 January 1998.
79 Dali L. Yang, "Economic Crisis and Market Transition in the 1990s."
80 *Renmin ribao*, overseas ed., 7 March 1997.
81 Jiang Zemin, "Hold High the Great Banner of Deng Xiaoping Theory for an All-round Advancement of the Cause of Building Socialism with Chinese Characteristics to the Twenty-first Century," Xinhua News Agency, 21 September 1997.
82 Interestingly, Luo Gan, state councillor and the outgoing Secretary-General of the State Council, presented the government restructuring plan to the NPC.
83 All substantive information on the restructuring in this section is based on "Further on Restructuring Plan," Xinhua, 6 March 1998.
84 The Ministry of Labor and Social Security was charged with setting up a unified social security administrative system.
85 The Ministry of Personnel oversees the management of technical personnel and civil servants, the appointment and removal of leaders of large enterprises under the supervision of the State Council, and the dispatching of supervisory commissioners to large enterprises.
86 Most of these universities have been transferred to the supervision of the Ministry of Education and local governments.
87 "Further on Restructuring Plan," Xinhua, 6 March 1998.
88 Bian Hongwei, "Reform Doubters Out of Line," *China Daily*, 13 March 1998.
89 *Guangzhou ribao*, 24 May 1999.
90 There have been reports that some government staff who were let go during the reorganization had been rehired, sometimes because they possessed key bureaucratic skills that were sorely missed. But this phenomenon is of minor significance in relation to the overall trend.
91 *Zhongguo gaige bao* (China reform news), 15 April 1999. For a scholarly study of the *shiye danwei*, see Huang Hengxue, *Zhongguo shiye guanli tizhi gaige yanjiu* (The reform of China's shiye management system) (Beijing: Qinghua daxue chubanshe, 1998).
92 The educational system is exempt though budget pressures have prompted universities to adopt reforms of their own.
93 *China Daily*, 12 April 1999; interviews.
94 *China Daily*, 12 March 1999.
95 *Liaowang* (Outlook), no. 29 (1999); *Guangzhou ribao*, 20 July 1999.
96 *China Daily*, 13 March 1998.
97 Kenneth Lieberthal and Michel Oksenberg, *Policy Making in China*, 1988.
98 Interviews in July 1998.
99 *China Daily*, 20 July 1999.
100 *Zhongguo jingji shibao*, 19 November 1997.

2 Reappraising central–local relations in Deng's China

Decentralization, dilemmas of control, and diluted effects of reform

Jae Ho Chung

China's track record of economic reforms has been more than impressive. Its turbo-charged development over the last two decades with a real average gross domestic product (GDP) growth per annum of 9.8 percent (1978–97) made China the seventh largest economy in the world and second largest on a purchasing power parity basis.[1] China's remarkable accomplishments constitute a stark contrast with the serious troubles that Russia has been facing since the collapse of the Soviet Union. As a matter of fact, China has quite successfully dispelled the ungrounded concern that it might disintegrate politically and even territorially. There is no doubt that both drastic and significant changes have occurred in China's central–local relations in the last twenty years, but, overall, they do not appear to have been as centrifugal as we would normally take for granted. Rather, Beijing has certainly been more adept and astute than Moscow in preserving hierarchical authority and utilizing the political mechanisms to enforce its priorities in the complex processes of reform.[2]

China's reform of the last two decades may be epitomized as the changes toward decentralization, marketization, and privatization. Through decentralization, the extent of which seems to have so far been the largest among the three, a wide range of decisional authority was devolved from the central government to the provinces and below for the sake of promoting local incentives and initiatives for reform.[3] Through marketization, state-plan controls were significantly weakened and the principles of competition and comparative advantage were diffused. Through privatization, the extent of which remains quite limited, individual and non-state property rights as well as foreign capital have gradually increased their influence over China's economy.

This chapter, evaluating China's reform from a central–local relations perspective, takes up the issue of decentralization not only because it has been most directly related to the restructuring of central–local relations but also because it encompasses the policy measures most extensively implemented in the post-Mao era. While marketization has also had some significant bearing upon central–local dynamics, it is treated here only as a supplementary theme. Privatization is perhaps most thinly linked to the reform of central–local relations.[4] The adoption of decentralization (defined here as a "downward transfer of power and authority between different levels of government") as the key concept is helpful for the understanding of China's central–local relations as, in a descriptive sense, it permits us to chart the major devolutionary changes in a wide range of functional areas. On the other hand, it also enables us to identify the issue areas where decisional authority was not significantly devolved or even recentralized. This crucial variation then allows us to gauge the intricate balance between central control and local discretion in China.[5]

The remainder of this chapter consists of three sections. The first provides the background to the earlier reform phase in which the "seeds" of transformation were planted during the late 1970s and early 1980s. More specifically, the Maoist norms of local suppression and the post-Mao leadership's strenuous efforts to de-ideologize Beijing's management of localities are discussed. The second section delineates and assesses the principal measures of decentralization and recentralization implemented for the last twenty years in a total of nine issue areas, both economic and non-economic. The third section offers a balance sheet that appraises the post-Mao decentralization reform, along with key implications and prospects for China's central–local dynamics.

"Seeding the transformation": norm changes in China's central–local relations

Decentralization entails more than simple structural and procedural readjustments. Genuine intergovernmental devolution of authority must be accompanied by concerted efforts to weaken the dominant norms of centralization that take local compliance for granted. In systems where a majority of key local officials are appointed rather than popularly elected, the problem of "bureaucratic careerism" – a tendency of career bureaucrats to become highly opportunistic to advance their careers largely by complying with orders from above – is particularly pervasive. The symptoms of bureaucratic careerism can be pushed to an extreme in socialist systems where advocating local interests against the center's priorities may easily be interpreted as following an "incorrect" ideological line. Under the fears of persecution, however important local interests might appear, they could never become as crucial as the careers of the officials involved and, consequently, most local implementors would choose to play safe by doing precisely what they are told by the center.[6]

Central–local relations in the Maoist era: norms of uniform compliance

Decentralization was by no means an unfamiliar experience in pre-reform China. As a matter of fact, Maoist China constantly oscillated between centralization and decentralization. No evidence suggests, however, that decentralization experiences during Mao's rule produced a genuinely expanded scope of local discretion. Rather, rigid ideological control dominated the policy process, depriving local leaders of the incentives to risk their political fate for local interests. Consequently, uniform compliance became the norm and local discretion a dangerous luxury: not only were local leaders not allowed to revolt, they were not even permitted to be unhappy with the center. In sum, however decentralized it appeared in theory and intention, the administrative *modus operandi* in Mao's China was generally for strengthening central control at the expense of local discretion.[7]

Systemic norms against local deviation in Maoist China were rigid beyond casual imagination. Particularly since 1957 after the traumatic anti-rightist purges, the principle of *yindi zhiyi* became largely an empty slogan.[8] During the successive phases of the "Great Leap Forward" (1958–9), the "Socialist Education Campaign" (1962–5), and the Cultural Revolution (1966–76), all of which involved large-scale purges, local incentives were dictated solely from above and genuine regional variations became nearly extinct. Beijing's intermittent calls for provincial discretion and adaptive implementation fell on deaf ears, standardization (*yidao qie*) became widespread, and swift total compliance was regarded as the key expression of ideological conformity and loyalty to the center and Mao in particular. The implementation processes of the communization drive, the "walking on two legs" movement, "mass irrigation campaigns," "grain production wars," and the "iron and steel movement" demonstrate the point well.[9]

The willful neglect of *yindi zhiyi* during the Cultural Revolution decade is best exemplified by Beijing's imposition of "single models" for nationwide emulation, most notably the Dazhai model for agricultural production, the Daqing model for industrial management, and the "eight model works" for theatrical performances. The gross violation of *yindi zhiyi* was also highlighted by the nationwide application of standardized policy in a wide range of issue areas. The policies of "take grain as the key link" (*yiliang weigang*) and "across-the-board mechanization" (*quanpan jixiehua*) were imposed indiscriminately on all localities during the Cultural Revolution decade, irrespective of regional meteorological and topological variations.[10] Even the central–provincial budgetary sharing arrangements of this period now appear to have been mostly nominal. Despite the stipulations of a "fiscal contract" system (*shouzhi baogan*) for 1971–3 and of a "fixed-ratio retention" system (*guding bili liucheng*) for 1973–5, it was later suggested that both systems had been implemented only in name and this five-year period was in fact one of "total centralization" (*tongshou tongzhi*).[11] Furthermore, as a result of Beijing's decade-long emphasis on local autarchy, the tendency for "cellular" development was accelerated with the correlation coefficients for provincial per capita agricultural and industrial outputs rising from −0.16 in 1957 to 0.75 in 1980, indicating a sharp decline in economic specialization.[12]

A crucial question remains to be answered: how was Beijing able to maintain its control over localities in the midst of policy oscillations and organizational breakdown during the periods discussed above? The question becomes all the more interesting if we consider that most of central policy directives during the Maoist era were "opinions" (*yijian*), "notifications" (*tongbao*), and "regulations" (*guiding*) of a less binding nature, as opposed to "orders" (*mingling*) and "decisions" (*jueding*), and that, equally importantly, the center then had only a very primitive capacity for administrative monitoring.[13] The answer lay in the norm sharing among local implementors. Through organizational learning, provincial officials had known from their past experiences of policy oscillations and subsequent purges that deviations were not to go unpunished. The internalization of such norms dictated that local officials follow central policy to the letter out of genuine fear. An editorial in the *People's Daily* paraphrases the nature of such fear:

> Under the circumstances where people are constantly told that they must not revise central documents and must follow them in everything they do, how can they solve new problems and difficulties which arise from the new conditions, and whose solutions are not provided by the central documents? … [The most important problem is that] they dare not speak of irrational orders, inflated production statistics, and policies unsuitable for local conditions. … [The core reason lies in] nothing but fears. The fear of being labeled as a "capitulationist"; the fear of being dismissed from one's post; the fear of being expelled from the party; the fear of being divorced by one's wife; the fear of serving a prison term; and the fear of being beheaded.[14]

When systemic norms bred constant fears on the part of local implementors, the faithful representation of local interests became impossible. Further, the norm of vertical control against local deviation was constantly supplemented by the horizontal operation of self-policing "metanorms." As ideological conformity constituted the ultimate criterion of career advancement, everyone sought to escape punishment by exposing the deviant acts by others. As a result, everyone strove to detect someone else's deviation so that their own allegiance became known and their careers were promoted at someone else's expense. When betrayal and informing were rewarded, there was little room left for interpretive discretion or adaptive implementation.[15]

The foregoing overview of the Maoist era suggests the following points concerning what would make decentralization genuine in China. First, without weakening the center's ideological control mechanism – that is, unless the norms of decentralization became widely accepted and internalized – local discretion would continue to be deemed ideologically problematic and politically unsafe. Second, economic and fiscal decentralization alone would not suffice to make the center genuinely committed to the cause of decentralization. That is, without administrative decentralization, the ever-impatient center might always find it convenient to revert to intervention. Third, as long as the central government remained the "center" of power and policy making, as is true in many unitary systems, antinomies of decentralization also stay with it. With the strengthening of its monitoring capacity to check pro forma compliance, Beijing might now find it easier to enforce its preferences with regard to national priority policies.[16]

Central–local relations in the reform era: the norm changes

The post-Mao reform has differed significantly from the Maoist precedents in that some key measures of administrative decentralization had preceded the devolution of substantive decision-making authority in the allocation of fiscal and material resources. This contrast may reflect the post-Mao reformist leadership's painful recognition that its economic reform platforms were bound to fail without first transforming the norms and rules of local policy implementation.[17] Only with fundamental changes in the perceptions of local implementors concerning the permissible boundaries of their discretion could their fears of persecution and the ensuing problems of bureaucratic careerism be mitigated. The most distinctive aspect of post-Mao reforms concerned the reformist leadership's strenuous efforts for the "emancipation of mind" (*sixiang jiefang*) in order to redress the pernicious effects of excessive ideological control over human relations in general and over economic management in particular. It was a painstaking decision on the part of the post-Mao leadership since it had to carry out the task as completely as possible yet without critically damaging the legitimacy of the regime dependent heavily on the control by the center, the Communist Party, and Mao Zedong Thought.[18]

During 1977–82, official news media were literally flooded with numerous attacks on "ultra-leftism." These attacks were conveniently launched against the then disgraced "Gang of Four" but they were in fact disguised criticisms of the Maoist era and Mao in particular. They initially took the subtle form of theoretical debates through which ultra-leftist policies were severely criticized for their excessive idealism. Urgent need for empiricism was emphasized.[19] Theoretical debates soon gave way to calls for "independent thinking" based on objective facts, not on empty ideological tenets.

As a concrete manifestation of the post-Mao leadership's determination to shake the ideological yoke off local implementors, large-scale pardons were granted to many of those who had been stigmatized as "rightists" and other "bad elements" and severely persecuted during the successive campaigns and purges since 1957. The pardoned included a large group of former provincial and local cadres who had dared to speak out against the policies that they had considered unsuitable for their localities.[20] These measures, along with the leadership's efforts to weed out "leftists" and beneficiaries of the Cultural Revolution, must have contributed to the mitigation of doubts held by many concerning the intentions of the central leadership.

The reformist leadership's efforts to transform the norms governing central–local relations were soon translated into a strong emphasis on the *yindi zhiyi* principle. The following excerpt well illustrates the leadership's commitment to avoid policy standardization:

> [T]o uphold the principle of seeking truth from facts … we must combine the spirit of the central directives with the actual conditions of our localities … and rectify any tendency for policy standardization through "whipping up a gust of ideological wind." … Our country is vast and populous and has

varied conditions. Since different localities have their own distinct conditions … we must not allow the same pattern everywhere.[21]

Beijing's stress on *yindi zhiyi* meant that local discretion in interpreting and implementing central policy should be permitted to account for varied local conditions and that the past malpractice of imposing "blanket policies" (*yidaoqie* or *yiguozhu*) should be avoided. Subsequently, the practice of promoting a single model for the whole country also came under severe criticisms, eventually to be abolished.[22]

The post-Mao reformist leadership employed a wide range of measures to minimize ideological influence over central–local policy dynamics. First, many central and provincial policy documents over and over again stressed the stability of post-Mao reform policies. Concerning the decollectivization reform, for instance, frequent reminders were issued that, unlike the past, the new rural policy would not change in tandem with abrupt ideological shifts at the center. Since the new leadership was keenly aware of the prevalent local fears of policy change, guarantees were made to ensure that the local perceptions based on the long-held belief that "it is safer being left than right" (*ningzuo huyou*) were groundless. Beijing also sought to prohibit rushed implementation rooted in another popular belief that it was "safer being faster than slower" (*ningkuai human*) in executing central policy.[23]

Second, in its efforts to rationalize the processes of policy making and implementation, the center called for the redress of the widespread practice of reporting inflated statistics. The prevalence of fraudulent reporting and its deleterious ratchet effects forced the new leadership to reconsider that under-achievement was not necessarily an act of non-compliance and, therefore, should not automatically be stigmatized. In order to halt the malpractice of distorting local performance statistics, for instance, the State Planning Commission, the Ministry of Agriculture, and the State Statistical Bureau issued a joint circular in 1980, which supplied five multiple indices for grain production and four for animal husbandry, replacing the hitherto single index of "per *mu* grain output" and the "number of livestock in possession."[24]

Third, the reformist leadership also made a pledge to reduce the government's use of overly ambitious and militant slogans as a key instrument of policy implementation. A derivative of these efforts was in part the disappearance, or at least a considerable reduction, of direct quotations from Mao Zedong Thought in the formulation and implementation of policy. Also related were strenuous efforts to criticize the widespread use of "hackneyed slogans" for the imposition of standardized policy.[25] Fourth, measures were also taken to promote the comparative advantages of different regions and localities. In 1978–80, a series of regional planning conferences were convened to identify regional economic conditions and developmental priorities on the basis of which central policy was to be formulated. Furthermore, multiple models were promoted to reflect these regionally variant conditions.[26]

Fifth, in order to expand provincial initiatives and enhance local adaptability in implementation, the reformist leadership might also have assumed that the appointment of provincial leaders well tuned to local conditions was desirable. Since the personnel decisions for provincial first party secretaries (PFPSs) were handled exclusively by the Central Organization Department with the *nomen-klatura* power, the increased share of PFPSs assigned to their native provinces and neighboring ones seems to have reflected Beijing's intention to expand local policy discretion. While the share of PFPSs assigned to their native provinces was only 5 percent in 1969–71 and 21 percent for 1949–79, by 1983 it rose to 26.6 percent. With the inclusion of PFPSs assigned to the neighboring provinces, the figure rose from an average of 41.3 percent for 1949–78 to 53.3 percent in 1983.[27]

Charting the changes: an overview of major issue areas

Any review of central–local relations in China, or in any system for that matter, is a complex task not only because the pertinent interactions take place between at least two different levels of government (and analysis) but because the dynamics also concern a wide range of policy issues. Yet, the predominant majority of studies on China's central–local relations have to date focused on their economic dimensions, and most notably the fiscal aspect (largely on budgetary arrangements and investment controls). It should be noted that the superfluous use of fiscal indicators expressed mostly in percentage terms reinforces the dichotomous zero-sum conceptualization of central–local relations. Such a conceptualization seems erroneous or highly debatable at the least, since such formal arrangements as budgetary allocations and transfers do not tell everything about the delicate balance between central control and local discretion.[28] This points to an acute need for us to opt for a more comprehensive view of China's central–local dynamics that are being rapidly diversified over time. Such a comprehensive perspective may enable us to explore a multitude of issue areas in which Beijing and localities have most frequently interacted and thus to draw a picture that more closely resembles the intricate balance of power poised between them.

Weakening the state planning system

Compared with the former Soviet Union, China's plan control was relatively weak and disorganized, permitting more decisional latitude for local governments. As a matter of fact, plan refinement was frequent, interunit bargaining rampant, relational contracting prevalent. Even the margin of error, as high as 25 percent officially, was allowed for plan fulfillment in pre-reform China.[29] Despite all these weaknesses and problems, China was undoubtedly a system of state plans, in which both macro plan items and micro-quotas were generated and imposed on lower level government units and enterprises by the state and the "little State Council," the State Planning Commission (SPC), in particular.[30]

Due to the mandatory nature of plan fulfillment and the politico-ideological costs implicated in the cases of failure, "ratchet effects" were constantly produced and simply "meeting the quotas" without due regard for quality became the *modus operandi*. Particularly when Beijing lacked an optimal capacity to collect and analyze the pertinent information on local performance, decentralization appeared to be a cost-effective alternative.[31]

The post-Mao changes introduced to China's planning system can be summarized as follows. First, as Table 2.1 well demonstrates, the total number of plan items controlled by SPC was drastically reduced over the years. Second, the reduction also represented a dual process: one in which the total number of binding "mandatory targets" (*zhilingxing zhibiao*) was sharply cut down; and the other in which less binding "guidance targets" (*zhidaoxing zhibiao*) were introduced to replace the mandatory ones.[32] Third, annual plan instructions (*niandu jihua*) were less emphasized and instead mid- and long-term economic planning (*zhongchangqi guihua*) were stressed. That is, the principal function of state plans has gradually changed from mechanically issuing micro-quotas to devising viable long-term strategies for development. Also present was the increase in the use of indirect means of control such as macro financial instruments as opposed to direct administrative measures of imposition.[33]

Table 2.1   Number of mandatory plan items under SPC's control, 1979–98

	Agricultural production	*Industrial production*	*Material allocation*	*State procurement*	*Price control* *	*Export control*
pre-1979	25	200+	256	65	1,336	–
1980	–	120+	–	–	–	900+
1981	20	–	–	–	–	–
1982	13	–	–	–	–	–
1985	0	60+	20+	–	1,021	31
1990	0	–	19	–	–	–
1991	0 (17)	–	–	–	737	29
1992	0 (9)	59	19	21	89	29
1993	0 (7)	36	12	16 (3)	–	22
1994	0	33	11	14 (4)	–	–
1998	0	–	–	–	58	16

Sources: Gui Shiyong, *Zhongguo jihua tizhi gaige* (The reform of China's plan system) (Beijing: Zhongguo caizheng jingji chubanshe, 1994), pp. 7–11; Terry Sicular, "Agricultural Planning and Pricing in the Post-Mao Period," *The China Quarterly*, no. 116 (December 1988), p. 677; *Dangdai zhongguo de wuzi liutong* (Materials allocation in contemporary China) (Beijing: Dangdai zhongguo chubanshe, 1993), p. 103; State Planning Commission, "Woguo zhongyang yu difang jingji guanli quanxian yanjiu" (Boundaries of economic management between China's central and local governments), *Jingji yanjiu cankao*, no. 434/435 (1 March 1994), pp. 5, 19–23; Lu Jiang (ed.), *Neimao daili chutan* (Exploring the agency system in internal trade) (Beijing: Zhongguo wuzi chubanshe, 1995), p. 17; Yin Jiqing (ed.), *Zhongguo duiwai jingji maoyi gaige ershinian* (Twenty years of reform in China's foreign economic relations and trade) (Zhengzhou: Zhongzhou guji chubanshe, 1998), pp. 43, 74–5, 91; Cheng Zhiping (ed.), *Zhongguo wujia wushinian* (Fifty years of prices in China) (Beijing: Zhongguo wujia chubanshe, 1998), pp. 479, 922; and Wu Shaojun, *Guojia fazhan jihua gailun* (Introduction to state development planning) (Beijing: Zhongguo renmin daxue chubanshe, 1999), pp. 84–7.

Notes: Figures in parentheses denote the number of items under guidance planning; * refers to that of production materials controlled by the State Bureau of Commodity Prices (*guojia wujiaju*).

Fourth, the weakening of central plan control was also in line with the reformist leadership's efforts to take into consideration varied local conditions in its economic policy making. From 1983, several large-scale surveys and investigations were conducted in various sectors, producing numerous sectoral and regional development guidelines and strategies.[34] Fifth, in organizational terms, the planning bureaus and commissions in the ministerial units were all abolished while those in the provincial government units survived, clearly suggesting that the reformist leadership sought to strengthen the "horizontal" (*kuai*) planning authority of the regions vis-à-vis the "vertical" (*tiao*) power of the functional system. Furthermore, the relationship between SPC and provincial planning commissions was also gradually changed from that of vertical leadership (*lingdao guanxi*) to that of business transaction (*yewu guanxi*).[35]

The implications are three-fold. First, much of what had previously been controlled solely by state plans was marketized. For instance, the share of the value of industrial outputs generated under SPC's responsibilities in gross value of industrial outputs (GVIO) declined sharply from 95 percent in 1979 to only 7 percent in 1993.[36] We can also find a similar trend in the area of material allocation. As of 1993, the share of steel and timber allocated centrally by the plan mechanism in their total production was 19.9 and 9.9 percent, while the comparable figures for 1979 were 77.1 and 85.0 percent, respectively. The share of the state-allocated grain in the total amount of grain distributed in 1994 was only 50 percent, with the remaining half handled by the market.[37] Second, the changes also point to a much expanded scope of discretionary planning authority granted to the provinces and sub-provincial authorities.[38] Third, more importantly, as Table 2.2 illustrates, quite a considerable degree of interprovincial variations existed in terms of production items under plan control, reflecting the renewed emphasis on *yindi zhiyi* in regional economic planning.

The budgetary dimension: "back to the single mess hall?"

Central–local budgetary arrangements of the post-Mao reform era are characterized by the extreme complexities not only in their diversities among different provinces but also in their frequent changes over time. Such complexities may in part reflect the reformist leadership's experimental spirit in recognizing regional variations and promoting local incentives for reform. On the other hand, they

Table 2.2   Number of plan items for industrial production in selected provinces

	Mandatory (1984)	Mandatory (1992)	Guidance (1984)	Guidance (1992)
Jiangsu	28	8	91	90
Ningxia	2	1	15	32
Shandong	25	6	–	42
Hubei	15	3	–	7
Guangxi	171	24	–	51

Source: Gui Shiyong, *Zhongguo jihua tizhi gaige*, p. 14.

may also represent a series of Beijing's efforts to redress its loss of control over intergovernmental fiscal flows. Since the central–local budgetary arrangements of the Maoist era and their post-Mao changes have well been documented elsewhere,[39] we confine the scope of our discussion to the following three issues: (1) principal reasons for Beijing's loss of revenue control; (2) key changes introduced by the 1994 "tax-sharing system" (*fenshuizhi*); and (3) a preliminary assessment of the impact of the new system.

The "state-capacity" argument is nowhere more appealing than in this budgetary dimension. As the provinces gradually became adept in taking advantage of intense central–local bargaining, the fiscal reform that had initially begun as a measure of promoting local incentives paradoxically produced a situation where Beijing found it increasingly difficult to rein in the provinces. For instance, the share of total state revenues in gross national product consistently dropped from 31.2 percent in 1978 to 16.2 percent in 1993, clearly indicating the dwindling capacity of the state in controlling the revenue flows. More importantly, Beijing successively failed to increase its share of budgetary revenues, which went down from 57 percent in 1981 to 33 percent in 1993.[40]

Several reasons account for Beijing's failure to regain its fiscal control. First, overly diversified patterns of revenue sharing, which permitted individual provinces with "hidden information" to engage in one-to-one bargaining with Beijing, were responsible for its weakened fiscal control. Particularly after the "fiscal contract system" (*caizheng baogan zhi*) became the norm, Beijing had to keep giving more leeway and concessions to the provinces. For instance, while the shared revenue of 1990 increased over that of 1988 by RMB 46 billion, the total amount remitted to the center only increased by RMB 1.8 billion, a mere 3.9 percent.[41] Second, another key reason concerned the rapid increase in the size of extra-budgetary funds (EBFs) and "extra-establishment funds" (EEFs). EBFs increased eleven times between 1978 and 1992, while the budgetary revenues only tripled in the same period. EBFs as a percentage of budgetary revenues grew from 31 in 1978 to 98 in 1992. It was estimated that by 1991 the sum of EBFs and EEFs accounted for almost three-quarters of all revenue incomes collected by the government.[42]

Third, rampant tax evasion also contributed significantly to the relative decline in state and central revenues. Examples included arbitrary granting of the "tax reduction and exemption" (*jianmianshui*) privilege to the enterprises with false identities of foreign-invested firms and fabricating "artificial losses" by raising the costs to reduce their tax liability. In addition, when local governments did most of the tax collection for the center, there was bound to be some room for problems. According to the Ministry of Finance, a nationwide auditing in 1989 generated RMB 95 billion in penalties, and an internal source projected that the average size of tax evasion in the 1990s might well reach RMB 100 billion annually.[43] Fourth, despite the relative decline in central revenues, the size of central government expenditures continued to rise, including "price subsidies" (*jiage butie*) and "enterprise deficit subsidies" (*qiye kuishun butie*), as well as such normal expenditures as administrative expenses, defense spending, payments for bonds, and so on. While a Ministry of Finance source argued that the share of budgetary revenues in national income should reach at least 28 percent to secure the absolutely necessary expenditures, the ratio was already down to 19.2 percent in 1988.[44]

Fifth, Beijing's intermittent resorting to various *ad hoc* measures proved unsuccessful most of the time.[45] Consequently, in stark contrast with the center undergoing successive deficits throughout 1981–93 except for 1989, local governments reaped seven-year surpluses during the same period.[46] Given that tax revenues constituted more than 80 percent of all budgetary incomes in 1993, readjusting the way tax revenues were to be distributed among different levels of governments must have been most appealing to the center in search of a way out. Subsequently, at the Third Plenum of the 14th Party Central Committee held in late 1993, Beijing decided to adopt the tax-sharing reform by reversing its earlier pledge that the fiscal contract system would remain at least for the 1991–5 period.[47] Beijing drew its final card to regain its long-lost fiscal control over the provinces.

Since the details of the tax-sharing reform are provided elsewhere,[48] only a brief discussion is offered here with the main focus placed on its implementation since 1994. The tax-sharing reform has entailed the following key measures. First, it involved a reclassification of tax categories. Most importantly, by dividing the consolidated industrial–commercial tax into the business tax as a local revenue and the product circulation tax as a shared revenue, Beijing managed to take a big bite out of the most voluminous single tax category. Second, the standardized tax rate of 33 percent, formerly reserved only for foreign-invested firms, was imposed on all domestic enterprises. The adoption of a unified tax rate for all enterprises was to plug an important loophole in the collection of tax revenues. Furthermore, the authority to grant the "tax reduction and exemption" privileges was recentralized back to the State Council. Third, in its efforts to tightly monitor the process of tax collection, Beijing set up national-level tax bureaus (*guoshuiju*) and local tax bureaus (*difang shuiju*). While the division of labor between the two is easy to discern, it is interesting to note the specific arrangement that all shared taxes are first to go to the national tax bureaus which then, according to the fixed ratio, allocate them to local governments.[49]

Provincial responses to the tax-sharing reform varied although most provinces were generally resentful of the changes to the status quo that they considered highly beneficial.[50] The negative sentiments among the provinces were clearly manifested by the number of votes that opposed the legislation of the budgetary law at the second plenary session of the National People's Congress in March 1994.[51] Regardless of the provincial sentiments, however, Beijing has remained determined and even adamant in pursuing its priorities.[52] Many provinces and localities have since 1994 complained of their dwindling bases of revenues. For instance, Shanghai reported that its remittances to Beijing amounted to RMB 17.3 billion and 18.5 billion in 1994–5, indicating that its size of remittances increased over the 1993 baseline by 57 and 68 percent, respectively. Shandong, too, was resentful of the much slowed pace of budgetary increases since 1994.[53]

Overall, however, sufficient evidence is not yet available for us to make a comprehensive and confident assessment of the impact of the new tax system. Simply to compare 1993 with 1994–8, the center's share in total budgetary revenues certainly increased from 33 percent in 1993 to 56, 52, 49, 49, and 50 percent during 1994–8. The share of central revenues in GNP also rose from 5.4 percent in 1993 to 6.3 percent in 1998.[54] To what extent these aggregate indicators sincerely reflect the scope of actual changes made in central–local fiscal relations remains rather unclear. As the 1994 system has constantly been revised – and it is officially a "transitional system" – we probably need a few more years before coming up with a more precise assessment of the reform.[55] In fact, Beijing and the provinces have been engaged in the tenuous processes of bargaining over such issues as: (1) delineating the expenditure responsibilities of the central and provincial governments; (2) controlling local EBFs;[56] and (3) choosing between the baseline figure method (*jishufa*) and the factor analysis method (*yinsufa*) in determining budgetary allocations. Various internal reports indicate that these issues have been debated over and over without clear-cut answers.[57] Whichever route the tax-sharing reform may eventually take, its outcomes will offer crucial evidence as to the evolving balance of fiscal power between Beijing and the provinces.

Investment controls

Investment is another key dimension closely related to the decentralization reform in the post-Mao era. Since 1984, a considerable degree of decisional latitude was permitted initially to the provincial-level governments and later to various sub-provincial units and development zones in authorizing large-scale investment projects without first obtaining Beijing's approval.[58] The expanded local discretion in investment decisions was accompanied by the rapid diversification of funding sources. Compared with the Maoist period during which almost all state investments had been financed within the planned budget, the post-Mao reform era witnessed a much reduced role of state budgetary investment. In 1975, the share of locally funded investments in total budgetary investments amounted to 27 percent, with the remaining 73 percent financed by the center. As of 1990, of all state investments, only 21.5 percent were financed by SPC's unified fund allocation, with the remainder financed by various levels of local governments. Even that figure went down to 17.2 percent in 1992.[59]

The rapid expansion of EBFs under local control, the large-scale intakes of foreign funds, and the utilization of bank loans have all contributed to the increased leverage local governments came to possess over investment sources. In 1997, for instance, the share of budgetary investment in total investment constituted a mere 2.8 percent, while those of "self-raised funds" (*zichou touzi*), bank loans, and foreign investment were 55.7, 19.2, and 10.8 percent, respectively.[60] The rise of domestic bank loans – through the policy of "replacing budgets with loans" (*bo gai dai*) since 1985 – merits our attention in two respects. First, on the surface, it represented the introduction of some rational elements into investment decisions by resorting to economic rationales. Second, on the other hand, it also permitted local governments to exert political influence over local branches of banks to help finance their pet projects.[61]

The emphasis on "small investments, quick returns" combined with local governments that possessed considerable influence over banks led to nationwide investment sprees at all levels of administration. Every locality was involved in the numbers game to maximize their discretion to invest in projects that would guarantee higher returns with small investments in a relatively short period of time, most notably breweries and tobacco factories. In 1996, China had over 40,000 *baijiu* distilleries and the famous Qingdao Brewery had less than a 3 percent share of the domestic beer market in 1994. The scope of duplicate investment went well beyond brewing. As of 1987, over 300 factories in 28 provinces produced washing machines and over 100 factories in 26 provinces manufactured television sets. The outcome was a duplicated production structure throughout the country, which grossly violated the principles of efficiency and comparative advantage.[62]

Other serious problems that accompanied the nationwide investment sprees were successive strings of inflation, which Beijing strove very hard to contain during most of the 1980s, but failed. Yet the enhancement of central control over local investment behavior in the 1990s seems to have led to an increased level of local compliance. While different assessments have been offered of Beijing's control capacity and provincial discretionary power in the realm of investment, the drastic decrease of the inflation rate from 21.7 percent in 1994 to 6 percent in 1996 suggests that Beijing's political imposition has mattered in the longer run.[63]

The "opening" of foreign economic relations

One of the most important dimensions in China's post-Mao reform is that of "opening" of foreign economic relations, most notably characterized by preferential deregulation. Preferential deregulation refers to policy measures designed to grant preferential policies to select localities deemed to possess more development potentials.[64] Starting with the establishment in 1979 of the four special economic zones (SEZs) in Guangdong and Fujian, by 1995 China designated a total of 260 "coastal open areas," 14 "coastal open cities," 30 "economic and technological development zones," 18 "open provincial capitals," 13 "bonded zones," 52 "hi-tech industrial development zones," 6 "riverine open cities," and 13 "border open cities," all of which were permitted various preferential policies designed to promote foreign trade and to attract overseas investment. As of 1993, a total of 1,053 counties and county-level cities (49 percent of all county-level units) were "opened" and the total number of various open development zones nationwide was estimated to be around 3,000.[65]

Provinces, cities, development zones, and many counties have actively participated in the creation of "outwardly oriented economies." In foreign trade, local initiatives and participation were promoted with the number of foreign trade corporations rising sharply from a mere dozen controlled solely by Beijing in 1979 to over 7,000 in 1994.[66] To further promote local incentives, most provinces were permitted to retain 25 percent of their foreign exchange earnings generated through exports during 1982–90, while the four SEZs retained 100 percent and Guangdong and Fujian 30 percent. While the item-based retention rate (generally 50 percent), instead of the region-based one, was used during 1991–3, the retention system itself was abolished in 1994 and Chinese exporters were then required to deposit all of their foreign currencies at thirteen designated banks under Beijing's control. For foreign-invested projects, over twenty provincial-level governments in the coastal region (including SEZs and "central economic cities") were empowered to authorize projects involving up to US$ 30 million. For most inland provinces, autonomous regions, and central economic cities (except Wuhan), the ceiling was initially set at US$ 10 million and later in 1992 readjusted to US$ 30 million.[67]

Through the schemes of preferential deregulation and "local–foreign pairing" (such as the well-known dyads between Liaoning and Japan, Shandong and South Korea, Guangdong and Hong Kong, and Fujian and Taiwan), subnational authorities have gradually developed vested interests in maintaining and expanding their own overseas linkages, sometimes bypassing Beijing.[68] Relatedly, many overseas liaison offices were set up by provinces, prefectures, and cities, and numerous local friendship associations were formed with foreign local counterparts. As of 1995, a total of 169 branches or liaison offices were established by China in South Korea. Among these, over half of regional liaison offices were presumably set up without official endorsements by using the titles of business firms. As of 1998, 821 pairs of "sister cities" were formed between Chinese cities and foreign counterparts.[69] Beijing apparently is trapped in a dilemma: it wishes to see a great increase in foreign economic relations to promote foreign trade and investment and yet wants to rein in excessive local discretion. For instance, in late 1993, Beijing abolished about 2,500 development zones approved by the provincial and sub-provincial authorities, leaving only 495 nationwide.[70] If we have no reservations talking about "California's foreign policy," it will not be too long before we talk about "Guangdong's foreign policy." In sum, the long-term implications of the emerging local–global nexuses for China's central–local relations remain to be explored.[71]

Personnel control: the heel of Achilles

Unlike the four economic issue areas discussed above, the extent to which the post-Mao decentralization reform has affected non-economic issue areas appears much more difficult to gauge. The reason is two-fold: not only because post-Mao reforms have to date been more economic in nature, but also because the political and administrative issue areas have no readily available quantifiers for researchers to utilize. Personnel management is perhaps one of the few dimensions least affected by the decentralization reform, although many important changes were introduced to the system of managing cadres' appointments, transfers, and retirement. The most notable change in personnel control pertaining to central–local relations concerned the reduction of the central *nomenklatura* in 1983, by which the party center's authority in personnel appointment was reduced from "managing two levels" (*xiaguan liangji*) to "managing only one level" (*xiaguan yiji*) to the provinces. Consequently, the number of *nomenklatura* positions managed by the Central Organization Department dropped sharply from over 13,000 to about 7,000.[72]

The restructured *nomenklatura* did not bring about any significantly adverse impact on Beijing's personnel control over the provinces (although more power was delegated to the provinces in managing personnel for the counties). Despite the 46 percent reduction in the number of centrally controlled *nomenklatura* positions, such core positions as the provincial secretaries, deputy secretaries, governors, and deputy governors still remained tightly controlled by the Central Organization Department. Furthermore, a scheme of recentralization was implemented in 1990, according to which the personnel management authority concerning key party and government positions at the prefecture-level governments as well as "central economic cities" (*jihua danlie shi*) reverted to the party center.[73]

In the post-Mao reform era, we have been acquainted with the reports that some provincial-level positions were filled with the candidates unsupported by the party center. A well-known example concerns the case of Ge Hongsheng, Zhejiang's governor, who was voted out of office due to his failure to get enough votes at the Provincial People's Congress in 1993. What remains uncertain concerns: (1) why Beijing let these incidents happen despite its near-omnipotent personnel power; and (2) to what extent these instances are generalizable to the center's capacity for personnel control. It seems that such instances still constitute exceptions rather than the norm. Quite to the contrary, abundant evidence is available to support that, once Beijing seeks to solicit local support at all costs, provinces will have very few options to choose from due mainly to the former's personnel control over the latter. Despite the decline of ideology as the omnipotent criterion of loyalty and conformity, the reform era has instead generated a substitute criterion – "the fruits of reform." That is, the extent to which local cadres have been successful in bringing about economic development (i.e., growth) has become an important standard for determining one's career path, thus producing another cycle of compliance succession.[74] Further, the establishment of the Bureau of Auditing and the Ministry of Supervision also made the center's personnel assessment institutionally easier.[75]

Administrative monitoring and information control

Manipulating performance statistics has long been a salient characteristic of the policy process in Maoist China where local officials would at all costs avoid lagging behind others in implementing central policy. The "hidden transcript" of bureaucratic careerism dictated that they report distorted (inflated or deflated) information on local performance. While the Great Leap fiasco is best noted for the rampant over-reporting of local production statistics, there is no indication that such malpractices were halted thereafter.[76] Instead, many studies suggest that central leaders utilized multiple means of monitoring local performance. Since central leaders (particularly Mao) did not wish to rely exclusively on local government reports, they took trips to localities themselves by way of such formats as "to the countryside" (*xiaxiang*), "squatting at a point" (*dundian*), routine inspection (*diaocha*), and investigation (*jiancha*), as well as dispatching central work teams to localities of concern. The official propaganda apparatus was also fully harnessed to provide the central leaders with pertinent information on local performance, including the New China News Agency's "internal reference" (*neibu cankao*) series produced twice daily.[77]

Several post-Mao measures strengthened Beijing's capacity for administrative monitoring and information control. First, by emphasizing *yindi zhiyi*, the central government strove to prevent the widespread practice of distorting local production statistics.[78] Second, the post-Mao era also witnessed a gradual strengthening of Beijing's institutionalized control over local information, performance, and statistics. Starting with the rehabilitation of the State Statistical Bureau (SSB) in 1978, the center's grip over statistics was further consolidated with the legislation of the "statistics law" (*tongjifa*) by the National People's Congress in 1983. By 1992, twenty-five provinces, municipalities, and autonomous regions adopted various penalties against the violation of the statistics law. SSB's power continued to expand during the reform era. In terms of personnel control, SSB could veto the appointments of key officials at the provincial- and county-level statistical bureaus. Their administrative expenses and procurement funds were financed mainly by the central budget in order to minimize the interference from the respective territorial (*kuaikuai*) administration. SSB also maintained more than 1,000 sampling survey teams at the county and city levels (*xianshi chouyang diaochadui*). The staff size of SSB also rose sharply from 280 in 1981 and 580 in 1988 to more than 1,000 in 1994.[79]

Third, the post-Mao publication of a wide range of provincial and sub-provincial gazetteers, yearbooks, and chronicles containing key local information and statistics can be fully utilized by Beijing in its making and implementation of policy.[80] Fourth, whereas there were only 186 newspapers nationwide in 1978, by 1998, 2,053 newspapers were published, of which 1,842 were produced at the county to provincial levels.[81] If properly monitored, these publications may also offer Beijing crucial information on localities. Fifth, both ordinary people and officials of all ranks were also encouraged to write letters (*xinfang*) to central and local government units, individual leaders, and media to voice their concerns and file their complaints. These activities would offer yet another channel of information for the center to utilize in monitoring localities.[82]

What can be made out of all these? While Beijing's capacity for administrative monitoring and information control has certainly strengthened in the reform era, distorted reporting has nevertheless continued. Various official and media reports warned against inflated reporting by local officials who sought promotions by way of exaggerating their accomplishments and against the local-ities which provided deflated reports on enterprise profits and revenue incomes to evade taxation.[83] As long as key personnel appointments, and subsidies and perks for local statistical bureaus, depended upon the territorial governments, such statistics as total grain output, per capita income, inflation rate, and average birth rate would continue to be first approved by the local leaders before being reported upward.

China's information system, at least to the insiders and to the center in partic-ular, will become increasingly more institutionalized and transparent. Properly monitored and analyzed, it may offer Beijing a distinct edge by providing it with what localities cannot possess. While the center's media control appears to have become loose at the sub-provincial level, that does not mean that the "alternative media" emerged to challenge Beijing. As the recent centralization and tight monitoring of Internet services in China suggest, the center's strengthened grip over information and statistics seems to be the major trend.[84] Nina Halpern, for instance, observed that "[A]lthough the dispersal of other resources contributed to the fragmentation of authority in the post-Mao era, the changes stemming from changing information flows were more complicated and probably, on balance, produced greater centralization."[85] After all, economic decentralization is not mutually exclusive with informational centralization.

Administrative reorganization: toward more complex dynamics

Principally, three changes may be noted for the organizational dimension of central–local relations in the post-Mao reform era. First, there emerged new administrative units in line with the new demands of the reform. More specifi-cally, various measures of preferential deregulation produced such new administrative units as SEZs, "coastal open cities," "economic and technological development zones," and "central economic cities," with differential functions and privileges. The emergence of these several dozens of cities and zones with their own discretionary power has further complicated central–local dynamics.[86]

Second, new layers of authority were also formed. With the "city in charge of county" (*shi guan xian*) policy adopted in 1983, prefecture-level municipal govern-ments became a crucial layer of local administrative hierarchy and, by 1991, one-quarter of China's counties were directly administered by these prefecture-level cities. The rise of the prefecture-level cities (*dijishi*) officially heralded the formation of a new layer of authority between provinces and counties, replacing prefectures (*diqu*) which, as field offices of the provincial administration, had had an ambiguous administrative status.[87] As a result of the rapidly rising levels of urbanization, many rural counties became county-level cities (*xianjishi*) with an enhanced degree of autonomy in economic management. The number of sub-provincial cities rose dramatically from 191 in 1978 to 664 in 1998.[88] Most importantly, the creation of "central economic cities" and "deputy-provincial cities" (*fushengji shi*) has undercut the power of the provincial and central authorities, further compounding central–local dynamics as well as intra-provincial politics.[89]

Third, with the weakening of state plans and the formation of markets, numerous "horizontal linkages" (*hengxiang lianxi*) were developed as a new coordinating mechanism to reduce regional conflicts and local protectionism and to promote reciprocal cooperation on the basis of comparative advantage. Some were initiated from the top down by the State Council and central ministries, others were linked up through the conventional networks for "relational contracting," and still others were voluntarily established on the basis of reciprocity. The number of these various dyadic, collective, centrally induced, and voluntarily formed interregional horizontal linkages at all levels amounted to several thousands at least.[90]

Interregional and intercity diplomacy also looms large. All provinces and an increasingly large number of prefectures and cities set up liaison offices in other local units. For instance, as of 1995, over 280 liaison offices were established in Qingdao by other provinces, prefectures, and cities. In Dalian, too, over 200 liaison offices were established by other regional authorities, while the number of corporate representative offices from other regions amounted to 3,300. Henan, for instance, maintains seven liaison offices in Shanghai, Guangzhou, Tianjin, Shenzhen, Shandong, and Xiamen.[91] A series of annual meetings were also institutionalized, where leaders of "coastal open cities" and "central economic cities" discussed common problems and strategies to cope collectively with Beijing. Overall, the rise of new units, new layers of authority, and horizontal linkages has introduced a highly complex equation into central–local dynamics and it is not entirely inconceivable that Beijing has been cultivating them as a counterweight to the fast-growing autonomy of the provinces.[92]

Local legislation and legislature

Since the granting of legislative powers to the Provincial People's Congresses (PPCs) in 1979, 2,483 provincial laws were promulgated by 1991. Not only the provinces but "special zones" like Shenzhen (1992), Xiamen (1994), Shantou and Zhuhai (1996), as well as nineteen "relatively large cities" (*jiao da de shi*) designated by the State Council, were also granted considerable legislative powers. Though involving mostly administrative and economic laws, PPCs have gradually expanded their legislative and supervisory powers so as to sustain some horizontal leverages over their governmental counterparts as well as to enhance the possibilities of conflict with the center. Particularly regarding the latter possibility, concerns were raised for the cases in which "sectoral regulations" (*bumen guizhang*) came into conflict with "local laws" (*difangxing fagui*). While a contingency was created by the State Council in 1990, according to which "in such cases, the National People's Congress (NPC) is to mediate upon the request by the State Council," there still exists ample room for disputes.[93] Positive aspects of PPCs can also be identified, the most important of which is their function as an "information broker," taking advantage of the dual roles of being the spokes-people for the NPC as well as remonstrators for local interests.[94]

Military, internal security, and grass-roots control

The military organizations and networks of the People's Liberation Army (PLA) provide a crucial conduit of local and social control in China. If this conduit is somehow blocked by, say, a collusion between provincial governments and local PLA units, it may then signal an ominous beginning of the "dynastic cycle." In the People's Republic, there exist formidable obstacles to such a local–military collusion against the center. Most importantly, while the highest sub-national PLA organization consists of the seven military regions, their civilian counter-parts are situated one level down at the provinces. Therefore, the chances for a meaningful military–civilian collusion against Beijing are rather slim. Moreover, the provincial government's teaming up with the provincial-level military district poses at best an insignificant threat since the latter possesses little control over the PLA main force units. Additionally, given that the movement of troops larger than a battalion must be authorized beforehand by the Central Military Commission, Beijing's control over the local military seems secure. Furthermore, military region commanders and political commissars now serve three years on average before their transfers to other geographical locations, while in the past they stayed in one place for as long as ten years or more.[95]

Despite such structural impediments, some concerns have been voiced with regard to the genesis of regionalism within the PLA. More specifically, the PLA's profitable "military-run businesses" have become highly diversified not only in their sectoral scope but also in their geographical foci covering all the provinces. Its growing financial ability and the corresponding decline in professionalism may become catalytic for the center's loss of control over local PLA forces which may choose to collude with local authorities to obtain more autonomy from Beijing's direction.[96] How feasible is this scenario? Interestingly, almost all studies that touch upon the PLA's regionalism stop short of linking this region-alism with disloyalty. In fact, many argue that PLA forces would still be similarly compliant to Beijing if they were to be subject to the same situation as that of June 1989.[97]

Aside from military regionalism, multiple sources of instability have emerged in the post-Mao reform era. They include the turbulent situations in some national minorities regions (particularly Xinjiang and Tibet), the growth of "invisible economies" (*yinxing jingji*) in various sectors nationwide that are well beyond taxation and regulation, the signs of institutional decay at the grass-roots level caused in part by the influence of local clans over basic-level party units, the prevalence of cross-border smuggling and drug trafficking, widespread pros-titution, rampant corruption, farmers' discontent with heavy levies, the breakdown of the *hukou* and *danwei* systems and the rise of the "floating popula-tion," the rapid increase of laid-off workers, the rise of religious sects (most notably *falungong*), and so on.[98] Measuring the impact of these developments on

China's central–local relations is not as easy as it seems. One point of contention, however, is that the state-capacity argument that is widely but rather too casually employed in the field needs to be differentiated from the center's ability to rein in local governments. Comparatively speaking, for instance, an increase in crime rates at the street level in the United States would not necessarily be the responsibility of the federal government.

The balance sheet: agency problems, dilemmas of hierarchical solutions, and diluted effects of reform

In the foregoing discussion, we have charted the major changes in nine different issue areas in addition to the norm changes introduced in the reform era. In a nutshell, the impact of the post-Mao decentralization reform on China's central–local relations has not been very straightforward. While there is no doubt that localities have obtained a significantly expanded scope of discretionary power in the last twenty years of reform, it nevertheless appears that the critical balance of power between Beijing and localities has not predominantly tilted toward the latter as is too casually taken for granted. Several concluding observations are offered below with regard to the diluted effects of decentralization.

First, central–local relations of the reform era constitute an outstanding example of agency problems best characterized by the conflicting incentives for the agent to become discretionary and for the principal to regulate and discipline. The fundamental dilemma of control versus autonomy inherent in central–local dynamics was tackled by the post-Mao reformist leadership which relied on contract systems in various issue areas ranging from agricultural production and enterprise management to budgetary sharing and foreign trade management. These contract systems devised initially to promote local incentives within certain limits did not always work in line with the center's intentions as localities were often strongly tempted to venture out into the hitherto unaccepted realm of discretion in order to maximize their short-term interests. The final arbiter, however, has almost always been the political mechanism – through its personnel control and policy amendment – which proved strong enough to override any type of contractual constraint.[99]

Second, Beijing's power and will to enforce its priorities, or their absence, have not been uniformly demonstrated in all issue areas across the board. Two principal variations can be noted here. One concerns the distinction between economic and non-economic issues. Generally speaking, the center may possess more patience with local discretion and deviations in economic issue areas as long as they promote growth at the system level. On the other hand, the same cannot be said of local discretionary behavior in political and organizational realms regulated more by political reasoning than economic rationality. The other variation concerns national priority policies, the implementation of which Beijing would very closely monitor. The nationwide adoption of the tax-sharing reform in 1994 and afterwards constitutes a key example. With the gradual improvement in Beijing's capacity for administrative monitoring discussed earlier, the center may find it increasingly easier to enforce its priority policies in the years to come.[100]

Third, despite the resilient power of Beijing over localities, the overall pattern of central–local interactions has become much more complex and diversified. Aside from a few exceptions, uniform compliance has largely become a bygone concept in the post-Mao reform era. Several factors contributed to this crucial change: (1) the consistent emphasis on *yindi zhiyi*; (2) the dramatic rise in the number of new local actors at various levels; (3) the rapid increase in the number of policy areas that require local discretion and bottom-heavy information (e.g., foreign economic relations and environmental protection); (4) the extent of diversity inherent in a wide range of contract systems customized for individual localities; and (5) the size of variation in the pace and pattern of economic development in different regions and sectors.[101] If this trend continues, perhaps, a new type of "cellularization" may appear on the horizon. As Beijing's policy provision is considered a special blessing for local development, dyadic patterns of interaction between Beijing and each province or a sub-provincial locality will become increasingly crucial so far as territorial deregulation matters.

Fourth, the rise of local actors and centrifugal forces poses a much-asked question regarding the unitary system which China, despite its sheer size, has consistently held on to. Some view reform era China as actually implementing "behavioral federalism" or executing "federalism, Chinese style."[102] Yet, since the real meaning of federalism lies in the specific power-sharing arrangement by which the center is not permitted to introduce arbitrary changes to the structure that governs central–local relations, such modifiers as "Chinese" and "behavioral" do not give full credit to the fundamental changes that a genuine federalist structure can and should bring about. Given that China has not even opted for the nominal federal structure, as the former Soviet Union had, the issue of "centrifugality" must be more real to its leaders than we would normally assume.

Fifth, in the longer run, the marginal space (both functional and territorial) under Beijing's tight control may decrease in proportion to the overall duration of the reform. That is, while the post-Mao reform era has been replete with cycles of decentralization and recentralization, each cycle at its end has generated a set of structures and interests more favorable to local incentives and discretion. If the tenure of the reform is further elongated, therefore, the scope of local discretion at $t + 2$ would become wider than that at $t + 1$, all other things being equal. To what extent this spiral model of central–local relations will succeed in making forecasts remains to be seen. Equally importantly, although rarely treated, how the intensification of marketization and privatization is going to interact with the decentralization reform constitutes another key question to consider. Of course, whether genuine privatization can be created bureaucratically remains to be answered.[103] How the processes of internationalization and globalization are going to affect central–local relations is also a crucial question. The overall power of the center in China had been rather excessive in the past and much of it was delegated and devolved to sub-national levels. Yet, it should be noted, various programs (i.e., poverty alleviation, interregional equalization, welfare provision, and so on) need the center's hierarchical involvement and they may be better implemented with the cooperation of local governments with abundant bottom-heavy information.

Notes

1 For overviews, refer to the Development Research Center of the State Council, "Zhongguo gaige kaifang fazhan de huigu yu zhanwang" (China's reform, opening and: retrospect and prospects), *Jingji yanjiu cankao* (Reference Materials for Economic Research), no. 1259 (22 February 1999) and "Twenty Years of Reforms," *China News Analysis*, no. 1624 (15 December 1998). Also see the ten-page special on China in *Financial Times*, 1 October 1999.

2 See Steven L. Solnick, "The Breakdown of Hierarchies in the Soviet Union and China: A Neoinstitutional Perspective," *World Politics*, vol. 48, no. 2 (January 1996), pp. 209–38.

3 In this study, the term "center" refers to the national-level party and government apparatus. Throughout the chapter, the term "local" denotes all tiers of sub-national administration, although it generally means "provincial" when juxtaposed with "central."

4 It may be argued that China's reform had started out in the late 1970s with a thrust of decentralization that stressed "local adaptation" (*yindi zhiyi*) and offered preferential local incentives such as the designation of the special economic zones in 1979. In the mid-1980s and thereafter, the role of market was emphasized with such *tifa* as "planned commercial economy" (*you jihua de shangpin jingji*) initially and later with "socialist market economy" (*shehuizhuyi shichang jingji*). The resolution of the ownership issue, particularly pertaining to privatization, took longer as its "co-optation" came only at the 15th Party Congress of late 1997. See, for instance, Wang Shunsheng et al., *Cong bada dao shiwuda* (From the Eighth to Fifteenth Party Congress) (Fuzhou: Fujian renmin chubanshe, 1997), pp. 246–51, 299–309, 432–9, 507–14.

5 The concept of decentralization adopted here is more than structural or organizational. As will be discussed shortly, the concept also encompasses the norm dimension: that is, without fundamental norm changes, decentralization more often than not fails. For the importance of norm changes, see John Echeverri-Gent, "Between Autonomy and Capture: Embedding Government Agencies in Their Societal Environment," *Policy Studies Journal*, vol. 20, no. 3 (1992), pp. 342–64.

6 For the issue of bureaucratic careerism in general, see Joel S. Migdal, *Strong Societies and Weak States: State–Society Relations and State Capabilities in the Third World* (Princeton: Princeton University Press, 1988), pp. 239–42. For the persistence of bureaucratic careerism in the reform era, see Jae Ho Chung, *Central Control and Local Discretion in China: Leadership and Implementation during Post-Mao Decollectivization* (Oxford: Oxford University Press, 2000), ch. 5.

7 For the paradox between intentions and outcomes of decentralization during Mao's rule, see David Zweig, "Agrarian Radicalism as a Rural Development Strategy, 1968–1981," in William A. Joseph, Christine P. W. Wong, and David Zweig (eds.), *New Perspectives on the Cultural Revolution* (Cambridge, MA: Harvard University Press, 1991), p. 66.

8 For the deleterious impact of the anti-rightist campaign, see David Bachman, *Bureaucracy, Economy, and Leadership in China: The Institutional Origins of the Great Leap Forward* (Cambridge: Cambridge University Press, 1991), p. 5; and William A. Joseph, "A Tragedy of Good Intentions: Post-Mao Views of the Great Leap Forward," *Modern China*, vol. 12, no. 4 (October 1986), pp. 427–8. And for the predominance of ideological and political criteria in China's policy process in the Maoist era, see Carl

Riskin, "Neither Plan Nor Market: Mao's Political Economy," in Joseph, Wong, and Zweig (eds.), *New Perspectives on the Cultural Revolution*, pp. 138–9.

9 See, respectively, Frederick C. Teiwes, "Provincial Politics: Themes and Variations," in John M. H. Lindbeck (ed.), *China: Management of a Revolutionary Society* (Seattle: University of Washington Press, 1971), p. 172; Alfred L. Chan, "The Campaign for Agricultural Development in the Great Leap Forward: A Study of Policy-Making and Implementation in Liaoning," *The China Quarterly*, no. 129 (March 1992), pp. 54–5; Benedict A. Stavis, *The Politics of Agricultural Mechanization in China* (Ithaca: Cornell University Press, 1978), p. 121; Chu Han, *Sannian ziran huihai changbian jishi* (Records of natural calamities during the three years of 1959–61) (Chengdu: Sichuan renmin chubanshe, 1996), pp. 105–42; and Li Rui, *Dayaojin qinliji* (Personal recollections of the Great Leap Forward) (Shanghai: Shanghai yuandong chubanshe, 1996), pp. 119–28.

10 See Marc Blecher and Wang Shaoguang, "The Political Economy of Cropping in Maoist and Dengist China: Hebei Province and Shulu County, 1949–90," *The China Quarterly*, no. 137 (March 1994), pp. 73–80; and Jae Ho Chung, "The Politics of Agricultural Mechanization in the Post-Mao Era,1977–87," *The China Quarterly*, no. 134 (June 1993), pp. 265–80.

11 See Song Xinzhong, *Zhongguo caizheng tizhi gaige yanjiu* (Study of China's fiscal reform) (Beijing: Zhongguo caizheng jingji chubanshe, 1992), pp. 48, 51; and Penelope B. Prime, "Central–Provincial Investment and Finance: The Cultural Revolution and Its Legacy in Jiangsu Province," in Joseph, Wong, and Zweig (eds.), *New Perspectives on the Cultural Revolution*, p. 212.

12 For the correlation coefficients, see Thomas Lyons, *Economic Integration and Planning in Communist China* (New York: Columbia University Press, 1987), p. 174.

13 See Kenneth Lieberthal, *Central Documents and Politburo Politics in China* (Ann Arbor, MI: Center for Chinese Studies, 1978), pp. 11–15; and Huang Yasheng, "Information, Bureaucracy, and Economic Reform in China and the Soviet Union," *World Politics*, vol. 47, no. 1 (October 1994), pp. 102–34.

14 *Renmin ribao*, 7 December 1978.

15 For the concept of "metanorms," see Robert Axelrod, "An Evolutionary Approach to Norms," *American Political Science Review*, vol. 80, no. 4 (1986), pp. 1101–2. For such metanorms in operation, see Dorothy J. Solinger, "Politics in Yunnan Province in the Decade of Disorder," *The China Quarterly*, no. 92 (December 1982), pp. 628–62; and Anne F. Thurston, *Enemies of the People: The Ordeal of the Intellectuals in China's Great Cultural Revolution* (Cambridge, MA: Harvard University Press, 1987).

16 During the Maoist era, local variations were manifested mostly in the implementation of low-priority policies. For instance, variations characterized the provincial policies toward the size of private plots since 1962 as they gradually entered the realm of the "gray economy" which Beijing was not highly motivated to monitor or regulate. See William L. Parish and Martin K. Whyte, *Village and Family in Contemporary China* (Chicago: University of Chicago Press, 1978), pp. 34–5, 118–19.

17 Such recognition is implicitly, and often explicitly, manifested in *Guanyu jianguo yilai dang de ruogan lishi wenti de jueyi* (Resolutions on some historical problems of the Party since 1949) (Beijing: Renmin chubanshe, 1985). More specifically, in his personal recollections of the Maoist era, Bo Yibo points out the deleterious symptoms of the "right-aversive disease" (*kongyouzheng*), referring to the widely shared norm that cadres sought to avoid anything that could at any time be perceived and labeled as a "rightist" act regardless of its practical utility. See *Ruogan zhongda juece yu shijian de huigu* (Recollections of some crucial decisions and events) (Beijing: Zhonggong zhongyang dangxiao chubanshe, 1993), vol. 2, p. 778.

18 For an excellent overview in this regard, see Ma Licheng and Ling Zhijun, *Jiaofeng: dangdai zhongguo sanci sixiang jiefang shilu* (Sword-crossing: records of the three emancipations of ideas in contemporary China) (Beijing: Jinri zhongguo chubanshe, 1998).

Also see Dai Yuanchen, "Sixiang jiefang tuidongle gaige kaifang he jingji fazhan" (The "Emancipation of Mind" pushed forward the reform, opening and economic development), *Shehuikexue yanjiu cankao ziliao* (Reference Materials for Social Science Research), no. 588 (20 February 1999), pp. 1–6.

19 See, for instance, Xinhua Domestic Service, 2 March 1977 in *Foreign Broadcast Information Service: Daily Report-China* (*FBIS*), 7 March 1977, pp. E17–21; *Renmin ribao*, 23 January, 17 July, and 7 December 1978; and *Guangming ribao* (Guangming Daily), 9 August 1979 in *FBIS*, 16 August 1979, pp. L8–9.

20 See *Renmin ribao*, 17 November 1978. For this process of "verdict-reversing" (*pingfan*), see Hong Yung Lee, *From Revolutionary Cadres to Bureaucratic Technocrats* (Berkeley and Los Angeles: University of California Press, 1991), chs. 7–8. In the case of Shandong, for instance, previous verdicts on 2,458 cases were reversed between October 1976 and November 1978. Between 1977 and 1986, 81 percent of the verdicts on 68,000 cases involving persecuted local cadres were reversed, and 91 percent of those on 76,000 cases involving basic-level cadres were reversed. See Research Office of the Shandong Provincial Party Committee, *Shandong sishinian* (Shandong in the last forty years) (Jinan: Shandong renmin chubanshe, 1989), pp. 133–41.

21 *Renmin ribao*, 3 July 1979. Also see ibid., 15 October 1979 and 20 July 1980 for similar messages.

22 For the process in which the Dazhai model was severely criticized and abolished, see Tang Tsou, Marc Blecher, and Mitch Meisner, "National Agricultural Policy: The Dazhai Model and Local Change in the Post-Mao Era," in Mark Selden and Victor Lippit (eds.), *The Transition to Socialism in China* (Armonk, NY: M. E. Sharpe, 1982), pp. 286–95. Also see Sun Qitai and Xiong Zhiyong, *Dazhai hongqi de shengqi yu duoluo* (The rise and fall of Dazhai's red flag) (Huixian: Henan renmin chubanshe, 1990), pp. 285–363.

23 See "How Change and No Change in Policy Should be Understood," in *Hongqi* (Red Flag), February 1981, pp. 24–6 in *FBIS*, 11 March 1981, pp. L21–5; Beijing Xinhua Domestic Service, 9 July 1980 in *FBIS*, 15 July 1980, T3–6; Guizhou Provincial Service, 20 November 1981 in *FBIS*, 25 November 1981, pp. Q1–2; and *Renmin ribao*, 4 August 1981.

24 See *Renmin ribao*, 16 November 1977; and Beijing Xinhua Domestic Service, 24 October 1980 in *FBIS*, 27 October 1980, pp. L4–5.

25 *Renmin ribao*, 23 December 1977; *Dongxiang* (Trend), 16 July 1979, pp. 27–9 in *FBIS*, 20 July 1979, pp. U1–2; and *Zhejiang ribao* (Zhejiang Daily), 30 September 1980 in *FBIS*, 21 October 1980, O5–6. Also see Michael Schoenhals, *Doing Things with Words in Chinese Politics: Five Studies* (Berkeley, CA: Institute of East Asian Studies, 1992), pp. 20, 44; and Zhang Wenhe, *Kouhao yu zhongguo* (Slogans and China) (Beijing: Zhonggong dangshi chubanshe, 1998).

26 For the proceedings of agricultural planning conferences, see *Nongye buju yu nongye quhua* (Agricultural production composition and regional planning) (Beijing: Kexue chubanshe, 1982).

27 In retrospect, this was only the beginning of a long-term trend. By 1988, 44 percent of all provincial party secretaries and governors in China were natives. See Xiaowei Zang, "Provincial Elite in Post-Mao China," *Asian Survey*, vol. 31, no. 6 (June 1991), p. 516. For a similar trend at the sub-provincial level, see Cheng Li and David Bachman, "Localism, Elitism, and Immobilism: Elite Formation and Social Change in Post-Mao China," *World Politics*, vol. 42, no. 1 (October 1989), pp. 71, 80–1.

28 See Kenneth G. Lieberthal, "Introduction: The 'Fragmented Authoritarianism' Model and Its Limitations," in Kenneth G. Lieberthal and David M. Lampton (eds.), *Bureaucracy, Politics, and Decision Making in Post-Mao China* (Berkeley: University of California Press, 1992), p. 20. For a fuller discussion of central–local government relations as positive-sum and issue-variant games, see Jae Ho Chung, "Studies of Central–Provincial Relations in the People's Republic of China: A Mid-Term

Appraisal," *The China Quarterly*, no. 142 (June 1995), pp. 501–6. And for an in-depth study of central–provincial policy dynamics focusing on a non-fiscal issue area, see Chung, *Central Control and Local Discretion in China*, chs. 3–6.

29 See Lyons, *Economic Integration and Planning in Communist China*, pp. 218–22; Dorothy J. Solinger, "Urban Reform and Relational Contracting in Post-Mao China," *China's Transition from Socialism: Statist Legacies and Market Reforms* (Armonk, NY: M. E. Sharpe, 1993), pp. 107–25; and Barry Naughton, *Growing out of the Plan: Chinese Economic Reform 1978–1993* (Cambridge: Cambridge University Press, 1995), pp. 41–2.

30 For the bureaucratic process of plan making, see Lyons, *Economic Integration and Planning in Communist China*, p. 217; and for the power of SPC, see Wang Lixin and Joseph Fewsmith, "Bulwark of the Planned Economy: The Structure and Role of the State Planning Commission," in Carol Lee Hamrin and Suisheng Zhao (eds.), *Decision-Making in Deng's China: Perspectives from Insiders* (Armonk, NY: M. E. Sharpe, 1995), p. 61.

31 See Huang, "Information, Bureaucracy, and Economic Reform," pp. 102–34.

32 See Thomas Lyons and Wang Yan, *Planning and Finance in China's Economic Reforms*, Cornell University East Asia Papers, no. 46 (Ithaca: Cornell University Press, 1988).

33 Gui Shiyong, *Zhongguo jihua tizhi gaige*, pp. 16–18, 50.

34 Ibid., pp. 2–4, 38–9.

35 Lyons and Wang, *Planning and Finance in China's Economic Reforms*, pp. 14–17.

36 See State Planning Commission, "Woguo zhongyang yu difang jingji guanli quanxian yanjiu," p. 19; and Joseph C. H. Chai, *China: Transition to a Market Economy* (Oxford: Oxford University Press, 1997), p. 186.

37 Gui Shiyong, *Zhongguo jihua tizhi gaige*, pp. 9–10.

38 See Wu Shaojun, *Guojia fazhan jihua gailun*, pp. 84–5.

39 See, for instance, Michel Oksenberg and James Tong, "The Evolution of Central–Provincial Fiscal Relations in China, 1971–1984: The Formal System," *The China Quarterly*, no. 125 (March 1991), pp. 1–32.

40 *Zhongguo tongji nianjian 1994* (China Statistical Yearbook 1994) (hereafter *ZGTJNJ*) (Beijing: Zhongguo tongji chubanshe, 1994), pp. 20–1.

41 "Dangqian caishui gaige bage beijing jieshao" (Eight backgrounds to the current fiscal and tax reform), *Caizheng yanjiu ziliao* (Fiscal Research Materials), no. 2 (20 January 1994), p. 3.

42 For the data on EBFs, see *Zhongguo tongji zhaiyao 1994* (Statistical survey of China 1994) (Beijing: Zhongguo tongji chubanshe, 1994), p. 40; and Yu Tianxin, "Guipin he shudao yusanwai zijin de gaigeshi zai bixing" (The reform of merging and channeling the extra-budgetary funds is inevitable), *Jingji yanjiu cankao*, no. 417 (7 May 1994), pp. 30–1.

43 See Xiang Huaicheng, *Jiushiniandai caizheng fazhan zhanlue* (Strategies of fiscal development for the 1990s) (Beijing: Zhongguo caizheng jingji chubanshe, 1991), p. 65; "Dangqian caishui gaige bage beijing jieshao," p. 2; and "Tongyi caizheng: gaige yu fazhan de biran xuanze" (Unified finance: the inevitable choice for reform and development), *Jingji yanjiu cankao*, no. 889 (9 June 1996), pp. 10–11.

44 See Song, *Zhongguo caizheng tizhi gaige yanjiu*, pp. 63, 65, 68–70. See Xiang, *Jiushiniandai caizheng fazhan zhanlue*, p. 16.

45 These measures ranged from specialized levies imposed on EBFs and the mandatory provincial quotas for the purchase of national bonds to "forced loans" and other demands for extra fiscal contribution to the center. See *Dangdai zhongguo caizheng* (Contemporary China's finance) (Beijing: Zhongguo shehuikexue chubanshe, 1988), vol. 1, pp. 309–11; Department of National Bond Management of the Ministry of Finance, *Zhongguo guozhai zhanlue wenti yanjiu* (Study of China's national bonds strategy) (Beijing: Jingji kexue chubanshe, 1991), p. 75; and Guo Yanzhong, "Fenshuizhi yanjiu zhuanji" (Special edition on the study of the tax-sharing system), *Jingji yanjiu cankao*, no. 401 (1 January 1994), p. 37.

46 For budgetary balances in 1981–93, see *ZGTJNJ 1994*, p. 220.

47 See Guo, "Fenshuizhi yanjiu zhuanji," pp. 14–16.

48 See Jae Ho Chung, "Beijing Confronting the Provinces: The 1994 Tax-Sharing Reform and its Implications for Central–Provincial Relations in China," *China Information*, vol. 9, no. 2–3 (Winter 1994/1995), pp. 1–23.

49 See State Council Document no. 85 issued on 15 December 1993 published in *Caizheng* (Finance), no. 2 (1994), p. 19; and *Renmin ribao*, 23 November 1993.

50 For detailed discussions of provincial responses to the tax-sharing reform, see Chung, "Beijing Confronting the Provinces," pp. 16–23.

51 *Ming Pao*, 23 March 1994.

52 See *Renmin ribao*, 13 December 1993; *Guangming ribao*, 21 March 1994; and *Renmin ribao*, 29 November 1994.

53 "Xinshuizhi yunxing de zongti pingjia yu jianyi" (Evaluations of and suggestions for the implementation of the new tax system), *Jingji yanjiu cankao*, no. 1023, (7 March 1997), p. 24.

54 See *ZGTJNJ 1994*, pp. 21, 213, 220; *ZGTJNJ 1999*, pp. 20, 275.

55 For a generally positive assessment but with a concern that the tax-sharing reform might end up producing only a nomimal centralization, see Barry Naughton, "Fiscal and Banking Reform: The 1994 Fiscal Reform Revisited," in Maurice Brosseau, Kuan Hsin-chi, and Y. Y. Kueh (eds.), *China Review 1997* (Hong Kong: The Chinese University Press, 1997), pp. 254–67. For a mixed evaluation, also see Le-Yin Zhang, "Chinese Central–Provincial Fiscal Relationships, Budgetary Decline and the Impact of the 1994 Fiscal Reform," *The China Quarterly*, no. 157 (March 1999), pp.130–40.

56 Beijing has been very determined to rein in local EBFs, as its nationwide campaign in 1996 led to a very successful survey and appropriation of local EBF bases. See He Shengming, *Zhongguo caizheng gaige ershinian* (Twenty years of fiscal reform in China) (Zhengzhou: Zhongzhou guji chubanshe, 1998), pp. 76–7.

57 "Lun fenshuizhi de zhidao yuanze ji qishishi yunzuo wenti" (On the leading principles and implementation problems of the tax-sharing reform), *Caizheng yanjiu*, no. 3 (March 1994), p. 15; "Yijiujiusinian zhongguo gongshang shuizhi gaige pingxi" (An analysis of the 1994 industrial-commercial tax reform in China), *Jingji yanjiu cankao*, no. 1022 (4 March 1997), pp. 2–28; Wang Qingyun, "Shenhua fenshuizhi gaige" (Intensify the tax-sharing reform), *Neibu canyue* (Internal Reference), no. 404 (1 April 1998), pp. 10–15; and Xiang Huaicheng (ed.), *Zhongguo caizheng wushinian* (Fifty years of China's finance) (Beijing: Zhongguo caizheng jingji chubanshe, 1999), pp. 535–40.

58 Initially in 1984, concerning domestically financed projects, the ceiling for provincial approval had been set at RMB 10 million for some coastal regions (while SPC tightly controlled those in other areas). For projects related to energy, transportation, and raw materials, the ceiling was set much higher. For areas like Guangdong and Fujian, the ceiling was set much higher at RMB 200 million as early as 1985, which was later applied to Hainan in 1988. Regarding foreign-invested projects, different ceilings were set for different regions depending upon their levels of "opening." Over time, the preferential ceiling was upgraded from US$ 5 million in 1984 to 10–30 million since 1988. Currently all province-level units, "central economic cities," and some state-level development zones enjoy the same privilege. See Yao Zhenyan, *Zhongguo touzi tizhi gaige* (Reform of China investment system) (Beijing: Zhongguo caizheng jingji chubanshe, 1994), pp. 5–8; and Zeng Peiyan, *Zhongguo touzi jianshe wushinian* (Fifty years of investments in China) (Beijing: Zhongguo jihua chubanshe, 1999), pp. 233–7.

59 Gui Shiyong, *Zhongguo jihua tizhi gaige*, p. 16; and Peng Guilan and Huang Shutian (eds.), *Zhongguo gaige quanshu: touzi tizhi gaige juan* (Compendia on China's reform: volume on the reform of investment systems) (Dalian: Dalian chubanshe, 1992), p. 6.

60 See *ZGTJNJ 1998*, p. 185.

61 See Peng and Huang (eds.), *Zhongguo gaige quanshu*, pp. 55–78. For the leverage local governments have over local banks, see Wu Jinglian, "China's Economic and Financial Reform," in On Kit Tam (ed.), *Financial Reform in China* (London: Routledge, 1995), pp. 95–7.

62 See Anjali Kumar, "Economic Reform and the Internal Division of Labor in China: Production, Trade and Marketing," in David S. G. Goodman and Gerald Segal (eds.), *China Deconstructs: Politics, Trade, and Regionalism* (London: Routledge, 1994), pp. 99–109. As of 1989, the correlation coefficient of the industrial structure among twenty-eight provincial-level units was already 0.81. See Development Research Center of the State Council, *Zhongguo quyu xietiao fazhan zhanlue* (Strategies of regionally coordinated development in China) (Beijing: Zhongguo jingji chubanshe, 1994), p. 19. For a good overview of this problem, see Lance L. P. Gore, "The Communist Legacy in Post-Mao Economic Growth," *The China Journal*, no. 41 (January 1999), pp. 32–47.

63 For Beijing's failures in the 1980s, see Shaun Breslin, *China in the 1980s: Centre–Province Relations in a Reforming Socialist State* (London: Macmillan, 1996), ch. 4. For two different assessments, compare Yasheng Huang, *Inflation and Investment Controls in China: The Political Economy of central–local relations during the Reform Era* (Cambridge: Cambridge University Press, 1996), ch. 8, with Linda C. Li, *Centre and Provinces: China 1978–1993* (Oxford: Oxford University Press, 1998), ch. 7. For the data, see *South China Morning Post International Weekly*, 4 January 1997.

64 For the centrality of preferential policies, see Jae Ho Chung, "Shandong: The Political Economy of Development and Inequality," in David S. G. Goodman (ed.), *China's Provinces in Reform: Class, Community and Political Culture* (London: Routledge, 1997), pp. 127–57; and Jae Ho Chung, "A Sub-provincial Recipe of Coastal Development in China: The Case of Qingdao," *The China Quarterly*, no. 160 (December 1999), pp. 924–6, 931–8.

65 "Cujin diqu jingji xietiao fazhan yanjiu" (Study of promoting regionally coordinated economic development), *Jingji yanjiu cankao*, no. 914/915 (25 July 1996), pp. 33–4; and Li Haijian, *Jouxiang pinghengshi kaifang* (Towards a balanced opening) (Beijing: Shehuikexue chubanshe, 1999), p.165.

66 "Yijiujiusinian zhongguo waimao jiben zhuangkuang de huigu yiji dui yijiujiuwunian zhongguo waimao qianjing de zhanwang" (A retrospect on China's foreign trade in 1994 and its prospect for 1995), *Jingji yanjiu cankao*, no. 601 (1 January 1995), p. 21.

67 See Nicholas R. Lardy, *Foreign Trade and Economic Reform in China, 1978–1990* (Cambridge: Cambridge University Press, 1992), pp. 55–7; and State Planning Commission, "Woguo zhongyang yu difang jingji guanli quanxian yanjiu," pp. 20–1.

68 See Brantly Womack and Guangzhi Zhao, "The Many Worlds of China's Provinces: Foreign Trade and Diversification," and Gerald Segal, "Deconstructing Foreign Relations," in Goodman and Segal (eds.), *China Deconstructs*, pp. 131–76, 322–55; and You-tien Hsing, *Making Capitalism in China: The Taiwan Connection* (New York: Oxford University Press, 1998), chs. 5–7.

69 Wang Yukai (ed.), *Zhongguo xingzheng tizhi gaige ershinian* (Twenty years of administrative system reforms in China) (Zhengzhou: Zhongguo guji chubanshe, 1998), p. 158.

70 *Zhongguo gaige kaifang shiwunian dashiji* (Chronology of China's fifteen years of reform and opening) (Beijing: Xinhua chubanshe, 1994), p. 240.

71 "California's foreign policy" is the title of an article that appeared in *Foreign Affairs* (Spring 1993). In this regard, see Earl H. Fry, *The Expanding Role of State and Local Governments in US Foreign Affairs* (New York: Council on Foreign Relations, 1998).

72 For the 1983 changes to the *nomenklatura* control, see John P. Burns, "China's Nomenklatura System," *Problems of Communism*, vol. 36, no. 5 (September–October 1987), p. 38.

73 See John P. Burns, "Strengthening Central CCP Control of Leadership Selection: The 1990 *Nomenklatura*," *The China Quarterly*, no. 138 (June 1994), pp. 470–4.

74 See Lance L. P. Gore, *Market Communism: The Institutional Foundation of China's Post-Mao Hyper-Growth* (Hong Kong: Oxford University Press, 1998), ch. 3. The widely used practice of putting provincial leaders in charge of overseeing the implementation of central policy constitutes another source of local compliance. See, for instance, "Liangshi shengzhang fuzebi: maodun he wenti" (The Governor's responsibility system in grain production: contradictions and problems), *Jingji yanjiu cankao*, no. 1208 (24 September 1998), pp. 21–8.

75 See Yasheng Huang, "Central–local relations in China during the Reform Era: The Economic and Institutional Dimensions," *World Development*, vol. 24, no. 4 (April 1996), pp. 661–2; and Wang Yongxiang and Yang Shijian (eds.), *Zhongguo xiandai jiancha zhidu shi lun* (On the history of administrative supervision in modern China) (Fuzhou: Fujian chubanshe, 1998), pp. 228–64.

76 For the falsification of statistics in this period, see Kenneth Lieberthal, "The Great Leap Forward and the Split in the Yenan Leadership," in Roderick MacFarquhar and John K. Fairbank (eds.), *The Emergence of Revolutionary China 1949–1965*, vol. 2, *The Cambridge History of China* (Cambridge: Cambridge University Press, 1987), p. 309.

77 See Michel Oksenberg, "'Methods of Communication within the Chinese Bureaucracy," *The China Quarterly*, no. 57 (January–March 1974), pp. 21–2; and Michael Schoenhals, "Elite Information in China," *Problems of Communism*, vol. 34, no. 5 (September–October 1985), p. 66.

78 *Renmin ribao*, 16 November 1977; and Beijing Xinhua Domestic Service, 24 October 1980 in *FBIS*, 27 October 1980, pp. L4–5.

79 See SSB, *Zhongguo tongji gongzuo nianjian 1993* (China statistical work yearbook 1993) (Beijing: Zhongguo tongji chubanshe, 1993), pp. I-51–54, III-13–14; *South China Morning Post*, 28 October 1994 and 21 January 1995; and Yasheng Huang, "The Statistical Agency in China's Bureaucratic System: A Comparison with the Former Soviet Union," *Communist and Post-Communist Studies*, vol. 29, no. 1 (March 1996), pp. 59–75.

80 For a categorization of various materials on local issues, see Jae Ho Chung, "Reference and Source Materials in the Study of Provincial Politics and Economics in the Post-Mao Era: A Select List," *Provincial China*, no. 1 (March 1996), pp. 2–8.

81 See Liu Kao and Shi Feng (eds.), *Xinzhongguo chuban wushinian jishi* (Chronicle of fifty years of publication in China) (Beijing: Xinhua chubanshe, 1999), pp. 404–5.

82 See Diao Jiecheng, *Renmin xinfang shilue* (History of popular letter-writing) (Beijing: Beijing jingji xueyuan chubanshe, 1996).

83 See *Zhongguo tongji gongzuo nianjian 1993*, p. I-52; *Renmin ribao*, 17 August 1994 and *China Daily*, 11 September 1994.

84 See Yuezhi Zhao, *Media, Market, and Democracy in China: Between the Party Line and the Bottom Line* (Urbana and Chicago: University of Illinois Press, 1998), pp. 158–60, 168–70, 177; and *Wall Street Journal*, 9 September 1999 and 25 January 2000.

85 Nina P. Halpern, "Information Flows and Policy Coordination in the Chinese Bureaucracy," in Kenneth G. Lieberthal and David M. Lampton, *Bureaucracy, Politics, and Decision Making in Post-Mao China* (Berkeley: University of California Press, 1992), p. 126.

86 For instance, Shandong, Qingdao, and Huangdao Economic and Technological Development Zone (located in Qingdao) all enjoy the same US$ 30 million ceiling for approving foreign-invested projects. Administratively, too, Qingdao became a deputy-provincial city (only a half-grade lower than Shandong) and Huangdao became a prefecture-level unit (only a half-grade lower than Qingdao). For the complexities, see Jae Ho Chung, "Study of Provincial Politics and Development in the Post-Mao Reform Era: Issues, Approaches, and Sources," in Peter Cheung, Jae Ho Chung, and Zhimin Lin (eds.), *Provincial Strategies of Economic Reform in Post-Mao China: Leadership, Politics, Implementation* (Armonk, NY: M. E. Sharpe, 1998), pp. 437–9.

87 See Diao Tianding, *Zhongguo difang jigou gaiyao* (Overview of local government organizations in China) (Beijing: Falu chubanshe, 1989), pp. 169, 204–8; and Liu Junde, *Zhongguo xingzheng quhua de lilun yu shijian* (Theory and practice of administrative zoning in China) (Shanghai: East China Normal University Press, 1996), pp. 160–9.

88 For the number of cities, see Wu Peilun, *Dangdai zhongguo zhengfu gailun* (Overview of contemporary China's government) (Beijing: Gaige chubanshe, 1993), pp. 25, 182–3; and *ZGTJNJ 1999*, p. 3.

89 Currently, there are fifteen deputy-provincial cities composed of six central economic cities and nine provincial capitals. For the conflicts involving these cities with the provinces, see Zhu Limin et al., "Zhongyang yu difang zhengfu shiquan huafen yu zhineng peizhi wenti yanjiu" (Study of how to distribute the powers and functions of central and local governments), in Wu Peilun (ed.), *Difang jigou gaige sikao* (Thoughts on the reform of local organizations) (Beijing: Gaige chubanshe, 1992), pp. 182–7; and Liu Junde and Wang Yuming, *Zhidu yu chuangxin* (Institutions and innovations) (Nanjing: Dongnan daxue chubanshe, 2000), pp. 154–61.

90 See Zhang Wanqing, *Quyu hezuo yu jingji gangluo* (Inter-regional cooperation and economic linkages) (Beijing: Jingji kexue chubanshe, 1987), pp. 34–50, 100–17; *Zhongguo hengxiang jingji nianjian 1992* (1992 Yearbook of horizontal economies in China) (Beijing: Zhongguo shehuikexue chubanshe 1993); State Planning Commission, *Woguo diqu jingji xietiao fazhan yanjiu* (Study of co-ordinated regional economic development in China) (Beijing: Gaige chubanshe, 1996).

91 See *Qingdao nianjian 1992* (Qingdao yearbook 1992) (Qingdao: Zhongguo baike quanshu chubanshe, 1993), pp. 70–1; interviews in Jinan, Qingdao, and Dalian; Liu Menglin (ed.), *Henan zhuwai gongzuo huigu yu zhanwang* (Retrospect and prospects for Henan's external liaison work) (Zhengzhou: Henan renmin chubanshe, 1994), p. 8.

92 This speculation has benefitted from Vivienne Shue, *The Reach of the State: Sketches of the Chinese Body Politic* (Stanford: Stanford University Press, 1988), pp. 54–5.

93 See Sen Lin, "A New Pattern of Decentralization in China: The Increase of Provincial Powers in Economic Legislation," *China Information*, vol. 7, no. 3 (Winter 1992–93), pp. 27–38; and Liu Xingyi, "Zhongyang yu difang de lifaquan huafen" (Delineating the legislative powers between the center and localities), in Wei Liqun (ed.), *Shichang jingji zhong de zhongyang yu difang jingji guanxi*, pp. 139–40.

94 See Ming Xia, "Informational Efficiency, Organisational Development and the Institutional Linkages of the Provincial People's Congresses in China," *Journal of Legislative Studies*, vol. 3, no. 3 (Autumn 1997), pp. 10–38; and Zhang Yuankun, *Difang renda gongzuo gailun* (Introduction to the work of Local People's Congresses) (Beijing: Zhongguo minzhu fazhi chubanshe, 1997), chs. 2–3.

95 See Michael D. Swaine, "Chinese Regional Forces as Political Actors," in Richard H. Yang et al. (eds.), *Chinese Military Regionalism: The Security Dimension* (Boulder: Westview Press, 1994), pp. 63–7; and David Shambaugh, "China's Military in Transition: Politics, Professionalism, Procurement and Power Projection," *The China Quarterly*, no. 146 (June 1996), p. 283. For the average duration of service by regional commanders, see *Hong Kong Standard*, 9 October 1994.

96 See Tai-Ming Cheung, "Profits over Professionalism: The PLA's Economic Activities and the Impact on Military Unity," in *Chinese Military Regionalism*, pp. 85–110; and *South China Morning Post International Weekly*, 7 September 1996.

97 See, for instance, David S. G. Goodman, "The PLA in Guangdong Province: Warlordism and Localism," in *Chinese Military Regionalism*, pp. 220–1; and Gerald Segal, *China Changes Shape: Regionalism and Foreign Policy* (London: International Institute for Strategic Studies, 1994), pp. 24–5.

98 Most of these problems are dealt with in David Shambaugh (ed.), *Is China Unstable?: Assessing the Factors* (Washington, DC: Sigur Center for Asian Studies, 1998). While this volume has no individual chapter covering central–local relations as a key source of instability, I have treated the question earlier in "Central–Provincial

Relations," Lo Chi Kin, Suzanne Pepper, and Tsui Kai-yuen (eds.), *China Review 1995* (Hong Kong: Chinese University Press, 1995), pp. III-31–3.

99 See Huang, *Inflation and Investment Controls in China*, pp. 312–13; and Richard Baum and Alexei Shevchenko, "The 'State of the State'," in Merle Goldman and Roderick MacFarquhar (eds.), *The Paradox of China's Post-Mao Reforms* (Cambridge, MA: Harvard University Press, 1999), pp. 334–8.

100 For these two variations, see Chung, "Studies of Central–Provincial Relations in the People's Republic of China," pp. 504–6.

101 For the variation argument, see Jae Ho Chung (ed.), *Cities in China: Recipes for Economic Development in the Reform Era* (London: Routledge, 1999); and Cheung, Chung, and Lin (eds.), *Provincial Strategies of Economic Reform in Post-Mao China*.

102 See Yong-Nian Zheng, "Perforated Sovereignty: Provincial Dynamism and China's Foreign Trade," *The Pacific Review*, vol. 7, no. 3 (1994), p. 320; and Gabriella Montinola, Yingyi Qian, and Barry R. Weingast, "Federalism, Chinese Style: The Political Basis for Economic Success in China," *World Politics*, vol. 48, no. 1 (October 1995), pp. 50–81.

103 See János Kornai, *Highway and Byways: Studies on Reform and Postcommunist Transition* (Cambridge, MA: MIT Press, 1995), pp. 99–100.

3 China's agricultural reforms

A twenty-year retrospective

Robert F. Ash[1]

This essay addresses aspects of the development of China's farm economy since 1978, set against the historical perspective of agricultural change during the previous 30 years.[2] The nature of such a retrospective exercise invites an eclectic approach, which is here reflected in the cursory treatment of some important issues. Only brief consideration is, for example, given to an analysis of farm output and productivity growth, both having been examined in some detail elsewhere. Nor, except *en passant* and in the concluding comments, are institutional aspects of agricultural reform addressed, these being the subject of two excellent recent analyses.[3] More generally, in what follows I have tried to combine quantitative inquiry, empirical analysis, and reflective comment in order to address the nature, rationale, and impact of China's farm policies during the last two decades.

Some may question the choice of agriculture as the sole focus of economic analysis in this book. That other sectors of the economy also deserve consideration is undeniable. But even at the turn of the century, when the most aggregate measures would appear to highlight the relatively insignificant economic contribution of farming,[4] the case for focusing on the farm sector remains compelling. China remains a predominantly rural society, in which 69 percent of the total population are officially classified as rural residents.[5] It is also still a poor society, in which the most obvious manifestations of poverty are to be found in the countryside – above all, among farmers.[6] Under the impact of reforms, China's agricultural record displays many positive features, including consistently buoyant growth in fishing and livestock sectors, and significant improvements in both the output and structure of crop farming.[7] Perhaps most striking of all has been the remarkable series of grain harvests since 1995, which have raised average per capita supplies of grain to a record high[8] and, for the time being, confounded predictions of enforced and rising imports in the face of increasingly severe domestic grain shortages.[9] In fact, China has not only maintained basic self-sufficiency in grain, but been a net exporter of cereals and cereal flour.[10] Analysis of China's trade in *all* foods meanwhile reveals a rapidly growing surplus that has risen from US$ 58 million (1980) to US$ 3.3 billion (1990) to US$ 6.4 billion (1998).[11]

These achievements have their origin in the positive response by farmers to improved incentives associated with growing agricultural marketization. For a long time, market forces had their greatest impact on aquaculture, animal husbandry, and the farming of some economic crops, although such influences have recently been extended to grain and cotton farming. For a variety of reasons, however, the welfare consequences have frequently lagged behind economic progress in the agricultural sector.[12] Following a narrowing of differentials between the rural and urban sectors in the wake of the earliest agricultural reforms, such gaps have, since the mid-1980s, once again widened. The geographical complexion too is important, the coastal–interior divide showing up most strongly for rural incomes.[13] This context is important, serving to highlight the perceived threat to economic and social stability in the countryside resulting from the continuing exploitation of farmers, through the imposition of fees and other illegal or quasi-legal levies, which they are ill-equipped to pay and which, in any case, frequently do nothing to improve their own well-being.

These are some of the considerations, although they are not the only ones, which help explain the potency of the forty-year-old slogan, which insists that agriculture remains "the foundation of the national economy."[14] The peasant-based nature of the Chinese Revolution, as well as resonances associated with the human tragedy and economic impact caused by the collapse of agriculture during the Great Leap Forward and the subsequent great famine, are still part of the mindset of the third generation of Chinese leaders. Meanwhile, resource constraints and the need to accommodate further increases in income and consumption highlight the challenge of maintaining farm productivity growth in a context in which the orthodoxy of preserving domestic food self-sufficiency still prevails. From the central government's perspective, no less important is the need to improve farmers' welfare in order to obviate social and even political pressures associated with lagging and stagnating farm incomes.[15]

The agricultural legacy on the eve of reform

The essential developmental role of agriculture is to generate a surplus, albeit one that assumes various forms. A basic imperative is to produce a real surplus: of food, especially for industrial workers and their urban dependants; of raw materials for light industry; and of exports in order to earn foreign exchange. The farm sector may also be the source of a financial surplus, whether extracted through fiscal policy or, as in China, through the imposition of quotas set by the state that shift the net barter terms of trade against the farmers. Finally, it may facilitate modernization by making available the labor resources needed by an expanding industrial sector.

In 1978, following three decades of communist rule, agriculture remained a cornerstone of the Chinese economy. On the eve of reforms, almost 30 percent of national income still derived from agricultural activities.[16] As a source of food, the farm sector had achieved limited success: except for the years of famine following the Great Leap Forward, China met basic food security during the

Mao period,[17] but did so without accompanying quantitative or qualitative improvements in diet.[18] Nor, as the estimates in Table 3.1 show, was there strong growth in the domestic availability of other major farm products. (Underlying these figures were quite wide regional variations in agricultural development. To give just one example, agricultural growth between 1953 and 1978 was driven by strong performances in central-eastern and southern China, whereas growth in many northern and north-eastern provinces was below the national average – a profile that was dramatically reversed during the later 1980s and early 1990s.)

Dependence on agriculture for light industrial raw materials and exports also remained high throughout the period. In 1978, almost 70 percent of light industrial output relied on the farm sector for raw materials, and 63 per cent of exports were either raw or processed farm products.[19] Although the importance of the farm sector as a provider of raw materials was subsequently maintained, its role as a source of exports declined rapidly after 1978.[20]

From the 1950s, high capital–labor ratios associated with the heavy industrialization thrust of China's development strategy minimized the demand for labor from outside the urban sector. During the 1950s, quite large-scale voluntary rural–urban migration did take place, but by the end of the First Five-Year Plan (1953–7), the implementation of a household registration (*hukou*) system provided an effective control mechanism that remained in place until after the initiation of the post-1978 reforms. As a result, the principal employment challenge facing China's farm sector during the Mao period was to maximize employment within the countryside. Between 1957 and 1976, the proportion of the total labor force engaged in farming fell by less than 6 percentage points,[21] and in 1978, almost three-quarters of the workforce were still engaged in farming. In general, the process of agricultural collectivization was instrumental in providing an institutional framework that went some way toward maximizing rural employment opportunities, albeit at the expense of waste, inefficiency, and the concealment of large numbers of surplus farm laborers.[22] This is not to suggest that large-scale

Table 3.1   Average per capita output (kg) of major items of agricultural production (1952–78, selected years)

Year	Grain	Cotton	Oil seeds	Pork, beef, and mutton	Fish
1952	288.0	2.3	7.4	6.0	3.0
1957	306.0	2.6	6.6	6.3	4.9
1962	240.5	1.2	3.0	2.9	3.4
1965	272.0	3.0	5.1	7.7	4.2
1970	293.0	2.8	4.6	7.3	3.9
1975	310.5	2.6	5.0	8.7	4.8
1976	307.5	2.2	4.3	8.4	4.8
1978	318.5	2.3	5.5	9.0	4.9

Source: Ministry of Agriculture, *Zhongguo nongcun jingji tongji daquan (1949–1986)* (Compendium of rural economic statistics (1949–1986)), (Beijing: Zhongguo nongye chubanshe, 1989), p.127.

transfers out of agriculture did not occur before the 1980s. In the first half of the 1970s, for example, when there were major increases in the accumulation rate and in construction investment throughout China, the average annual addition to the workforce engaged in industrial and construction activities rose sharply, while the corresponding figure for farm labor declined. To what extent this break in the previous trend reflected farm labor absorption associated with the ongoing Third Front industrialization programme, as well as other non-agricultural rural initiatives, is something that deserves further investigation. Even so, not until the dismantling of the collective edifice in the 1980s did the burden on the rural and other sectors to find productive employment opportunities for the huge number of underemployed farm workers really manifest itself.

Acceptance of official statistics at face value would confirm a widely held view that from the 1950s until the late 1970s, Chinese agriculture derived a net gain as a result of intersectoral resource flows. However, data limitations throw such findings into doubt.[23] It is true that direct taxes on farmers were falling during this period, but this decline was offset by the increasing burden of the state's monopoly procurement policies in the countryside.[24]

Meanwhile, a growing emphasis on self-reliance – above all, on grain self-sufficiency – minimized structural change within the farm sector. In 1957, crop farming accounted for 81 percent of agricultural gross value output (GVAO); twenty-one years later, the corresponding figure was still 77 percent.[25]

Finally, China inherited from the Mao period a significant legacy of rural poverty. Even allowing for pockets of relative prosperity, per capita disposable income in the countryside remained very low – in 1978, averaging a mere 145 yuan. This was less than half of the corresponding figure (346 yuan) for urban residents, and only 80 percent of the national average for the entire population.[26] The persistence of such low living standards, in absolute and relative terms, highlights what has become an increasingly serious threat to China's economic and social stability since the second half of the 1980s.

The record of agricultural reform in China

The challenge of agriculture in transition: an introductory remark

Economic planners in socialist systems have argued that agriculture, like industry, has the potential to realize economies of scale over the entire range of its activities. This orthodoxy lasted for many years in China, where a collectivist ethos defined the nature of the institutional framework of farming from the mid-1950s until the early 1980s.[27] In reality, however, the large size of collectives was the source of serious organizational problems that have been largely absent under capitalist agriculture, where farms usually involve only a few workers. Far from economizing on human labor and capital, China's collective institutional framework generated huge resource waste.

In ancillary farming activities (research, irrigation, crop spraying, processing, and marketing), there does exist considerable potential to realize scale economies and secure the benefits of cooperation. Typically, capitalist agriculture is characterized by the use of small manpower units devoted to the main farm tasks, combined with a significant degree of cooperation in such activities. Farm policy in China during the post-Mao period has increasingly sought to provide institutions that would preserve these valuable aspects of cooperative activity. From the 1980s, for example, efforts were made to put in place a new kind of institutional framework, which would realize the advantages of decentralized, household-based field operations and secure the benefits of cooperation in areas susceptible to more centralized management, such as mechanized ploughing, irrigation, and the procurement of basic agricultural inputs. That such efforts continue is clear from the CCP Central Committee's 10th Five-Year Plan Proposals, which call for the stabilization of the "two-tier system that combines unified and independent management on the basis of contracted household operations."[28]

Financing agricultural development

Agricultural decollectivization in China did not presage the establishment of private property rights over farmland. Instead, the village retained ownership rights and sought to control the terms on which land was used, endeavoring to give farm households equal access to it.[29] Selective and gradual privatization of farm machinery did, however, take place following the first agricultural reforms. In the first half of the 1980s, most small, collectively owned means of production were sold to individual peasants.[30] At the time, many larger items remained under collective ownership, although in the second half of the decade peasants began more actively to purchase large farm machinery too.[31]

The identification of fundamental problems associated with collective farming does not of itself suggest an easy way in which policies designed to raise agricultural productivity can be formulated. Such policies have to be seen in the context of a wide range of other issues, one of which is investment. In the 1950s, Chinese agriculture was starved of such funds; in the mid-1970s, it still absorbed only about one-tenth of total state capital construction investment.[32] But funding of agriculture support industries (especially farm machinery and chemical fertilizers) had meanwhile risen steadily, as had investment undertaken from within the collective sector itself. The farm sector's purchases of agricultural inputs grew especially rapidly, averaging almost 12 percent p.a. between 1957 and 1978.[33] Its share of steel products rose from 8 to 17 percent, and that of cement from 9 to 25 percent during roughly the same period.[34]

Before 1978, irrigation was largely organized by the state or the collective. Side by side with decollectivization of farmland, the 1980s saw rapid growth in private investment and ownership of such facilities by individual households or groups of households.[35] In the provision of irrigation, as in that of other farm inputs, the burden on the collective sector declined as individual involvement increased. As this process took place, collective funds were increasingly made available for other purposes.[36]

The government was traditionally responsible for the administration of water conservancy facilities, as well as for funding new capital construction. But in the apparent belief that increasing rural prosperity was a potential source of indigenous funding by the peasants themselves, the central authorities sought during the 1980s to reduce their role in the provision of irrigation facilities. This decision was later acknowledged to have been misplaced and at the end of the 1980s it was reversed. But in the interim the level of capital construction investment in irrigation undertaken by the central authorities remained depressed.[37]

The decline in the state's contribution to irrigation investment mirrored a reduction in its investment role in agriculture as a whole. From the mid-1960s until the late 1970s, agriculture's share in capital construction investment remained fairly stable. But within the space of a single decade, the corresponding figure had been halved; and within another five years, it again fell sharply.[38] In nominal terms, agricultural construction investment grew impressively (by 12.7 percent p.a.) during the Seventh Five-Year Plan (7FYP) period (1986–90), and accelerated to 26.7 percent annually under the Eighth Plan (1991–5).[39] But if the investment estimates are deflated by the retail price index, the average annual rates of growth are reduced to a more modest 2.7 percent (1986–90) and 13.7 percent (1991–5). Typically, about two-thirds of agricultural construction investment have been directed to irrigation work, although in the second half of the 1980s, this figure fell to 55 percent.[40]

Reference was made earlier to sources of financial support for agriculture other than funds generated through the state budget for capital construction purposes.[41] Between the 7FYP period and the early 1990s (1991–4) the share of capital construction funds in total agriculture support expenditure fell from 28 to 21 percent.[42] As a proportion of total public spending under the central budget, agriculture's share fell from a peak 13.6 percent (1978) to 7.9 percent (1986). Recent years have seen something of a recovery, although budgetary spending on agriculture (excluding rural relief funds) still accounted for only 8.8 percent of total government expenditure during 1991–5.[43] In 1997 – the most recent year for which I have access to relevant data – the corresponding figure had fallen to 7.9 percent.[44]

Depressed real investment growth in agriculture during 1986–90 may have strengthened the government's commitment to the establishment of a "two-tier operational system" that sought to combine decentralized, household-based farming with a collectively operated "socialized service system" (see above). Whatever the reality, the outcome was to give added impetus to a process that was already underway: namely, the expansion in the provision of farm inputs and services by village (*cun*), township (*xiangzhen*), and other specialist service groups. This is confirmed by the findings of a survey of over 5,300 villages throughout China (excluding Tibet), which revealed that between 1986 and 1990, the provision of irrigation, mechanized ploughing, plant protection and veterinary services, and supplies of seeds and chemical fertilizers by socialized service organizations (especially at village level) expanded rapidly.[45] As a result, by 1990, individual farm households were responsible for only 30 percent of drainage and irrigation, less than a quarter of 23 percent of both mechanized ploughing and the supply of chemical fertilizers, 15 percent of plant protection services, and less than 3 percent of veterinary services.[46]

The extent to which the "new collectives"[47] can perform the role for which they are designed depends critically on their financial strength. If the evidence indicates no lack of demand for their services, it also suggests that they have sometimes faced a quite severe financial challenge. Finance for the expansion of socialized service activities should ideally come from fee income generated by the service activities themselves and covered by collective dues from farmers. But in less rurally industrialized regions, collective levies have often been sufficient (sometimes not only that) only to finance public utilities and general administrative expenses – hence the frequent need to rely on local government subsidies, derived from the profits of rural, non-agricultural enterprises. The further inference is that only in more affluent rural areas of the country, where collectively owned rural industry and services are more highly developed, has sufficient funding been available to fulfill the economic rationale of the two-tier system, and additionally to finance social welfare and subsidize other activities under a "unified management" system.

In many poor countries, institutional and other factors have led to widespread and enforced reliance on informal, high-interest credit generated within the rural sector. Such practices often inhibit investment by potentially efficient farmers and trap poor peasants in a network of dependency on traditional moneylenders.

In the wake of unprecedented farm output and income growth in the early 1980s, the net savings ratio of China's peasants increased sharply from 16 percent (1979) to 22.9 percent (1984).[48] Subsequent difficulties that emerged in the farming sector reversed this upward trend and by the end of the 1980s, the ratio had fallen back to a level (11 percent) that was significantly below that which had prevailed at the beginning of the first reform decade. Recovery has gradually taken place in the 1990s, although the 1984 peak was not matched until 1997.[49]

Big increases in the absolute value of rural savings deposits were a corollary of these changes, although internal inconsistencies in given official sources and conflicting estimates between different sources make it difficult to estimate between the level of such savings with confidence.[50] That rural savings rose rapidly throughout the 1980s and into the 1990s is, however, not in doubt. Suffice to say here that an increase in rural household savings from 184.2 billion to 481.6 billion yuan between 1990 and 1994[51] contained the potential to add hugely to prevailing levels of state investment in agriculture. For example, the 1994 savings figure was nine times greater than total government spending on agriculture. In 1998, *agricultural* deposits alone totalled 174.8 billion yuan and were 2.7 times higher than total central government spending in support of agricultural production and associated operating expenses.[52]

Peasants' savings were mostly deposited in official financial institutions (especially the Agricultural Bank and rural credit cooperatives),[53] where the funds were secure but earned a low rate of return. Available evidence suggests that the role of such institutions as a source of credit to farmers was uneven and sometimes disappointing. In 1994, for example, only 15 percent of all the loans extended by the Agricultural Bank were for farm purposes.[54] In rural credit cooperatives too, agricultural loans 'proper' constituted a small and declining part of the total loan portfolio of rural credit cooperatives. There was also a strong bias against extending agricultural loans to *individual* farm households.[55] Neither the Agricultural Bank nor the cooperatives were a significant source of capital for fixed investment.[56] Most loans – for example, 68.5 percent of those extended by the Agricultural Bank in 1994 – were used for "commercial purposes" (especially purchases of agricultural and sideline products).

That rural credit should have been directed increasingly toward non-farming activities (especially rural industry and commerce)[57] in the 1980s and 1990s is not surprising, given the higher returns available from this rapidly expanding sector. Whether informal financial institutions would have been a more effective source of funding to China's farm sector is an open question, although the experience of some other Asian countries (e.g., South Korea) highlights the potentially positive role of this sector.

Agricultural marketization

The ultimate thrust of agricultural policy since 1978 has been to transform China's farm sector from a supply-orientated to a market-responsive, demand-oriented system. The cost of establishing an integrated wholesale capacity has been a significant constraint on the pace of marketization in China. Nevertheless, agricultural commercialization accelerated after 1978 and the rapid proliferation of private markets facilitated the free exchange of many farm products.[58] On the eve of reform, the marketed share of many farm items was already quite high, although supply and marketing cooperatives and other state agencies remained the dominant channel for such sales. In the second half of the decade, more and more output of this kind came to be sold in free markets.[59] By contrast, however, a large part of the marketed output of staple products (grain, edible oil, and cotton) remained subject to compulsory procurement throughout the 1980s.[60] As late as 1992, 84 percent of marketed grain and over 90 percent of cotton were still being sold through state commercial channels.[61]

During the 1980s, free-market transactions in grain grew much more slowly than those of meat, fish, vegetables, and fruit.[62] In the 1990s, this situation changed. Between 1990 and 1998, comparable sales of grain and edible oil grew, on average by 33 percent p.a., to reach 146.5 billion yuan. This rate of expansion exceeded that of meat, poultry, and eggs, and matched the sales growth of fish and vegetables.[63] But until the government was prepared to sanction rises in retail prices, even such rapid growth failed to alleviate the budgetary burden associated with the state's continuing involvement in grain purchases. The physical increase in grain sales through state channels – from 50.7 (1978) to 90.6 (1985) to 122.6 million tonnes (1990) – would on its own have added considerably to that burden.[64] When allied to the persistent increase in purchase price, it generated severe fiscal difficulties. This was the background against which the central authorities were compelled, in 1991–2, to sanction unprecedented rises in retail prices of staple foods, thereby abandoning the former rationing system in urban areas.[65]

Subsequently, in the wake of successive post-1994 bumper harvests – a likely reflection of the regionally directed "grain bag" policy[66] – increases in grain supply exceeded rises in consumer demand, causing stockpiles to grow and once more placing an increasingly heavy fiscal burden on the government. A further consequence was a growing reluctance by state grain enterprises to buy surplus grain at the protective prices supposedly guaranteed by the state. This made it difficult for farmers to offload their produce. Meanwhile, farmers' residual inclination to stress output maximization was reflected in neglect of grain variety and quality.

These more recent developments were the background against which, in May 1999, Premier Zhu Rongji announced that administrative price protection for grain varieties of poor quality and/or in excess supply was gradually to be phased out.[67] The decision foreshadowed further reform of the grain distribution system, designed to facilitate production in accordance with the dictates of the market. Significant too was an announcement, in August 1999, that the fixed purchase price of *cotton* set by the central government would also be abolished.

The most striking manifestation of the government's determination to create a truly market-orientated grain economy came in announcements, made in January 2000, that urged reductions in both the sown area and total production of grain, as well as those of other staple agricultural products.[68] Such decisions reflected the recent unprecedented run of bumper harvests, but also highlighted the government's intention that higher incomes for grain farmers should derive less from physical increases in output, but more from deliberate market-orientated adjustments in the *structure* of production – not least, by producing more high-quality grains, more grain for processing, and more feed grain.[69] Implied too was the determination to generate a pattern of production, based on regional comparative advantage and designed to meet consumption requirements, as expressed through market demand. To these ends, protective price guarantees were withdrawn from low-quality cereals, while prices of high-quality cereals were increased. Farmers were meanwhile warned to expect widening price differentials, in line with varying qualitative, seasonal, and regional production conditions.[70]

But the central government has also been explicit in recognizing some of the obstacles to successfully implementing the changes. These include the inadequacy of capital funds to facilitate comprehensive structural adjustment and modernization of the farm sector, as well as the absence of effective systems to provide checks on product standards and quality, and to disseminate technological information (including information on improved seed varieties). The inability of many localities to differentiate clearly between differing grades of farm products has also adversely affected farmers' incentives to produce superior products, thereby undermining efforts to make farming responsive to market needs.

Farm input purchases

Before 1978, almost all farm *inputs* were purchased by collectives through state supply networks. The lack of direct involvement by farmers in purchasing decisions sometimes resulted in inappropriate technologies being forced upon them, while the absence of commercial pressures deterred them from making qualitative improvements in farming methods. From such perspectives, the growth of free markets for farm inputs after 1978 was highly beneficial. But it is noteworthy that throughout the reform period, the growth of free-market sales of agricultural producer goods has been slower than that of any other category of farm product. For example, even allowing for accelerated growth after 1990, the average annual rate of expansion of such transactions between 1980 and 1994 was 21.4 percent – and this from a negligible base (0.71 billion yuan in 1980).[71]

In short, state agencies have remained a dominant channel through which farm inputs have been made available to peasants. Measures, such as the introduction of decentralized pricing for extra-plan marketing of manufactured and imported inputs, did encourage free-market exchange of agricultural inputs. But in circumstances in which excess demand for inputs at state prices often existed, the adoption of dual-track pricing was reflected in an increase in input prices after the mid-1980s.[72, 73]

At the end of the 1970s, the state engineered a major improvement in the relative price at which farm produce was bought from farmers. Between 1978 and 1980, the net barter terms of trade between agriculture and industry[74] moved in favor of farm produce by 23 percent.[75] Thereafter, the fiscal burden of further rises in farm purchase prices, unaccompanied by matching increases in urban retail food prices, resulted in a slower improvement in the "price scissors." Indeed, in 1988 the narrowing of the price gap between agriculture and industry was halted and during the next four years the terms of trade once more turned against farmers. This deterioration was temporarily reversed in 1993–5, but thereafter again declined.[76]

Water and chemical fertilizers have probably contributed most to crop output growth. Until the mid-1980s, the irrigated area failed to increase, but thereafter significant expansion took place (including the share powered by electro-mechanical means).[77] Between 1985 and 1999, chemical fertilizer use more than doubled (from 17.8 million to 41.2 million tonnes), with potash and compound products registering the biggest increases.[78]

Overall, access to items of fixed farm capital has also improved significantly under the impact of reform. Sample survey data show that between 1990 and 1998, for example, ownership of tractors of all kinds almost tripled, while there was a 2.5 times increase in that of motorized threshing machines; the corresponding increase for irrigation and drainage pumps was 3.5 times.[79] Even so, ownership of such items was, even in 1998, far from universal: only 14 percent of farm households possessed walking tractors and water pumps, and less than 10 percent owned motorized threshing machines.[80] There were also marked regional variations, reflecting the impact of both demographic and developmental factors.

To what extent the realignment of collective, state, and individual in the 1980s and 1990s impacted on the frequency and severity of natural disasters in China is a subject that deserves further investigation.[81] From some perspectives, there is evidence that only quite small improvements in flood prevention, water, and soil conservation have taken place since the 1980s.[82] Taken at face value, official statistics reveal that the incidence of natural disasters has worsened during this period. For example, whereas during the latter years of the Mao era and its aftermath (1970–8) some 37.75 million hectares were, on average, "covered"[83] by natural disasters each year, the corresponding figure rose to 41.11 million hectares (1978–90) and to 50.78 million hectares (1991–9).[84] Not only has the incidence of such disasters increased, but so have their severity: for example, between 1991 and 1999, some 25.99 million hectares suffered average annual crop losses in excess of 30 percent, compared with only 11.55 million hectares during 1970–8.[85] The human cost too appears to have increased: during 1953–67, some 92,643 lives were lost as a result of natural disasters (on average, 6,176 p.a.); between 1978 and 1994, the corresponding figure was 115,465 (6,792 p.a.).[86]

Output and productivity growth

The output performance of Chinese agriculture under the impact of post-1978 reforms has been analyzed in detail elsewhere and only brief consideration is given here to this aspect.[87] Sources are agreed that 1978 constitutes a real watershed in terms of agricultural growth. In the period under Mao, for example, China's real growth rate of farm output (GVAO) averaged 3.6 percent p.a. (1957–78),[88] compared with 6.6 percent during 1978–97. Estimates of net agricultural growth indicate that in contrast to the Mao period, real *net* agricultural growth since 1978 has easily exceeded population expansion and has been more than twice the previous long-run trend rate of farm growth.

The macroeconomic profile in Table 3.2 of China's agricultural performance since 1978 is taken from official GVAO estimates.

Throughout the post-1978 period, non-crop farming activities have grown

Table 3.2   Agricultural growth (% p.a.) in China, 1978–99

	GVAO	Crop farming	Forestry	Animal husbandry	Fishing
1978–99	6.54	5.09	5.35	9.57	12.01
1978–84	7.62	6.79	9.09	9.59	7.67
1984–9	3.92	1.13	0.63	8.71	15.15
1989–94	6.81	4.30	7.10	10.35	14.18
1994–9	7.49	5.87	4.01	9.58	12.10

Sources: *TJZY* (2000), p. 95; *TJNJ* (1993), p. 336; (1998), p. 390.

much faster than crop cultivation and forestry. In the 1980s, the share of live-stock farming and fishing in GVAO rose from one-fifth to one-third; by 1999, it had reached nearly 40 percent. Meanwhile, the share of crop farming (not including forestry) fell from 76 to 57.5 percent (1980–99).[89] These structural changes mainly reflected increases in income that enabled consumers, especially in the cities, to choose a more varied diet based on higher intakes of meat, fish, and dairy produce.

The most disappointing feature of China's agricultural performance was the marked slowing in the growth of the grain sector in the second half of the 1980s. Under the impact of the early agricultural reforms, average per capita grain output rose rapidly, increasing from 317 to 394 kilograms between 1978 and 1984. But as a result of output stagnation in the second half of the 1980s and faltering growth in the first half of the 1990s, the 1984 peak level of per capita output was not subsequently reattained (and surpassed) until the record harvest of 1996.[90] In the mid-1990s, one apocalyptic scenario suggested that a declining supply response, combined with inexorable demand pressures, would generate an increasingly large domestic grain deficit in China, ultimately necessitating imports of up to 369 million tonnes by 2030.[91] Scholars and analysts inside and outside China have been strongly critical of Brown's projections and, by coincidence, a run of fine harvests since 1995 has taken per capita grain output to a new record high (412.2 kg in 1996).[92] From the present perspective, it is unlikely that Brown's extreme scenario will be fulfilled, although some of his warnings remain salutary and it may yet be premature to assume that China's food security, defined in terms of the maintenance of basic grain self-sufficiency, is permanently assured.[93]

Assessing the efficiency of China's agricultural performance is difficult. Table 3.3 seeks to measure labor productivity in selected years between 1978 and 1997. The figures suggest that until the mid-1980s, all branches of farming except for grain shared in the impressive growth of agricultural labor productivity. Thereafter, there was a distinct slowing of productivity growth in crop farming activities and the continuing upward momentum of GVAO owed most to further labor productivity improvements in meat and aquatic production.

A distinctive feature of crop farming's performance under the impact of

Table 3.3   Farm sector productivity in China, 1978–98 (1978 = 100)

	1980	1985	1990	1995	1998
Average output per farm worker:					
Grain	102.3	113.2	121.6	131.3	143.2
Cotton	121.4	174.1	172.6	188.7	177.0
Oil seeds	143.3	275.2	256.6	369.9	377.9
Meat	136.9	187.0	243.6	427.2	569.6
Fish	93.9	137.8	220.6	463.8	715.0
Average GVAO per farm worker (index based on comparable prices)	106.1	147.0	150.3	233.1	307.7

Sources: *TJNJ* (1999), pp. 138, 395–6, 401, and 403; *TJZY* (2000), p. 95.

reform has been the achievement of rapid growth in average yields (output per sown hectare) (Table 3.4). For staple crops, the burden of growth was over-whelmingly (in the case of cotton) or entirely (in that of grain) carried by such improvements. In the absence of significant yield growth, potentially serious imbalances between domestic demand and supply of these crops would have emerged. Even so, sown area adjustments remained an important source of growth for oil bearing crops and economic crops, such as sugar and tobacco. Indeed, the case of tobacco is remarkable, its entire output growth being depen-dent on area extension.

Finding a reliable measure of the capital–output ratio in Chinese agriculture after 1978 is difficult, not least because it is impossible to be sure of the propor-tions of village assets used for agricultural and non-farm work. It does, however, seem quite likely that in the wake of early farm reforms (say, between 1978 and 1984), the long-run trend decline in agricultural capital productivity was temporarily reversed. Subsequent trends are harder to interpret, although a steep increase in purchases of farm inputs side by side with slowing GVAO growth may signal a renewed decline in capital productivity.

Table 3.4   The relative importance of improvements in yields and sown area adjustments in generating output growth (1980 = 100)

	1985	1990	1995	1998	1999
Food grains:					
Total output	118.3	139.2	145.6	159.8	158.6
Average yield	127.4	143.8	155.1	164.7	164.3
Sown area	92.8	96.8	93.9	97.1	96.5
Oil-bearing crops:					
Total output	205.2	209.8	292.6	300.9	338.2
Average yield	137.9	152.6	177.6	184.6	192.8
Sown area	148.8	137.5	165.2	163.0	175.4
Cotton:					
Total output	153.2	166.5	176.1	166.3	141.4
Average yield	145.9	145.9	158.4	181.8	185.2
Sown area	104.5	113.6	110.2	90.6	75.7
Sugar cane:					
Total output	226.0	252.6	286.8	365.8	327.5
Average yield	112.3	120.1	122.2	125.2	
Sown area	201.5	210.6	234.9	292.5	
Sugar beet:					
Total output	141.5	230.4	221.8	229.4	
Average yield	111.7	152.0	141.3	174.1	
Sown area	126.6	151.2	156.9	131.6	
Flue-cured tobacco:					
Total output	289.4	315.1	289.0	291.2	304.7
Average yield	105.8	92.6	87.3	95.9	
Sown area	271.3	338.0	329.7	302.3	

Sources: *TJNJ* (1999), pp. 391–7; *TJZY* (2000), pp. 97–9.

Welfare aspects of agricultural reform: a brief note

Under the impact of rising per capita incomes, rural households have experienced quite a sharp fall in the share of total spending on staple foods since 1978, expenditure on non-staples having meanwhile increased. But compared with their urban counterparts, rural households continue to spend more on food and less on clothing. Moreover, if direct grain consumption has just about peaked for the rural sector as a whole, in poorer parts of the countryside it will continue to increase. Meanwhile, consumption of meat, fish, poultry, and dairy produce in the countryside remains well below urban levels. A heavier burden of spending in deregulated sectors – health, education, and transport – is also evident among rural households. The obvious inference is that rural residents remain a long way behind their urban cousins.[94]

Access to a wider variety of consumer goods has certainly improved among rural residents. Consumption of basic household goods – bicycles, sewing machines, wristwatches, and radios – all jumped dramatically between 1978 and 1985 and may have peaked in the first half of the 1990s. Meanwhile, in the mid-1980s, demand for larger consumer durables – TV sets, sofas, washing machines, and refrigerators – began to increase. Between 1990 and 1995, villagers bought 24.2 million color TV sets and 8.3 million motorbikes. Yet on average, in 1998 there were still only 33 color TV sets, 32 radio cassettes, and a mere 13.5 motorbikes per 100 rural households.[95] This is one obvious respect in which China's continuing status as an overwhelmingly rural society has enormous importance. For the time being, electric fans are the only consumer durable to which access has become the norm among rural households. Demand for goods, markets for which are already saturated in the cities – radio and TV sets, washing machines, etc. – is likely to stay buoyant in rural areas. For other goods, associated with even higher incomes, markets remain almost wholly unexploited.

Conclusion: themes and perspectives

Excessive emphasis on the historical significance of the Third Plenum of the 11th CCP Central Committee carries the danger of ignoring elements of continuity that flow from earlier to later years across that watershed. In fact, recurrent themes characterize China's agricultural development since 1949. Like leitmotifs in an opera, their recurrence is not coincidental. Rather, they highlight profound dilemmas that have confronted Chinese governments in their efforts to promote the rapid and sustained growth of the farm sector and assist in the fulfillment of its developmental role. Recognizing these dilemmas is important, if prejudicial or glib assessments of the economic and other implications of the vagaries of Chinese agricultural policies are to be avoided.

For example, arguments about the relative merits of private and public resource ownership – in agriculture, especially land ownership – demand careful and dispassionate consideration. So do investigations of the supposed strengths and weaknesses of centralized and decentralized decision making in the farm sector. Central to both issues are questions of incentives and efficiency. But finding the most appropriate balance between the forces of control and *laissez-aller* that will maximize both is difficult and complex. The contrasting experiences of China in the second half of the 1950s and after the mid-1980s highlight profound policy dilemmas, associated with the differing motivations of farmers acting individually and under state guidance in the wake of the devolution or centralization of decision-making powers in the agricultural sector. It is no coincidence that following collectivization in the mid-1950s, the Chinese government found it prudent to allow farmers to retain private plots. But it is also telling that current farm policies should, through the establishment of a two-tier system (see above), seek to integrate family-based farming into a framework of socialized services.[96]

Identifying and implementing the most desirable scale of farming is also far from easy. On theoretical and empirical grounds, there are strong cases to be made in favor of both small-scale, household-based farming and large-scale, collectivized agriculture. But as China's experience in the Mao and Deng periods shows, unambiguous policy advocacy of either is likely to pose fresh dilemmas for policy makers, to which there is no easy resolution. What does seem clear is that the massive reservoir of surplus farm labor in China is and will remain in the foreseeable future a major constraint on the adoption of a truly capitalist mode of agriculture, associated with large-scale, private-owned land-holdings and the use of a farm technology that embodies high capital–labor ratios. Except in some north-eastern and north-western parts of the country, mechanization no longer commands a high premium in official agricultural policy, emphasis on the application of science and technology being couched more in terms of the need to improve farmers' access to better working capital (especially superior seed strains). Moreover, ideological considerations apart, the introduction of a private land market would, through its likely effect on average farm size, merely exacerbate the pressures of underemployment. For the time being, therefore, a significant increase in the scale of farming can be considered unlikely. Rather, the government's greater preoccupation will be how to accelerate the transfer of existing redundant farm laborers, whether through the restructuring and further development of township and village enterprises, or the integration of farming operations "proper" with ancillary activities, such as agricultural processing and the distribution of farm-based products. In short, under current circumstances, tolerating farms of sub-optimal size[97] may be regarded a price worth bearing, if the alternative is heightened social tension resulting from an even greater displacement of agricultural labor.

In China, many of the issues raised above are strongly interrelated. Given heavy population pressure and an adverse person–land ratio, the implementation of an egalitarian land reform based on private ownership is bound to lead to small-scale farming. The outcome may be to enhance personal incentives to the benefit of agricultural yields and farm incomes. Such was the experience of China in both the early 1950s and early 1980s, although in the latter period privatization did not embrace the ownership of land.[98] But the result may also be to impede important technical improvements, as well as undermining state control needed to secure desirable economic and distributional objectives. Ideological imperatives ensured that under Mao, the underlying policy dilemma was resolved through the establishment of a collective agriculture. By contrast, the ethos of post-1978 reforms has precluded the possibility of a return to a collective agriculture of the kind that existed in the Mao era. On the contrary, the conviction that agriculture's traditional supply orientation should give way to the primacy of demand considerations has increasingly facilitated the introduction of free-market elements in farmers' decision making. Yet at the beginning of a new century, thanks to policy dilemmas as well as ideological shibboleths, China's agriculture is still some way from typifying an unconstrained free-market system.

Moral economy considerations also deserve to be addressed.[99] A central issue here – one that has profound economic and political implications – is the nature of elite–mass relations in the countryside, most dramatically captured in the struggle over the disposal of the harvest. Recent interpretations of China's rural development in the early twentieth century have highlighted the positive impact of domestic and foreign market developments on farm efficiency, agricultural growth, and peasant living standards.[100] As such, they have come to define a new orthodoxy that challenges the previous, more conventional view of pre-1949 rural society, which stressed supposed agricultural stagnation and peasant impoverishment.[101] Consideration of the issues raised in these interpretations is beyond the scope of this essay. But the continuing debate counsels caution in accepting at face value the argument that landlordism, tenurial practices, and other related modes of behavior are inherently inimical to agricultural efficiency and growth.

The implications of "Maoist" and "Dengist" farm policies for the disposal of the harvest also deserve consideration. Jean Oi has described the post-collectivization pattern of clientelist rule in the Chinese countryside as a relationship between "two actors of unequal status."[102] In contrast to the Soviet Union, where, in the 1930s, collectivization and "de-kulakization" conferred absolute authority on the Stalinist state, in China a more ambiguous clientelist relationship emerged, reflecting new patterns of collusion and evasion. The response to early post-1978 rural reforms no doubt highlights the growing power of Chinese peasants vis-à-vis the state in this period.[103] But if such evidence underlines the constraints on farmers' maneuverability imposed by the former collective framework, subsequent developments have demonstrated the limits to such power in the evolving institutional framework of the 1990s.

Indeed, out of the reforms have emerged new forms of exploitative behavior against farmers.[104] The immediate sources of such exploitation are two-fold. The first is the practice of issuing IOUs (*baitiaozi*), instead of cash, for produce delivered for sale to commercial agents of the state. The second – the more intractable problem – is the imposition of illegal exactions (*tanpai*) on peasants in order to fund development projects or other schemes whose benefits to farmers may be questionable. That such practices have generated dissatisfaction and anger among many crop farmers is undeniable. Ultimately, however, both forms of exploitation are symptoms of a more profound malaise – that of poverty. It is the consequences for social and even political stability of such poverty, as much as – perhaps more than – the fulfillment of agriculture's economic role, that have come to resonate most strongly in official pronouncements on agricultural policy.

Kate Zhou has used an acronym – SULNAM[105] – to describe developments in the countryside since 1979. Whether or not one accepts the force of the argument contained in the SULNAM designation, the Chinese government is clearly aware of the dangers of exceeding the limits of rural tolerance. Defining, let alone measuring, such limits is notoriously difficult in a peasant context, although circumstantial evidence would suggest that they may already have been passed in some regions. A notable instance is that of a township in Hubei Province, where, according to the local party secretary, financial levies had become so severe that many farmers could no longer afford to farm their land. The outcome was massive blind migration that reduced the local workforce from 18,000 to 3,000 (*sic*), and threatened to leave 65 percent of the township's arable land abandoned and uncultivated.[106] The extent to which conditions had deteriorated was revealed in the finding that whereas in 1995, 85 percent of local villages had access to a positive balance of accumulated funds, by 2000, the same proportion of villages were suffering losses (90 percent of them in debt to the extent of 600,000 yuan or more, on which they incurred a monthly rate of interest of 20 percent).[107] Meanwhile, in neighboring Jiangxi Province, Hong Kong sources reported that in August 2000, some 20,000 farmers in Jiangxi Province had been involved in riots against excessive taxation, requiring the deployment of 2,000 police in order to re-establish order.[108] At the time of writing, it is by no means clear that the government will be able to achieve the early resolution of these and associated problems.

The moral economy dimensions, as well as an awareness of the policy dilemmas mentioned earlier, are a vital part of the backcloth against which an assessment of China's agricultural reforms should be made. It is precisely the heightened economic and social tensions inherent in these dilemmas that make the future trajectory of China's agricultural sector so uncertain and difficult to predict. Until the mid-1980s, there was a strong case for regarding agriculture as the leading sector, in the sense of driving China's national economic growth; thereafter, the situation changed, as industrialization accelerated and assumed the pivotal role in the economy.[109] To argue that the economic role of agriculture has diminished is of course not to deny the significance of that lesser role. But it is perhaps to suggest that the *social* dimensions of farm policy – above all, those stemming from the poverty of certain groups of farmers – have come to assume the even greater importance. The effort simultaneously to accommodate the economic requirements of agricultural growth and meet the legitimate welfare demands of these farmers remains a huge challenge for the Chinese government. What is more, its scale and complexity will intensify as the government prepares to meet new challenges, including possible demands for protectionist measures on behalf of the farm sector, associated with China's impending accession to the World Trade Organization. Such considerations suggest that the process of agriculture's transition to an unconstrained market system will continue to be protracted, and perhaps halting. The economic and social imperatives of farm growth also point to a continuing and important residual involvement by the state in China's agricultural development. From all these perspectives, there is no hint of paradox in the designation of China's agricultural sector, even at the beginning of the twenty-first century, as the "foundation of the national economy."

Notes

1   I am pleased to acknowledge the valuable comments made by an anonymous referee on an earlier draft of this essay. They have helped greatly in the task of revision. My thanks too to Professor Peter Nolan (Sinyi Professor of Chinese Management, Judge Institute of Management Studies, University of Cambridge) for the stimulation of exchanges on many of the issues raised in this essay. It is a particular pleasure to express the debt of gratitude I owe to the editors of this volume. Their patient encouragement enabled me to undertake the revision of this essay at a time when non-academic preoccupations might easily have deterred me from the task.

2   The legacy of the past cannot be ignored. As Dwight Perkins once observed, "even in areas where the People's Republic has instituted radical change, one cannot comprehend the magnitude of significance of that change unless one can answer the question, change from what?" ("Introduction: The Persistence of the Past," in D. Perkins (ed.), *China's Modern Economy in Historical Perspective* (Stanford: Stanford University Press, 1975)), p.1.

3   Yiping Huang, *Agricultural Reform in China: Getting Institutions Right* (Cambridge: Cambridge University Press, 1998); Jean C. Oi, "Two Decades of Rural Reform in China: An Overview," *The China Quarterly* (hereafter *CQ*), no. 159 (September 1999), pp. 616–28 (reprinted in Richard Louis Edmonds (ed.), *The People's Republic of China after 50 Years* (Oxford: Oxford University Press, 2000), pp. 54–66).

4   In 1999, the share of agriculture (crop farming, fishing, and animal husbandry) in national GDP was only 17.3 percent. The corresponding figures for secondary and tertiary sector activities were 49.7 percent and 32.9 percent (estimates taken from State Statistical Bureau (SSB), *Zhongguo tongji zhaiyao* (China statistical abstract), *TJZY* (Beijing: Zhongguo tongji chubanshe, 2000), p. 16.

5   The total number of rural residents was estimated to be 870.17 million in 1999 (*TJZY* (2000), p. 34).

6   Although in decline in the 1990s, in 1999 there were still 329 million people engaged in farming (agriculture, forestry, fishing, and livestock husbandry) (*TJZY* (2000), p. 93). By comparison, the number engaged in rural construction, industry, services, and other rural occupations was 140 million.

7   Average annual rates of growth of fishing and livestock value output between 1978 and 1999 were 12 percent and 9.6 percent, compared with 5.1 percent for cropping. In the most recent past, aquaculture and animal husbandry have maintained these long-term trend rates of growth (cf. average annual growth of 12.1 percent and 9.6 percent during 1994–9), while growth of crop farming has accelerated to 9.6 percent p.a. (data from *TJZY* (2000), p. 95). For an analysis of improvements in China's cotton market in the even more recent past, see Hunter Colby and Stephen MacDonald, "China's New and Improved Cotton Market," US Department of Agriculture (USDA), *International Agriculture and Trade Reports: China* (Washington, DC: USDA, March 2000), pp. 21–3.

8   Per capita grain output during 1995–9 averaged 402.4 kg. The record level was achieved in 1998 (410.5 kg) (*TJZY* (2000), pp. 34 and 98).

9   The most extreme proponent of this view was Lester Brown (*Who Will Feed China?: Wake-Up Call for a Small Planet* (New York and London: W. W. Norton, 1995)), although many others, including the present author, predicted China's growing involvement, as an importer, in the international grain market.

10 During 1997–9, China's net exports of cereals and cereal flour averaged 4.4 million tonnes p.a., earning US$ 640 million p.a. See SSB, *Zhongguo tongji nianjian* (China statistical yearbook), *TJNJ* (Beijing: Zhongguo tongji chubanshe, 1999), pp. 587 and 589; and *TJZY* (2000), pp. 141–2.

11 Data for 1980 and 1990 from Lu Feng, "Comparative Advantage and China's Food Trade Pattern: A Third Option for China's Food Policy Adjustment" (Organization for Economic Cooperation and Development (OECD)), *Agricultural Policies in China* (Paris: OECD, 1997), p. 258; data for 1998 from *TJNJ* (1999), p. 581.

12 China is of course not alone, either among socialist or non-socialist countries, in having had to accommodate potential price and income volatility associated with greater reliance on prices and markets as the main arbiters of production and distribution. Grain farmers in China have often been the most disadvantaged group: thanks in part to payment for their produce being made in IOUs (*baitiaozi*), in 1989, when grain output reached an all-time high, income per head registered negative growth (see Wen Guifang, "Guanyu shenhua liangjia gaige de jige wenti" (Some problems associated with the deepening of grain price reforms), *Jingji yanjiu cankao* (Economic Research Reference Materials), vol. 183, no. 383 (November 1993), p. 25.

13 I have pointed out elsewhere that as one moves into the interior of China, fewer rural workers are engaged in better-paid rural non-agricultural activities and more in farming "proper." Moreover, of those engaged in agriculture, more depend on low-return activities, such as grain farming, which offer relatively low incomes. See Ash, "Challenges and Opportunities Facing the Rural Sector in China," in Joseph Y. S. Cheng (ed.), *China Review 1998* (Hong Kong: Chinese University Press, 1998), esp. pp. 437–40. See also World Bank, *Sharing Rising Incomes: Disparities in China* (*China 2020 Series*) (Washington, DC: The World Bank, 1997), esp. ch. 2.

14 From the early 1960s until the 1990s, Deng Xiaoping was consistent in his advocacy, for both economic and social reasons, of agriculture as the prime strategic focus. For a detailed exposition of Deng's views, see Chinese Academy of Agricultural Sciences, *Deng Xiaoping nongye sixiang yanjiu* (An investigation of Deng Xiaoping's thinking on agriculture) (Beijing: Zhongguo nongye chubanshe, 1998).

15 The "Proposal for drawing up the 10th Five-Year National Economic and Social Development Plan" (2001–5), adopted at the Fifth Plenum of the Chinese Communist Party on 11 October 2000, is the latest authoritative document to stress the pivotal economic and social role of agriculture. Its first main section is devoted to the agricultural sector and continuity of policy thinking is evident in the first sentence, which states "strengthening agriculture is an important aspect in the adjustment of the economic structure, and also the foundation for maintaining economic development and social stability" (see British Broadcasting Corporation, *Summary of World Broadcasts: Part 3 Asia-Pacific*, hereafter *SWB*, FE/3979 (24 October 2000), S1/2).

16 The primary sector's contribution to GDP fell from 40.3 percent to 28.1 percent between 1957 and 1978. See SSB, *Zhongguo tongji nianjian* (China statistical yearbook), *TJNJ* (Beijing: Zhongguo tongji chubanshe, 1998), p. 56.

17 For a quantitative analysis of the origins and impact of famine, see Kenneth R. Walker, "Food and Mortality in China during the Great Leap Forward," in Robert F. Ash (ed.), *Agricultural Development in China, 1949–1989: The Collected Papers of Kenneth R. Walker* (Oxford: Oxford University Press, 1998), pp. 106–47. Food security is defined here in terms of an average per capita availability of 300 kg of raw grain. This figure is thought sufficient to accommodate basic energy requirements and contributes something toward seed and animal feed needs.

18 Grain output growth only just exceeded the rate of natural increase in total population. During 1957–78, total grain production grew, on average, by 2.15 percent p.a.,
compared with population growth of 1.9 percent. Average per capita grain output
remained virtually unchanged between 1955 and 1957 (303 kg) and 1975 and 1976
(305 kg).

19 SSB, *Zhongguo nongcun tongji nianjian* (China rural statistical yearbook), *ZGNCTJNJ*
(1989), pp. 24–5.

20 By 1991, only 42 percent of exports derived from farm products. But as late as 1998,
68.2 percent of light industrial output was still dependent on agricultural raw materials (*ZGNCTJNJ* (1995), p. 53).

21 From 81.2 percent to 75.8 percent (SSB, *Zhongguo laodong gongzi tongji ziliao, 1949–1985*
(Statistical materials on China's labour force and wages, 1949–1985) (Beijing:
Zhongguo tongji chubanshe, 1987), p. 8). Not until 1980 did the agricultural share
fall below 80 percent.

22 For a contrary view on the extent of surplus agricultural labor, see Chris Bramall,
Sources of Chinese Economic Growth, 1978–1996 (Oxford: Oxford University Press, 2000),
pp. 167–8. Bramall does, however, concede the existence of "an on-farm incentive
system that did little to encourage high levels of productivity" (ibid.).

23 For further consideration of these issues, see the excellent account in Nicholas R.
Lardy, *Agriculture in China's Modern Economic Development* (Cambridge: Cambridge
University Press, 1983), esp. pp. 98–128. Also relevant is Robert F. Ash, "The Peasant
and the State," *CQ*, no. 127 (September 1991), pp. 516–18.

24 As Yiping Huang observes,

> [l]ower than market equilibrium agricultural prices secured lower subsistence
> costs for industrial workers and, in turn, ensured low wages and cheap raw mate-
> rials. Lower production costs, in turn, enabled industry to generate high profits
> which were then re-invested in industrial development.
>
> (1998, p. 28)

25 Ministry of Agriculture, *Planning Office, Zhongguo nongcun jingji tongji daquan, 1949–1986*
(Compendium of statistical materials on China's rural economy, 1949–1986), hereafter *Daquan* (Beijing: Nongye chubanshe, 1989), pp. 110–11. The shares of forestry,
animal husbandry, and aquaculture in 1978 were 3.6 percent, 16.8 percent, and 1.5
percent, respectively.

26 Joseph C. H. Chai, "Consumption and Living Standards in China," *CQ*, no. 131
(September 1992), p. 723.

27 The collapse of agriculture during the Great Leap Forward admittedly led to a
temporary retreat, even to the extent of sanctioning contractual arrangements with
individual farm households. But this was only a temporary expedient and between
1965 and 1978, the average size of commune, production brigade, and production
team steadily increased. By 1980, a brigade and team contained, on average, 449 and
56 workers (SSB, *Zhongguo tongji nianjian, 1981* (China statistical yearbook, 1981), hereafter *TJNJ* (Beijing: Zhongguo tongji chubanshe, 1981), p. 132).

28 SWB, FE/3979 (24 October 2000), S1/3.

29 In the early 1980s, the distribution of contracted land was carried out on an egalitarian basis: equality of access, rather than growth maximization, was the guiding
principle and it served to avoid the unequal outcome which would have resulted from
a free-market auction.

30 By 1984, individual households owned over 90 percent of carts and more than 80
percent of small walking tractors (*ZGNCTJNJ* (1985), p. 242). By 1988 the corresponding figures were 98 percent and 94 percent (*ZGNCTJNJ* (1989), p. 268). But not
all farmers had access to such machinery: as recently as 1998, ownership of walking

tractors averaged only 14.34 per hundred farm households (*ZGNCTJNJ* (1999), p. 71).

31 In 1984, the collective sector still owned 56 percent of large and medium-size tractors, 51 percent of mechanical threshers, 48 percent of farm trucks, and 65 percent of drainage and irrigation equipment (*ZGNCTJNJ* (1985), p. 242). By 1989, the corresponding figures were 28 percent, 23 percent, 30 percent, and 32 percent (*ZGNCTJNJ* (1990), p. 237). It is hard to know to what extent earlier peasant involvement in these forms of fixed asset formation was deterred by lack of savings, lack of confidence in the permanence of the new, reformist thrust of agricultural policy, or a perception that large-scale fixed capital formation in agriculture remained the prerogative of the state.

32 Agriculture's share of such investment rose from 7.6 percent (1970) to 10.9 percent (1975) (*ZGNCTJNJ* (1995), p. 114), although both these figures were below the 1965 level (14.8 percent). See also Nicholas R. Lardy, *Agriculture in China's Modern Economic Development*, p. 130.

33 Peter Nolan, *State and Market in the Chinese Economy: Essays on Controversial Issues* (London: Macmillan, 1993), p. 245.

34 Peter Nolan, *The Political Economy of Collective Farms* (Cambridge: Polity Press, 1988), p. 60.

35 Peasant households' share of total drainage and irrigation machinery (measured in terms of horsepower) rose from 35 percent to 53 percent between 1984 and 1988; the number of pump-sets sold by the state and by supply and marketing cooperatives more than doubled during the same period, to reach almost 1.1 million in 1989 (66 percent of the total stock) (*ZGNCTJNJ* (1985), p. 242; (1990), pp. 157 and 237).

36 As rural industry and commerce expanded, such funds were not necessarily used for farming-related purposes.

37 In nominal terms, such investment averaged 31.5 million yuan during 1976–80; 18.6 million yuan during 1981–5; 28.7 million yuan during 1986–90; and 83.6 million yuan during 1991–5 (*ZGNCTJNJ* (1996), p. 97). Note that if budgetary outlays on irrigation capital construction are deflated by the retail price index for agricultural means of production, such expenditure can be shown to have fallen by 22 percent between 1983 and 1989.

38 Between the second half of the 1970s and the first half of the 1980s, the agricultural share of "basic capital construction investment" declined from 10.5 percent to 5 percent. The corresponding figure for 1986–90 was 3.3 percent (*TJNJ* (1993), p. 158).

39 *ZGNCTJNJ* (1997), p. 92.

40 Ibid.

41 See also Ash, "The Peasant and the State," in Brian Hook (ed.), *The Individual and the State in China* (Oxford: Clarendon Press, 1996), p. 77.

42 *ZGNCTJNJ* (1997), p. 91.

43 The relevant figures can be found from data in *TJNJ* (1999), pp. 265 and 273.

44 Ibid.

45 The data, published in 1991 by the Ministry of Agriculture, were drawn from a survey of 5,389 villages (*cun*) in 205 counties (*xian*) in 29 provinces, autonomous regions, and directly administered municipalities, excluding Tibet. Socialized service organizations include the following: (1) *xiangzhen* (township) technical departments (agro-technology stations, plant protection stations, etc.); (2) *xiang* and *cun* collective economic organizations (including *cun* service companies, service stations, and teams set up by the *cun* people's committees and *cun* people's small groups); (3) different special service groups (including specialist associations, research associations, joint service groups, specialized households, and different forms of popular cooperative groups).

46 Chai cites a Chinese source to the effect that "by 1990, 50 percent of mechanized ploughing, irrigation, procurement of farm inputs, and veterinary services were …

carried out by the new collectives" (Joseph C. H. Chai, *China: Transition to a Market Economy* (Oxford: Clarendon Press, 1997), p. 26).

47 See the previous footnote.

48 Y. Y. Kueh, "Food Consumption and Peasant Incomes," in Y. Y. Kueh and Robert F. Ash (eds.), *Economic Trends in Chinese Agriculture: The Impact of Post-Mao Reforms* (Oxford: Clarendon Press, 1993), p. 235.

49 Between 1990 and 1995, the net savings ratio rose from 14.8 percent to 17 percent. In 1996 and 1997, it was 18.4 percent and 22.6 percent (*TJNJ* (1998), p. 344).

50 Until 1996, *TJNJ* provided separate estimates of "urban savings deposits" (*chengzhen chuxu cunkuan*) and "rural deposits" (*nongcun cunkuan*). But since 1998, the same source has shown a consolidated estimate of "urban and rural savings deposits" (*chengxiang chuxu cunkuan*), as well as for the first time introducing a new category of "agricultural deposits" (*nongye cunkuan*). Data for 1994 highlight the difficulties of interpretation: according to *TJNJ* (1996), p. 614, urban savings (1,584.5 billion yuan) and rural deposits (19.5 billion yuan) generated a total (urban + rural) of 1,604 billion yuan. Yet the following year, the same source (*TJNJ* (1997), p. 622) gave a figure of 2,151.9 billion yuan (some 34 percent higher than the previous estimate) for urban and rural savings deposits. A further anomaly, as yet unexplained, is that the last *TJNJ* to record rural and urban savings deposits separately indicates a fall from 141.8 billion to 13.5 billion yuan in rural deposits in a single year (1993–4) (*TJNJ* (1996), p. 614). Meanwhile, another authoritative source suggests that "rural household deposits" (*nonghu chuxu*) in 1994 totaled 481.6 billion yuan (Agricultural Bank of China, *Zhongguo nongcun jinrong tongji nianjian* (Chinese rural financial statistical yearbook), hereafter *JRTJNJ* (Beijing: Zhongguo tongji chubanshe, 1996), p. 241).

51 *JRTJNJ* (1995), p. 241.

52 *TJNJ* (1999), p. 273; *TJZY* (2000), p. 58. Lack of data makes it impossible to relate agricultural deposits to aggregate government spending on agriculture (including capital construction, and science and technology promotion): an informed guess would, however, suggest that the ratio was around 3:1.

53 Deposits lodged by farming households with rural credit cooperatives increased from 5.6 to 619.6 billion yuan between 1978 and 1995 – an average annual rate of growth of 32 percent. During the same period, deposit balances held by agricultural collective units rose by 14 percent p.a. (from 9.4 to 89.2 billion yuan) (*TJNJ* (1996), p. 617). The corresponding figures for rural deposits held in the Agricultural Bank appear not to be readily available, although it is known that such deposits increased from 29.8 to 173.1 billion yuan between 1978 and 1988 (Ash, "The Peasant and the State," p. 523).

54 *JRTJNJ* (1995), p. 34.

55 Between 1986 and 1992, individual farm households' share of all agricultural loans from the Agricultural Bank and rural credit cooperatives fell from 59.6 percent to 49.2 percent. In absolute terms, the cooperatives were a more important source of credit for individual households than the Agricultural Bank (cf. 6.4 and 12.6 billion yuan extended to such households by the Agricultural Bank in 1986 and 1992, compared with 25.8 and 75.95 billion by credit cooperatives (*JRTJNJ* (1991), pp. 28 and 70; (1993), pp. 33 and 81)).

56 The proportion of all Agricultural Bank loans used for fixed capital formation rose from 1.3 percent (1985) to 2.3 percent (1994) (*JRTJNJ* (1995), p. 34).

57 "Industrial loans" and "loans to township and village enterprises" became increasingly important during the 1990s, rising from 13.5 percent of all loans (1990) to 24.3 percent (1994) (*JRNCTJNJ* (1995), p. 34); also Ash, "The Peasant and the State," pp. 81–2).

58 Between 1978 and 1990, the number of urban free markets in China increased from a negligible level to over 13,000; in villages, the number grew from 33,000 to more

than 59,000. By 1998, there were over 27,000 urban markets and more than 67,000 rural markets (*ZGNCTJNJ* (1999), p. 203).

59 For example, in 1978 virtually the entire marketed output of eggs, fish, and fattened pigs was sold through state or quasi-state marketing channels. By 1985, the proportion of such items exchanged in free markets had reached 67 percent, 61 percent, and 48 percent (*ZGNCTJNJ* (1989), pp. 158 and 162). See also Terry Sicular, "Redefining State, Plan and Market: China's Reforms in Agricultural Commerce," in Andrew G. Walder (ed.), *China's Transitional Economy* (Oxford: Clarendon Press, 1996), pp. 58–84.

60 See Wen Guifang, op. cit.

61 *ZGNCTJNJ* (1993), pp. 162 and 166.

62 Between 1980 and 1989, sales of grain and edible oil in free markets rose from 3.4 billion to 14.27 billion yuan. The implied average annual rate of increase (17.3 percent) compared with 33.6 percent (meat, poultry, and eggs), 37 percent (fish), and 30.6 percent (vegetables) (*TJNJ* (1988), p. 709; (1991), p. 605).

63 Cf. 24.4 percent (meat, poultry, and eggs), 31.8 percent (fish), and 30.4 percent (vegetables) during 1990–7 (*TJNJ* (1999), p. 553).

64 See *ZGNCTJNJ* (1989), p. 158; (1993), p. 166. After 1990, grain purchases by state commercial departments and supply and marketing cooperatives fell. Purchases through state agencies absorbed 70 percent of the incremental marketed output of grain during 1978–85, and 84 percent during 1985–92 (but 99 percent in 1985–90).

65 By the end of 1993, a mere 25 out of 2,000 counties had failed to implement comprehensive grain marketing reforms, including price liberalization (Yiping Huang, op. cit., p. 100). See also Huang's excellent analysis (pp. 101–3) of some of the problems that emerged in the wake of the 1991–2 initiatives. Also useful is Colin A. Carter and Scott Rozelle, "How Far Along Is China Developing its Food Markets?" Joint Economic Committee of the US (ed.), *China's Economic Future: Challenges to U.S. Policy* (Armonk, NY: M. E. Sharpe, 1996), esp. pp. 146–9.

66 This was the policy that placed direct responsibility for grain production on the shoulders of provincial governors in an attempt to counter declining output, especially in some central and southern provinces.

67 *SWB*, FE/3539 (20 May 1999).

68 For example, see *SWB*, *Weekly Economic Report*, FEW/0621 (5 January 2000), FEW/0622 (12 January 2000), and, citing Chen Yaobang (Minister of Agriculture), FEW/0623 (19 January 2000).

69 The regional implications of the structural adjustments were dramatic, some 70 percent of the grain area contraction being carried by just five provinces in southern China (Jiangsu, Anhui, Zhejiang, Hubei, and Sichuan).

70 The structural adjustments no doubt also sought to accommodate some of the challenges associated with China's impending accession to the World Trade Organization.

71 *TJNJ* (1988), p. 709; (1996), p. 563.

72 See Terry Sicular, "Ten Years of Reform: Progress and Setbacks in Agricultural Planning and Pricing," in Kueh and Ash (eds.) (1993), p. 71.

73 A modest reduction in the proportion of total chemical fertilizer supplies sold through state agencies occurred in the first half of the 1980s (from 94 percent to 85 percent between 1980 and 1985). Following the re-establishment of the state's monopoly, the corresponding figure had risen to 97 percent by 1989; it subsequently fell again to 88 percent in 1992 (*ZGNCTJNJ* (1989), pp. 187 and 271; (1992), pp. 174 and 267; and (1993), pp. 169 and 257).

74 That is, the index of farm and sideline purchase prices divided by the index of retail prices of industrial products in the countryside.

75 *TJNJ* (1990), p. 250.

76 *TJNJ* (1998), p. 302. Reference has already been made to difficulties associated with the interpretation of official price indices (also see *TJNJ* (1995), p. 233). But there is

little doubt that sharp rises in input prices were responsible for a deterioration in the farmers' barter terms of trade in the second half of the 1980s.

77 Between 1990 and 1999, the irrigated area rose from 44 million hectares to 53 million (the power or motorized-driven share having increased from 56 percent to 67 percent) (*TJZY* (2000), p. 97).

78 Ibid. and *TJNJ* (1999), p. 385.

79 *TJNJ* (1999), p. 389.

80 On average, 48 percent of rural households owned a draft animal, compared with 57 percent in 1990 (ibid.).

81 Some relevant analysis can be found in Ash and Richard Louis Edmonds, "China's Land Resources, Environment and Agricultural Production," in Edmonds (ed.), *Managing the Chinese Environment* (Oxford: Oxford University Press, 1998), esp. pp. 135–48, for an analysis of the interrelationship between environmental factors and agricultural productivity.

82 For example, see *TJNJ* (1999), p. 386; also Ash and Edmonds, op. cit.

83 The Chinese term is *shouzai* and refers to farmland that has suffered a crop loss of less than 30 percent. It contrasts with the area "calamitously affected" (*chengzai*) by natural disasters, on which crop losses of more than 30 percent have occurred. See Y. Y. Kueh, *Agricultural Instability in China, 1931–1991: Weather, Technology and Institutions* (Oxford: Clarendon Press, 1995), p. 112.

84 Cf. also an early benchmark figure of 30.49 million hectares p.a. The relevant *shouzai* data can be found in *Daquan*, pp. 354 and 356; *TJNJ* (1999), p. 408; and *TJZY* (2000), p. 102.

85 Comparable figures for 1953–66 and 1978–90 are 14.08 million hectares and 19.73 million hecatres. Ibid.

86 SSB and Ministry of Civil Affairs (ed.), *Zhongguo zaiqing baogao, 1949–1995* (Report on natural disasters damage in China, 1949–1995) (Beijing: Zhongguo tongji chubanshe, 1995), p. 315. The same source reveals an average annual livestock loss of 1.78 million animals during 1978–94, compared with only 87,500 during 1953–67.

87 For example, see Robert Michael Field, "Trends in the Value of Agricultural Output, 1978–1988," and Kenneth R. Walker, "Trends in Crop Production," in Kueh and Ash (eds.) (1993), pp. 123–60 and 161–201. See also Ash, "Agricultural Development since 1978," in Ash and Kueh (eds.) (1996), pp. 55–87.

88 *Daquan*, pp. 112–13.

89 *TJNJ* (1993), p. 335, and *TJZY* (2000), p. 95.

90 Per capita grain production was 412 kg in 1996 (*TJNJ* (1999), pp. 111 and 395).

91 Lester Brown, *Who Will Feed China?*, p. 97. Note that Brown's estimate is given in terms of trade grain, which, if converted to raw grain, would yield a figure of about 490 million tonnes.

92 Average per capita grain output for 1996–9 was 406.5 kg (*TJZY* (2000), pp. 34 and 98).

93 In November, a report from Hong Kong noted that in the wake of a 9.3 percent reduction in summer grain output and a further expected fall in the autumn harvest, China was likely to face an annual shortfall of about 5 million tones of grain in 2000 (*Zhongguo Tongxun She* (China News Agency), 5 November 2000, quoted in *SWB*, FE/3993, 9 November 2000).

94 But regional differentials are wide. Among rural inhabitants in provinces "proper" (i.e., excluding Beijing, Tianjin, and Shanghai), the share of food in total consumption spending varied (1997) from a high of 70 percent (Guizhou and Tibet) to a low of 47–48 percent (Zhejiang and Jiangsu). See *TJNJ* (1999), p. 342.

95 *TJNJ* (1998), p. 353. Note, however, that as recently as 1990, the corresponding figures were 4.7, 17.8, and 0.9 (ibid.).

96 For example, cf. Jiang Zemin in Hefei (28 September 1998):

The general target for deepening rural economic structural reform is to establish a rural economic structure suited to the development of the socialist market economy, based on the household output-related contract system and supported by the agricultural socialized service system, the agricultural products market system, and the state assistance and protection system for agriculture.

(Quoted in *SWB*, FE/3344, 29 September 1998)

97 "Sub-optimal," as used here, would be measured in terms of lost efficiency.

98 During 1949–52, disentangling the general impact of rehabilitation from the specific effects of early land reform makes it difficult to make a comparative assessment of the economic consequences of the first and second land reforms. For what it is worth, between 1978 and 1983, average grain yields grew, on average, by 6.1 percent p.a., compared with 6.3 percent during 1949–53 – this despite average yields in 1978 being 92 percent higher than in 1953 (see *Daquan*, pp. 146 and 148).

99 The seminal investigation of the peasant economy as a moral economy is that of James C. Scott, *The Moral Economy of the Peasant: Rebellion and Subsistence in Southeast Asia* (New Haven, CT: Yale University Press, 1976). The most insightful application of some of Scott's themes to the context of the Chinese countryside is provided by Jean C. Oi in her *State and Peasant in Contemporary China: The Political Economy of Village Government* (Berkeley: University of California Press, 1989). See also Vivienne Shue, *The Reach of the Chinese State: Sketches of the Chinese Body Politic* (Stanford: Stanford University Press, 1988).

100 An early influential example is Ramon H. Myers, *The Chinese Peasant Economy: Agricultural Development in Hopei and Shantung, 1890–1949* (Cambridge, MA: Harvard University Press, 1970). Two more recent examples are Loren Brandt, *Commercialization and Agricultural Development: Central and Eastern China, 1870–1937* (Cambridge: Cambridge University Press, 1989), and David Faure, *The Rural Economy of Pre-Liberation China: Trade Increase and Peasant Livelihood in Jiangsu and Guangdong, 1870 to 1937* (Hong Kong: Oxford University Press, 1989).

101 Someone whose work has extended both the old and new orthodoxies of analysis of pre-1949 rural development is Philip C. C. Huang. See his *The Peasant Economy and Social Change in North China* (Stanford: Stanford University Press, 1985) and *The Peasant Family and Rural Development in the Yangzi Delta, 1350–1988* (Stanford: Stanford University Press, 1990).

102 Oi, p. 128. The actors she refers to are the state and the individual Chinese farmer.

103 The clearest and most explicit account of the growing power of Chinese peasants in the wake of early rural reforms is given in Daniel Kelliher, *Peasant Power in China: The Era of Rural Reform, 1979–1989* (New Haven, CT, and London: Yale University Press, 1992). See also Kate Xiao Zhou, *How the Farmers Changed China: Power of the People* (Boulder, CO: Westview Press, 1996).

104 Reference to the weakening authority of the CCP in recent years has become a cliché. But it is also an important truth. The view that the party's treatment of farmers is an exploitative one has also apparently become quite widespread – some rural inhabitants, in a nice play on words, even describing the CCP as the "fleece-the-people" party (*guamindang*). This, as well as considerable evidence of corruption amongst cadres and officials, has tarnished the party's image and undermined its legitimacy in the countryside.

105 That is, a "spontaneous, unorganized, leaderless, non-ideological, apolitical movement" (*How the Farmers Changed China*, op. cit., p. 1).

106 *SWB*, FE/3945, 14 September 2000, quoting *Nanfang Zhoumo* (Guangdong), 24 August 2000.

107 Ibid.

108 *SWB*, FE/3933, 31 August 2000.

109 See Chris Bramall, *Sources of Chinese Economic Growth, 1978–1996*, esp. ch. 3.

Part II

The social consequences of economic reform

4 Clashes between reform and opening

Labor market formation in three cities

Dorothy J. Solinger

Up through 1996, nearly two decades of marketizing restructuring in China spelt spiraling increases in output, living standards, and incomes throughout the economy. Despite a rash of ominous social externalities, such as heightened corruption and widening inequalities, the consensus was that, insofar as the economy itself was concerned, markets were a success. Even times of over-heating and occasional inflation – as in the mid-1980s, the late 1980s and the early to mid-1990s – were terminated relatively rapidly through officially trig-gered recessions; even interfirm debts seemed capable of being brought under control by 1995.

In the cities, though some small proportion of state workers were being laid off as early as 1988,[1] in the main managers refrained from dismissing employees openly well into the 1990s. Even then, because of each firm's responsibility to see to the future of its own displaced workers, a range of disguised forms of unemployment emerged, including early retirements and "long holidays," often entailing reductions in benefits and underpayment or non-payment of wages, but without calling the worker "unemployed."[2] Meanwhile, numbers of peasants moving off the land and into the municipalities to take on urban jobs ranged between some 60 to 80 million by the late 1990s, and on the whole they found work to do.[3] Indeed, it appeared near the end of the century that once-socialist China was truly turning into a market society, in the process producing an urban labor market of national scope that could accommodate both city workers and sojourners from the countryside. Internal economic reform and external opening (*gaige* and *kaifang*) seemed congruent and mutually reinforcing.

But the year 1997 saw sudden shifts that were fundamentally to undermine this optimism about the ease and the outcomes of market transition. The finan-cial crisis that began its ominous journey across Asia in summer 1997 was soon joined temporally by the Chinese Communist Party's 15th Congress, convened in September that year, in spelling momentous economic change for the country. Probably more by coincidence[4] than design, the two events had parallel outcomes: both boded ill for the fate of the famous iron-rice-bowl-provisioned city worker in China, and indeed for any laborer, whether of urban or rural origin, hoping to hold a city factory job. The *China Daily Business Weekly* reported in a late August 1998 edition that an unnamed China trade expert had admitted that: "Devaluations in East Asia have greatly reduced the competitiveness of Chinese exports in the world market,"[5] while officials at the Ministry of Labor and Social Security revealed around that time that the crisis had "reduced our competitiveness," and that "it will influence our employment."[6]

In the several years since these events coalesced, the nation has seen surging unemployment for urbanites – probably exceeding 10 or even 20 percent in a number of urban areas[7] – coupled with greater uncertainty than had been the case in a decade for the job prospects of peasant migrants in the metropolises. Regime leaders remain vitally concerned about resettling those among the city-born who have been laid off, getting them retrained, finding them new placements, and compelling localities to issue them basic living allowances when necessary. Yet at the same time, as Teh-chang Lin and Jae Ho Chung's chapters indicate, top officials continued to proclaim their unaltered aims of economic reform, growth, enterprise restructuring, and labor market formation. According to Premier Zhu Rongji, speaking at a January 1999 State Council meeting on state enterprise laid-off workers:

> The central authorities have laid down the major policy on state enterprise reform. As long as we resolutely implement the central authorities' policy; do not engage in duplicate construction; adjust and reduce the redundant and backward portion of the productive forces; cut personnel and improve efficiency; do a good job in ensuring the basic livelihood of state enterprises' laid-off workers and in providing reemployment for them; and improve the leading groups of enterprises, we will be able to free most of the large and medium-sized loss-incurring state enterprises from predicament in about three years so that most of the key enterprises can initially establish a modern enterprise system.[8]

While throwing millions out of work may be the first step in forcing the jobless to fend on a newly forming non-state-directed job market, at the same time party chiefs are not content to leave these people wholly to their own devices. But the rising competition thrust on the country as currency devaluations ran rampant around its borders in 1998–9 meant that many localities and firms preferred to hire on the cheap, which often meant employing peasant labor – a move that was beneficial to the formation of a genuine labor market but threatening to the jobs of urbanites.

Thus, clearly, there are fundamental contradictions between two sets of goals. As against what Jae Ho Chung argues, modernizing, marketizing, and making competitive and prosperous the national economy and its labor market – to meet the challenge of global rivalry for markets but also ultimately, leaders hope, to provide jobs for currently dismissed urbanites – is only one of these. Simultaneously, central leaders also order that local bureaucrats succor city workers whose jobs disappear as their former firms try to save money – or, more frequently, to cease losing money in such large quantities as they have been of late.

This essay uses interview and documentary material from three cities to examine how three very diverse localities were coping with these essentially opposed imperatives in autumn 1998. These are Guangzhou at the core of the southeast region, Shenyang in the northeast, and Wuhan in central China. Each of these is the site of a different type of political economy, the product of its geographical location, its resource endowment, and its treatment over time by the central government. These factors have produced local economies of quite varying levels of economic health in recent decades.[9]

Guangzhou and its surrounding area, as the recipient of preferential central policies, has been the part of the country most involved in the external economy since reforms began, both as the recipient of foreign investment and as exporter. Shenyang is an old industrial base, where central governmental investment over the decades devoted much capital to the creation of heavy industrial infrastructure, equipment, and output, but where the level of industrial losses has been especially high in recent years. Wuhan, though like Shenyang also the home of many aging and failing industrial, state-owned plants, is a marketplace as well. The city is notable too for serving as one of the chief hubs of the national transport network and as a major national-level emporium, as it lies at the intersection of the Guangzhou–Beijing trunk rail line going north–south and the Yangtze River, along the east–west axis.

The diverse characteristics that location, resources, and treatment have shaped in each – characteristics seen in the overall health of the local economy, the level of domestic market activity in the city, the extent of international economic interactions, and the degree of labor market absorptive capacity resulting from these characteristics – would lead one to expect differences in their rates of unemployment, their abilities to reabsorb the laid-off and to form a labor market, and in their receptivity to migrant labor. In fact, as I will show, this spate of what the Chinese are calling "layoffs" (*xiagang*)[10] has been variously met in Guangzhou, Shenyang, and Wuhan by what we could term a Thatcherite, a Keynesian, and a mixed response, respectively. But in them all after 1997 open markets shut at least a bit, in a bid to placate the old proletariat, some numbers of whom have gone out on strike and demonstrated, and with increasing frequency across urban China.[11]

Policy and policy contradictions in labor markets

The new surge of people needing jobs has clearly presented the leadership with a quandary. There is a direct conflict between the desire to develop a locals-only job market to absorb the *xiagang* or "laid-off" workers, who are the product of the switch to a market economy, on the one hand, and the need to reduce costs to meet external competition, an imperative that is yet another outcome of China's mesh with markets, in this case the global one, on the other.

Policy makers at all levels are well aware that the real solution to the problem of state-induced unemployment is, at least in the longer run, to strengthen a genuine national labor market. As announced in a State Council decision of early June 1998, this should entail "establish[ing] and perfect[ing] the market mechanism, and under state policy direction carry[ing] out a combination of workers' autonomous job selection, labor market adjustment of employment, and government promotion of employment."[12]

Given this understanding, city administrations have been handed the daunting and probably impossible task of facilitating the formation of a national, unified labor market that can at once manage outside labor and yet guarantee locals' full employment.[13] This takes concrete form in local versions of a national "Reemployment Project,"[14] a monumental effort which originated in April 1995 with the ambiguous aim of somehow arranging the settlement of the laid-off workers. As Jae Ho Chung's chapter shows, localities have discretion in balancing the goal of promoting enterprise reform – with its call for efficiency and layoffs – and of establishing a genuine labor market, while also addressing leaders' persisting but antithetical concern about placing locals.

Indeed, in the wake of the Asian crisis and the 15th Party Congress, there was ambivalence about the very effort at re-employment itself – its proper direction and the strategies that could achieve it. As one interviewee quite aptly phrased it, "the Reemployment Project is a half-planned economy method, which has the goal of developing a market."[15] One study referred to its various prongs as "really, just one welfare system replacing another... [a program that is] trying to protect urban residents' original superior position under market conditions."[16] Yet a third critic charged: "This governmental guidance is merely a way of temporarily alleviating employment pressure, not a sign of a healthy market economic system."[17] These remarks all point to a certain tendency of the leadership to revert to the old default position of the command economy when the economy seems under threat, despite, as Dali Yang demonstrates, a weakening commitment to the state sector.

But at the same time, the project is also touted as one that – in forcing at least some workers out of the factory and providing them with preferential treatment (such as tax exemptions and reductions, cancellation of licensing, management, sanitation, and other fees, provision of market sites and stalls, etc.) if they start new businesses – can be seen as "symbiotic with the development of a market economy." Moreover, unemployment is a "necessary product of the law of value, the law of competition, and the law of supply and demand," according to this line of thought.[18] For those who believe this, unemployment (a term used today in China to refer to those whose firms have altogether disappeared due to economic loss) and layoffs should be the wedge that forces China to switch from "arranging" to marketizing labor, from the dominance by state and collectively owned enterprises to the growth of non-governmental firms, and from contracted to more flexible forms of employment.[19]

Also, as layoffs drive former state industrial workers to find jobs in the private and tertiary sectors, the project "readjusts the industrial structure and deepens enterprise reform,"[20] claims one advocate. And, some hope, "the diversion and arrangement of surplus labor [will] make the flow of labor follow the demands of the market economy's laws."[21] Thus, depending on one's perspective – and on the particular push of various local enforcers – the project may have either a Keynesian or a Thatcherite thrust, as we will see when we turn to the three cities.

I go on to consider how the three cities are grappling with these issues – issues which concern the economy as a whole. Each of them has a distinctive political economy and thus a different set of structural factors driving its unemployment – and either facilitating or obstructing a solution. As an overview, Wuhan planners put primary emphases on placing workers in the tertiary sector and in the district and street-level economy, both official and both of which were showing the most vitality and ability to absorb laid-off personnel.[22] In Guangzhou, however, the private sector was to be the chief recipient of laid-off workers, while in Shenyang, leaders seemed most concerned with preferential policies for laid-off people and with merging giant plants. Overall, at both central and local levels, leaders were forced to confront the very fundamental contradictions inherent in openness and market involvement, contradictions especially poignant for a once-socialist state.

Three cities

Three variables have a bearing on the positions different cities adopt toward three tightly linked issues: the issues are the formation of (and involvement in) a labor market; the employment (and, lately, more importantly, unemployment and re-employment) of locals; and receptivity toward outsiders. These variables are: (1) the health and wealth of a city's economy (principally a function of the nature of its industrial structure – including factors such as how much of its industry is heavy industry, how large is its GDP and GVIO, and how fast is its growth in recent years); (2) the vitality of its domestic markets (as measured by such factors as its level of retail sales, the number of its market sites, the proportion occupied by its tertiary sector – meaning chiefly its service (thus, informal) sector – and the vigor of its non-state industry); and (3) its international involvement – as seen in levels of foreign investment and exports. All of these variables are functions of geographical location, resource base, and central governmental policy. (See Tables 4–1 to 4–7.)

As of the time covered in this study (1998), Guangzhou's industry was clearly the healthiest of the three cities, its domestic markets the most vibrant, and its international involvement by far the greatest, the result of geographical and policy factors. Shenyang, by contrast, had the most ailing industrial economy, the least active domestic markets, and a level of international involvement far below Guangzhou's, but slightly above Wuhan's. Wuhan's industrial economy was not notably stronger than Shenyang's, and its amount of foreign trade and investment was a bit lower, but its domestic markets – and thus its attraction for migrant labor as well as its ability to reabsorb the unemployed – were more developed. A final point is that the populations of the three cities were roughly comparable (Table 4.1).

Table 4.1   Population distribution in the three cities, 1997 (unit = 1,000,000)

City	District population[23]	City district population	Of which non-rural
Guangzhou	6.56	3.90	3.22
Shenyang	6.71	4.77	3.84
Wuhan	7.16	5.17	3.82

Source: Urban Statistical Yearbook 1997.

Guangzhou

Geography quite vividly sets the context for the crucial disparities among the three cities. Guangzhou, along the southeast coast, has had the benefit since 1980 of the central government's preferential policies, and also of proximity to Hong Kong and the world beyond. Its industrial development, thwarted in Maoist times because of its perceived vulnerability along the coast, never saw the intensive investment in huge and heavy industrial plant that occurred inland and in the north.

Perhaps these features help to explain why only 31 percent of the city's firms were suffering loss in 1997, as the negative offshoots of marketization began to be felt – a relatively small proportion when placed in a national context, even then. Moreover, the city's light industrial output represented a full 61.3 percent of GVIO in 1997 (see also Table 4.2). The state-owned sector accounted that year for just 33.5 percent of ownership, the collectively owned for 18.3 percent, and "other" categories (private and foreign-invested) for as much as 48.2 percent. In the province as a whole, the urban private and individual economies provided 51.7 percent of new jobs in 1997, while the city's tertiary sector's output value accounted for 48.4 percent of GDP.[24] Thus, it is not surprising that one scholar commented in late summer 1998 that "*Xiagang* in Guangzhou is not serious there are more and more jobs in the informal sector."[25]

In line with this economic profile, as of late 1997, Guangdong chose to focus on a particular aspect of the 15th Party Congress's message: its leadership emphasized the call for actively readjusting the ownership structure and making the private economy into a new growth point.[26] But it was not long before a less optimistic outlook began to appear in provincial and urban statements. Indeed, even before the Asian crisis broke, a national economic slowdown beginning around 1994 had started to have adverse effects in the area. An analysis of the provincial economy prepared late in 1997 or early in 1998 noted that: "Because the market is very active in Guangdong, when supply surpasses demand nationally, restraints on production created by low demand are most obvious here."[27] As for Guangzhou itself, although the city had "emphasized competitive employment in the past," by early 1998 a city paper announced that: "This year we will turn the keypoint to guaranteeing employment."[28] (See also Table 4.3.)

Once the effects of the Asian crisis began to be felt, Guangzhou was first forced to face a problem it had not fully encountered up to then: international competition. As an early 1998 study of the city's economy noted: "In 1998 the Southeast crisis will cause Guangzhou's industrial firms to face greater difficulty

Table 4.2   Health of the local economy

(a) District GDP, 1996 (unit = RMB 10,000)	
Guangzhou	14,449,358
Shenyang	7,718,047
Wuhan	7,821,325

Sources: Zhongguo tongjiju chengshi shehui jingji diaocha zongdui bian (Chinese Statistical Urban Social and Economic Research General Team (ed.)), *Zhongguo chengshi jingji nian jian 1997* (1997 Chinese urban statistical yearbook) (Beijing: Zhongguo tongji chubanshe, 1998), hereafter Urban yearbook, pp. 164, 153, 163.

(b) District GVIO (current prices), 1996 (unit = RMB 10,000)	
Guangzhou	20,685,796
Shenyang	10,212,166
Wuhan	10,126,592

Source: Urban yearbook, pp. 244, 233, 243.

(c) Profits and taxes (lishui) of all independent accounting industrial enterprises (city and surrounding suburbs), 1996 (unit = RMB 10,000)	
Guangzhou	14,360,389
Shenyang	5,742,538
Wuhan	6,246,777

Source: Urban yearbook, pp. 264, 253, 263.

(d) District fixed investment total assets, 1996 (unit = RMB 10,000)	
Guangzhou	3,392,397
Shenyang	1,220,038
Wuhan	2,897,650

Source: Urban yearbook, pp. 364, 353, 363.

(e) District local financial in-budget income, 1996 (unit = RMB 10,000)	
Guangzhou	725,203
Shenyang	376,228
Wuhan	343,259

Source: Urban yearbook, pp. 464, 453, 463.

(f) Average annual growth indices, GDP, 1991–6	
Guangzhou	118.97
Shenyang	111.60
Wuhan	–

Sources: Guangzhou shi tongji ju bian (Guangzhou City Statistical Bureau (ed.)), *Guangzhou tongji nianjian 1996* (Guangzhou statistical yearbook 1996) (Beijing: Zhongguo tongji chubanshe, 1997), p. 15 and n.a.; *Guangzhou nianjian 1997* (Guangzhou yearbook 1997) (Guangzhou: Guangzhou nianjian chuban she, 1997), hereafter Guangzhou 1996, 1997 yearbook, p. 448; *Shenyang nianjian 1997* (Shenyang 1997 yearbook) (Beijing: Zhongguo tongji chubanshe, 1997), hereafter Shenyang 1997 yearbook, p. 551.

in expanding their use of foreign capital and in increasing their exports."[29] Guangzhou, it warned, had lost its "original superiority" because of international and domestic competition. Already in late 1997, international competition had pushed Guangzhou's export growth rate down to 15.7 percent while the national average remained at 20.9 percent.[30] By the end of the summer, even the

Table 4.3   Domestic markets

(a) Proportion of city district population employed in tertiary sector (%), 1996

Guangzhou	53.8
Shenyang	42.1
Wuhan	44.1

Source: Urban yearbook, pp. 144, 133, 143.

(b) City district tertiary sector as percentage of GDP, 1996

Guangzhou	53.6
Shenyang	52.7
Wuhan	46.9

Source: Urban yearbook, pp. 184, 173, 183.

(c) District social commodities retail sales, 1996 (RMB 10,000)

Guangzhou	6,864,426
Shenyang	3,655,427
Wuhan	3,800,808

Source: Urban yearbook, pp. 424, 413, 423.

(d) Numbers employed in private enterprises; numbers self-employed in urban areas, province, end 1997

Province	Numbers in private enterprises		Numbers self-employed	
	Firms	People	Firms	People
Liaoning	40,000	548,000	638,000	1,004,000
Hubei	24,000	335,000	682,000	1,418,000
Guangdong	89,000	1,058,000	717,000	1,380,000

Source: Zhongguo tongji ju bian (Chinese Statistical Bureau (ed.)), *Zhongguo tongji nian jian 1998* (Chinese statistical yearbook 1998) (Beijing: Zhongguo tongji chubanshe, 1998), pp. 153, 154.

official *China Daily* had admitted that: "The monetary disorder in Southeast Asia has thwarted the city's foreign trade."[31] Accordingly, by the end of 1997, the city's economists had concluded that "only by reducing personnel can we quickly increase labor productivity and get a slight increase in economic results."[32] (See also Table 4.4.)

By the end of 1997, slower growth, along with state enterprise reform, was perceived to be making "employment and reemployment increasingly serious" in the view of local analysts.[33] Although Guangzhou had the lowest number of *xiagang* personnel among the nation's ten largest cities, and also the lowest proportion of its workforce laid off – officially 53,400 or 2.67 percent of all staff and workers, in comparison with a national official average rate of 8.18 percent[34] – still, even these figures were disturbing in an area that had had nothing but good news for nearly two decades. (See also Table 4.5.)

As the provincial economic study remarked: "In 1996, urban unemployed staff and workers' reemployment suddenly became a hot point of social concern, and it did so even more in 1997," when the numbers of layoffs saw an increase of 13.3 percent over the year before.[35] Accordingly, the term "*mingong*" – loosely, a label used to specify casual labor, which had formerly referred to surplus rural

Table 4.4   International involvement

(a) Actually utilized foreign direct investment, 1996 (unit = US$ 10,000)	
Guangzhou	260,002
Shenyang	78,783
Wuhan	50,100

Source: Urban yearbook, pp. 431ff.

(b) Total imports and exports, 1996 (unit = US$ 10,000)	
Guangzhou	65,140
Shenyang	9,330
Wuhan	8,040

Source: Wuhan nianjian bianzuan weiyuanhui zhubian (Wuhan Yearbook Compilation Committee (ed.)), *Wuhan nianjian 1997* (Wuhan 1997 statistical yearbook) (Wuhan: Wuhan nianjian she, 1997), pp. 359–61.

(c) Average annual growth indices, actually utilized foreign capital, 1991–5	
Guangzhou	153.2
Shenyang	136.8
Wuhan	–

Sources: Guangzhou 1996 yearbook, p. 21; Shenyang 1997 yearbook, p. 550.

Table 4.5   Unemployment

(a) Numbers of registered unemployed at year end, 1996	
Guangzhou	48,237
Shenyang	72,000
Wuhan	56,955

Source: Guojia tongjiju renkou yu jiuye tongjisi, Laodongbu zonghe jihua yu gongzisi, bian (State Statistical Bureau, Population and Employment Statistics Department, Department of Overall Planning and Wages, Ministry of Labour (ed.)), *Zhongguo laodong tongji nianjian 1997* (China labour statistical yearbook) (Beijing: Zhongguo tongji chubanshe, 1997), hereafter Labor yearbook, pp. 100, 105, 106.

(b) Numbers of laid-off (LO) SOE workers as percentage of total SOE workers, by province, 1996 (1,000 people)

Province	SOE total workers	LO SOE workers	LOs as % of total
Liaoning	6,684	638.8	9.50
Hubei	5,661	379.2	6.69
Guangdong	5,518	255.3	4.60

Source: Labor yearbook, pp. 227, 213.

workers from the interior – in 1998 began to designate the urban laid-off and unemployed as well.[36] (See also Table 4.6.)

By 1998 the city for the first time took reemployment as "important work,"[37] adopting a distinctive approach to the campaign, one much in line with the city's prior pro-market and non-state-sector-based growth: of the three cities, it was the one closest to a Thatcherite, marketist strategy. When the provincial leadership first turned its attention to the issue of reabsorbing the newly jobless in

Table 4.6   Migrants

(a) Employment of rural labour

	Rural labor employed outside their homes, 1995	Of which, employed in other counties in own province
Guangdong	1,572,800	1,493,300
Liaoning	300,460	250,500
Hubei	1,700,000	600,000

(b) Employment of rural labor from other localities

Province	End of 1995	End of 1996	1996 as % of 1995
Guangdong	3,940,300	4,672,100	+18.57
Liaoning	464,600	308,200	33.66
Hubei	850,000	853,500	+00.41

Source: Labor yearbook, pp. 126, 127.

1996, its members determined that maintaining growth and supporting the non-state economy were to be their thrust.[38] Later, even as the city's economy seemed to falter, official statements continued to emphasize that "the precondition for solving reemployment is to guarantee a certain growth speed."[39] Forcefully developing the tertiary sector and promoting the non-public economy were held to be the winning tactics through 1998.[40]

And despite Guangzhou's leaders having joined the rest of urban China in worrying about reemployment – including relying like other cities on a series of supportive active labor market policies, such as preferential rents, loans, provision of sites, reduction of fees, and free licensing[41] – they adopted a version of the project that explicitly aimed at "pushing labor toward the market, using the labor market to arrange labor resources."[42] Thus, in promoting reemployment, unlike the governors of the other two cities, Guangzhou used the program as a means of entrenching a non-state market employment mechanism.[43] And, also unlike the other two cities under review, Guangzhou's authorities believed they could control the rate of the flow and the scale of the numbers of layoffs so that they matched the city's absorptive capacity.[44]

The strategy appeared to be working fairly well as of summer 1998. In the first half of the year the rate of registered unemployed had dropped 0.19 (*sic*) percent compared with the same period a year earlier.[45] And in a survey of 10,000 respondents later in the year, 46.58 percent of those reemployed claimed to have joined the private sector.[46] It is quite striking that as of the end of 1997, only 340,000 were known to the authorities to be without work in all of Guangdong Province, while in the cities of Wuhan and Shenyang at that point at least that many were officially counted as without work just at the city level alone.[47]

Against this background, one would expect that peasant migrants into the city would not be much of a cause for concern. The press frankly acknowledged that there were "jobs with no one to do them" in the city – partly for the simple reason that urbanites would not do catering, sanitation work, or clothing and footwear manufacturing, and partly because of unmet needs for highly educated, technically trained, or specially skilled professionals. The solution to both these gaps was to depend on outside labor, whether peasants to meet the former need or urbanites from elsewhere for the latter one.[48]

But despite the marketist orientation here, by early 1998 concerns about layoffs had led officials to decide that it would no longer do just to allow the market to remedy the city's shortages. Since the locally laid-off were often not as suited as outsiders, ran one commentary, "We can't entirely let the market economy govern whom enterprises hire"; "Guangzhou must restrict the proportion of outsiders in certain trades to solve the reemployment of local labor," it read.[49]

According to the then US Consul-General in the city, Edward McKeon, events seemed in accord with this policy. Not just foreign enterprises but Chinese companies in the city as well, he noted, were sending outside labor home because business had fallen off, with both foreign investment and exports down.[50] And the Program Officer at the Ford Foundation, Stephen McGurk, drawing on the foundation's various field research projects, concurred that Guangzhou had indeed tightened up against incoming peasants because of the Southeast Asian crisis.[51]

Also evincing a growing concern to stem the tide of immigrants, the province reported in 1997 that – relying on a nine-province interregional program organized years before – it had undertaken stronger macrocontrol measures toward the labor market, toward rural surplus labor flowing across regions, in particular. As a result, the numbers of incomers declined for the first time in 1996; in 1997 new entries from other provinces coming for work dropped by 9 percent, according to a study of Guangdong's economy.[52] A new public security regulation appearing on the city's walls in summer 1998 illustrated this posture against outsiders: it decreed that one's identification card should be merged with one's household registration card and that the items on it would be increased to include blood type and height, along with a photograph.[53]

The province also demanded that employers engage urbanites before ruralites, locals before outsiders, and provincials before those from other provinces, with priority for the unemployed and the laid-off. This would mean, regulators acknowledged, a "serious attack on peasant workers' hopes for equal competition in employment and to stay in the city."[54] "Even in rich Guangdong," commented Hong Kong's frank-speaking *Ming Pao*, "dealing with local workers' livelihoods would have to entail extending a [regulatory] hand toward the labor market."[55]

In sum, Guangzhou was surely the city of the three best situated to generate jobs and absorb labor of all kinds, whether peasant or unemployed local worker. Initially it shrugged off the concerns besetting other places, not really paying attention to the problem of re-employment until 1996, 1997, or even later. It also chose to stress the marketist prong of the decisions of the 15th Party Congress. But even in this wealthy and open metropolis, the fallout of those decisions – when combined with the financial crisis affecting neighboring countries and domestic factors slowing down the national economy – caused city officials to constrain their earlier receptivity toward migrants. And there are signs that their policies may have had some results.

Shenyang

Among our three cities, Shenyang stands at the other extreme from Guangzhou, in many ways. Not only were there substantially more laid-off workers, but there were fewer peasants as well. The three-fold set of factors identified above – the health of the local economy, the nature of urban domestic markets, and the extent of global economic involvement, itself a function of geography and history – explain these differences. Situated in the northeast, Shenyang became a regional trade center in the mid- to late 1980s, but not a national or international one. Location also meant that the city was industrialized early, first as a part of the Japanese imperial system in the 1930s and 1940s and later as the recipient of Soviet aid in the First Five-Year Plan. This early development meant the placement of a disproportionate number of the nation's large state-owned enterprises here.[56] According to informants from the provincial Planning Commission, the non-state economy accounted for about 17 or 18 percent of GVIO in 1997, whereas the non-state economy in Guangzhou was 48 percent of GDP at that time.[57]

But for the problems of the late 1990s, geography also offered a blessing: Liaoning Province, of which Shenyang is the capital city, boasts the largest non-agricultural population nationally. According to one interviewee, 53.1 percent of its population was counted as urban then.[58] It also has more open land and thus more land per peasant than many other areas (see Tables 4.7(a) and (b)). So even if the province led the nation in numbers of industrial enterprise staff and workers, it did not have to contend with inflowing peasants to the same extent as the rest of eastern China did.[59]

Table 4.7   Per capita arable acreage

(a) Average arable per capita acreage (district), urban areas, 1996 (mu)	
National	1.10
Shenyang	1.27
Wuhan	0.47
Guangzhou	0.29

Source: Urban yearbook, p. 91ff.

(b) Average arable per capita acreage, provincial, 1996 (mu)	
National	2.30
Liaoning	2.96
Hubei	1.60
Guangdong	0.88

Source: Guojia tongjiju bian (State Statistical Bureau (ed.)), Zhongguo tongji nianjian 1997 (1997 Chinese statistical yearbook) (Beijing: Zhongguo tongji chubanshe, 1997), p. 379.

Once large plant was set in place in the 1950s, little was done to modernize it: renovation was too costly, so the original equipment, generally unaltered, was still in operation in the 1990s, turning out limited varieties.[60] Moreover, Shenyang mainly produces for the internal market, with vastly less foreign investment than Guangzhou attracts, and, since its enterprises' results were already poor in the 1980s, the economy there could not absorb much new labor.[61] By 1997, 51.7 percent of state-owned firms were suffering losses (as compared with 31 percent in Guangzhou).[62] And in the first eight months of 1997, when Liaoning's financial income was RMB 11.77 billion, an increase over 1996 of only 8 percent, Guangdong's was 32.92 billion, having grown 21.2 percent.[63] Over the first ten months of the year, Liaoning's GVIO rose at the rate of 9.4 percent, Guangdong's at 18.2 percent.[64]

As for market activity in the city, one-third of Liaoning's workers were employed in the tertiary sector,[65] but before 1996 such workers had represented only one-fourth of total staff and workers. In 1996 and 1997, however, there had been much governmental investment and a set of official preferential policies, so that the original 300,000 workers rose to over 500,000 in just a year or so.[66] Foreign involvement, as Tables 4.3(a) and (b) indicate, was not insignificant in Shenyang. But as of mid-1998 a mere 5 percent of the province's workers were employed in foreign-invested firms, and only one-fifth of the economy was internationally involved.[67]

Problems in the Shenyang economy were both structural and cyclical. Structurally, Shenyang, like all of the northeast, had been the heartland of the planned economy, dependent upon generous state investment, reliant on guaranteed state purchases whatever the quality of the output, and free from paying back any debts incurred. Assured support provided no incentive to turn out marketable products, so that even the city's name-brand goods got stocked in warehouses, where they generated mounting storage costs. The problems caused by excessive and unbalanced investment in heavy industry became quite apparent once the economy shifted to the market mechanism, especially given the low level of science and technology in the city's industry.[68] With that vital switch, steep losses began to emerge and the demand for labor plummeted with the drop in demand for local products, particularly those of such "sunset industries" as steel, coal, chemicals, and energy, the chief components of the area's economy.

The cyclical dimension was one Shenyang shared with the rest of the nation, when the total demand for labor fell after 1994 as national policy dictated slower growth.[69] Following the 1994 Third Plenum of the 14th Party Congress, the proportion of output taken by state purchases declined sharply.[70] Against this background, the call for speeding up reform, restructuring assets, and putting increased emphasis on competitiveness and efficiency hit the city with a severe blow. The only way its leaders could imagine raising productivity and meeting the demands of the new market economy was to implement drastic cuts in staff.[71]

The Southeast Asia financial crisis exacerbated the local economy's difficulties.

For instance, one-fourth of the exports in the machinery trade had gone to that region before the crisis began; by mid-1998 the amount had been cut in half. And where the trade's export growth rate had been in the range of 10 to 20 percent in the early 1990s, in 1997 it grew a mere 2.5 percent.[72] The Southeast Asia crisis was also a contributing factor in the city's problems with mounting unemployment:[73] The *China Daily Business Weekly* declared in August 1998 that in Liaoning investment from Asian countries in 1998 had fallen by 32.6 percent, with that from Japan alone declining by 55 percent. This was particularly serious since over half the investment in the province in recent years had come from Japan, South Korea, and Thailand.[74]

And although Liaoning leaders chose to interpret the party's 15th Congress primarily as a call to readjust the ownership structure in the state sector, and to intensify state enterprise reform,[75] the meeting's credo of emphasizing efficiency and competition definitely had an impact as well. For instance, even as a senior engineer at the provincial Machinery Bureau bragged that no other Chinese city's products could possibly compete with Liaoning's, he (almost mindlessly, it seemed) professed that: "We have to increase our competitiveness; to increase our efficiency, we must cut off some workers."[76]

Resulting from a combination of these domestic and international factors, the numbers of laid-off staff and workers across the northeast were notoriously higher than in most of the rest of the country. Already in mid-1996, when the problem was only just beginning to be noticed in Guangzhou, the city of Shenyang announced publicly that over 300,000 people had been *xiagang*'d, of a total of 2.3 million.[77] By the end of that year, when the average rate of registered "unemployed" (those whose firms had been merged, bankrupted, or otherwise shut down, so that the workers no longer had any ties with their previous enterprises) plus "laid-off" personnel was 10.3 percent nationally, in Liaoning it was 16.7 percent.[78]

By early 1998, the officially admitted figure had shot up to 378,000, of whom 249,000 remained without any placement; even of those who had been settled, about 30 percent were engaged in only temporary or seasonal work, and so would soon need a new "arrangement."[79] During the summer, informants put the likely figure of layoffs at at least 400,000, with one even estimating that some 40 percent of Shenyang's staff and workers were either laid off or unemployed.[80]

Of the three cities, Shenyang's reemployment policy was the most Keynesian, on balance relying more on state initiatives than on leaving people to the market. Liaoning instituted its "Reemployment Project" in 1994, initially placing the focus on readjusting the province's industrial structure and deepening enterprise reform. Under this program, Shenyang created seventeen large enterprise groups in electronics, automobiles, and clothing, among other industries, a plan, it was claimed, that could solve the arrangement of surplus labor. So the "Reemployment Project" (hereafter REP) was to be an opportunity for the province and the city to take advantage of their comparative superiority in being the site of many very large plants.[81] As in Robert Ash's chapter on agriculture in this volume, in some places state channels still counted for a lot.

But in Shenyang the project had another dimension: this was to create a "new iron rice bowl" for the idle workforce of the city, as one booster article in the local press described the effort in the city's hardest hit district, Tiexi.[82] The mission of this program was to organize neighborhoods and enterprises; and to develop preferential policies for laid-off workers that would both encourage them to set up businesses and spur firms to employ sizable numbers of them.[83] The city government invested RMB 6.5 million in Tiexi district alone to create the most complete center in the province for the provision of work opportunities for the local *xiagang*'d.

By autumn 1996 Shenyang boasted thirteen reemployment "bases" providing free training; by the start of 1998 the city government had set up over 250 basic-level job introduction stations and six specialized labor markets, and had allocated funds to open some 128 new commercial markets, to build new factory sites, and to offer training.[84] But despite a multitude of measures aimed at providing new opportunities for employment, Shenyang like the northeast in general was plagued by two stubborn obstacles: a serious shortage of funds and a gross insufficiency of jobs. As one writer lamented:

> The financial situation of the state-owned enterprises all over the Northeast is below the average level in the other regions. And because the financial situation is inferior, there are so many *xiagang*'d staff and workers; it is also the cause of the low level of compensation [that can be offered to those without jobs].[85]

Seconding this statement, one article reported that in Shenyang those who had been let go were getting less than one-third the relief they ought to have received, with "capital sources unstable, [appearing] irregularly and in small fragments."[86] Training programs were affected by the shortfall too, as it was not possible to invest in skill development.[87] Consequently, whereas the rate of re-employment of the laid-off nationwide ranged between 40 and 50 percent, with the city of Shanghai actually able to reemploy as many as 70+ percent, in Liaoning, the rate did not even reach 40 percent.[88] Indeed, as against what Teh-chang Lin reports, many workers of the late 1990s had so far failed to develop any sort of dependable livelihoods independent of the state.

As for the city's effort to construct a labor market to absorb the jobless, problems abounded here as well. First of all, former state workers were reluctant to settle for jobs outside the state sector: in one survey, over half (53.5 percent) insisted on returning to a state-owned firm.[89] And with most district- and street-level firms not participating in pension pooling, and with no way to transfer one's pension relationship, workers were very leery of cutting themselves off from their original firms.[90] Even concerted exertions on the part of the city directly to construct a labor market beginning in October 1995 fell far short of the mark.[91] The intention was to connect the city – along with its subordinate counties, districts, townships, and towns – with other Liaoning cities, so as to shift laborers needing work to spots where they could be employed.

Reportedly, all the way from the metropolitan level right down to the residents' committees, professional introduction networks, labor adjustment exchange meets, specialized talk hotlines, and newspapers were created to serve the laid-off. But as of the end of 1997, information channels proved inadequate: only the Labor Department was able to install communication networks, while job placement organs run by the trade unions, women's federation, and other social groups had not yet managed to do this.

For the most part, though a Northeast Labor Market was established in 1996 centered in Shenyang, labor exchange remained quite localized: though the city Labor Department claimed to have formed five information networks, interlinked via a microcomputer network, of these four were just within the city itself, the fifth being with eight nearby cities in the province. And as of early 1998, when the numbers of the laid-off approached at least 400,000, a mere 10,000 workers had been moved around among trades and firms;[92] meanwhile, fewer than 5,000 workers had gone to other regions during all of 1997.[93]

As in Guangzhou, by late summer 1998, the spontaneous labor market was dwindling as well. Here too there was a perception among residents that the numbers of outside peasants in town had decreased. In earlier years, when urban construction had flourished in Shenyang, there were enough rural laborers migrating into the city that as of early 1998 local economists maintained that their presence rendered the solution of urban unemployment more difficult.[94] Just what the actual numbers were is impossible to gauge, given the quite discrepant figures at my disposal: an account in an early 1998 study of reemployment cited about 300,000 peasants and persons from other cities entering Shenyang annually to work;[95] but a contemporaneous study of Liaoning claimed that by 1998 only 400,000 outsiders were arriving in all of Liaoning per year.[96] Perhaps as evidence that the situation had really changed over the course of the 1990s in response to stricter bars against outsiders, another source, depicting the situation three years earlier (as of 1995), claims that at that time as many as 900,000 rural surplus laborers were moving into the cities of the province every year.[97] An administrator from the provincial textile system remarked that:

> We can't deal with the *xiagang* workers, [so] how could we hire peasants? Those who have finished their contracts have already left, and the enterprises suffering losses are reducing personnel, not adding anyone.[98]

Another sign comes from an outdoor produce market, where *xiagang*'d ex-workers, now market salespeople, confirmed that in the past, before the city's industrial workers had been laid off in great numbers, the business there had been conducted mainly by peasants.[99]

As early as 1995, the provincial government formulated a directive entitled "Methods to Strengthen the Management of Outside Labor," which requested various levels of government to restrain the speed and scale of the movement of rural surplus labor into the cities, to create more openings for unemployed and surplus native workers. And by 1997, managers in over 100 work categories in the machinery, chemical, electronics, and building materials trades were ordered to reduce their use of outside labor and to hire their own surplus workers first. Only if there were no way at all to meet their needs using locals could any unit recruit outsiders. Firms behaving otherwise were to be fined.[100] That regulations had stiffened with time and were at least somewhat effective was confirmed by one local scholar who noted that peasants were perceived as employment competitors with locals and so were being made to pay money and get certificates to enter town, whereas no such controls had existed previously.[101]

In sum, Shenyang's government began to focus its energies on the over-whelming issue of its laid-off workers as early as 1995. Because of its shortage of capital and its dearth of posts, there was more laying off in the first place and more difficulties addressing those dismissed than in most of the rest of the nation. Peasants were surely restricted to some degree here, but probably the work of officialdom was spent more on job creation than on active expulsion of outsiders. In any event, the weakness of the local labor market was apparent and not readily rectified despite much official effort.

Wuhan

Wuhan's local economy combined elements of those of both Guangzhou and Shenyang. While its geographical situation – which has earned it the popular label of "the thoroughfare of nine provinces" – renders it a national-scale communications, trade, and transport center, at least as critical to the domestic economy in this regard as is Guangzhou, it is at the same time an old industrial base like Shenyang, similarly favored in the initial heavy industrial push of the 1950s and hence hampered by outdated technology, obsolete facilities and equipment, and uncompetitive products.

This mix of features meant that Wuhan's commercial centrality had a pull on peasantry from its own region; it also enabled the city to offer possibilities for reabsorbing some of the city's mounting numbers of laid-off workers. But its historical legacy of large, heavy industrial plant made for massive layoffs. Thus its *xiagang*'d workforce approached Shenyang's in size, but its magnetism for peasants resembled Guangzhou's.[102]

Although the state sector was decidedly dominant (state and collective sectors combined accounted for 80.6 percent of employment in 1996),[103] the non-state sector was vibrant. Compared with Shenyang, where a labor bureau administrator described this sector's advance as slow, in Wuhan (whose population was just over 6.7 million in 1997 – see Table 4.1 above) more than a million people were reportedly working in the sector in mid-1998.[104] And the tertiary sector accounted for 45 percent of GDP in 1997.[105]

The Asian financial crisis was not a critical component of Wuhan's *xiagang* problem, but it did contribute to it. In the past, enterprises with good results could export, and Wuhan's products did find a market in Southeast Asia. But with the drop in receptivity there to Chinese imports, many goods which were once exported had to be sold domestically, where heightened competitiveness then increased the pressure on local employment.[106] Light industrial firms had been the chief exporters, so these were the ones most influenced by the Asian crisis, with most layoffs in these firms. Some products that had once been exported not only could no longer be exported but instead had to be imported because their Southeast Asian versions had become so low priced. The crisis had also had an effect on steel exports, as Korean and Russian output had become so much cheaper.[107] The new stress on competitiveness in national policy in 1998 also found its echo in Wuhan, intensifying problems of unemployment.[108]

By the end of 1996, Wuhan's laid-off workers were said to total 289,000 or 13.7 percent of the total of staff and workers in enterprises.[109] That year the registered unemployed and the laid-off together comprised 10.3 percent of staff and workers nationally, but 13.2 percent in Hubei Province (as against 16.7 percent in Liaoning, as noted above).[110] A year later the official figure had mounted to 300,000; but another estimate that year was 340,000, or 16.5 percent of 2.08 million staff and workers.[111]

Reflective of its middling position between Guangzhou and Shenyang economically and geographically, Wuhan's approach to reemployment partook of both a Keynesian emphasis and a Thatcherite/marketist one. Many of the city's solutions remained within the state sector, with government departments being pressured to arrange the laid-off[112] and both government offices and enterprises being told to create more jobs for those without work.[113] The city directly guided much of the process, as by arranging labor exchange and forming "reemployment bases" – such as evening markets that offered preferential policies just for the *xiagang*'d (and not for peasants) – and mandating that firms and trades set up "reemployment service centers" to which their laid-off workers could be entrusted, where they were to be trained, and which were to find new jobs for them.[114] The city also invested in infrastructure and the private sector, in the hope of maintaining 15 percent economic growth.[115] The local leadership admitted in mid-May 1998 that the city would aim to solve its problems of employment "basically" within five years, as against the three years being urged at the central level.[116]

Like Shenyang, Wuhan got started with reemployment early, in the second half of 1994; in 1996, when Guangzhou was just getting underway, Wuhan's effort was picking up speed.[117] The city put primary emphasis on placing workers in the tertiary sector, and in the district and street-level economies, both official and both of which were showing the most vitality and ability to absorb laid-off personnel.[118] Wuhan also demonstrated a certain flexibility of approach, as in its tolerance of seemingly hundreds of pedicabs clogging the streets, a picture absent in the other three cities I visited in 1998 (besides Guangzhou and Shenyang, I also was in Beijing).[119] Moreover, in 1995 Wuhan eliminated the management fee for the members of its private sector, something done in Shenyang only two years later.[120]

The most outstanding obstacle to reemployment that the city faced, as in Shenyang, was its woeful deficiency of funding for the program. In 1995 a special fund was created of just RMB 10 million, with another 10 million added in 1996 and 1997, so that by 1997 the city had 30 million in the till, at a time when Shanghai had over 200 million just for its two service centers and 626 million in all.[121] None the less, its administrators took the project very seriously. For instance, in 1997 the party and government leaders of the city named this work the number one topic for research that year and issued over ten separate policy documents concerning it.[122]

The other crucial issue was the limitation on posts that could be provided.[123] These two core problems informed many of the other ones. For instance, since 70 percent of the laid-off came from firms with losses, funds for their sustenance while off the job and for their social insurance were hard to come by.[124] Plus, as one example, it was so difficult to get former workers who were temporarily based in the textile trade's reemployment service center hired that only 130 of the 400 placed (of the 10,000 laid-off in the center) managed to hold onto a job for at least three months. Thus, in cities such as Shenyang and Wuhan, unlike what Teh-chang Lin reports in his chapter in this volume, many workers' exit from their original posts was not a matter of their own choosing.

And for those who did get positions, their new employers usually refused to sign a work contract or to turn in any pension fees; they were also grossly underpaid.[125] Some of those reemployed rapidly turned into new unemployed.[126] And the publicity about the program was so poor that those in need of it were usually unable to obtain accurate and timely employment information. The absolute majority of the 300 who did find work in a summer 1997 survey took over two years to do so, while most did not understand anything about the city government's preferential policies that were supposedly aimed at themselves.[127] Of these, 26 percent were working in state firms, 21 percent in collectives, 14 percent in joint ventures, another 31 percent in private firms, and the last 7 percent in individual operations.

Were peasant migrants a source of these difficulties? Again Wuhan is middling in its hospitality to labor from elsewhere, as compared with Shenyang and Guangzhou. Table 4.6(b) shows that in the period running up to 1996 Guangdong Province was increasing its immigrants, as was Hubei, though those coming into Guangdong represented a far larger increase (+18.57 percent into Guangdong as against +0.41 percent for Hubei). Wuhan had from the start of the reform period extended a special welcome to outsiders, under the auspices of a slogan coined by Wuhan University Professor Li Chonghuai, which made Wuhan famous as the home of the "two *tong*s" (*jiaotong* and *liutong*, or communications and circulation), and because of then Mayor Wu Guanzheng's effort to make Wuhan into a regional central city.

And again there are signs of flexibility. For instance, in the hotel in which I stayed in Beijing, a maid told me that there had been people working in that hotel from other provinces more than two years before, but not at the time I was there, because of "regulations" (*guiding*).[128] But at my hotel in Wuhan the staff were Wuhan *xiagang*, Hubei peasants, and also people from other provinces, all mixed in together.[129] And among pedicab drivers, despite the occupation's capacity to absorb and thus mollify displaced workers, it was not reserved for locals: operators included peasants and other outside workers.[130] Perhaps these signs reflect the attitude of city leaders: unlike what one hears about other cities, according to one informant, "The enterprises *and* the city government don't want to limit incoming peasant workers."[131]

The outside rural labor entering Wuhan was mostly from nearby counties and provinces: altogether 81 percent of the total was from Hubei province alone (Guangzhou, by contrast, attracted just 50 percent of its outsiders from its province and a full 30 percent from elsewhere).[132] But rather than organizing an interregional macrocontrol program such as the one attempted in Guangdong, the city allowed rural workers to come in spontaneously. Densely populated countryside around the city (provincial average arable in Hubei was 1.6 mou whereas it was 2.96 in Liaoning in the late 1990s, as shown in Table 4.7(b)), plus Wuhan's geographical position – which meant that the city naturally attracted people in transit – combined to raise the numbers of outsiders.[133]

Estimates vary, but most placed the figure of peasants working in the city in the mid- to late 1990s at about 700,000.[134] They were clearly numerous in particular occupations. Unlike in Shenyang, everyone interviewed in Wuhan on this topic agreed that peasants remained at work in the textile trade there despite efforts to reemploy the natives.[135] The city's labor officials reported that an enterprise needed to invest RMB 30,000 to hire one urban worker, but just 10,000 for a peasant one. The result of this was that: "Though the city controls peasant workers, their seizure of employment posts is still serious."[136]

As in other places, but as distinct from Guangzhou which only did this in 1998, the city government began as early as July 1995 to issue rulings dividing job categories into those that could and could not hire peasant workers. But given the laxity in the city leaders' stance and the difficulties of supervising every firm, these rulings did not stick.[137] Many outsiders entered the city without going through any procedures, and went on to do business without reporting their presence.[138]

Perhaps one obstacle to tightening up control was that as of mid-1998 the city still had not been able to levy an "adjustment fee" (*tiaojiefei*) on firms that employed outsiders. The reason for this was that Hubei's leaders, concerned about the whole province where rural labor was in surplus, hoped to have these workers absorbed in Wuhan, and so refused to authorize the fee.[139] Moreover, at the end of May 1998, in a local menu of five suggested solutions to unemploy-ment, the problem of outside labor was not even mentioned at all.[140] Relatedly, most informants believed that Wuhan's recent economic development had opened up new jobs over time, so that overall there were no fewer peasants than in the past.[141]

Surprisingly in light of Wuhan's geographical and commercial centrality, even its own publicists lamented its inability to realize the formation of a labor market, even within the confines of the city itself, much less beyond it. There were plans to make Wuhan into the core of a regional labor market, ideally forged out of professional introduction organs and an active information network, but they were running into snags as of 1998.[142]

Though there were arrangements underfoot for a nationwide labor market based on seven regional centers, Wuhan had not yet even begun to establish its own portion as of September 1998.[143] One sticking point appeared to be conflicts among the cities involved. For instance, a Yangtze liaison committee (*lianxihui*) preparing to serve the mid- and lower Yangtze and proposed by the Ministry of Labor to run from Wuhan to Shanghai, got stuck, its members grappling with pleas from Chongqing to join.[144] Possibly the problem was that the huge numbers of surplus rural laborers from the Chongqing area were perceived to threaten to overwhelm the trade in workers between Wuhan and Shanghai.

In lieu of joining or facilitating the formation of a larger network, Wuhan concentrated its efforts on developing a computer network for jobs just within the city, and establishing one large building where the jobless could come to try to locate positions.[145] The other main thrust of the city's efforts was to decree that each of the city's seven districts install a localized labor market of its own, each of which was to share job information with the city's central labor market computer network and organize reemployment meetings.[146] But even these smaller scale projects fell short. In April 1998 the press held the city's labor market development to be "seriously behind, far from satisfying employment needs." This judgment rested chiefly on the sorry fact that the urban-level market had not yet connected up even with the city's own districts and the neighborhoods within them, much less with various places within the central China region.[147]

One of the main difficulties continuing to obstruct the flow of labor was ongoing blockages between ownership systems;[148] another was inadequate publicity. A telling illustration of the latter problem was my attempt in September 1998 to find the building administering the Jiangan district labor market, which had opened in June 1998, by then a full three months earlier. As my taxi drove up and down the street where it was situated, no pedestrian knew of the place.[149] Other obstacles included the gross mismatch between the types of employees in urgent need in many reform-era firms – highly skilled salespeople – and the mass of ordinary, ill-trained laborers left over from the planned economy.[150]

All told, Wuhan was striving to use its traditional strength in the state sector to settle its laid-off workers, at the same time that its location and its markets provided possibilities for tertiary and private sectoral placements. But in early autumn 1998 there was not much sign of local labor market formation to absorb its numerous unemployed.

Conclusion

This essay has revealed the complexity of China's openness, especially as it relates to the shifting implications for both employment and labor market formation. The year 1997 uncovered a new sort of underside to domestic marketization and entry into the global marketplace, as a financial crisis that began among China's immediate neighbors intensified pressures of competitiveness that the central political leadership had been stirring up already. Since these pressures came to the fore with great force and immediacy in late 1997 and throughout 1998, localities were compelled simultaneously to handle problems of enterprise reform – which meant rising lay-offs and unemployment, plus calls for cheaper labor – and also of finding work for the displaced.

Thus, economic openness can create a labor market, but it also creates unemployment under certain economic conditions. Besides, even under favorable circumstances, a policy of openness cannot quickly forge a labor market upon the ruins of a planned economy. I drew upon data from three cities, Guangzhou, Shenyang, and Wuhan, which differ in location, industrial health, extent of domestic marketization, and involvement with the world economy, to illustrate how the relationship between openness and the formation of a labor market can take varying forms, depending on the economic environment. As Jae Ho Chung's chapter in this volume shows, these differences have been greatly amplified with the increasing discretion for local governments in the reform era.

To some local leaders it has appeared as if generating the growth requisite to meeting the need for jobs – and necessary for besting international competition – depended upon cheap labor; this meant hiring workers from the countryside without benefits or security for over a decade and a half within China. But other leaders elsewhere focused rather more on protecting their own local workers, especially in the late 1990s, which made for more closed doors among cities than it did for greater domestic openness. Even in the most marketized city in this study, Guangzhou, new pressures meant some reduction in openness in the labor market; in Shenyang, which was less tied into the markets to begin with, it appears that the reduction was greater. Wuhan, which shares some traits with each city, seems to have been in between in this regard.

In the process, cities also chose to interpret the state's REP in variable ways, emphasizing either a more Keynesian approach, in which government assistance almost substituted for the market in creating jobs, or a more Thatcherite one, which stressed forcing people onto the market, and, for China, thereby assisting in the creation of a labor market *de novo* with the termination of the planned economy. The cities also differed both among themselves and over time in the extent to which they viewed the peasant laborer as a stimulus to the economy or as a competitor for their own people's posts. And each had somewhat different roots for its unemployment and differing attractions and degrees of attraction for migrant workers.

In sum, the failure to install a truly free national labor market at least as late as 1998, despite widely touted "market reform," was in large part the result of an effort to meet contradictory economic imperatives. For given simultaneous pressures both to be competitive and yet to provide employment for locals, each city's economy and its labor market remained rather separate, more or less protected, and run according to different rules. Indeed, after mid-1997 the Chinese state's program of marketization and opening crafted a political economy that embodied opposed objectives. Whether one objective will triumph over the other in the medium term, or whether an uneasy amalgam of the two will linger on, may turn out to be settled locally rather than nationally.

Notes

1 Shi Yongfeng and Xiao Binchen, "Chinese Workers Faced with the Perplexity of Unemployment," *Liaowang Overseas*, 5 September 1988, pp. 5, 6, in US Foreign Broadcast Information Service (*FBIS*), 14 September 1988, pp. 36–7; Andrew G. Walder, "Workers, Managers and the State: The Reform Era and the Political Crisis of 1989," *China Quarterly (CQ)* (1991), no. 127, p. 477.

2 Andrew Watson, "Enterprise Reform and Employment Change in Shaanxi Province" (Paper presented at the Annual Meeting of the Association for Asian Studies, Washington, DC, March 28, 1998), pp. 15–16; and Antoine Kernen, "Surviving Reform in Shenyang – New Poverty in Pioneer City," *China Rights Forum* (1997), Summer, p. 9.

3 Dorothy J. Solinger, *Contesting Citizenship in Urban China: Peasant Migrants, the State and the Logic of the Market* (Berkeley: University of California Press, 1999), chs. 1, 6.

4 At a January 1997 State Council National Work Conference on State Enterprise Staff and Workers' Reemployment – months before the crisis broke – attendees were told that solving their firms' difficulties depended upon enterprise reform, system transformation, cutting staff, normalizing bankruptcies, and encouraging mergers. This is noted in Yang Yiyong et al., *Shiye chongji bo* (The shock wave of unemployment) (Beijing: Jinri zhongguo chubanshe, n.d. (probably 1997)), p. 220.

5 *China Daily Business Weekly (CDBW)*, 23 August 1998, p. 2.

6 Interview at the Ministry's Employment Section, September 1, 1998.

7 According to Jim Mann, writing in the *Los Angeles Times*, 17 February 1999, p. A5, citing the Chinese paper, the *Economic Times*, a *conservative* estimate puts the figure at 9.3 percent in the cities as of early 1999. Kathy Wilhelm states there are more than 17 million laid off, or more than one in five workers, in "Out of Business," *Far Eastern Economic Review*, 18 February 1999, p. 12.

8 *Xinhua* (hereafter *XH*) 14 January 1999, in *Summary of World Broadcasts* (hereafter *SWB*), FE/3436, January 19, 1999, p. G/4.

9 On Wuhan's fate in the first decade and a half of reform, see Dorothy J. Solinger, "Despite Decentralization," *CQ* (1996), no. 145, pp. 1–34.

10 "Laid-off" or *xiagang* workers are those who have left their production and work post and are not doing any other work in their own unit owing to the enterprise's production and work situation, but who retain their labor relationship with the unit. See "Woguo di shiye renyuan he xiagang zhigong tongji diaocha" (A statistical investigation of our country's unemployed personnel and layoffs), *Zhongguo laodong* (Chinese Labor), *ZGLD* (1998), no. 5 , pp. 15–16.

11 See Dorothy J. Solinger, "The Potential for Urban Unrest," in David Shambaugh (ed.), *Is China Unstable?* (Armonk, NY: M. E. Sharpe, 2000), pp. 79–94.

12 *Guangming ribao* (Bright Daily) (*GMRB*), 23 June 1998, p. 4.

13 Yan Youguo, "Wanshan laodongli shichang shixian" (Realize the perfection of the labor market), *ZGLD* (1998), no. 1, p. 17.

14 Ru Xin, Lu Xueyi, and Dan Tianlun (eds.), *1998 Nian: zhongguo shehui xingshi fenxi yu yuce* (1998: Analysis and prediction of China's social situation) (Beijing, Shehui kexue wenxian chubanshe, 1998), p. 86.

15 Author's interview with Professor Yao Yuchun, People's University sociologist, September 1, 1998.

16 Beijing daxue zhongguo jingji yanjiu zhongxin chengshi laodongli shichang ketizu (Beijing University Chinese Economy Research Center Urban Labor Market Task Group), hereafter Beijing University, "Shanghai: Chengshi zhigong yu nongcun mingong di fenceng yu ronghe" (Shanghai: Urban staff and workers and rural labor's strata and fusion), *Gaige* (Reform) (1998), no. 4, p. 109.

17 Kong Pingsheng, "Jiejue jiuye xu xingcheng heli" (To solve employment we must pool efforts) *Laodong neican* (Labor Internal Reference), *LDNC* (1998), no. 3, p. 42.

18 Wang Baoyu, "Zai jiuye gongcheng renzhong dao yun" (Reemployment Project: the burden is heavy and the road is long), Unpublished manuscript prepared for the Wuhan City People's Congress, Wuhan, 1997.

19 Liu Zhonghua, "Guanyu zaijiuye gongcheng yu laodongli shichang jianshe di sikao" (Thoughts on the Reemployment Project and labor market construction), *LDNC* (1998), no. 2, p. 42.

20 "Yi bashou gongcheng zai Liaoning" (Number one project in Liaoning), *Zhongguo jiuye* (Chinese Employment) (1998), no. 3, p. 13.

21 Li Zhonglu, "Zai jiuye gongcheng di diaocha yu jishi" (An investigation and on-the-spot report of the Reemployment Project), *Gongyun cankao ziliao* (Workers' Movement Reference Materials, *GYCKZL* (1997), no. 11, p. 17.

22 *GMRB* (probably), 21 December, and Wuhan planning commission interview, 9 September 1998.

23 "District" is my definition for the Chinese term "*diqu*"; I translate "*shiqu*" as "city district."

24 Guangzhou shi jihua weiyuanhui (Guangzhou City Planning Committee) hereafter, Guangzhou shi (ed.), *Jingji shehui bai pishu* (Ecocomic-social white paper) (Donghuang: Guangdong jingji chubanshe, 1998), pp. 79–81, and p. 156 for Guangzhou; and, for Guangdong, Zheng Zizhen, "Dui Guangdong sheng renkou qianyi liuru wenti di zhanlue sikao" (Strategic considerations about the issue of Guangdong's population migration and inflow), *Zhongguo renkou kexue* (Chinese Population Science) (1997), no. 3, p. 43; and Li Zhao and Li Hong (eds.), *Guangdong jingji lanpishu: jingji xingshi yu yuce* (An analysis and forecast of the Guangdong economy) (Chaoqing: Guangdong renmin chubanshe, 1998), pp. 237, 242.

25 Author's interview with Professor Huang Ping (the CASS Institute of Sociology), September 3, 1998.

26 Li Zhao and Li Hong, *Guangdong jingji*, p. 237; and *Yangcheng wanbao* (Sheep City Evening News) (*YCWB*), 26 November 1997.

27 Li Zhao and Li Hong, *Guangdong jingji*, p. 236.

28 *YCWB*, 3 January 1998.

29 Guangzhou shi, *Jingji shehui*, pp. 132, 159.

30 Guangzhou shi, *Jingji shehui*, p. 185. The tariff reduction of October 1997 on nearly 5,000 products was expected to intensify domestic market competition (pp. 126 and 159).

31 *China Daily*, 24 August 1998, p. 5.

32 Guangzhou shi, *Jingji shehui*, p. 125.

33 Guangzhou shi, *Jingji shehui*, p. 234.

34 *Shijie ribao* (World Daily), 25 April 1998, p. A9. According to *Ming Pao* (Bright Daily) *MP*, 13 January 1998, the city's mayor claimed that only about 40,000 were *xiagang*'d but that more than an additional 60,000 were officially unemployed as of the end of 1997. However, *XH*, 26 October 1998, in *SWB* FE/3369, 28 October 1998, p. G/5, cited, quite discrepantly, that 55,600 workers who had been laid off by state firms had found new jobs in 1997(!).

35 Li Zhao and Li Hong, *Guangdong jingji*, p. 241.

36 *MP*, 12 February 1998.

37 Article from July or August 1998 in *Guangzhou ribao* (Guangzhou Daily), hereafter *GZRB*. Unfortunately there is no citation because I received this article from a Beijing University student who did not note the article's date. But photos of the summer floods on the same page as the cut-out article place it in either July or August.

38 Li Zhao and Li Hong, *Guangdong jingji*, pp. 236–7.

39 *Caijing zhoukan* (Asian-Pacific Economic Times) (the paper has these two names on its masthead), *CJZK*, 2 April 1998, p. 1.

40 *CJZK*, 2 April 1998, p. 1, and *GZRB*, July or August 1998.

41 *MP*, 17 May 1998, and *Jingji ribao* (Economic Daily) *JJRB*, 24 March 1998.

42 *CJZK*, 2 April 1998, p. 1.
43 *JJRB*, 24 March 1998.
44 *YCWB*, 26 February 1998.
45 *GZRB*, July or August 1998.
46 *SWB*, FE/3369, G/5.
47 For Guangdong, *MP*, 17 May 1998; for the other two cities, see below.
48 *YCWB*, 26 November 1997 and 3 January 1998.
49 *MP*, 13 January 1998.
50 Author's interview, August 11, 1998.
51 Author's interview, August 28, 1998.
52 Li Zhao and Li Hong, *Guangdong jingji*, p. 243. The program, or "agreement plan" (*xieyi jihua*), that the nine provinces devised involved setting up labor coordination centers in each province responsible for channeling and modulating the outflow of workers (interview, Zhongshan University, May 12, 1992); see also *XH*, 17 December 1991, in *FBIS*, 24 December 1991, p. 38; and Liaowang (Overseas Edition) (1992), no. 12, pp. 5–6, in *FBIS*, 7 April 1992, p. 30. By the spring of 1995, a Center for Information Exchange on the Labor Needs of South China, created to provide estimates of demand and to integrate information on regional supply and demand conditions, was at work, with the support of ministries and commissions under the State Council, as well as with the cooperation of the provinces involved in the network (*JJRB*, 20 December 1994, p. 1, in *FBIS*, 16 March 1995, p. 34).
53 Document observed on the street, August 7, 1998.
54 "Guangdong sheng zhigong duiwu di zhuangkuang ji zhuyao tezheng" (The situation and important special characteristics of Guangdong's staff and worker ranks), no documentation. This article was given to me by a Beijing University student who acquired it from "a friend."
55 *MP*, 17 May 1998.
56 Author's interview, Shenyang City Industrial and Commercial Bureau, August 19, 1998.
57 Author's interview, Planning Commission of Liaoning Province, August 14, 1998. See note 24 on Guangzhou.
58 Planning Commission interview.
59 *Singdao Daily*, 20 July 1995; interviews with officials from the Liaoning Planning Commission, at the Liaoning Academy of Social Sciences (LASS), and with Professor Yao Yuchun, People's University.
60 Interview at LASS, August 18, 1998.
61 Author's interview with Jin Weigang, Division of Strategy in Ministry of Labor and Social Security's Institute for Labor Studies, August 27, 1998.
62 Xu Jinshun, Gao Xiaofeng, and Zhang Zhuomin, *1997–1998 nian Liaoning sheng jingji shehui xingshi fenxi yu yuce* (1997–1998 Liaoning Province economic social situation analysis and prediction) (Shenyang: Liaoning renmin chubanshe, 1998), p. 28.
63 Xu, Gao, and Zhang, *1997–1998 nian*, p. 142.
64 Li Zhao and Li Hong, *Guangdong jingji*, p. 404.
65 Planning Commission interview.
66 Author's interview, Shenyang Labor Bureau, August 18, 1998.
67 Planning Commission interview.
68 Author's interview with provincial Textile Industrial Council, August 17, 1998.
69 Author's interview, LASS, and Xu, Gao, and Zhang, *1997–1998 nian*, pp. 143, 274–6, and 280–1.
70 LASS interview.
71 Xu, Gao, and Zhang, *1997–1998 nian*, p. 276, and author's interview with an official from the Shenyang Labor Market Management Committee's Office and the city's Employment Work Leadership Small Group Office, August 18, 1998.
72 Author's interview, provincial Machinery Bureau, August 19, 1998.

73 Author's interview, City Labor Bureau, August 18, 1998.

74 *CDBW*, 23 August 1998, p. 7.

75 Xu, Gao, and Zhang, *1997–1998 nian*, p. 274.

76 Author's interview, August 19, 1998.

77 *Liaoning ribao* (Liaoning daily) *LNRB*, 17 October 1996. *LNRB*, September 1996, p. 4, gives the number of staff and workers as of early September; if the laid-off people were being counted as members of the staff and workers this would mean that 13.04 percent of the total had already been laid off.

78 "Woguo dengji shiyelu gediqu bupingheng" (The imbalance among various districts in our country's registered unemployment rate), *ZGLD* (1998), no. 1, p. 44.

79 Wang Chengying (ed.), *Zhongguo zaijiuye* (Reemployment in China) (Chengdu: Sichuan daxue chubanshe, 1998), p. 201.

80 Interviews with the city Industrial and Commercial Administration, August 19, 1998, and with Zhou Qiren of Beijing University's Chinese Economy Research Center on September 1, 1998.

81 "Yi bashou," pp. 13–14.

82 *LNRB*, 1 June 1995.

83 The preferential policies were essentially the same as those offered in Guangzhou or in any other city to deal with the local laid-off, including free business licenses for the first year, no management fees, sites for carrying out their new businesses, tax exemption for the first year, reduction in commercial and other types of management fees for the first year. Firms where over 60 percent of the workers had been previously unemployed or laid off could escape income tax for three years. But Shenyang's government seemed more energetic in pursuing these policies than Guangzhou's did.

84 For instance, Wang Chengying, *Zhongguo zaijiuye*, pp. 201–4; "Shishi 'zaijiuye gongcheng' jingyen jieshao" (Enforce the introduction of experience on the reemployment project), *GYCKZL* (1996), no. 1, pp. 12–15; *LNRB*, 5 September 1996; interviews with city's labor official, August 18, 1998, and with officials at the city's Industrial and Commerical Administration, August 19, 1998. See also Shenyang renmin zhengfu (Shenyang People's Government), "Pizhuan shi laodongju guanyu shishi zaijiuye gongcheng anshan fenliu anzhi qiye fuyu zhigong yijian di tongzhi" (Circular transmitting the city labor bureau's opinion on implementing the reemployment project, properly diverting and arranging enterprise surplus staff and workers), Shenyang, 1996, p. 31. This document was obtained for me by a student at Beijing University and there is no further documentation.

85 Niu Renliang, "Xiagang zhigong chulu sikao" (Thoughts on the way out for the laid-off staff and workers), *Lingdao canyue* (Leadership consultations) (1998), no. 1, p. 10. Similarly, Xu, Gao, and Zhang, *1997–1998 nian*, p. 283; and "Yi baoshou," p. 14.

86 Huang Jian, "Yanjun di wenti yu changqi di tiaozhan" (Severe problem and long-term challenge), *NBCY* (1998), no. 400, pp. 7, 8. According to Xu, Gao, and Zhang, *1997–1998 nian*, p. 278, once Mu Shi became mayor, he allocated RMB 100 million for the REP; the context, plus Wang Chengying, *Zhongguo zaijiuye*, p. 203, which was published in early 1998 and which also speaks of an allotment of 100 million "this year," reinforces my guess that this was the amount for 1997. But "Yi bashou" states that the original REP fund was 100 million and that in 1997 there had been an increase of RMB 20 million for training.

87 Xu, Gao, and Zhang, *1997–1998 nian*, pp. 282–3.

88 Niu Renliang, "Xiagang zhigong," p. 9.

89 Wang Chengying, *Zhongguo zhigong*, p. 204.

90 Li Zhonglu, "Zai jiuye gongcheng," p. 18.

91 The following draws on Li Zhonglu, "Zai jiuye gongcheng," p. 18; *LNRB*, 5 September 1996; "Yi bashou," p. 15; and author's interview with official from the city labor bureaucracy, August 18, 1998.

92 Wang Chengying, *Zhongguo zaijiuye*, p. 203.

93 Xu, Gao, and Zhang, *1997–1998 nian*, p. 282. "Yi bashou," p. 15, which saw publication at just the same time, claims that the province had organized nearly 20,000 unemployed and *xiagang*'d to go to other provinces and other countries to work. Even so, this is still not very many, given that just one city in the province contained twenty times that many in the category of *xiagang*, not to mention those fully "unemployed."

94 Xu, Gao, and Zhang, *1997–1998 nian*, p. 305.

95 Wang Chengying, *Zhongguo zaijiuye*, p. 203.

96 Xu, Gao, and Zhang, *1997–1998 nian*, p. 277.

97 "Shishi," p. 13.

98 Author's interview, August 17, 1998.

99 Author's talks with marketers, August 20, 1998.

100 Li Zhonglu, "Zai jiuye gongcheng," p. 19; Xu, Gao, and Zhang, *1997–1998 nian*, p. 277; Wang Chengying, *Zhongguo zaijiuye*, p. 203; and interview with labor bureau official, August 18, 1998.

101 LASS interview.

102 Interviews with Huang Ping; the Wuhan Labor Employment Management Bureau of the city's labor bureaucracy, September 7, 1998 (labor interview); and Wang Baoyu, former Head of the Wuhan Social Science Academy and former Vice-Chair of the City People's Congress's Finance and Economics Committee, September 9, 1998.

103 Author's interview, Wuhan Planning Commission, Tertiary Sector Planning Coordination Office, September 9, 1998.

104 Wuhan labor interview.

105 Interviews, labor bureau and planning commission.

106 Labor interview.

107 Author's interview, Wuhan Economic Commission, September 8, 1998.

108 *Changjiang ribao* (Yangtze Daily), *CJRB*, 9 April 1998, p. 1; Si Yuan and Zeng Xiangmin, "Wuhan 1998 hongguan zhengce shou xuan mubiao-zaijiuye" (Reemployment – Wuhan's 1998 macro policy's first objective), *Wuhan jingji yanjiu* (Wuhan Economic Research) (1998), no. 3, p. 56.

109 Jianghan daxue ketizu (Jianghan University Project Group), "Wuhan shi shishi zaijiuye gongcheng duice yanjiu" (Policy research on Wuhan City's implementation of the reemployment project), Wuhan, 1998, p. 2.

110 "Woguo dengji shiyelu," p. 44.

111 The first report was from, I believe, *GMRB*, 21 December 1997 (the article was clipped for me without the source having been noted); the second from Jianghan daxue ketizu, *Wuhan shi*, p. 2.

112 Author's interview with planning commission officials.

113 Instructions from the mayor, in *CJRB*, 9 April 1998, p. 1.

114 Labor interview.

115 *CJRB*, 9 April 1998, p. 1, and 30 May 1998; and "Wuhan shi zhuazhu sanxiang gongzuo da da zaijiuye gong jianzhan" (Wuhan city grasps three items of work, boldly storms the strongholds of the battle of reemployment), *ZGJY* (1998), no. 2, p. 17.

116 *CJRB*, 30 May 1998; a report on the central-level meeting can be found in *JJRB*, 18 May 1998, p. 1.

117 *JJRB*, 2 May 1998; labor interview, September 6, 1998.

118 *GMRB* (probably), 21 December 1997, and planning interview.

119 According to *Sing Tao Jih Pao*, 22 February 1998, in *SWB*, FE/3162, 27 February 1998, p. G/8, the Chinese Information Center for Human Rights and Democratic Movement reported that Tu Guangwen, a pedicab driver who organized a demonstration in Wuhan in October 1997, had been sentenced to three years in prison by the city's Jiangxia District People's Court for the crime of gathering people to

disrupt traffic. He stood accused of blocking traffic for up to six hours. The information center said that to improve the city's appearance, the Wuhan city government had issued a circular on rectifying the pedicab trade in October 1997. The rectification cut the drivers' incomes sharply, and also meant that drivers without temporary permits would be unable to continue their trade. The drivers are mainly laid-off workers. When repeated negotiations with the government proved fruitless, some 1,000 workers held a demonstration on October 16 in Zhifang town, in Wuhan's Jiangxia district. The authorities sent in police to suppress the demonstration and arrested five people, one of whom was Tu. The government neither eliminated this conflict, nor held talks to resolve it, according to the center.

120   For Wuhan, author's interview with industrial and commercial officials, September 10, 1998; for Shenyang, interview with the same office there on August 19, 1998.

121   On Wuhan, "Wuhan shi zhuazhu," p. 16, *JJRB*, 2 May 1998, and Jianghan daxue ketizu, "Wuhan shi," p. 61; on Shanghai, Yang Yiyong, *Shiye chongji bo*, p. 230. On both, Si Yuan and Zeng Xiangmin, "Wuhan 1998," p. 56.

122   *CJRB*, 5 November 1997, and another article from the same paper sometime just after the 9th National People's Congress (article clipped for me but without the date).

123   *CJRB*, 1 December 1997, p. 11, and *JJRB*, 2 May 1998.

124   "Guanyu Wuhan shi zaijiuye wenti di diaocha baogao" (An investigation report on Wuhan City's re-employment problem), Wuhan, n.d., p. 3, and *JJRB*, 2 May 1998. For comparison, Guangzhou shi, Jingji shehui, p. 84, states that "at many levels the social security system is gradually being completed and unemployment coverage is expanding."

125   *CJRB*, 2 June 1998, p. 2.

126   Wang Baoyu, "Zai jiuye," p. 2.

127   *CJRB*, 2 June 1998, p. 2, and Jianghan daxue ketizu, "Wuhan shi," pp. 57, 58.

128   Author's interviews, August 25 and 28, 1998.

129   Author's interview, September 5, 1998.

130   Street interview, September 6, 1998.

131   Author's interview with Professor Yang Yunyan, Central China Finance and Trade University, Wuhan, September 6, 1998.

132   Zeng Yanhong, "Wuhan shi yu qita da chengshi liudong renkou bijiao yanjiu" (Comparative research on Wuhan city and other large cities' floating populations), *Zhongguo renkou* (1997), no. 4, p. 32.

133   Also see Si Yuan and Zeng Xiangmin, "Wuhan 1998," p. 56.

134   Though the labor bureau officials claimed a figure of 800,000, many other sources said 700,000, and one (an undated newspaper clipping from 1997 or 1998) said 600,000. The planning commission officials and *CJRB*, 1 December 1997, p. 11, both said 700,000, and Si Yuan and Zeng Xiangmin, "Wuhan 1998," p. 56, noted that in 1995 there was a floating population of 1.5 million in the city but that only about 700,000 of them were working.

135   "Among those still working in textiles, some are peasants," according to the planning commission informants; and Professor Yang Yunyan claimed that: "Textiles uses peasants on a large scale." But Wang Baoyu said that "the factories are shrinking, so peasants are leaving."

136   Jianghan daxue ketizu, "Wuhan shi," p. 3. Wang Baoyu said much the same thing in my interview with him.

137   Labor interview.

138   "Guanyu Wuhan shi," p. 4. In *Contesting Citizenship in Urban China*, I note that this has tended to be more the case in cities further from Beijing and where the market is more active.

139   Labor interview.

140   *CJRB* 30, May 1998.

141 Wuhan Economic Commission interview, September 8, 1998.
142 "Wuhan shi zhuazhu," pp. 16–17.
143 Planning commission interview, September 9, 1998.
144 Wuhan labor interview, September 7, 1998.
145 "Wuhan shi zhuazhu," p. 17; labor interview; planning commission interview; *CJRB*, 18 December 1997.
146 Planning commission interview; *Wuhan wanbao* (Wuhan Evening News), 24 February 1998.
147 *CJRB shichang zhoukan* (Yangtze Daily Market Weekly), *CJRB SCZK*, 2 April 1998, p. 14.
148 *CJRB SCZK*, 23 April 1998, p. 14.
149 This occurred on September 16, 1998. We eventually found the building and learned that about 3,000 visits had been made there, eventuating in 800 persons' names being entered into the center's computer, only several tens of whom were peasants.
150 *CJRB SCZK*, 3 September 1997, p. 14.

5 The interdependence of state and society

The political sociology of local leadership

David S. G. Goodman

The restructuring of the Chinese economy and its subsequent rapid development have had a profound social impact at the county level and below.[1] New social classes and categories have been generated – most obviously private entrepreneurs; managers of the new forms of enterprises owned by rural communities or by other state sector enterprises; and a range of professionals including lawyers, psychologists, and merchant bankers – to service the increased needs of the economy and the associated social complexity.[2] At the same time, local political elites have had to adjust and adapt to their rapidly changing social and economic environments, including losing their monopoly of high status.[3]

The wider significance of these social changes has been a subject of considerable debate. Particularly outside China, commentators have disagreed in their explanations of the political dynamics involved, and even more in their prognoses for the future of state–society relations. The reduction of the role of the state in economic development,[4] the introduction of greater legal regulation – a rule of laws if not exactly the rule of law[5] – and the evolution of mechanisms for ensuring the public accountability of officials, especially in rural China,[6] are all clear markers that significant political change is underway. The difficulty has been in relating these political changes to the transformation of the social structure, particularly against the background of even more far-reaching questions about the potential for various forms of pluralism and democracy to develop in China.

The distinct liberalization of relations between state and society together with the development of a market sector of the economy and private entrepreneurship have led some to identify a new middle class that will be the harbinger of capitalism and democracy.[7] Without going nearly so far in the clarification of specific social categories, studies of rural China often identify the emergence of new and distinct social and economic interests.[8] Though by no means all such interpretations see these new interests as completely independent of the state, there are those who regard the new categories of entrepreneurs as a fundamental challenge to the existing state.[9]

Far less dramatic positions are taken by those who argue that the social forces unleashed by reform have launched China on a slow but inevitable transition somewhat similar to democratization in Taiwan;[10] and those who see the potential for, rather than the realization of, pluralism and the emergence of civil society in the emergence of new local elites.[11] The new entrepreneurs and particularly the business and social organizations that have developed to serve their need for wider organization are seen as the building blocks of these future changes. Any hesitancy about the speed of change reflects an understanding of the continued economic involvement of local governments, local government and the Chinese Communist Party (CCP) officials acting individually, entrepreneurs who had been officials, and entrepreneurs who depend on networks with officials and government agencies in what is clearly an economy that has not only grown out of state socialism but that still retains some of its institutional influences.

Similar concerns inform another set of interpretations about the impact of social change under reform that focus on the corporatist and government-dominated aspects of economic development. While private entrepreneurship has been a more publicized dimension of reform, a substantially larger proportion of economic growth is attributable to enterprises active in the market sector of the economy but owned by local governments, villages, and state sector enterprises.[12] The economic elites of these enterprises are neither private entrepreneurs nor state officials, though they may in the past have been either (and sometimes even both.) Moreover, in general, entrepreneurs of all kinds still need to operate in both state and society, and to network widely in both, in order to be successful. One view of these phenomena completely rejects any pluralist tendencies in reform at all, with the party–state regarded as exercising even more control over society than was the case during the pre-reform era, as it now has to work within a more complex social environment.[13] Others emphasize the continued centrality of the CCP and the party–state, and the absence of political pluralism, while at the same time acknowledging a nascent social pluralism and the more ambiguous positions of private and local corporate entrepreneurs in state–society relations.[14]

These varying interpretations of state–society relations are not necessarily mutually exclusive, not least because there have been changes over time and there are considerable differences across China.[15] Moreover, in part any discussion of the changing nature of state–society relations in China is a debate about the definition of the state which places either Beijing and central government, on the one hand, or the influence of the CCP through the structures of the party–state, on the other, at the center. If the center of emphasis in the conceptualization of the state is placed on the organization of government in and from Beijing, then clearly reform has almost by definition seen the reduction of the state as government has withdrawn from many areas of direct economic management and introduced large-scale decentralization. The border between state and society would then occur somewhere below the county level of administration. However, if the roles of the CCP in the party–state are placed at the center of the definition of the state, then the borders of state–society relations will largely be determined by local CCP influence. This may result in an extremely localized version of the party–state: a different but not necessarily a reduced form of state power that will be determined by the local party's political organization and its social networks.

There can be little doubt that the relationships between state and society in China are changing and becoming more complex. It is the speed and trajectories of change which require clarification and it is not necessary to always expect cataclysmic or immediate outcomes. A recent and wider comparative study of the prospects for civil society and democratization is particularly instructive for China in this respect: it emphasizes that authoritarian regimes which practice corporatist inclusionary politics and are successful in being associated with economic prosperity are not likely to change quickly, not least because few opportunities are provided to encourage the emergence of counter-elites.[16]

The evidence from interviews with local political and business elites in Shanxi Province reinforces the view that the party–state – in the form of the CCP and local government – continues to play a central role in not only the economic but also the social formation of the new economic elites. A comparison of the personal backgrounds, careers, and standards of living of local political and business elites provides somewhat conflicting indications with respect to the emergence of distinct social and economic interests under reform. There are social, economic, and political differences beginning to emerge between local political and business elites, which might conceivably become entrenched inter- ests, and given changes in the wider environment provide the social bases for a form of political pluralism.

At the same time, it is far from clear that the emerging differences between political and business elites are more significant than those among different cate- gories of the local political and economic elites, some of which leave elements of the business elites having more in common with their equivalent-level political elites. Moreover, the sustained and continuing influence of the party–state is clearly visible in the formation of the local elites. Entrepreneurs have emerged from within the party–state, have benefited from the intergenerational transfer of privilege brought by the party–state, or have been incorporated into the party–state. The party–state may not subsume society as in the past and there may be more space for social activities of various kinds and even for certain kinds of political activity. All the same the state–society relationship is better characterized in terms of interdependence and accommodation rather than separate development.

Local elites in Shanxi

Shanxi is a north China province, which in 1997 had 31.41 million people, a GDP of RMB 148 million, and a GDP per capita of RMB 4,736.[17] Although it is one of the country's major heavy industrial bases, based on exceptionally large and high-quality resources of coal, its reputation within China is for peasant radicalism. It was the site of the major front-line base areas against Japanese invasion during the War of Resistance of 1937–45; and the later Mao-era model production brigade of Dazhai is located in its east. None the less, since the 1920s

Shanxi has been an established major center for heavy industry, and it continues to produce large proportions of China's coal, coke, aluminum, electricity, and specialist steels. Until the 1990s provincial economic development had depended heavily on central government investment, growing fastest during the mid-1950s and mid-1980s: it was only during the mid-1990s that sustained, though still only moderate, above-national-average rates of growth were achieved without that support.[18] This less spectacular economic profile, and other aspects of its economy, mean that Shanxi had more in common with many of China's provinces – particularly those inland – than the more spectacular-performing coastal provinces (Guangdong, Zhejiang, and Jiangsu) and large municipalities (Beijing and Shanghai).

In the 1990s Shanxi's economic structure ceased to be dominated by the central state sector, though it still played a sizable role in provincial development. There was very little foreign interaction with the province though there was considerable domestic investment from and trade with other parts of China, particularly in the development of the collective and private sectors of the economy. By 1997, 32 percent of the gross value of industrial output (GVIO) was produced by the state sector all of which was in heavy industry (the national average was 25.5 percent); 37.1 percent of provincial GVIO was derived from the collective (or local government) sector of the economy based on coal industry support activities and by-products (the national average was 38.1 percent). A much higher than the national average 26.8 percent of provincial GVIO came from the private sector, with production based in the new technologies, food-stuffs, and textiles[19] (the national average was 17.9 percent). Moreover, within Shanxi itself there was suspicion that the real figure for the size of the private sector was considerably higher, with many private entrepreneurs masquerading for political reasons as part of the local government economy.[20] In 1997, only 4.1 percent of GVIO was derived from the foreign-funded sector of the economy, compared to a national average of 18.5 percent.[21] These figures necessarily understated the size of the private and collective sectors of the economy (in that order). Industrial production was 47.5 percent of GDP in Shanxi, agricultural production was 13 percent of GDP, while the retail and other service sectors were dominated by private entrepreneurs.[22]

Before reform the local leaders of the party–state were effectively the local elite. By the late 1990s this had changed so that it became possible to identify a political, an economic, and, even to some extent, a social and cultural elite. The political elite remained the leading cadres of the party–state, while the economic elite were the private entrepreneurs and managers of economic enterprises. Both broad categories had high social status in addition to their political or economic standing. In contrast, the emerging local social and cultural elite – for example, media personalities, designers, writers, artists, singers, and performers – were popularly acknowledged by virtue of being politically recognized or economically successfully.

During 1996–8 just under 300 members of the political and business elites in Shanxi Province were interviewed about their work, their lives, and their attitudes to change.[23] The interviewees were drawn from every district in Shanxi; from rural areas and urban areas; from different sizes of enterprises; from different sectors of the economy; and from different levels of the administrative system, where this was appropriate. All the interviewees were socially defined local leaders, by virtue of their position of leadership in either their enterprise or administrative unit within the party–state.

Shanxi's local political elite could be estimated at the 204,708 people who were leading cadres in the province (as of the end of 1997). The province's role in the development of the communist movement, and its history of heavy industrialization, mean that the CCP has deep social roots here and partly explains the high number and proportion of cadres. Contemporary estimates suggested that in Shanxi the ratio between cadres in the party–state and staff in other social organizations was about 1.6 times greater than the national average.[24] In addition to the leading cadres there were an additional 594,446 ordinary cadres in the province, with the vast majority at the sub-county section level.

Formally in terms of the CCP's appointments policies and procedures there are five levels of cadres of which three – sub-provincial department and district, county and section – represent the local political elite. However, there are significant political and social differences between workplaces and formal cadre ranks which make it more analytically rigorous to discuss the local political elite in terms of four categories of cadres: provincial administration, district offices, county authorities, and (within county) section-level cadres.[25] In broad terms, cadres in the provincial administration represent the province's technocratic elite; those in district offices are the more conservative, political cadres; the county level is the testing ground for the potential senior cadres of the future; and section-level cadres are locality based and production related.[26]

It is much harder to assess the size of Shanxi's economic elite. It was estimated that there were about 994,154 economic enterprises in the province during 1997. According to official provincial statistics there were 93,288 state sector enterprises; 109,183 collective sector enterprises; 75,564 private enterprises; 1,345 share-based companies; and 774 enterprises financed either in whole or in part by investors from Hong Kong, Taiwan, or elsewhere in the world outside China.[27] In addition, according to national statistics, there were 714,000 enterprises in the service sector not differentiated by ownership system.[28]

Not all of these enterprises could necessarily be considered successful, leading examples, or best practice in any sense. At the same time, while many privately owned enterprises had only one or at most two individuals (the owner and spouse) at their head, other bigger enterprises in the state and collective sectors had several leading managers who could reasonably be regarded as part of the local economic elite. As a crude estimate it would seem likely that the local economic elite during the late 1990s might therefore have been about 300,000 people, but might also conceivably have numbered more.

The entrepreneurs and managers of the local economic elite came from a bewildering array of different types of companies, which often effectively masked their status as owners and managers. Not all managers were managers, particularly in the collective local government sector where some were owners; and ownership was more usually mixed than the official categorization of the economy into state, collective, private, and foreign-funded sectors implies. Indeed, the question of ownership or management was probably a less important characteristic of the contemporary economic elite than entrepreneurship as the exercise of risk (political as well as financial).[29] Formally, the state sector is the planned part of the economy; the collective sector is the unplanned part of the state economy, with enterprises owned by the workers in the company (mainly in urban areas) or by a locality (mainly in rural areas); and the private sector is that for owner–operators. However, in practice these distinctions had become increasingly less meaningful as explanations of economic structures and activities.

The biggest change was that with reform it became possible to identify the emergence of a larger public sector, which grew out of the collective sector often through cooperation with local government, in between the state and private sectors. It included a range of companies with a variety of ownership structures and management systems, as well as of registration and method of incorporation, and significant differences in scope and scale of operation. These public sector enterprises all competed in the market sector of the economy and all involved an element of public as opposed to state sector ownership. They included companies owned by other, often state sector or collective, enterprises; by social units (such as schools and trade unions); by units of local government; by townships and villages; and by individuals in cooperation with collectives, state sector enterprises, villages, townships, local governments, and social units. It included urban and rural collectives, shared-based companies, and equity-based enterprises; and may have included investors from elsewhere in China as well as from Hong Kong, Taiwan, and beyond.[30]

Within this more complex economic structure of state, public, and private sectors it was possible to identify seven broad categories of the local economic elite: state sector managers, public sector urban enterprise managers, public sector rural entrepreneurs, public sector private entrepreneurs, joint venture managers, private enterprise managers, and owner–operators. Each was differentiated by workplace and organizational context, which seemed likely to lead to social and political differences. Table 5.1 provides information on the scale and

Table 5.1 Average fixed assets and profits after tax for different categories of enterprise by sector (RMB million yuan per annum, 1997)

Sector	Fixed assets	Net profits
State sector enterprises	1,258.39	24.31
Public sector:		
Urban enterprises	107.71	29.82
Rural enterprises	19.45	4.22
Private enterprises	31.00	6.35
Foreign-funded joint ventures	42.36	1.78
Private sector enterprises	7.68	0.28

size of the different kinds of enterprises (as indicated by the size of average fixed assets and net profits) which were identified in interviews with entrepreneurs and managers in the state, public and private sectors.

Managers of state sector enterprises were the most easily identified category of the local economic elite. Typically of very large scale, as Table 5.1 indicates, state sector enterprises often have a large management leadership team, each member of which has wealth, status, and position sufficient for them to be considered part of the local economic elite. State sector enterprises are an essential part of the party–state. Its managers are recruited in similar ways to cadres and it would be reasonable to expect state sector managers to have a similar profile.

The public sector can be sub-divided into four general types of enterprise, differentiated by the locus of activities, the major source or sources of investment, and by the scale of activity. Each type of enterprise generated at least one separate category of the local economic elite.

The urban enterprises within the public sector include collectives and share-based companies established by state sector enterprises and social units, as well as urban collectives of more pre-reform types. Urban enterprise managers are therefore likely to be drawn from the same broad employment pool as to be found in state sector enterprises and social units, with high levels of educational achievement and of mobility. At the same time it would be reasonable to expect urban enterprise managers to share some of the characteristics of others operating in the market sector of the economy.

The rural enterprises within the public sector include collectives and stock companies established by townships, villages, and rural districts. Although originally fairly small scale and village based, many have taken advantage of the rural sector's preferential economic regulation to develop sizable industrial concerns, especially in mining and associated activities. The growth of rural enterprises has been particularly spectacular in suburban areas where villages have been able to benefit from their rural status as well as access to markets and technical inputs. Rural entrepreneurs were most likely to be local residents who have mobilized the locality behind the particular idea that has led to the development of the enterprise.

The foreign-funded joint ventures in the public sector were those enterprises supported in whole or in part by investors from Hong Kong, Taiwan, and the rest of the world. In Shanxi during the late 1990s there were few of these by any standard but they tended to be larger and developing versions of private or state sector enterprise, though there were also rural collectives and social unit owned companies that had transformed themselves into joint ventures. The profile of joint venture managers is likely to some extent to reflect the nature of the enterprise from which the Shanxi side of the joint venture developed. Though depending on the skills and techniques required, they may also have been professional managers hired for the specific task.

The fourth type of public sector enterprise were private enterprises which had become either collective enterprises through cooperation with local government or share-based public companies, but where the original individual entrepreneur remained in the senior management position. The public sector private entrepreneurs were likely in consequence to have the profile of more experienced owner–operators. The identification of public sector private enter- prises may seem oxymoronic but was actually a function of the political determination of economic development. Private enterprise was initially sanc- tioned by the CCP during the 1980s as small-scale economic activities – such as retail and service provision – which were more efficiently provided in this way according to market needs. There was virtually no thought given to individual enterprise development and, indeed, when small-scale private entrepreneurs started to accumulate and wanted to reinvest in new areas, and especially wanted to become small-scale industrialists, they found themselves without access to bank loans, or the additional labor, machinery, and land that they required.[31] As a consequence, private entrepreneurs wanting to expand or to develop into new areas usually cooperated with local government, villages, townships, or occasion- ally with state sector enterprises to form new companies. Consequently, as Table 5.1 indicates, private sector enterprises were still subject exclusively to the economic direction of their owner–operators and remain fairly small scale.

The sixth category of the local economic elite were the owner–operators of the private sector. In addition to those who owned and ran the entire economic infrastructure of private sector enterprises, this category also includes entrepreneurs who ran businesses based on village, local government, state, or collective sector enterprise ownership of capital where the operation of the plant was then contracted out. Owner–operators were frequently characterized as young and poorly educated.[32]

The seventh and final category of the local economic elite were the managers of the larger private enterprises hired as managers in either the private or the public sectors.[33] Even in the private sector there were some fairly sizable enter- prises, e.g., restaurants and luxury hotels, while the public sector private enterprises include a number which were as large as large-scale state sector enterprises.[34] Because private enterprise had not really developed in Shanxi until after 1992, private enterprise managers were also likely to be young, but unlike private entrepreneurs and owner–operators were likely to be well-educated professionals imported precisely for that reason.

Personal background

An analysis of the personal backgrounds of members of the local political and business elites interviewed provides some evidence of difference both between and within those two broad categories. Data on age (at the end of 1998), native place, parental membership of the party–state, and peasant background are provided in Table 5.2 for each category of the local political and economic elites. Both political and business elites were fairly middle aged, the only exceptions being those entrepreneurs and managers involved with private enterprise. There would appear to be an inverse relationship between parental membership of the

Table 5.2   Shanxi local elites: demographic background (interviewees, 1996–8)

	Average age (years, end 1998)	Native to workplace county (%)	Parents in party–state (%)	Former peasants (%)
Cadres:				
Provincial administration	55	n.a.	18	38
District offices	54	n.a.	0	90
County	45	0	42	64
Section level (within county)	48	60	0	71
Entrepreneurs:				
State sector managers	48	32	22	42
Urban enterprise managers	48	25	25	32
Rural entrepreneurs	47	63	34	48
Private entrepreneurs	42	50	47	38
Joint venture managers	46	64	43	38
Private enterprise managers	30	33	45	0
Owner–operators	41	54	40	48

party–state and current employment within it: on the whole entrepreneurs and managers in private enterprise were considerably more likely than cadres to have a parent who had been a member of the party–state.

The age structure of Shanxi's local elite reflected both a maintenance of the traditional relationship between seniority and status, as well as the relative youthfulness of those involved in private enterprise. With the exception of private entrepreneurs, private enterprise managers, and owner–operators, the average age for each category of business elite was the late forties, as it was for section-level and county cadres. These are quite high averages and would seem generally to indicate the need for individuals to work their way up a hierarchy over twenty years or more if they wish to reach the top, rather than relying on innovation or initiative to short-circuit the process. The exceptions were all in private enterprise where it was clearly possible for both entrepreneurs and managers to achieve wealth and status when young. Indeed, sometimes the younger entrepreneurs in private enterprise were selected precisely because of their age to become "model entrepreneurs" for emulation, or delegates to people's congresses.

Those of Shanxi's local elites interviewed were almost all natives of the province, and there were few differences between or amongst the local political and economic elites in this respect.[35] While no county-level cadres were stationed in either their place of birth or native place,[36] the majority of section-level cadres did work in their native place. To some extent this reflects the nature of their work in encouraging local enterprise in much the same way as undertaken by rural entrepreneurs, though with less of the direct economic management responsibility. The high proportion of rural entrepreneurs, private entrepreneurs, and joint venture managers who worked in their native place indicates the local origins of much of the new entrepreneurialism.

The social impact of the party–state in the formation of local economic elites begins to emerge when data on family background are considered. With the exception of county-level cadres, very few of the local political elite (17 percent for all cadres) had at least one parent who was a member of the party–state (a member of the CCP or holder of a formal position in the state). In contrast 47 percent of private entrepreneurs, 43 percent of joint venture managers, 40 percent of owner–operators, and 45 percent of the private enterprise managers had a parent who had been a member of the party–state. Cadres were recruited overwhelmingly from the peasantry. (Shanxi has officially about 38 percent of its population classified as peasants.) On the whole, lower proportions of the economic elites came from a peasant background.

Those interviewed were also almost all men: the only significant (yet still small) number of women were to be found in private enterprise. Only two cadres interviewed were women: one a mayor, the other a county cadre. Among the economic elite, two of the urban enterprise managers interviewed were women, one of the private enterprise managers, and nine of the owner–operators. On the other hand, many of the entrepreneurs and managers interviewed worked together with their wives in the same company, with the latter often as the company accountant: 47 percent of private entrepreneurs, 46 percent of owner–operators, and 37 percent of rural entrepreneurs fitted this pattern, as more surprisingly did 39 percent of state sector managers.

Education and work experience

The interdependence of state and society, as well as differences among the various categories of the local political and business elites, can be seen in the career backgrounds of those interviewed. The interdependence is highlighted not only by the large numbers of former local leading cadres who became entrepreneurs, and the recruitment into the CCP of those successful entrepreneurs who were not previously members, but also by the recruitment into the political elite of individuals with specialized non-political skills. The differences are highlighted by differential access to higher education and CCP membership, yet equally neither was no longer an exclusive predictor of advancement and it had certainly become possible to pursue wealth independently.

On the whole cadres were better educated than members of the local economic elite; urban-based elites were better educated than rural-based elite groups; and those from the leadership of the state and public sector enterprises were better educated than entrepreneurs in the private sector. Data on the highest educational levels achieved by interviewees are presented in Table 5.3.[37] Despite their peasant backgrounds and the intercession of the Cultural Revolution, most of the political elite graduated from university. This presumably reflects the party–state's cadre recruitment procedures – by intellectual merit through institutions of higher education – and its reform-era emphasis on more formal qualifications. The exceptions are the more locally (and rurally)

Table 5.3   Shanxi local elites: highest educational level (interviewees, 1996–8, % of known cases)

	University	College	Middle school
Cadres:			
Provincial administration	78	12	12
District offices	67	8	
County	50	50	
Section level	9	64	9
Entrepreneurs:			
State sector managers	49	21	27
Urban enterprise managers	31	34	34
Rural entrepreneurs	6	19	69
Private entrepreneurs	40	7	47
Joint venture managers	36	27	18
Private enterprise managers	70	30	
Owner–operators	16	16	59

oriented section-level leading cadres, a majority of whom had attended technical colleges, or district and county-level party schools.

Among the economic elites, private enterprise managers had a similar rate of university education to the political elites; and if levels of tertiary education (rates of university and college education combined) are taken into account then state sector, urban enterprise, and joint venture managers also have comparable levels of education. One explanation of the high rate of tertiary education achievement recorded among private enterprise managers is to be found in the contrasting educational backgrounds of owner–operators and private entrepreneurs. Moreover, in interviews it became apparent that many entrepreneurs, despite their own considerable economic achievements, not only greatly respected intellectual endeavor but felt the need for highly educated assistants.

Table 5.4 provides a calculation of the average length of service in the enterprise or unit where they were currently working when interviewed for each category of the elite, as well as information on the careers of local elites before their current appointment. The calculation of average lengths of service (which includes the period of the current appointment) does not seem to indicate a high degree of work or even social mobility for either the political or the economic elites. On the contrary, given that rural reform in Shanxi did not really start until the mid-1980s, and that the urban economy did not start to change dramatically until 1992, these figures suggest strongly that economic change was led by individuals from within existing structures.

Average lengths of service seem relatively high for all categories of the elite, except as might be expected for private enterprise managers who were both young and hired specifically for their skills and qualifications. The long average lengths of service for section-level cadres and rural entrepreneurs would appear to be consistent with the high degree of commitment to their work location that can be assumed from other aspects of their profiles. On the other hand, given usual policies on the circulation of cadres, the average figures for provincial

Table 5.4   Shanxi local elites: careers (interviewees, 1996–8; percentages have been rounded up and may exceed 100 percent)

	Average length of service in current enterprise or unit (years, end 1998)	Predominant career before appointment (% of known cases)				
		Party–state	Technocrat or intellectual	Business	Worker	Peasant
Cadres:						
Provincial administration	8.2	61	33	6		
District offices	7.3	75	25			
County	5.0	67	33			
Section level	9.5	90	10			
Entrepreneurs:						
State sector managers	12.8	39	41	8	23	
Urban enterprise managers	11.3	25	54	13	8	
Rural entrepreneurs	12.0	52	10		29	10
Private entrepreneurs	6.6	50		31	19	
Joint venture managers	6.4	64	18	9	9	
Private enterprise managers	3.7	70			30	
Owner–operators	6.8	23	19	10	31	17

administration and district office cadres seem particularly high, though not as high as for the state sector and urban enterprise managers, some of whom had been in the same company or enterprise (or their predecessor institutions) for thirty or forty years.

Information on former careers highlights the centrality of the party–state as a source of leadership for the public sector of the economy. The percentages provided in Table 5.4 reflect in large part the impact and influence of village leaders and local party secretaries who took the lead in mobilizing local populations behind new economic initiatives, particularly in rural areas. Entrepreneurialism in this context has been more characterized by its organizational capacities than (as was more the case in Western experiences of modernization) its technical innovations. The pattern in urban areas was somewhat different where economic leadership has been exercised by those with a technocratic background in urban enterprises, a pattern repeated to some extent in the development of the state sector.

As might be expected, most of the political elite had worked their way up the administrative hierarchy. However, substantial proportions of the cadres interviewed from the provincial administration, district offices, and county authorities had not spent the majority of their working lives within the offices of the party–state. In all cases these were technocrats, intellectuals, and businesspeople who had been politically suspect in the Mao-dominated era of China's politics. Though a few had been permitted to join the CCP even before the reform era, all had chosen to make their careers elsewhere. With the advent of reform they were recruited to political office by a provincial leadership anxious to utilize their skills and expertise.

This pattern of incorporation into the party–state for a segment of the technocratic elite is also visible in Table 5.5 which presents data on CCP membership for each category of the local elite. When the information in Table 5.5 on the average age on entry, and the era of entry to the CCP, is read together with the information on average ages from Table 5.2, the extent of political incorporation during the reform era for cadres in the provincial administration is emphasized. Individuals on track to be promoted quickly up the political hierarchy would usually appear to be admitted to the CCP at the age of 22 to 24 years. For the cadres in the provincial administration who have been interviewed, the average age on entry was 32 years, while their average age (at the end of 1998) was 55 years.

As Table 5.5 indicates, membership of the CCP was high for all categories of the local economic elite interviewed. Even the figures of 56 percent of private entrepreneurs and 39 percent of owner–operators as party members were not low given the age difference with other categories of the local elite. More interesting is the extent to which the statistics presented reflect the existence of a substantial portion of the economic elite who had been involved in the party–state even before reform, as well as the extent to which CCP members, technocrats, and entrepreneurs have sought accommodation during the reform

Table 5.5   Shanxi local elites: membership of CCP (interviewees, 1996–8)

	Membership of CCP (%)	Average age on entry to CCP (years)	Entry into CCP:	
			Pre-reform (before 1978) (%)	Reform era (after 1978) (%)
Cadres:				
Provincial administration	100	32	67	33
District offices	100	23	91	1
County	100	24	58	42
Section level	100	23	83	17
Entrepreneurs:				
State sector managers	100	28	30	70
Urban enterprise managers	71	30	41	59
Rural entrepreneurs	77	31	46	54
Private entrepreneurs	56	25	13	87
Joint venture managers	73	26	63	37
Private enterprise managers	66	22		100
Owner–operators	39	29	21	79

era. Sizable proportions of those interviewed who were state sector managers, urban enterprise managers, rural entrepreneurs, and joint venture managers had been members of the CCP even before 1979. At the same time, as the relatively high average ages on entry to the CCP emphasize, even greater proportions of the state sector and urban enterprise managers, as well as rural entrepreneurs, were only admitted to the party after 1978.

In addition, the CCP has clearly sought to incorporate most of the more successful owner–operators and private entrepreneurs into the activities of the party–state. Often this has been through recruitment into the CCP, as Table 5.5 indicates, though this technique is not used exclusively. A number of high-profile, successful private entrepreneurs (most usually responsible for fairly large-scale enterprises) have quite explicitly not been permitted to join the CCP, even though party branches have been established in their enterprises. Instead they are publicized as "model entrepreneurs" and become delegates to the Provincial and National People's Congresses, which can certainly be regarded as other forms of membership in the party–state.[38]

Standards of living

Despite problems of observation and measurement, consideration of the standard of living of those members of the various categories of the local elite interviewed would appear to indicate clear differences between political and economic elites. Even allowing for various forms of hidden income, cadres had considerably less real disposable income than members of the economic elites. On the other hand, cadres had considerably more access to various public goods than their business counterparts. However, there is also evidence of differences within both the political and economic elites, particularly those which more accurately reflect the rural–urban divide. The village-based section-level cadres and rural entrepreneurs might have been able to live in relatively large private houses, but their children were relatively less likely than those of other parts of the political elite, and indeed sections of the economic elite, to attend university. While it is difficult to assess the wealth and access to privilege of the local elite, the attempt has been made by presenting information on wages and housing (Table 5.6) and the number and education of children (Table 5.7) for each category of the local elite interviewed.

Table 5.6 provides data on the average monthly monetary wage for each category of the local elite interviewed, as well as the average housing size. Monthly wages have been calculated at 1997 costs with appropriate adjustments made for individuals interviewed in 1996. It is common practice for all entrepreneurs to be paid a monthly wage, even when they may be the effective owner of an enterprise and the primary or exclusive recipient of any net profit. There are essentially two types of housing: public housing which is provided through the state, available only to those working in the party–state, state sector enterprises, or other state activities (such as schools and universities) and heavily subsidized; and private housing which must be built (and paid for) individually or rented.

Table 5.6   Shanxi local elites: living standards (interviewees, 1996–8)

| | Average wages per month (yuan) | Average size of dwelling (m²) for individuals occupying: | |
		Public housing	Private housing
Cadres:			
Provincial administration	798	78	
District offices	705	88	90
County	490	45	90
Section level	496	70	120
Entrepreneurs:			
State sector managers	1,342	71	97
Urban enterprise managers	1,408	72	98
Rural entrepreneurs	1,477		163
Private entrepreneurs	2,159	77	197
Joint venture managers	2,203	69	218
Private enterprise managers	1,367		
Owner–operators	2,158	50	139

The extent to which (as is indicated in Table 5.6) individual members of the economic elite in the public and private sectors access public housing is another indicator of state–society interdependence, even when (as was sometimes the case) some of those interviewed explained that public housing was provided through the employment of either their spouse or a parent.

Certainly, figures for monthly wages are not accurate representations of the incomes of either cadres or economic elites. Cadres have considerable hidden income. In addition to heavily subsidized housing costs,[39] they have no health and insurance costs, guaranteed pensions, and often free education for their children. They also receive small cash supplements and bonuses. All of the economic elites have additional income. Some whose jobs are closely tied to or part of the party–state – such as state sector and urban enterprise managers – also have hidden income similar to cadres. Managers and entrepreneurs in the public and private sectors may be able to offset personal costs – housing is probably the most substantial – in various legitimate ways as enterprise costs. Additional monetary income for the managers and entrepreneurs in the public and private sectors comes from their share of profits. An essential characteristic of the public sector is that entrepreneurs and managers all have a production-related income. In addition, private entrepreneurs and owner–operators have access to most or all of an enterprise's net profits. State sector managers are usually remunerated more like cadres, with a performance-based bonus system, rather than having their wages linked directly to production or the market.

Even were it possible to take all these various and competing factors into account, it is still likely that the local political elite would still have had less real disposable income than the local economic elite once the latter's bonuses and other shares of enterprise output were taken into account. However, these differences in general are not likely to be as great as the crude figures presented in Table 5.6 would seem to suggest. Interviewees in Taiyuan (the provincial capital of Shanxi) during 1998 estimated that a market sector monthly income of about RMB 2000 was equivalent to a monthly cadre's income of about RMB 800. All the same, cadres at county and section level were still likely to be considerably poorer than their equivalents in the economic elite. These were the cadres who dealt routinely with rural and private entrepreneurs and owner–operators who had immediate access to sizable financial and non-financial resources.

Housing may not be as reliable an indicator of real disposable income in China as it is generally elsewhere, and there are clearly differences in the housing market between rural and urban areas, and even across different regions of Shanxi. It is entirely conceivable, for example, that the average house size of 163 m^2 for rural entrepreneurs might be regarded as an equivalent indicator in either wealth or status of the average apartment size of 78 m^2 for cadres in the provincial adminis-tration living in central Taiyuan. None the less, information about housing provision does reinforce suggestions that managers and entrepreneurs in the public and private sectors were considerably better housed than the local political elite. The differences are not simply those of square meters. In most cases members of the economic elite were in private housing which they had built themselves. In contrast, the majority of the political elite were housed publicly, having been allo-cated to existing buildings, most of which were very poor-quality, old housing stock.

The number of children in a family is perhaps a more reliable indicator of real disposable income for members of the economic elite, particularly since the intro-duction of the "One-child Family Policy" in 1979. Preferences for sons and the introduction of the "One-child Family Policy" have led to pressures for larger families. State sanctions against more than one child have meant that it is expen-sive to have additional children as there are often punitive costs to be covered, as well as the loss of benefits and the additional costs of an extra person. These developments have meant that in general it is only the wealthy who can afford larger families. As Table 5.7 indicates the average family size for each category of the local economic elite was well in excess of the state norm. As might be expected given the evidence that the "One-child Family Policy" is both less enforced and less enforceable in China's villages,[40] there was a slightly higher average for the families of rural entrepreneurs. These figures are only marginally adjusted down-ward if controls are imposed to take account of those individuals whose children had been born before the introduction of the "One-child Family Policy".

As Table 5.7 also indicates, large family size would appear to be a general characteristic of elite status. However, in the case of the local political elite the ability to have more than one child was presumably a function of political status rather than wealth. Once again the figures for average family size for each cate-gory of the local political elite are only marginally adjusted downward if those children born before the introduction of the "One-child Family Policy" are excluded from calculations.[41]

The provision of public housing is one example of access to public goods. Attendance at university is another, with considerably more significance for the intergenerational transfer of privilege.[42] Before the Cultural Revolution and since the start of the reform era, university graduation has brought guaranteed, high-

Table 5.7   Shanxi local elites: number and education of children (interviewees, 1996–8)

	Average family size, no. of children	Children attended university (%)
Cadres:		
Provincial administration	2.8	71
District offices	2.1	82
County	1.7	56
Section level	1.9	40
Entrepreneurs:		
State sector managers	1.8	66
Urban enterprise managers	1.9	48
Rural entrepreneurs	2.5	21
Private entrepreneurs	1.9	46
Joint venture managers	2.7	50
Private enterprise managers	n.a.	
Owner–operators	1.9	25

status employment and the prospect of entry to the elite. In particular, with reform, as the example of the private enterprise managers bears witness, it can also bring a reasonable level of wealth at a fairly early stage in a career. The proportions of children who attended or had graduated from university for each category of the local elite are also presented in Table 5.7. These calculations have been based on only those children of the local elites who would have been old enough to attend university, had the opportunity presented itself. The children of three categories of the local political elite – cadres in the provincial administration, district offices, and at county level – had overwhelmingly attended university, a characteristic shared by the children of state sector managers. The exception among the local political elite were the children of section-level cadres. Their university attendance rate was not low, but it was lower than any other category of the local elite except for the children of rural entrepreneurs and owner–operators. The latter is partly explained by the relative average youth of owner–operators. The children of those owner–operators who were old enough to have attended university would have had almost no opportunities to do so because of the dislocations caused to the educational system by the Cultural Revolution and its aftermath.

Elite formation

The case could easily be made that Shanxi's political economy in the 1990s was structurally conservative: the CCP had deep social roots, the central state had considerable investment and presence, and the reform process had been extremely slow to get started in the province.[43] This may well explain the emphasis on the interdependence and accommodation of local political and economic elites that emerges in describing their development under reform. Specific social and economic interests for each category of the local elite became more identifiable with reform. However, this process of elite formation blurred rather than polarized the relationship between state and society.

The evidence from those interviewed in Shanxi about the formation of local elites emphasizes the centrality of the CCP socially, economically, and politically. However, in keeping with changed national priorities, the CCP's processes and mobilizatory techniques were inclusionary and accommodative rather than ideologically driven. This too may have changed the ways in which the party–state operated, and may even have affected the contents of policies being implemented, without necessarily weakening the party–state.

The social role of the CCP in the formation of the new economic elites was perhaps the most dramatic: cadres may have been recruited largely from the non-party peasantry, but their children moved on in disproportionate numbers to become managers and entrepreneurs in the public and private sectors of the economy. They almost certainly in most cases built on their parents' associations within the party–state to the extent that those who were small-scale owner–operators often did not see an immediate need to become members of the CCP themselves. Table 5.8 summarizes information about family membership detailing whether interviewees had at least one parent who had been a member of the CCP (at the time of the interviewee's birth) and then whether the interviewees were themselves party members. Overall, very few of the members of the local economic elite interviewed in Shanxi had no personal experience of the party–state in these ways: only 21 percent of the urban enterprise managers, 19 percent of the rural entrepreneurs, 27 percent of the private entrepreneurs, 13 percent of joint venture managers, and 37 percent of the owner–operators.

In economic development the local political and economic elites, particularly at the most local levels, established close communities of mutual interest where county and section-level cadres on the one hand, and rural entrepreneurs, private entrepreneurs, and owner–operators on the other, all worked together. Politically, as Table 5.8 also indicates, most of the local economic elite were members of the CCP. There were two predominant career paths for the managers and entrepreneurs of the public and private sectors: either they were

Table 5.8 Shanxi local elites: family membership of CCP (interviewees, 1996–8)

	Parent member of CCP		Parent not member of CCP	
	Interviewee:		*Interviewee:*	
	Member	*Not member*	*Member*	*Not member*
Cadres:				
Provincial administration		18	82	
District offices				100
County		42	58	
Section level				100
Entrepreneurs:				
State sector managers		24	76	
Urban enterprise managers	8	17	54	21
Rural entrepreneurs	10	24	48	19
Private entrepreneurs	7	27	27	27
Joint venture managers	13	38	38	13
Private enterprise managers	15	45	40	
Owner–operators	23	16	23	37

former senior members of the party–state at local levels who had taken the lead in developing economic initiatives and enterprises; or they were individuals who, having become successful entrepreneurs, were then recruited to the CCP. The relatively high proportion of owner–operators outside the CCP, though still not large, reflects the process of incorporation. Owner–operators were generally younger entrepreneurs with small-scale operations who as they became more successful would become private entrepreneurs, at which stage if they were not already CCP members it would be more likely for them to be invited to join.

The centrality of the CCP to elite formation might superficially suggest that not very much had changed with reform at the local level, at least in Shanxi. However, the local elite of the 1990s were not the former single, and fairly homogeneous, local power elite of the pre-reform era. They had been replaced by a more complex network, containing several distinct categories of interdependent political and economic elites.

At first sight the local political elite would still appear to have been fairly homogeneous, characterized by their non-party peasant backgrounds and high levels of educational achievement. While those characteristics undoubtedly accurately reflected the CCP's recruitment procedures for potential leadership cadres, they also masked significant differences within the political elite. Most obviously, there were significant differences in prospects if not in background between section-level cadres and those at other levels; significant differences in background between the cadres in the provincial administration and those at other levels; and age differences between the older cadres in the provincial administration and district offices, and the younger cadres in the counties.

Cadres in the provincial administration were a significant technocratic elite, having been largely responsible for the introduction of reform into the province. Largely university educated they were not notably from peasant families and a substantial proportion were only recruited to the party–state in the reform era. In contrast, those in the district offices were more long-standing activists of the party–state, as was more appropriate for cadres whose function was often much more political and required less interaction with the various categories of the economic elite.

County leadership cadres were on the whole a younger breed of more mobile individuals, testing themselves for future glory. The product of, in roughly equal proportions, party schools and universities, their main focus was economic development. Success at the county level would likely lead to rapid promotion. Section-level cadres within the counties were the most local of the political elites. They were usually natives or at the very least long-term residents of their workplace, and worked very closely with local entrepreneurs and managers, especially in the rural areas. Like the rural entrepreneurs and private entrepreneurs in the countryside, the life prospects of rural cadres were shaped largely by rural conditions. However, rural section-level cadres were usually better educated, though considerably poorer, than the entrepreneurs and managers with whom they worked.

Among the local economic elites, the managers of state sector enterprises and, even to some extent, the managers of urban enterprises had profiles very like those of cadres. Both were on the whole a more technocratically oriented version of a local cadre. University or college educated, they tended to work outside their native place but none the less to have been working for some considerable time in the same enterprise from which the current company had emerged. Their mone-tary wages were generally higher than those received by cadres, though they appeared to have access to public goods as did cadres. Urban enterprise managers were likely to have earned more than state sector managers through their greater exposure to the market, and were less likely to be members of the CCP.

Rural entrepreneurs were most likely to be former village heads or local party secretaries of their native place, with little formal education and large families. Rather than technical innovators they were the local leaders with the vision and ability to organize local communities behind specific initiatives. They worked very closely with section-level cadres, as did public sector private entrepreneurs who were essentially successful owner–operators who had expanded their economic activities. When owner–operators attempted to develop, or indeed as (on occasion) private entrepreneurs attempted to develop further, they needed to find additional investors and guarantors of land and labor, which often meant cooperation with units of local government. Private entrepreneurs were likely to have had parents with backgrounds in the party–state, to have been relatively well educated, and were themselves likely to have had earlier careers in the administration of the party–state or in business.

Somewhat surprisingly given the nature of their current employment, joint venture managers were not necessarily likely to have high educational qualifica-tions, though they were usually politically well connected. They were long-term members of the CCP whose parents had also been members of the party–state: members of the Cultural Revolution generation whose education was inter-rupted at that time, and who joined the CCP either in the late 1960s or in the early 1970s. The private enterprise managers interviewed in Shanxi were very young, fairly recent university (or sometimes college) graduates, usually single, and highly mobile. They were hired for their technical expertise and managerial skills. Most were the children of party members who had themselves joined the CCP at an early age when at university, in the past a marker for potential future political advancement.

Owner–operators were on the whole young, somewhat poorly educated, small-scale entrepreneurs. Although a substantial proportion had not joined the CCP, many had at least one parent who had been a member of the CCP or who had worked in the party–state. Fairly well-off in terms of real disposable income, most were natives of the place where they developed their enterprise. Quite apart from the opportunity to make money, many had gone into business on their own because they preferred to work for themselves.

Conclusion

Local elite formation in Shanxi during the reform era has been characterized by both increasing diversity and the centrality of the CCP. Although this may seem somewhat paradoxical, the party–state has changed to accommodate the social change that accompanied reform. Changes in the party–state – particularly its encouragement and incorporation of alternative social elites – have necessarily altered and had an impact on the relations between state and society. However, there is little evidence that these changes have led so far to increased polarization between state and society. On the contrary, the various elements of the local political and economic elites developed interdependently, even though reform may have created differences in wealth and access to public goods.

State and society both clearly changed in the process of reform. Local elites became inherently more diverse, and the former local elite were certainly not simply replaced by a single political elite and another single business elite. Moreover, sections of both political and business elites clearly had more in common across any imagined state–society divide, rather than being constrained by such differences. There were emerging politicized business elites, and at the same time local political elites changed and became more representative of society in a range of ways. As a result local political and business elites were more likely to have shared concerns, behaviors, and interests, including that of doing business.

Notes

1   Indeed, it is now often argued that the reform era has been led more from "below" than "above," as for example: Barbara Krug, "Moving the Mountains: Transformation as Institution Building from Below," in J. Backhaus and G. Krause (eds.), *The Political Economy of Transformation: Country Studies* (Metropolis: Marburg, 1997); Lynn T. White III, *Unstately Power*, vol. 1 of *Local Causes of China's Economic Reforms* (Armonk, NY: M. E. Sharpe, 1998); and Kate Xiao Zhou, *How the Farmers Changed China* (Boulder, CO: Westview, 1996).

2   See for example, and variously: David S. G. Goodman, "The People's Republic of China: The party–state, capitalist revolution and new entrepreneurs," in Richard Robison and David S. G. Goodman (eds.), *The New Rich in Asia: Mobile-phones, McDonalds and Middle Class Revolution* (London: Routledge, 1996), p. 225; Victor Nee, "Social Inequalities in Reforming State Socialism: Between Redistribution and Markets in China," *American Sociological Review*, vol. 56, no. 3 (1991), p. 267; Ole Odgaard, "Entrepreneurs and Elite Formation in Rural China," *Australian Journal of Chinese Affairs*, no. 28 (1992); Margaret M. Pearson, *China's New Business Elite: The Political Consequences of Economic Reform* (Berkeley: University of California Press, 1997); and Susan Young, *Private Business and Economic Reform in China* (Armonk, NY: M. E. Sharpe, 1995).

3   David S. G. Goodman, "The Localism of Local Leadership: Cadres in Reform Shanxi," *Journal of Contemporary China*, vol. 9, no. 24 (2000), pp. 159–83; and Richard Latham, "The Implications of Rural Reforms for Grass-Roots Cadres," in Elizabeth Perry and Christine Wong (eds.), *The Political Economy of Reform in Post-Mao China* (Cambridge, MA: Harvard University Press, 1985), p. 131.

4   See, most comprehensively: Barry Naughton, *Growing out of the Plan: Chinese Economic Reform, 1978–93* (Cambridge: Cambridge University Press, 1996).

5   See, for example: R. Benewick, "Towards a Developmental Theory of Constitutionalism," *Government and Opposition*, vol. 33, no. 4 (Autumn 1998), p. 442; and Carlos Wing-hung Lo, *China's Legal Awakening: Legal Theory and Criminal Justice in Deng's Era* (Hong Kong: Hong Kong University Press, 1995).

6   See, for example: Susan V. Lawrence, "Democracy, Chinese Style," *Australian Journal of Chinese Affairs*, vol. 32 (July 1994), p. 61; Kevin J. O'Brien, "Implementing Political Reform in China's Villages," *Australian Journal of Chinese Affairs*, vol. 32 (July 1994), p.

33; Kevin J. O'Brien and Lianjiang Li, "The Politics of Lodging Complaints in Rural China," *China Quarterly*, no. 143 (September 1995), p. 756; and Minxin Pei, "Citizens v. Mandarins: Administrative Litigation in China," *China Quarterly*, no. 152 (December 1997).

7 The most straightforward statement of this position is R. M. Glassman, *China in Transition: Communism, Capitalism and Democracy* (New York: Praeger, 1991).

8 See, for example: John Dearlove, "Village Politics," in R. Benewick and P. Wingrove (eds.), *China in the 1990s* (London: Macmillan, 1995), esp. p. 130; George C. S. Lin, "Transformation of a Rural Economy in the Zhujiang Delta," *China Quarterly*, no. 149 (March 1997), p. 56; and Ole Odgaard, "Entrepreneurs and Elite Formation in Rural China," *Australian Journal of Chinese Affairs*, no. 28 (1992).

9 For example:

> Rural industries were the most presentable outcome of this entrepreneurialism, and their resources created new local power. … The reform syndrome was generally foisted on China's most famous leaders by myriad ex-farmer leaders whose names are not publicly known. When the powerful lack enough resources to stay where they are, as Pareto suggested, the elite changes. This is now happening in China, as the centralist revolutionaries have already done all they can for most people.
>
> (Lynn T. White III, *Unstately Power*, vol. 1 in *Local Causes of China's Economic Reforms* (Armonk, NY: M. E. Sharpe, 1998), p. 151)

See also: Weixing Chen, "Peasant Challenge in Post-Communist China," *Journal of Contemporary China*, vol. 6, no. 14 (March 1997), p. 101.

10 For example: Gordon White, *Riding the Tiger: The Politics of Economic Reform in Post-Mao China* (London: Macmillan, 1993).

11 Jude Howell, "Refashioning State–Society Relations in China," *European Journal of Development Research*, vol. 6, no. 1 (1994), p. 197; Jude Howell, "Civil Society," in Benewick and Wingrove (eds.), *China in the 1990s*, p. 73; Gordon White, "Prospects for Civil Society in China: A Case Study of Xiaoshan City," *Australian Journal of Chinese Affairs*, vol. 29 (1993), p. 63; G. White, J. Howell, and X. Shang, *In Search of Civil Society: Market Reform and Social Change in Contemporary China* (Oxford: Clarendon Press, 1996).

12 Weixing Chen, "The Political Economy of Rural Industrialization in China: Village Conglomerates in Shandong Province," *Modern China*, vol. 24, no. 1 (1998), p.73; David S. G. Goodman, "Collectives and Connectives, Capitalism and Corporatism: Structural Change in China," *Journal of Communist Studies and Transition Politics*, vol. 11, no. 1 (March 1995), p. 12; Nan Lin, "Local Market Socialism: Local Corporatism in Action in Rural China," *Theory and Society*, no. 24 (1995), p. 301; J. C. Oi, "The Role of the Local State in China's Transitional Economy," *China Quarterly*, no. 144 (December 1995), p. 1132; Pei Xiaolin, "Township–Village Enterprises, Local Governments, and Rural Communities: The Chinese Village as a Firm during Economic Transition," in Eduard B. Vermeer, Frank Pieke, and Woei Lien Chong (eds.), *Cooperative and Collective in China's Rural Development: Between State and Private Interests* (Armonk, NY: M. E. Sharpe, 1998), p. 110; and Andrew Walder, "Local Governments as Industrial Firms: An Organizational Analysis of China's Transitional Economy," *American Journal of Sociology*, vol. 101, no. 2 (1995), p. 263.

13 Kristen Parris, "Private Entrepreneurs as Citizens: From Leninism to Corporatism," *China Information*, vol. X, nos. 3/4 (Spring 1996), p. 1; D. J. Solinger, "Urban Entrepreneurs and the State: The Merger of State and Society," in D. J. Solinger (ed.), *China's Transition from Socialism: Statist Legacies and Market Reforms 1980–1990* (Armonk, NY: M. E. Sharpe, 1993), p. 256; and Mayfair Mei-hui Yang, "Between State and Society: The Construction of Corporateness in Chinese Socialist Factories," *Australian Journal of Chinese Affairs*, vol. 22 (1989), p. 31.

14 Christian Henriot and Shi Lu, *La Réforme des Enterprises en Chine: Les enterprises shanghai-ennes entre État et marché* (Enterprise reform in China: enterprises in Shanghai between state and market) (Paris: L'Harmattan, 1996); Margaret M. Pearson, "The Janus Face of Business Associations in China: Socialist Corporatism in Foreign Enterprises," *Australian Journal of Chinese Affairs*, no. 31 (1994), p. 25; and David Wank, "Private Business, Bureaucracy, and Political Alliance in a Chinese City," *Australian Journal of Chinese Affairs*, no. 33 (1995), p. 55.

15 As Perry argues in "Trends in the Study of Chinese Politics: State–Society Relations," *China Quarterly*, no. 139 (September 1994), esp. p. 710ff., social science research is likely to prove more productive if it adopts a perspective of spatial difference across China rather than proceeding from the assumption of uniformity. Melanie Manion, "Survey Research in the Study of Contemporary China: Learning from Local Samples,"*China Quarterly*, no. 139 (September 1994), provides excellent guidance on the contextualization of local studies. See also: David S. G. Goodman, "China in Reform: The View from the Provinces," in David S. G. Goodman (ed.), *China's Provinces in Reform: Class, community and political culture* (London: Routledge, 1997); Lynn T. White III, *Unstately Power*, vol. 1 in *Local Causes of China's Economic Reforms* (Armonk, NY: M. E. Sharpe, 1998), esp. p. 54.

16 Mehran Kamrava and Frank Omora, "Civil Society and Democratization in Comparative Perspective: Latin America and the Middle East," *Third World Quarterly*, vol. 19, no. 5 (December 1998), esp. p. 894.

17 1997 economic development statistics are taken from Shanxi Statistical Bureau, "1997 Shanxisheng guojia jingji shehui fazhan tongji bao" (The 1997 Shanxi Social and Economic Development Statistical Bulletin), *Shanxi jingji ribao* (Shanxi Economics Daily), 27 February 1998, p. 2. A report on Shanxi's development during the 1990s may be found in Governor Sun Wensheng's speech to the 9th Shanxi Provincial People's Congress on January 8, 1998, "Quanmian guanche dangde shiwuda jingshen baxingjin fuminde hongwei daye duixiang ershiyi shiji" (Push forward the great task of invigorating and enriching Shanxi into the 21st century), *Shanxi zhengbao* (Shanxi Gazette) (February 1998), p. 32. RMB 8.3 (*Renminbi*, or People's currency) = 1 US$.

18 For further information on the development of Shanxi see: Shaun Breslin, "Shanxi: China's Powerhouse," in David S. G. Goodman (ed.), *China's Regional Development* (London: Routledge, 1989), p. 135; Donald G. Gillin, *Warlord Yen Hsi-shan in Shansi Province 1911–1949* (Princeton: Princeton University Press, 1967); and David S. G. Goodman, "King Coal and Secretary Hu: Shanxi's Third Modernisation," in Feng Chongyi and Hans Hendrischke (eds.), *The Political Economy of China's Provinces: Competitive and comparative advantage* (London: Routledge, 1999).

19 "Shanxi Jianhang xindai zhanlue he zhizhu chanye xuanze" (The Shanxi Construction Bank's credit strategy and selection of industries for support) *Touzi daokan* (Investment Guide), no. 1 (1 February 1996), p. 9.

20 Jia Lijun, "'Hongmaozi' zhende ganzhaima?" (Has the 'Red Cap' really been removed?), *Shanxi fazhan dabao* (Shanxi Development Herald), 19 May 1998, p. 2.

21 Statistics for 1997 are calculated from Zhonghua renmin gongheguo guojia tongji ju (ed.), *Zhongguo tongji nianjian 1998* (China statistical yearbook 1998) (Beijing: Zhongguo tongji chubanshe, 1998), p. 435. These national figures are used for comparative purposes as provincial and national compilations of statistics are often inconsistent. See: Carsten Herrmann-Pillath (ed.), *Wirtschaftliche Entwicklung in Chinas Provinzen und Regionen, 1978–1992* (The economic development of China's provinces and regions), (Baden-Baden: Nomos, 1995), esp. p. 35.

22 *Shanxi tongji nianjian 1998* (Shanxi statistical yearbook 1998) (Beijing: Zhongguo tongji chubanshe, 1998), p. 19.

23 293 individuals were interviewed across Shanxi Province during 1996 to 1998 as part of a project to investigate the emergence of political communities and the negotiation of identity in Shanxi Province, north China. The project was supported by a research

grant from the Australian Research Council. Professor Tian Youru of the Modern Shanxi Research Institute, and Li Xueqian of Shanxi University, provided help and assistance without which this project would not have taken place. Neither they nor indeed anyone else in Shanxi who has contributed to this project, including those interviewed, are in any way responsible for the interpretation or views expressed here.

24 Xu Guosheng, "Shanxi jingji luohou shei zhiguo?" (Who bears responsibility for Shanxi's economic backwardness?), *Shanxi fazhan dabao* (Shanxi Development Herald), 2 January 1998, p. 4.

25 Interviews with fifty-four leading cadres have provided the data presented here. Of these, eighteen were provincial administration cadres, twelve were district cadres, twelve were county cadres, and twelve were sub-county section-level cadres.

26 Additional specific information on cadres in Shanxi may be found in David S. G. Goodman, "The Localism of Local Leadership: Cadres in Reform Shanxi," *Journal of Contemporary China*, vol. 9, no. 24 (2000), pp. 159–83.

27 *Shanxi tongji nianjian 1998* (Shanxi statistical yearbook 1998) (Beijing: Zhongguo tongji chubanshe, 1998), pp. 26, 211.

28 *Zhongguo tongji nianjian 1998* (China statistical yearbook 1998) (Beijing: Zhongguo tongji chubanshe, 1998), p. 419.

29 Barbara Krug, "Political Entrepreneurship in China: The Political Economy at the Local Level," Unpublished paper, 1999.

30 Further detail and description of these processes may be found in: David S. G. Goodman, "Collectives and Connectives, Capitalism and Corporatism: Structural Change in China," *Journal of Communist Studies and Transition Politics*, vol. 11, no. 1 (March 1995); and Victor Nee, "Organisational Dynamics of Market Transition: Hybrid Forms, Property Rights, and Mixed Economy in China," *Administrative Science Quarterly*, vol. 37, no. 1 (1992), p. 237.

31 Susan Young, "Policy, Practice and the Private Sector in China," *Australian Journal of Chinese Affairs*, no. 21 (1989).

32 For example: Lynn T. White III, *Unstately Power*, vol. 1 of *Local Causes of China's Economic Reforms* (New York: M. E. Sharpe, 1998), esp. p. 127; and Susan Young, "Wealth but not Security: Attitudes Towards Private Business in China in the 1980s," *Australian Journal of Chinese Affairs*, no. 25 (1991).

33 Interviews with 230 members of the local economic elite have provided the data presented here. Of these, fifty were state sector enterprise managers, thirty-three were public sector urban enterprise managers, thirty-two were public sector rural entrepreneurs, eighteen were public sector private entrepreneurs, fourteen were managers of joint venture enterprises, twenty-three were managers of private enterprises, and sixty-three were owner–operators.

34 One of the largest and most colorful in Shanxi is the Antai International Enterprise Group Company, led by Li Anmin, which is based in and dominates Jiexiu County. Founded originally on coke production it has now expanded into a range of coal industry by-products, fashion and textiles, and owns its own trains. An early biography of Li Anmin is: Liu Liping et al. (eds.), *Zhongguo dangdai qiyejia mingdian – Shanxi tao* (Contemporary Entrepreneurs in China – Shanxi volume) (Beijing: Gongren chubanshe, 1989), p. 302.

35 The lowest proportions of provincial nativity are to be found amongst the urban enterprise managers (75 percent natives of Shanxi) and the cadres of the provincial administration (78 percent).

36 Chinese political culture differentiates carefully between the individual's place of birth and the family's native place which may often be a more potent form of identification.

37 The category of *University* has been employed exclusively for (minimum) four-year degree programs in universities and institutes. *College* refers more inclusively to all post-secondary two- or three-year programs, including adult colleges, party schools, and training courses.

38 For example: Li Anmin, Antai International Enterprise Group Company, Jiexiu; Liang Wenhai, Shanxi Huanhai Group Company, Yuci; and Han Changan, Lubao Coking Group Company, Lucheng, all of whom have been national model entrepreneurs of various kinds. Li and Liang have been delegates to the Provincial People's Congress, Han was elected to the National People's Congress in 1998. "Li Anmin," in Liu Liping et al. (eds.), *Zhongguo dangdai qiyejia mingdian – Shanxi tao* (Contemporary entrepreneurs in China – Shanxi volume) (Beijing: Gongren chubanshe, 1989), p. 302; and Wang Yonghai, Liu Yaoming, Wang Jikang, and Zhang Guilong, "Shanxi Huanhai jituan yougongsi zhongshizhang Liang Wenhai yu tade Huanhai shiye he huanbao zhanlüe" (General manager of the Shanxi Huanhai Group Company, Liang Wenhai, his Huanhai business and environmental strategy), *Shanxi Ribao* (The Shanxi Daily), 22 September 1996, p. 4. Additional information derived in discussions with Li Anmin, interviewed in Yi'an township, Jiexiu City, June 1, 1996; Liang Wenhai, interviewed in Yuci, October 29, 1996; and Han Changan, interviewed in Dianshang, Lucheng, October 14, 1998.

39 Housing costs vary not only between rural and urban districts but also among different cities or towns and markets. In Taiyuan, for example, in 1997 a publicly provided apartment of about 90 m^2 would cost about 30 yuan a month including utilities, whereas a private apartment of about the same size could easily cost 45,000 yuan just to purchase.

40 A. John Jowett, "Mainland China: A National One-child Program Does Not Exist," *Issues & Studies* (September, 1989), p. 48; Elisabeth Croll, Delia Davin, and Penny Kane (eds.), *China's One-child Family Policy* (London: Macmillan, 1985).

41 While the local economic elites had an equal number of boys and girls, the cadres had twice as many daughters as sons. This ratio remained constant even if children born before the introduction of the "One-child Family Policy" were excluded from calculations.

42 C. Montgomery Broaded and Chongshun Liu, "Family Background, Gender and Educational Attainment in Urban China," *China Quarterly*, no. 145 (March 1996), p. 53; and Gordon White, *The Politics of Class and Class Origin: The Case of the Cultural Revolution* (Australian National University, Contemporary China Centre paper, 1976).

43 Bai Suyu (ed.), *Dangdai Zhongguo de Shanxi* (Shanxi Today), 1 (Beijing: Zhongguo shehui kexue chubanshe, 1991), p. 17ff.

6 The reform of state-owned enterprises in mainland China

A societal perspective

Teh-chang Lin

Introduction

Under the planned economic system, the functions of the government and state-owned enterprises (SOEs) have performed very poorly in mainland China. SOEs, in particular, have become affiliated organs of governmental agencies. The government, through assigning quotas on product types, and quantity and quotas of labor and wages, directly intervenes in the production, operation, and management of SOEs. Alternatively, SOEs have also to bear a lot of responsibility for social affairs that should have been handled by the government, thus resulting in financial and administrative burdens. By the end of 1997, the number of formal employees of SOEs was 107.66 million, compared to only 28 million for urban collective-owned units.[1] Total labor insurance and welfare funds of SOEs reached RMB 257.8 billion in 1997. Moreover, the enterprises have to pay RMB 255.4 billion by themselves to cover such funds.[2] This system has resulted in the phenomenon of "enterprises running small societies," where SOEs need to utilize RMB 54 billion to subsidize public welfare and facilities.[3]

In societal terms, to establish an effective and coherent social security and welfare system nationwide is one of the major resolutions in the reform of SOEs. The construction of such an effective social security mechanism would certainly release the SOEs from their financial burdens in the running of their "small societies." However, there is also a clear signal that these SOEs, due to their malfunctions, are no longer able to offer social benefits for their workers as previously provided under a planned economy. As a result, the transformation will eventually lead to a change in the old connections between the workers and SOEs, and even between the workers and society. Under this changing context, the original state–society relationship in mainland China prior to 1978 would thus inevitably need to be redefined.

This chapter explores the issues confronted by the SOEs in mainland China from a societal perspective. In other words, this chapter claims that the core in the reform of SOEs is how to remove the social burdens and then to enhance their efficiency and production. In doing so, unemployment insurance, social pension for retirees, medical care, and housing policy all need to be reformed according to the principle of marketization before the SOEs' reform can be accomplished. To this end, this chapter will focus on the study of the issues of social burdens on SOEs. However, although the issues of unemployment insurance, social pension, and medical care are the main themes of this chapter, it does not endeavor to go into the details of each policy. Rather, the chapter focuses on the difficulties and implications of the establishment of a social security system in the context of SOE reform. In other words, if these societal problems cannot be solved jointly by the government and enterprises, the inherent weaknesses in SOEs would then be sustained and aggravated.

Unemployment insurance

The insurance for unemployment covers workers originally from SOEs that announced bankruptcy (or those dismissed as a result of reducing their payroll by enterprises on the verge of bankruptcy), and those contract workers whose contracts have been terminated or who have been dismissed by the enterprises. By the end of 1997, according to Yu's estimate, as for the number of workers who are not required for production by the SOEs and actually have little or no work to do, the most radical estimate of surplus workers is up to 30 million. The surplus workers are mainly concentrated on SOEs. For instance, among 11.5 million surplus workers, 7.8 million of them are affiliated to the SOEs.[4] Moreover, the number of displaced workers, or so-called *xiagang* (off-duty) workers in SOEs reached 6.3 million by the end of 1997.[5] In order to avoid social instability, the major issue for the government and SOEs is: who or what institution is responsible for solving the problem of these surplus laborers?

In order to solve the problem of surplus workers, in general, there are two policy orientations. First, the SOEs should adopt various measures to settle their surplus workers, and the government should also open social settlement channels to solve those issues the SOEs cannot solve by themselves. Second, SOEs have to do their best to create job opportunities for some of their own surplus workers and the remainder should then be turned over to the government and society for help.

For the past few years, several measures have been taken to solve the problem of surplus workers in SOEs. Enhancing the development of tertiary industry so as to absorb more surplus workers from SOEs is certainly a feasible way for Beijing. However, Beijing has confronted some problems in its domestic and international economic development, especially under the influence of the Southeast Asia financial crisis. This may have had a negative impact on mainland China's future development of tertiary industry.

The establishment of labor service enterprises is also useful in absorbing some surplus workers in the urban environment. At present, 200,000 such enterprises have been established and employ 9.15 million laborers in the country. When such enterprises were initially established, they tended to provide job opportunities for the unemployed. In order to deal with their current difficult situation, however, absorbing surplus workers has become one of their main tasks. When surplus workers go to work in labor service enterprises, their former employing enterprises regard them as settled in society. They need to know that the labor service enterprises might be only temporary employment units. The surplus workers are able to seek more appropriate job opportunities after some training in labor service enterprises. Furthermore, employment training agencies and labor exchange units have also been established for solving the unemployment problem in SOEs. In 1997, the numbers of the above agencies and units were 14,328 and 34,286, respectively.[6] It was estimated that 0.7 million displaced SOE workers entered the re-employment service centers in 1997.[7]

Another way to tackle unemployment in SOEs is to encourage jobless workers to seek jobs on their own. The policy toward those workers who take this option is to allocate their unemployment compensation in one installment as their starting and supporting fund, and then to guarantee the extension and connection of their social insurance. Because these employees from SOEs have for a long time enjoyed having a pension and free medical care, and if their departure from SOEs indicates a deprivation of their rights to such social welfare, then there will be few willing to leave the SOEs and give up the guaranteed social insurance. Therefore, corresponding policies should be adopted so that they will be able to continue to obtain their social benefits. However, this is a tough task. It goes without saying that different policies among the provinces have impeded labor mobility. Moreover, the disparity within a province is also conducive to *xiagang* workers' reluctance to move their job from one place to another.

Mainland China's current unemployment insurance system started in 1986, with the issuance of "Provisional Regulations on Insurance for Workers Waiting for Employment in State-Owned Enterprises" by the State Council on July 12, 1986.[8] The regulations in 1986 intended to adopt a unified ratio of unemployment insurance premiums, for the purpose of decreasing the pension burden on SOEs. However, with the deepening of enterprise reforms, the implementation of SOE bankruptcy from theory to practice and the provisions on dismissal of workers in Article 27 of the Labor Law, the fund must be accordingly expanded to cover more unemployed people. To collect the needed funds, an alternative to be considered, apart from the contribution of 0.6 to 1 percent of the enterprises' total wages in accordance with provisions of the "Regulations of Unemployment Insurance of the State-Owned Enterprises," is that individual workers should also pay a premium for their own unemployment insurance. In the case of Chengdu, for instance, in addition to the enterprise's contribution of 2 percent of total wages, individual workers in 1998 needed also to contribute 1 percent of their wages to a pooling fund of unemployment insurance.

For SOEs, if more unemployment compensation is available for distribution, it should imply that more surplus laborers could then be settled and the financial burden on enterprises eased further. However, the current maximum term for unemployment compensation is only two years. If new jobs cannot be found within that period, this would indicate that a large number of surplus workers would be left for society to take care for. Although they are no longer subject to unemployment insurance, the government has to rely on some other means (such as social subsidy) to maintain its subsistence for social stability. However, it is worth noting that, because of financial difficulties among SOEs, about 3 million *xiagang* workers were unable to get the minimum allowance from their enterprises for basic living.[9] In addition, a contradictory situation also exists in mainland urban areas: many people have nothing to do, while many jobs are available but without any people to perform them. The central point is that the quality of the labor force is generally low and they are not qualified for jobs requiring rather high qualifications. From this perspective, strengthening the training programs for the unemployed workers will be necessary to assist them in finding a job. Again, this task is not easy to accomplish. For those unemployed workers, because of their age, they have already lost the momentum to find another new job. This situation has increased the financial burden on the government and enterprises.

Unemployed workers and surplus laborers from SOEs have become a serious economic, societal, and political challenge to mainland China. In 1997, 5.7 million urban state workers were officially registered as unemployed, and another estimated 30 million were surplus workers.[10] The introduction of wage reforms, the labor contract system, and the establishment of a social security system, from the workers' perspective, have symbolized that they no longer enjoy a lifelong entitlement to employment. SOEs, many of which suffer from chronic inefficiency and inferior competitiveness in the socialist market economy, pay wages that on average lag behind those in the non-state sector, especially in foreign-invested and joint venture enterprises. SOE workers, including the *xiagang* workers, have become the most disgruntled segment of the working class under reform. Their deep-seated discontent sometimes finds expression in protests and strikes, such as in the cases of Sichuan and Liaoning, forcing the government to slow down SOE bankruptcies and to provide a minimum living allowance for the unemployed.[11]

Social pension for retirees

In the early 1950s, mainland China initiated a state welfare program. It was a comprehensive, work-based social welfare program including generous retirement pensions. A presumption of the program was based on universal lifetime employment among urban workers, working for SOEs and collective-owned enterprises. But the benefit package enjoyed by urban workers in general and state employees in particular, notably the retirement pension, is costly for a poor society in mainland China.

In 1978, 74.5 million SOE workers and 20.5 million urban collective workers were eligible for pension benefits. In 1978, 3.1 million retired workers and staff received pensions, 2.8 million from SOEs and 0.3 million from urban collectives.[12] The number of those retiring increased ten-fold from 3.1 million in 1978 to 30.9 million in 1995, including 24 million from SOEs and 6.2 million from collective sector employers.[13] It then amounted to 32.5 million in 1997, including 26.3 million from SOEs and 6.2 million from urban collective-owned enterprises.[14] This increasing number has certainly resulted in an increase in social insurance and welfare for the SOEs. For instance, total social insurance and welfare costs rose from RMB 7.8 billion in 1978 to RMB 236 billion in 1995, increasing the total wage bill in state enterprises from 13.7 to 29.2 percent.[15] Specifically, in 1997, the total social insurance and welfare funds for those retiring from SOE were RMB 173 billion and the medial care for them reached RMB 240 billion. As a result, these funds have greatly increased the financial burden for SOEs.[16]

Furthermore, mainland China's pension system has confronted two serious problems in the 1990s: namely, a rapidly aging population and a pension crisis in the SOEs. In the past ten years, the aging of the population in mainland China has accelerated, especially in urban areas. For those SOEs with a longer history, each worker has been assumed to support one retiree. But for some newly established state enterprises, there are virtually no retirees. Furthermore, in the mid-1980s, in some older SOEs the number of retirees exceeded the number of active workers. Consequently, SOEs were responsible for paying the pension fund for their retirees, and this placed a heavy financial burden on the SOEs that made reform more difficult. Some old enterprises in Sichuan and Liaoning have thus run into trouble financially. The proportion of total social welfare expenditure devoted to pensions in SOEs increased from 57 percent in 1992 to 72 percent in 1994.[17] In 1997, the retirement pensions of SOEs amounted to RMB 89 billion.[18] Currently, most SOEs are still unable to manage the financial burden of pensions by themselves.

The old pension system has also made SOE restructuring almost impossible. SOEs are like mini welfare states, with work units that look after workers' welfare from the cradle to the grave. The bankruptcy or sale of an SOE raises a tough issue concerning the social benefits of pensioners and *xiagang* workers. If an alternative arrangement, such as a healthy social security system nationally, cannot be worked out, enterprise reform seems doomed to failure. Liquidation, joint ventures, and mergers cannot proceed smoothly unless the social burden of SOEs is successfully removed.

In 1978, the State Council issued new pension regulations for SOEs, government workers, and non-profit organizations. The prevailing retirement ages in mainland China were reaffirmed as 60 for men and 55 for women. But according to the regulations of 1978, qualifications were eased, allowing a worker to retire after ten years of continuous service rather than twenty.[19] These regulations created a problem. They were obviously intended to encourage early retirement in order to create jobs for a large flow of new workers into the urban labor force, but this has produced a negative consequence: the number of retirements jumped five-fold between 1978 and 1985, and pension costs accordingly rose from 2.8 to 10.6 percent of the urban wage bill. As the increase in pension costs became apparent, the incentives to encourage retirement were terminated.

Some new regulations have been issued several times since 1986, and there have been many experiments in retirement pension systems. On October 1, 1986, pension reforms were accompanied by employment reforms for contract workers. New workers were to be hired on a contract basis, while original workers would continue to work permanently. As a result, separate city pension pools were established for contract workers and permanent workers. Contract workers had to make their own individual contributions, while permanent workers initially did not. However, enterprises had to contribute to both pools. In the late 1980s, the pension pools were extended to include workers in collectively owned enterprises in many cities. Other enterprises, such as joint ventures, joint stock companies, and foreign enterprises, have also been brought into the pension pools in some cities, although participation is generally far from complete.

However, among the SOEs themselves, three problems still need to be addressed. First, the pension burden on different industries is different. For some traditional industries, such as the mining industry, the contribution rate is as high as about 25 percent. On the other hand, for some newly established industries, such as banking and civil aviation, the contribution rate is less then 10 percent. Second, the regional disparity concerning this burden is rather large. The pension burden for old industrial cities is heavy, but for newly emerged industrial cities it is much lighter. Third, the unified pension system is implemented mainly in SOEs. Although this is conducive to balancing the burden among SOEs, it is actually not helpful for reducing this burden on SOEs in comparison with other types of enterprises. Private and foreign-invested enterprises, developed in the past few years, have the clear characteristic of young staff; but most of them are not included in the unified pension system. This might explain why the surplus workers of SOEs are unwilling to find new jobs in non-state enterprises, since transfer from SOEs to private enterprises implies that the workers would lose any social benefits they original possessed.

In the 1990s, Beijing decided to unify the pension system, in an attempt to include all types of enterprises under a single system. The spirit of the unified pension system based on management of the pension program should be handed over from enterprises to governmental agencies, and administrative management and fund management also needed to be separated. In 1995, nationally, over 2,000 city governments had managed to replace the responsibility for collecting funds from the SOEs.[20] In 1997, 55 million SOE workers and employees had contributed to overall pension insurance, and 16 million SOE retirees had joined pension insurance. However, notably, in 1997 there was a deficit of RMB 19 billion between pensions that should have been contributed and those actually contributed.[21] This again resulted in more financial burden on the SOEs.

On June 26, 1991, the State Council proposed a three-tier retirement insurance system for employees in urban enterprises, with the basic retirement program managed by the state, supplementary retirement programs funded by enterprises, and individual savings retirement accounts chosen by each employee. State Council Document 6 of 1995 further introduced two models for the basic retirement program. City and prefecture governments were given the right to select a reform design according to their own situations. Plan I focuses on the importance of individual accounts,[22] while plan II emphasizes the social component.[23] Although local governments have flexibility to choose either plan I or plan II, it inevitably violates the original intention to establish a unified retirement insurance. For instance, most pension pooling is conducted at the county, municipality, or prefecture level, and many localities have their own separate pools for state enterprises, collective enterprises, or other population groups.

Additionally, each municipality is also attempting to differentiate its scheme from that of others in order to retain control over the pension funds. This has led to the creation of hundreds of schemes all over the country, which seriously handicaps labor mobility from SOEs to private enterprises. In July 1997, the State Council further issued a "Decision on Social Pension System", and stipulated that each enterprise must contribute no more than 20 percent of the total wage as social pension funding. Individual workers had to pay 11 percent of their wages into their personal accounts.[24]

From the perspective of economic development in mainland China, factors of production must be able to move from one sector or region to another if it is to establish a socialist market economy and restructure its SOEs. For these purposes, the pension benefits of workers must be portable. The division of the national system into many separate unfunded municipal pools makes portability difficult and will become an increasingly serious impediment to labor mobility. As a result, pension funds and individual pension accounts must be able to be transferred throughout the province or even across provinces as workers change jobs.

The problems of the current pension system in mainland China are deep-seated and widely recognized. Policy analysts have engaged in extensive discussions about how to solve these problems and design a new, sustainable pension system. Although the broad directions of reform have been clarified, implementation has indeed proven difficult, hampered by misperceptions about the costs of transition and also by the political, economic, and social implications of the change. According to Table 6.1, it is quite clear that, even in the 1990s, the SOEs are still responsible for most of their own social pensions.

Table 6.1   Pensions for SOE retirees, 1980–97 (RMB 100 million)

Year	Total pensions	Paid by enterprises	Year	Total pensions	Paid by enterprises
1980	43.4	40.1	1989	252.7	245.2
1981	53.3	50.0	1990	313.3	306.1
1982	62.1	58.9	1991	372.9	365.3
1983	74.0	70.8	1992	465.7	456.5
1984	84.6	81.6	1993	612.9	600.9
1985	116.1	112.4	1994	861.5	844.0
1986	137.5	134.2	1995	1,074.2	1,054.8
1987	168.2	164.2	1996	1,285.4	1,265.3
1988	215.6	209.0	1997	1,517.6	1,493.0

Source: *China Labour Statistical Yearbook 1998*, p. 491.

Medical care

Two major concerns in mainland China's health sector are the declining health insurance coverage and the inadequate rural access to health services. In 1998, medical care mechanisms covered only 19.5 percent of the population, but accounted for 40 percent of health expenditures.[25] Official data indicate that only 30 million people, or 2 percent of the total population of mainland China, are eligible beneficiaries of the government health insurance system.[26]

Health insurance coverage still relatively tends to concentrate in urban areas. The government insurance system now covers about 30 million people, including current government workers and retirees, the military, and university students. Its annual spending per member is on average 389 yuan per member, compared to the national average of 110 yuan. Regarding the state enterprise insurance system, it covers an estimated 140 million employees and retirees. It spends about 259 yuan per member.[27] And, most important, health insurance coverage is tied to place of work, thus impeding the labor mobility essential for a modern market economy.

However, some state enterprises have been unable to cover the health care bills of their employees and retirees. Since the systems are pay as you go, state enterprises and government units with large numbers of retirees have particularly high financial burdens. According to the "labor-protection medical care" system introduced in 1951, it stipulated that all medical expenses incurred by an ill worker and salary subsidy during leave due to illness should be financially handled by the enterprise. The enterprise should also reimburse 50 percent of the medical expenses if any family member of the worker or employee suffers from a disease. To the workers and employees, this is no doubt very beneficial welfare. However, it also results in huge financial burdens for the SOEs. That is, SOEs were required to contribute an amount equal to 14 percent of their wage bill to cover health benefits. For instance, SOEs spent RMB 15.9 billion on medical care in 1997.[28]

Moreover, SOEs are also running a great number of hospitals and clinics for their own workers and employees. As statistics show, there are 110,000 medical institutions operated by SOEs and departments other than public health departments, employing 1.4 million staff and accounting for one-third of the country's total number of medical personnel. Such medical institutions mainly serve the workers and employees of their respective enterprises and their family members. Normally, the medical costs of these self-run institutions are lower than those of public hospitals, but such a financial burden is also actually shouldered by the SOEs.

In order to alleviate the burden of medical care in SOEs, one of the options considered by the government is to establish individual medical care accounts to which an amount of money is allocated, and workers would pay the medical expenses first from their individual accounts. The deposits in the individual accounts are a kind of designated consumption and can be used only for medical care; if the allocation for the year is not used completely, the remaining amount may be transferred for use in the following year. However, when all the allocation in the individual account is used up, individuals would have to pay a certain extra amount toward medical expenses by themselves. When these medical expenses paid by individuals exceed the stipulated limit, the unified social insurance fund will partially pay for them. In other words, the higher the medical spending, the bigger the part to be paid by the unified social medical insurance fund. At the end of 1997, thirty-two cities in mainland China had gradually adopted these measures.[29]

Another option is that minor diseases would have to be covered by the individuals themselves, but serious diseases would be covered by the unified social medical insurance fund. To this end, enterprises would contribute at the same ratio to establish a unified social medical insurance fund. If workers and employees suffer from the stipulated disease, their medical expenses would be reimbursed by the unified social insurance fund at the stipulated percentage. When workers and employees suffer from diseases other than those specified, the medical expenses would have to be paid by the individuals themselves. Under this option, the responsibility of the government is defined; that is, the medical expenses resulting from particular diseases are specified and easy to control. In 1997, more than 13 million in the population had been covered by this medical care policy.[30] Additionally, the contribution percentage from the SOEs is also specified.

The third option is to take a laissez-faire approach and allow private, voluntary insurance, with some government regulations, to close part of the gap in urban coverage. Employers could choose to offer health insurance and either self-insurance or membership of a larger insurance pool. Individuals could join their employer's plan, if there is one, or voluntarily purchase private health insurance. There are problems with this model, however, in that small employers may have difficulty purchasing private insurance. Moreover, workers would be in a risky situation of losing their insurance if they changed jobs. And people with high health risks would also have difficulty obtaining coverage.

In addition to the ongoing experiments with the government and SOE insurance systems, medical care coverage needs to be broadened to include those who are uninsured in urban areas. Again, to improve efficiency in the state enterprise sector, non-competitive enterprises must be allowed to fail or restructure, and labor must thus become more mobile. Delinking pension and health benefits from the enterprise helps to make this possible. The present system is an obstacle to economic modernization, which requires labor mobility and state enterprise reform. Pension and health finance reforms are needed to ensure that workers can change jobs without jeopardizing their pension and health benefits, to deal with the problems of pay-as-you-go finance and the cost of health care for retired workers, and to facilitate reform of the SOEs.

Conclusion

In this chapter, we have discussed the social burdens of SOEs in mainland China. The reform of SOEs is a very complex issue indeed and one that has been confronted by Beijing ever since the 1980s. This reform is not simply an economic issue, but also involves societal and political impacts on mainland China. This chapter has explored how to ease the social burdens on SOEs, especially from the perspectives of unemployment insurance, social pension, and medical care, and raised some difficulties and contradictions in the reform of a social security system. However, these issues cannot be dealt with independently. In other words, if the reform of SOEs needs to be successfully accomplished to a great extent, all of these social issues have to be solved as a whole package and also initiated at the same time. If there is a prospect of such social welfare reform, then there is also hope for successful SOE reform. In other words, the establishment of a healthy social security system has become one of the major factors in determining the success of SOE reform. Moreover, the current social security system is still in its "trial and error" stages, and with great disparities in its reformation from one province to another, or even from one city to another. On the whole, these issues have not only complicated the process of SOE reform, but also become a dilemma for Beijing's authority.

It is also worth nothing that the reform of SOEs in mainland China may also have a theoretical implication on reshaping state–society relations. The economic modernization since 1978 has had consequences for the character of society in mainland China. For instance, decollectivization, the potential separation of the party–state from the enterprises, and the growth of the private sector have given rise to new socio-economic groups,[31] and thus implicitly altered the structure of society. On the one hand the old intermediary institutions such as the All-China Federation of Trade Unions, the All-China Women's Federation, and the Communist Youth League have been trying desperately to adapt to the changing environment. On the other hand new intermediary organizations responsive to the needs of new socio-economic groups have emerged in the process of marketization. Moreover, the process of socialization of social insurance and welfare in mainland China is contributing to the perception that people should gradually eschew dependence on the state.[32] This also has an impact on the state–society relationship.

The new social organizations act as a bridge between the state and the people. They provide a new, indirect channel through which the party–state can impart policy to enterprises, households, and individuals. For example, some semi-official social organizations have begun to take on social welfare activities. The Self-Employed Workers' Association uses some of its membership fees for death or sickness expenses of its members or in helping households in dire economic straits. Moreover, another important theoretical implication in this essay is that, in the context of SOE reform, Beijing is now encountering a dilemma. If the reform of SOEs fails, it will certainly be a disaster for mainland China. However, if the reform of SOEs is to be successfully completed, a perfect social security system must be established as a precondition. It is worth noting that the establishment of a unified social security system signifies that most workers will lose any social benefits that they originally had during the planned economy. It also demonstrates that workers now realize that they have to rely on themselves to make their lives better, rather than passively depend on the work-place or the government. This might be conducive to another impact on the disconnection of the original state–society relationship.

Notes

1 *China Labour Statistical Yearbook1998* (Beijing: China Statistical Publishing House, 1998), p. 7.
2 Ibid., p. 3.
3 Ibid., p. 494.
4 Yu Yun-Shin and Fu Linn, *Toward 21st Century: The New Concept of Employment in Mainland China* (Beijing: Industry and Commerce Publisher, 1998), p. 14.
5 *China Labour Statistical Yearbook 1998*, p. 432.
6 Ibid., p. 121.
7 Ibid., p. 432.
8 Gao Shangquan and Chi Fulin (eds.), *China's Social Security System* (Beijing: Foreign Languages Press, 1996), pp. 105–9.
9 *China Labour Statistical Yearbook 1998*, p. 432.
10 Ibid., p. 3.
11 Ching Kwan Lee, "The Labor Politics of Market Socialism: Collective Inaction and Class Experiences among State Workers in Guangzhou," *Modern China*, vol. 24, no. 1 (January 1998), p. 4.
12 Mark Selden and Laiyin You, "The Reform of Social Welfare in China," *World Development*, vol. 25, no. 10 (1997), p. 1660.
13 Li Jen and Yen Bo, *The Report on Chinese Economic Problems* (Beijing: Economic Daily Publisher, 1998), p. 728.
14 *China Labour Statistical Yearbook 1998*, p. 479.
15 Selden and You, "The Reform of Social Welfare in China," p. 1661.
16 *China Labour Statistical Yearbook 1998*, pp. 497–8.
17 Selden and You, "The Reform of Social Welfare in China," p. 1662.
18 *China Labour Statistical Yearbook 1998*, p. 523.
19 For instance, workers who had worked for at least twenty continuous years would get a pension of 75 percent of the standard wage; those who had worked for fifteen to twenty years would get 70 percent; and those who had worked for ten to fifteen years would get 60 percent. There was a guaranteed minimum pension of 30 yuan per month.
20 Yu Chang-miao and Lee Chun, *China after CCP's 15th National Congress* (Beijing: People's Publisher, 1997), p. 139.
21 *China Labour Statistical Yearbook 1998*, p. 459.
22 According to plan I, the basic pension system for new workers would be individual accounts. A social pool would be responsible for the pensions for those who are already retired, for current workers not fully covered by individual accounts, and for certain adjustments for retirees drawing from individual accounts. Contributions to individual accounts, at approximately 16 percent of total wage, would consist of three parts: (1) an individual contribution of 3 percent of the total wage; (2) an enterprise contribution of 8 percent of each worker's total wage; and (3) an enterprise contribution of 5 percent of the average local wage. The intention is to increase the individual contribution over time and to decrease the enterprise contribution (by 1 percent every two years for ten years) until individuals are contributing half the total to their individual accounts.
23 Plan II puts more emphasis on social pooling than on individual accounts. The plan is designed mainly for cities that had chosen an earlier Ministry of Labor pension model, with a vesting period of ten years. For those whose contribution period is

longer than ten years, the pension will consist of the following parts: (1) a social pension equivalent to 20–25 percent of the local average wage; (2) a premium pension equivalent to 1.0–1.4 percent of the wage base for each year of contribution; and (3) an individual account pension that can be drawn as a lump-sum or an annuity equivalent to the funds in the individual account.

24 *The Social Blue Paper: The Analysis and Prediction of Chinese Societal Situation in 1998* (Beijing: Social Science Publisher, 1998), p. 26.

25 Li Jiang and Yen Bo, p. 745.

26 The World Bank, *Financing Health Care: Issues and Options for China* (Washington, DC: The World Bank, 1997), p. 23.

27 Ibid., pp. 6–7.

28 *China Labour Statistical Yearbook 1998*, p. 523.

29 *The Social Blue Paper*, p. 267.

30 Ibid., p. 268.

31 Jude Howell, "Refashioning State–Society Relations in China", *European Journal of Development Research*, vol. 6, no. 1 (June 1994), p. 199.

32 Linda Wong, "Privatization of Social Welfare in Post-Mao China," *Asian Survey*, vol. XXXIV, no. 4 (April 1994), p. 312.

Part III

Foreign policy and security issues

7 Reform and Chinese foreign policy

Lowell Dittmer

Although Chinese foreign policy certainly underwent a profound transformation with the inauguration of the "reform and opening policy" at the end of 1978, it also retained elements of continuity. Among these elements are:

1 An essentially goal-rational foreign policy that sets clearly prioritized strategic objectives. Some goals have been constant throughout, such as the emphasis on sovereignty, independence, and China's achievement of Great Power status. Others have been specific to a particular time period (the "general line") while retaining pragmatic flexibility with regard to tactics. This realism and pragmatism entails a willingness to reassess that foreign policy and make significant adjustments from time to time, without necessarily acknowledging doing so (e.g., Tiananmen).

2 A tendency toward rhetorical hyperbole and a love for the language of absolute values and norms ("principles"), often belying the pragmatism with which policies are actually implemented. While the PRC has been involved in wars or violent altercations more often than most countries in the course of its brief existence, it does so only on the (perceived) firm ground of "principle."

3 A penchant for "preceptorial diplomacy," i.e., persuading other countries to parrot certain "principles" to establish a common normative basis for further discussions. These principles may be general, as in the "Five Principles of Peaceful Coexistence," or they may be tailor-made for a particular relationship, as in the agreements set forth in the "three communiqués" (for Sino-American relations), the "three fundamental obstacles" to normalization of Sino-Soviet relations in the 1980s, the "basic agreements" set forth on three ceremonial occasions to govern Sino-Japanese relations,[1] or (most recently, to govern third nations' postures toward Taiwan) the "Three Nos." Extraordinary emphasis is typically placed on the preliminary enunciation of these principles, failing which the whole relationship may be declared in jeopardy, not "normal."

The basic differences between Maoist and reform policies are none the less profound. The fundamental difference is the practical abandonment of world revolution as the top-priority foreign policy goal in favor of the maximization of China's national interest. Granted, this shift was not as dramatic as it might appear, inasmuch as goals dictated by national interest were often smuggled into the definition of the functional requisites of world revolution – one may argue, for example, that the PRC never engaged in war unless its national interests were at stake. But the commitment to revolution was far more than rhetorical: after all, China did endorse and encourage wars of "national liberation," including sending weapons, military equipment, and sometimes advisors, risking war with the capitalist superpower; and it did become involved in a protracted altercation over ideological principles with the Soviet Union. None of these actions could easily be justified in terms of national interest. The Maoist focus on revolution pitched the whole approach to foreign policy in a provocative direction, emphasizing crises and contradictions in the capitalist world – stability is relative, struggle is absolute, even under communism. Revolution is necessarily violent (seizure of power via the ballot box, as in Italy or France, is "revisionist"), a third world war between capitalist and socialist forces inevitable. Amid this continuing world revolution, Mao relied on a few basic principles first clearly articulated during China's revolutionary war: isolate the "principal contradiction," unite with all others who can be induced to cooperate in dealing with the common enemy, do not allow secondary contradictions (e.g., conflicts about ideology, personality, etc.) to prevent you from being flexible on tactics so long as it serves your strategic objective. Thus in 1949 China after momentary hesitation and despite significant reservations adopted a "lean to one side" grand strategy to counter the hegemony of the United States, whose inveterate ideological hostility toward international communism (and concomitant containment policy) made it the principal external threat to PRC security. When the Sino-Soviet alliance soured and the Soviet military buildup along its Asian frontier compounded the ideological dispute between Beijing and Moscow, and as Washington demonstrated the limits of its military ambitions in Southeast Asia and signalled its plans for retrenchment in the Nixon/Guam Doctrine, Mao decided the Soviet Union was the superpower posing the more serious threat, and China adopted a "lean to the other side" strategy of Sino-American rapprochement. In retrospect, the 1971–2 *caesura* may be considered the first manifestation of the "reform" impulse in Chinese politics; although subsequently justified ideologically in terms of Mao's "Three Worlds" paradigm, it clearly came in response to power-political necessities.

Since the Third Plenum of the 11th Party Congress in December 1978, most of this revolutionary strategy has been postponed into practical irrelevance, and although "Mao Zedong Thought" remains an ideological cornerstone of the People's Republic, the official reconstrual has eviscerated it. Taking advantage of widespread disenchantment with the Cultural Revolution, Deng and his followers had by the Sixth Plenum of the 11th Congress (June 1981) largely dismantled Mao's doctrine of continuous revolution: "class struggle" (which Mao deemed the "key link") and "turbulent" mass movements were declared essentially *passé*, "politics in command" (viz., prioritization of the ideology and the "relations of production") was turned upside down, giving pride of place to the "forces of production" (i.e., the economic base). In foreign policy (now subordinate to domestic modernization priorities), the export of revolution and the support of insurgent liberation movements in the Third World gave way to a "peace and development" line (meaning in effect that China would support whomever was in its economic interest to support). Fresh analyses of the international correlation of forces resulted in the discovery that war was not inevitable, leading to reconciliation with the Soviet Union, a steady reduction in military spending, "a search for consensus while reserving points of contention."

The purpose of this essay is to describe and analyze this transformation in greater depth. The first section reviews the structural dimension of foreign policy change. In the second section, the evolution of foreign policy during the reform era will be chronologically reviewed and analyzed.

The organization of foreign policy

As in all aspects of politics and administration during the reform era, foreign policy making has been the beneficiary (or victim) of increasing institutionalization of the division of labor, higher educational preparation of officials, and more collective decision making. The three main institutional participants in the foreign policy process are the state, the Communist Party, and the PLA; several other organs have relevant auxiliary roles, such as the intelligence services.[2]

Of the seven organs of the state listed in the 1982 constitution, which has remained authoritative with only piecemeal amendment throughout the reform era, three are formally relevant to foreign policy making: the National People's Congress (in its capacity to ratify treaties), the restored (in 1982) position of chief of state (who receives and delegates ambassadorial personnel), and the State Council. As the first two are essentially ceremonial we shall focus on the State Council, which actually runs China's foreign policy apparatus. Four of the State Council's current complement of twenty-nine ministries and four commissions (as of March 1998) are concerned with foreign policy: the Ministry for Foreign Trade and Economic Cooperation (MOFTEC), the Ministry of Foreign Affairs (MFA), the Defense Ministry, and (in specialized cases) the People's Bank, which has ministerial rank. MOFTEC, a direct descendant of the Ministry of Foreign Economic Relations and Trade (MOFERT), was established adjacent to the MFA in 1982 (renamed in 1993) to administer foreign trade and investment in a tandem arrangement analogous to Japan's division between its Foreign Ministry and MITI; by the late 1980s MOFTEC had become, with the increasing emphasis on economic development and integration into world markets, the second most important ministry involved in foreign relations. The MFA (*waijiaobu*), the queen (and largest) of the ministries by dint of its long favored position under Zhou Enlai, is similar in structure to foreign ministries in other countries. It comprises a General Office (consisting of a Secretariat and a Confidential Communications Bureau), five internal affairs departments, and eighteen external affairs departments.[3]

The internal departments are functionally organized to manage personnel and direct information traffic. The external affairs departments include both regional departments (e.g., Africa, North America and Oceania, Taiwan Affairs, Western Europe, Hong Kong and Macao, Latin America) and functional departments (e.g., protocol, consular, international organizations, policy research, translation). Below the departments are divisions, such as the US Affairs Division under the North American and Oceanic Affairs Department.

Leading MFA personnel include the Foreign Minister, a series of vice foreign ministers (*fuwaizhang*), a score of assistants (*waijiao buzhang zhuli*), and the MFA spokesman (*waijiaobu fayanren*); below them is a small army of ambassadors, general consuls (*zongling shi*), consuls (*lingshi*), chargés d'affaires (*linshi daiban*), etc. These are career officials, who have had remarkable stability of tenure: fully 87 percent of all officials at or above ambassadorial rank in 1966 survived through 1979. Chinese diplomatic personnel are typically area specialists rather than generalists, often with excellent language training and cultural sensitivity to "their" area. At the apex of this pyramid, the reform era has seen three foreign ministers: Wu Xueqian (from November 1982 until being forced out in the wake of his son's involvement in the Tiananmen protests), Qian Qichen (1989–98), and Tang Jiaxuan (1998–). Of the three, only Qian could be considered a political heavyweight, one of the three foreign ministers (after Zhou Enlai and Chen Yi) to be promoted to the Politburo since Liberation (in 1992); though he yielded his position as Foreign Minister to Tang in 1997 (perhaps because Qian had been a known Qiao Shi acolyte, perhaps because some in the military considered him too "soft" on the West), he has retained Politburo membership and a visible presence in the foreign policy process.[4] Tang Jiaxuan, who did not receive regular membership in the Central Committee until his promotion, is a well-educated career MFA official with a grounding in Sino-Japanese affairs – and as such he seems to have been adversely affected by Jiang Zemin's confused and disappointing November 1998 Tokyo summit.

Given its constitutionally sanctioned "leading role," the Chinese Communist Party (CCP) has the final word over both state and armed forces in this as in all political decision making. Formally speaking the leading decision-making forum is the Central Committee (CC), which in turn delegates power to the twenty-four-person Politburo and thence to its still tinier (currently seven-member) Standing Committee (PBSC; in the early 1950s, and again briefly in the mid-1980s, the Secretariat eclipsed the Standing Committee, but since 1989 its leading role has been reaffirmed). Yet even the PBSC is deemed too large and cumbersome to make foreign policy decisions: during the Maoist era these were made by the team of Mao Zedong and Zhou Enlai (with Zhou increasingly relegated to the position of implementor). In the reform era the ambit was widened somewhat to a "leading nuclear circle" initially consisting of Deng, Chen Yun, Hu Yaobang, and Zhao Ziyang (1979–89), then of Deng, Yang Shangkun, Li Peng, and Jiang Zemin (1990–3), and finally of Jiang Zemin and Li Peng.[5] This "core" is given institutional status via the CPC Central (Committee) Foreign Affairs Leading Small Group (FALSG), consisting of key members of the PBSC and of government and party foreign affairs agencies. Inasmuch as this is a non-standing committee with no permanent staff, the Central Processing Unit (or *guikou*) for the implementation of its decisions is the Foreign Affairs Office of the State Council. Owing to its special status and problems, Taiwan alone does not fall under the jurisdiction of this *guikou*; in 1987, a CPC Taiwan Affairs Group (TALSG) was created, headed by Yang Shangkun, its CPU being the Taiwan Affairs Office of the State Council. These two committees, both now chaired by Jiang Zemin, have eclipsed what was for a long time the dominant non-standing foreign affairs committee, the CC International Liaison Department (*duiwai lianluobu*, ILD), with eight regional bureaus as well as functionally organized "movement" sections (union issues, peace commission, youth organizations, and women's leagues). But since the fall of the International Communist Movement in the early 1990s, the ILD has fallen into desuetude. Now chaired by a mere CC member, Dai Bingguo, the ILD has been relegated to the task of maintaining liaison with other political parties – at one time this meant communist parties, but since the collapse of the International Communist Movement in 1991 the ambit was broadened to include first socialist parties and eventually virtually all parties.[6]

Though the PLA, legatee of an historically close relationship with the CCP, has seen its political influence wax and wane over the years, since 1989 both the military and security forces seem to have been in the ascendancy, largely in reaction to the "turmoil" at Tiananmen and the ensuing collapse of the communist bloc. Whereas active military officers are eligible for any governmental or party positions (two currently serve on the Politburo), the highest venue for their official political influence is the CC's Central Military Commission. Somewhat unexpectedly, Jiang Zemin has been able to exert his command over this organ since his appointment as chair in the fall of 1989 despite his total lack of military experience – due to the unequivocal support of Deng Xiaoping, the early (1992) elimination of the "Yang brothers clique" (and the absence of rivals in the line of succession with better military credentials), plus Jiang's own skill in meting out promotions and other perquisites. Yet the other side of Jiang's successful control of the PLA is that the PLA has been able to utilize these appointments to enhance its collective political power. The PLA's power base is now extensive, enabling it virtually to articulate its own foreign policy. In 1997 alone, the PLA received over 150 delegations from 67 countries and five continents on visits to China, including 23 defense ministers; about 100 PLA delegations travelled to 70 foreign countries. Since being urged by Deng to go into business in the 1980s to compensate for steadily diminishing budget allocations, the military has acquired its own interests, and these are not only strategic. The foreign policy input of the military has increasingly reflected vested business interests – whether China should join the Missile Technology Control Regime (MTCR) or sign the Non-proliferation Treaty (NPT) or sell missile or nuclear technology to Pakistan – it is perhaps no coincidence that China cast a rare UN Security Council veto to prevent any public criticism or sanctions against Pakistan when the latter conducted underground nuclear tests (following India's tests) in May 1998. This may change following the PLA's forced relinquishment of economic interests in 1998, but it is important to bear in mind that this surprisingly swift divestiture involved only the services and not the national defense industrial sector. The PLA had many contacts with its US counterparts in the 1980s, but these were curtailed after Tiananmen and not resumed (partially) until 1997. Meanwhile, the military's interests with the Russian Federation have blossomed: since 1991 Russia has become China's major weapons supplier, selling tanks (T62s), supersonic fighters (Su-27s), submarines, and high-tech destroyers, even an old aircraft carrier (the *Varyag*). The military is officially represented in some high-level negotiations, such as the series of post-1991 five-power talks on frontier security with the former Soviet republics, leading to the April 1996 border treaty and the April 1997 treaty stipulating mutual frontier demilitarization and confidence-building measures.

In 1994, Deng in a sort of swan-song endorsed the functional division between party and state (*dang zheng fenkai*) as a primary constituent of reform, one of the most important operational implications of which was a systematic effort to reduce military influence in politics. This policy, however, proved an early casualty of Jiang's need to consolidate his power, as Jiang snapped up every available political office (including chief of state and chair of the CCP's Central Military Commission (CMC)) to consolidate his succession. In June 1994 Jiang appointed nineteen new generals, giving the PLA leadership his own imprimatur. In the mid-1990s the CR practice of seconding PLA officers to high political positions was revived, and the CMC was expanded (e.g., two new vice-chairs) to accommodate its added responsibilities in foreign affairs and reunification policy.[7] Military officers became most politically engaged in those issues deemed consistent with their professional responsibilities (and ardent nationalism), notably the Taiwan issue; after Lee Teng-hui's "alumnal" speech at Cornell in June 1995, military leaders began attending meetings of the FALSG and the TALSG (General Xiong Guangkai replaced civilian Wang Zhaoguo as Secretary-General of the TALSG), and the leadership was brought under such concerted attack that Qian Qichen and Wang Zhaoguo had to make self-criticisms. Yet the political results of this massive attempt at intimidation were so mixed in Taiwan (where Lee Teng-hui was re-elected by a landslide and popular interest in reunification nosedived) that their intervention damaged military credibility, enabling Jiang to replace Liu Huaqing and Zhang Zhen (with whom his relationship had been problematic) with loyalists Chi Haotian and Zhang Wannian at the 1997 15th Congress (whom, however, he excluded from the PBSC). The PLA's escutcheon had also been tarnished by widespread military involvement in illegal commerce, and perhaps by discomfiting popular memories of the history of military intervention in Chinese politics (martial law in 1949–54, military intervention in the Cultural Revolution, the Tiananmen crackdown).[8] Military participation in controlling the summer 1998 Yangtze flood, widely popularized in the media, has helped to alleviate that image, and in any event military preparations for "localized warfare under conditions of high technology" have continued to enjoy pride of place in China's annual budget allocations as well as in personnel appointments. Though it is difficult to measure the political impact of that buildup very precisely, it seems to have placed China somewhat out of step with most other powers in the region, who have been more interested in cashing in their peace dividends.

The role of China's secret service organs in the foreign policy process is for obvious reasons not well advertised. There are now three operational agencies: the Public Security Bureau, or PSB (*gonganbu*), the Bureau of State Security, or BSS (*guojia anquanbu*), and the Bureau of Investigation, or BI (*diaochabu*); these are all under the supervision of the Commission for Politics and Law, which since the involuntary retirement of Qiao Shi at the 15th Congress in 1997 has been chaired by Luo Gan, a former Qiao protégé with close links to Li Peng. The BSS is the descendant of the General Directorate of Intelligence (*qingbao zongshu*) established under the Government Affairs Council in 1949, eliminated in 1953, re-established as the party's Central Intelligence Department in 1955, shut down during the Cultural Revolution, and revived gradually under Zhou Enlai's auspices in the early 1970s. In 1983 the Party's CID was merged with the counterintelligence branches of the Ministry of Public Security's 1st Bureau to form the State Council's BSS (closely guided by the party's Central Security Committee, or *zhongyang baomi weiyuanhui*), designed mainly to cope with domestic dissidents or overzealous foreign journalists.[9] If the mission of the BSS is counterintelligence, that of the BI is intelligence – collecting sensitive information from abroad. Since the advent of reform its purview has broadened to include commercially relevant "high-tech," though as recent headlines surrounding release of the Cox Report attest, its interest in classic strategic secrets such as nuclear warhead miniaturization has not disappeared. As in the United States and many other countries, the PLA has its own foreign-policy-relevant security organs: the 2nd and 3rd Directorates of the PLA General Staff Department (the former concerned with human-source intelligence, the latter with signal and imagery intelligence gathering) and the so-called Liaison Directorate (*zhongzheng lianluo bu*) of the General Political Department all appear to be involved in collecting information relevant to military security, including high-tech weapons data. The most important source of unfiltered information to the foreign affairs establishment is the New China News Agency (Xinhua She), which publishes a series of news digests of varying degrees of confidentiality (e.g., Cankao Ziliao, Guoji Neican, Cankao Xiaoxi); according to some conspiracy theorists, the two journalists killed in the May 1999 bombing of the Chinese embassy in Belgrade were engaged in analysis of a downed US stealth bomber, for instance. Analytically processed information is routed through the foreign affairs research institutes: the Institute of International Studies is the official research arm of the MFA, which submits confidential briefing papers and also publishes *Guoji Wenti Yanjiu* (*Journal of International Studies*), but other "think tanks" include the Chinese Institute for Contemporary International Relations (the research arm of the BI), the China Institute of International Strategic Studies (established in 1979 under the General Staff Department), and the Chinese Academy of Social Sciences under the State Council. These think tanks acquired considerable prominence during the tenure of Zhao Ziyang, but whether the MFA pays much attention to their briefings is debatable.[10] Given the censorship and propagandistic distortion of the official news media, the role of intelligence in China's foreign policy learning process is vital.

Despite the growing salience and complexity of formal organization in the Chinese foreign policy process, the personal equation remains highly relevant, as manifest in the influence of informal groups in decision making and the occasional discrepancy between formal position and actual power. The organization of informal influence is a notoriously elusive quarry for research, as it is expressly forbidden, and thus one must rely on the grapevine (*xiaodao xiaoxi*) and occasional leaks. Informal networks are constructed on a combination of ascriptive and associational attributes, and although networks are often stable over long periods membership is by no means mutually exclusive and in a given showdown members usually have an option whether to participate and in what manner. In the context of reform the old nodes (e.g., the PLA field armies) have tended to become less relevant, replaced by new nodes such as old college ties (increasingly relevant with the higher educational attainments of the third generation), the "secretary clique," the "princelings" (*taizidang*), or Jiang Zemin's "mainstream faction" (*zhuliupai*). Informal groupings are amphibian, tending to surface only in the context of perilous uncertainty, as for example during succession crises. A notorious example is the 1972–6 cleavage between the followers of the "two maidens" (*liangwei xiaojie*), Mao's niece Wang Hairong and Tang Wenshang, young amateurs who had exclusive access to Mao during his terminal illness, and "Lord Qiao" (Qiao laoye, aka Qiao Guanhua), the foreign minister who represented the career professionals in the MFA. Even after one identifies a coherent "loyalty group" it is not always self-evident what its policy preferences are on a specific issue (which are generally irrelevant in any event, as key decisions are made at the top).

One noteworthy tendency during the reform era has been for personal loyalty groups to shift to bureaucratic politics, "where you stand is where you sit," as a consequence of the lower salience of ideology and reduced penalties for association on behalf of special interests. A bureaucratic base is not identical with a loyalty group (though they may overlap, as loyalty develops over time), inasmuch as it may be expected to dissolve immediately in the case of a personal career crisis. But it is more easily identifiable and its foreign policy interests may be rationally inferred from an organizational chart. Thus the MFA's geographically defined departments may be expected, *ceteris paribus*, to defend the interests of "their" country or region, and it is thus possible to identify (on the basis of bureaucratically vested interests) those governmental ministries, regions, and economic sectors more (and less) apt to support the policy of "opening to the outside world."[11] Thus the position of specific groups on any given issue should in principle be calculable from the conjuncture of their bureaucratic interests with international and domestic business cycles and other relevant economic data; more thorough and specific empirical research on this relationship is surely needed.

The evolution of foreign policy during reform

The evolution of China's foreign policy in the course of reform may be roughly sub-divided into four periods: the attempt to build an anti-Soviet united front culminating in "quasi-marriage" with the United States (1978–82), the implementation of Deng's "independent foreign policy" (1982–9), China's post-Tiananmen, post-Cold War reintegration into the international community (1989–95), and the current bid for Great Power status under Jiang Zemin (1995–9). During each period, without departing significantly from the "peace and development" line articulated at the outset of the reform era, Beijing undertook significant new policy measures to adapt to changes in the ongoing dialectic between domestic needs and the international environment.

Although Deng Xiaoping at the famous Third Plenum began to articulate the philosophical outlines of the new foreign policy orientation that would characterize his regime, for the first few years China's Great Power diplomacy was essentially continuous with the course set during Mao's waning years. This was dictated by the logic of the "strategic triangle," in which China's security depended on its relationship with the two superpowers, the Soviet Union was identified after 1969 as the world's most powerful "hegemonist" and main threat to China's national security, and China hence moved into closer collaboration with the United States as the cornerstone of a "united front" (including Japan and Western Europe) to be assembled to counter the "polar bear." The Sino-American "marriage" was celebrated by normalization of diplomatic relations, largely on Chinese terms, at the end of 1979, and was followed by good faith Chinese efforts on behalf of this quasi-alliance in its February incursion into Vietnam and its support for anti-Soviet *mujahideen* rebels in Afghanistan.

Yet the honeymoon proved remarkably brief. In 1982 Deng inaugurated a new "independent foreign policy of peace," announced by Hu Yaobang at the 12th Party Congress, and later the same year initiated a series of semi-annual "normalization" talks with the Soviet Union. Ideologically, the way was prepared for this shift to a more balanced (not equidistant, as that would also constrain China's room for maneuver) position between the superpowers with a deletion of "revisionism" from the polemical vocabulary and the inclusion of the United States (with the Soviet Union) under the epithet "hegemonists"; indeed, it put Beijing in a more defensible position vis-à-vis the Third World, where Reagan's "counterrevolutionary" foreign policies were highly unpopular. But the shift was strategically rather than ideologically motivated. With the doubling of US arms budgets and announcement of "comprehensive confrontation" under Reagan (and as Moscow became bogged down in Afghanistan and Cambodia) China deemed the strategic balance of power to be more stable, its security less at risk. Beijing could not get much more from Washington than it had already gotten, the CCP leadership probably reasoned, whereas further Chinese reliance on Western strategic collaboration would only trigger further Soviet armament efforts and hence indirectly aggravate its own security dilemma. Any consequent Chinese efforts to upgrade its own arsenal would not only detract from the other three "modernizations" but increase Beijing's growing dependency on Western arms markets, thus reducing its diplomatic freedom of maneuver.

In addition to shrewd triangular analysis a more visceral factor played a role in Beijing's shift, whose importance has frequently been underestimated: Taiwan. Normalization of Sino-American relations coincided with the advent of a new and unprecedentedly generous policy of "unification" with Taiwan, in which the island state was assured of "one country, two systems" with "a high degree of autonomy," and encouraged to engage in "three links" with the mainland. This new policy was in part meant to mollify Washington for breaking its mutual defense alliance with Taiwan in the absence of any guarantee not to use force by Beijing, but it also introduced to Taipei for the first time plausibly attractive terms for peaceful and prosperous unification. If China regained Taiwan, Beijing no doubt reasoned, that would be ample dowry for marriage to the world's leading bourgeois hegemonist. Hence Taipei's counterattack, in the form of a furious lobbying campaign that induced Congress to pass the Taiwan Relations Act within a few months of normalization, caught Beijing quite by surprise, and it was not pleased. The provisions of the Act seemed to erase, at one fell swoop, many of the gains of the Second Communiqué. Beijing's dismay was compounded by the election of Taiwan's "old friend" Reagan in November 1979 and by the resumption after a year's moratorium of US arms sales to Taiwan. This precipitated a rather stormy period in bilateral relations, only partially alleviated by the August 17, 1982 Third Communiqué, which promised (conditionally) to reduce and eventually curtail arms sales. "The change of our views on global strategies is affected above all by the changes the US has introduced," Deng stated in 1984. "The biggest shift that was caused by US changes is with regard to the Taiwan problem."[12]

As part of its move from revolutionary offensive to power balancing, China softened its "realism" somewhat to reassess the role of international organization, agreeing for the first time to participate in peacekeeping activities (even to help pay for them). China joined a wide range of intergovernmental organizations in the 1980s, including the IMF, World Bank, Asian Developmental Bank, International Atomic Energy Association, UNCTAD, UNICEF, UNESCO, WHO, MFA, and over 200 international agencies concerned with the development of science and technology. An active participant in UN discussions, it used its General Assembly vote (and Security Council veto) in support of various Third World proposals, criticizing both superpowers (although PRC economic relations with other Third World countries remained strictly business – no fraternal revolutionary aid, as in the Maoist era). China's position on arms control and disarmament issues was also redefined – thus Beijing participated in the activities of the UN Disarmament Commission, in 1982–7 attending seven of the eleven conferences of the commission in Geneva, contributing its critique of superpower nuclear arsenals.

Meanwhile, as to superpower relations, Beijing's frustration with Washington was soon put into perspective by disappointment with Moscow's dilatory response to Chinese calls to remove the "three fundamental obstacles." In the wake of Reagan's 1984 summit visit and Shultz's 1985 announcement of an end to further concessions and a strategic tilt toward Tokyo, Beijing thus set limits on its independent foreign policy posture, compromising on hitherto sensitive disputes and consolidating strategic ties with the United States. The Reagan administration reciprocated by increasing the flow of US technology to China and by minimizing public references to remaining differences over Taiwan.[13] Beijing's interest in rapprochement with the Soviet Union proved at the triumphant climax to their protracted negotiations to be relatively modest: the joint communiqué adopted at the May 1989 "normalization" summit did not project a vision of future cooperation in either the security or the economic realm.

The sharp international reaction to China's brutal suppression of the Tiananmen protest again seems to have caught CCP leaders quite by surprise. They seem to have expected things to blow over after a few months, but the coincidence of the crackdown with the collapse of communist regimes elsewhere dazzled the West with the prospect of an "end of history" and it was diverted from returning to China immediately. The Soviet Union's complete collapse, unrelieved by massive Western aid or spontaneous economic recovery, eliminated the third leg of the triangle, with the result that bilateral friction was no longer counterbalanced by either Washington's strategic need for Beijing or Beijing's strategic need for Washington, and tended to escalate. China's sudden relief from visible threats to its national security could not fully be appreciated in the context of a legitimacy crisis aggravated by an ideological vacuum, and military expenditures for the first time after nearly a decade of annual reductions[14] began to escalate annually by double digits, despite a temporary economic recession (1989–90) and no visible strategic threats looming on the horizon.[15]

Yet Beijing was able to rise to this grave foreign policy challenge by making four significant adjustments. First, given the unprecedented absence of Great Power threats, Beijing for the first time lowered its sites from the international chessboard to the regional arena. In the early 1990s Beijing normalized relations with all remaining ASEAN members on the basis of the Five Principles of Peaceful Coexistence (and non-recognition of Taiwan), and China's neighbors reciprocated by moving into the vacuum left by fleeing Western investors. Hong Kong, Taiwanese, and South Korean investment capital flooded into southern China in record quantities beginning in 1989 – thus demonstrating, perhaps, that the notion of "Asian values" had a germ of truth. Japan, too haunted by its own past to waste much time on recriminations, was the first major power to make steps toward reconciliation: on August 11, 1989 Premier Toshiki Kaifu announced that cooperation with China would continue in accord with the joint Sino-Japanese declaration of 1972, and (in response to Chinese urging) Japan the following year remitted the frozen yen loan promised by Takeshita in late 1988. This prepared the stage for the Kaifu visit in 1991 (the first visit by the leader of a leading industrialized democracy since the crackdown), and in the visit of the emperor himself in 1992, commemorating the twentieth anniversary of normalization (and offering a long-sought apology for Japanese war crimes).

The target of numerous Chinese complaints in the 1980s (Japanese investors had been frightened by Baoshan and other such abrupt Chinese economic reversals), Japan had become by the mid-1990s China's largest foreign trade partner (with whom China now enjoyed a consistent positive trade balance) and second or third largest investor.

Second, though barely avoiding a diplomatic *faux pas* when it considered recognizing the abortive conservative coup in August 1991, China quickly over-came its reservations about the collapse of European socialism and the inauguration of Yeltsin and normalized relations with the Russian Federation and all former Soviet Republics, and in the fullness of time the initially suspi-cious relationship was to develop into a quite warm one, as by 1991 China had become Russia's leading arms market (compensating the Russian Federation for declining international sales in the wake of the triumph of US "smart" muni-tions in the Gulf War). The evident failure of democratic capitalism to emancipate the Russian economy eliminated the danger of a Russian demon-stration effect, while China's embrace opened the way to Moscow's backdoor participation in the thriving Asian economic dynamo in the wake of its exclusion from an expanding NATO. Border talks with a diplomatic team consisting of all four former Soviet Republics (Russia, Kazakhstan, Kyrgyzstan, and Tajikistan) culminated in successful border treaties and agreements on frontier demilitariza-tion and confidence-building measures jointly signed in 1996–7, and in 1998 the demarcation of the Sino-Russian border was finally completed. True, the (non-military) economic relationship, after a promising beginning in the early 1990s, has proved disappointing to both sides (largely due to the collapse of the Russian economy), but the formation of a "strategic partnership" in 1997, by evoking the old Sino-Soviet "bloc" without actually reviving it, has improved both countries' diplomatic leverage at no visible cost.

Third, without in the least apologizing for its ferocious overreaction to the student demonstrations, Beijing for the time being quietly adopted a somewhat more progressive stance toward reform. Instead of retrenching, as had been anticipated, following Deng's 1992 "southern voyage" (*nanxun*), additional reforms were launched, further freeing domestic prices and opening China to international markets to an unprecedented degree; this ushered in a massive influx of private investment capital hoping to take advantage of China's poten-tially enormous market. The political arena having been placed out of bounds, China's officialdom and middle classes "plunged into the sea" (*xia hai*) of commerce with a vengeance, and the economy rebounded with double-digit growth (and initial high rates of inflation). While continuing to articulate its (now perforce increasingly anti-American) polemic against superpower hegemonism in international forums, China demonstrated a growing willingness to play by Western rules: it finally (after a final series of underground nuclear tests ending in 1996) joined the Nuclear Non-Proliferation Treaty (NPT) and the Comprehensive Test Ban Treaty (CTBT), as well as the Chemical Weapons Convention and Biological Weapons Convention, and vowed to abide by the MTCR.[16] Beijing even began to respond a bit more diplomatically to human rights concerns, preparing a series of plausibly argued white papers; particularly during annual Congressional deliberation of China's Most Favored Nation status, China was always willing to release a few dissidents and go on a shopping spree for US imports.

Fourth, as in previous periods when China's relations with the Great Powers frayed (e.g., the 1960s), Beijing revived its diplomatic contacts with the developing countries – none of whom had imposed sanctions or joined the world-wide chorus of recrimination. Thus a mid-1989 Politburo directive announced that "from now on China will put more effort into resuming and developing relations with old friends (in Africa) and Third World countries."[17] "In the past several years we have concentrated too much on one part of the world and neglected the other," Deng reflected during his summer 1990 vacation at Beidaiho. "The USA and other Western nations invoked sanctions against us but those who are truly sympathetic and support us are some old friends in the developing countries. ... This course may not be altered for 20 years."[18] Thus a series of high-level visits (by Yang Shangkun, Qian Qichen, and Li Peng) was conducted in 1989–90. China also joined Malaysia, Singapore, and assorted others in a defense of "Asian values" and developing countries' right to immunity from superpower intervention in the name of parochial Western values. China also supported the Third World proposal to launch a new international economic order, according to which developing countries, while retaining "full and eternal sovereignty" over their own natural resources, should be granted full access to Western markets without protectionist barriers or disadvantageous terms of trade. True, China's support for Third World causes remained essentially rhetorical, as it declined to join most Third World organizations, and in those mainstream groups that it did join it participated in debates but shied away from the functional committees and subsidiary bodies where business is actually transacted.[19] Still, to many in the Third World, the PRC remained the only major power willing to articulate some of their interests and concerns on the world stage.

Thus by the Fourth Plenum of the 4th CC in November 1994, the most plausible *de facto* dividing line marking the advent of Jiang Zemin's solo reign (Deng lived on until February 1997, but made no public appearances and was reportedly on life support), China seemed to have reintegrated itself into the international community far more successfully than seemed conceivable given its pariahdom only a few years ago. Deng, having been primarily responsible for this public relations disaster in the first instance, can take considerable personal credit for this miraculous recovery, urging colleagues not to panic but calmly to persevere in their work, staunching a revival of Sino-Soviet polemics during the Soviet collapse in 1989–91, successfully regenerating reform momentum in 1992, and, last but not least, setting forth and adhering to a succession regime with far greater surety than he had exhibited in the 1980s. As he was quoted in his "24-character principle" for handling world affairs enunciated in late 1989: "Observe developments soberly, maintain our position, meet challenges calmly, hide our capacities and bide our time, remain free of ambition, never claim leadership."

Despite having been chosen to succeed Zhao Ziyang as Party Secretary in the context of a legitimacy crisis, as a provincial dark horse with many career liabilities and few outstanding qualifications, Jiang Zemin in the course of time proved himself a worthy successor – not least by playing the delicate role of crown prince for so long without faltering. In a series of masterfully arranged confrontations he progressively eliminated a number of formidable rivals – the "Yang brothers clique," Chen Xitong, finally Qiao Shi – and was fortunate enough to see most of the older generation who might have attempted to assert seniority pass away. In an amazing series of personal appearances (he toured virtually every Chinese province and important city in the course of his internship, sagely evading the factional snarl in the capital), Jiang proved himself a commanding presence and a master of euphonious ambiguity. Within a year of his formal succession he had put all doubt about his staying power aside, eliminating some of the structural ambiguity of Deng's regime by having himself named to every formal leadership position available.

Filially hoisting the flag of Deng Xiaoping's Theory and claiming only to adhere to his patron's reform course, Jiang has not claimed any foreign policy innovations. Indeed, the fundamental reform line of peace and development has been retained, the primacy of domestic political economy with foreign policy in an auxiliary role,[20] the continued deradicalization of ideological rhetoric. As a younger and more vigorous man (indeed, an indefatigable traveler) and an orotund public speaker, Jiang has been in many ways a more capable representative of Dengist foreign policies than Deng himself. Inasmuch as Li Peng, Zhu Rongji, and Qian Qichen have also shown a penchant for the grand tour, China's interests and achievements have been amply showcased in national capitals and international forums.

Yet Chinese foreign policy has under Jiang's leadership already begun to show certain distinctive features – partly because Jiang is after all his own person, partly because of altered circumstances. Personally, Deng has displayed a paradoxical combination of extravagant showmanship and extreme caution. China's circumstances are no longer those of a scorned pariah but of a widely admired paradigm of market transition: after nearly two decades of reform and economic hypergrowth the prevailing mood has thus been that China has "arrived" – a mood encouraged by the obvious pride and optimism of "President Jiang" (Jiang zhuxi). I would argue that this has resulted in at least three foreign policy innovations that may be identified with the incipient "Jiang era." First, China has rejoined Great Power diplomacy, now riding the vehicle of "partnerships." Second, in its relations with the rest of the Asian region China has shown an inclination to revive a form of neotraditional diplomacy. And third, China has, despite profuse denials, shifted from Deng's policy of demilitarization to one of military modernization.

Notwithstanding Deng's admonitions to never seek a leadership position and never engage in power politics, China has embarked in what Jiang calls "Great Power strategy" (*daguo zhanlue*). The new international vehicle is not an alliance, not even a "friendship" alliance (for it is not mutually exclusive), it is decidedly not a "military bloc," nor is it a "united front" (for it is no longer based on common opponent); it is a vaguely privileged bilateral relationship based upon comprehensive cooperation. The first "partnership" was proclaimed with the Russian Federation on April 23, 1997, followed quickly by a partnership with France (May 16, 1997), and later by partnerships with Pakistan, the United States, South Korea, the European Union, even Japan (no socialist countries, oddly enough), all of which were hailed in similar rhetoric, aiming grandiosely toward the twenty-first century. At the center of such "comprehensive" cooperation within partnerships is "consultation" (*xieshang*), which seems to feature building a strong personal relationship with other leaders – thus the Sino-Russian and Sino-American partnerships have entailed the construction of "hotlines" to the Kremlin and the White House. A partnership is clearly a labor-intensive and quite ceremonial affair, entailing regularly scheduled summits and frequent between-summit consultations. But it is also more than that. It is in effect a practical realization of China's vision of a "new international order" (*jianli guoji xin zhixu*) through "multipolarization" (*shijie duojihua*), and concomitant rejection of "hegemonism, power politics, conflict and confrontation." This new international order is to consist of a series of carefully cultivated, discrete bilateral links based on reciprocal advantage. The international system will consist of a wheel (but a wheel without a rim, given Beijing's fear of collusion) with China at the center. The strategic logic of these partnerships seems to be essentially that of the triangle, with Beijing in the "pivot" position, but now extended indefinitely.

There is no direct evidence that China has any intention of establishing some sort of "neo-tributary" system among client states in East Asia, an argument by analogy that would no doubt be vehemently denied by those to whom it is applied. Yet it is striking the inordinate concern under Jiang with prestige and ceremonial ritual, betraying a decidedly hierarchical view of the international order. Great Power summitry presupposes a tacit agreement that status will be shared, but in other international relationships due deference is expected. This is to say that China (and its leaders) expects to be addressed in a manner appropriate to its status, failing which all communication is typically cut off, blocking communication when it is most needed. Such deference from abroad is duly celebrated in China's domestic media, bolstering the legitimacy of PRC leaders as international notables. Thus the historically troubled relationship with Taiwan or Vietnam seems at least in part to be attributable to the latter's annoying insistence on equality; the diplomatic relationship with Taiwan in particular is replete with intense (if usually petty) protocol disputes, which have made communication extremely difficult (though one must say in this regard that the Chinese on the eastern side of the Strait have had their own ways of inhibiting communication). In the case of the November 1998 Tokyo summit China let it be known just before it took place (after two delays) that it expected to receive a written apology for war crimes similar to that recently submitted to Seoul. When Tokyo refused, Jiang refused to sign the joint communiqué, leaving the statement unsigned.

China's post-Tiananmen military modernization and its budgetary accounting have been the focus of several studies with conflicting results, partly because the official budget figures do not include all expenditures that would be included in Western arms budgets, and the magnitude of unrecorded expenditures is inherently uncertain.[21] Less important in this context than the precision of the official budget figures is the trend line: following a decade of spending decreases, spending has begun to increase, according to the official figures, by some 11–14 percent per year. Initially this could understandably be attributed to the labile situation after Tiananmen, but after ten years, domestic tranquility has presumably been restored (and in any case responsibility has been transferred to the People's Armed Police). During the early 1990s high budget figures could be rationalized by double-digit inflation, but in the past few years inflation has been eliminated, indeed replaced by deflation, while military budgets have continued to rise at the same annual rate. It is true that much of China's arsenal is obsolescent and "objectively" requires modernization, that the PLA requires compensation for shutting down its commercial sector in 1998, and that international arms markets are glutted and hence offer cut-rate purchase opportunities. Moreover, China is not the only Asian country to have increased its arms spending lately (though it is the only one whose military budget survived the Asian financial crisis unscathed). The point is that this does represent a departure from Deng's legacy.

Jiang's innovations have resulted in what from the current vantage point looks like a mixed picture. The revival of Great Power relationships via partnerships appears to have been an outstanding success – with the sole exception of Japan, in which full partnership has been complicated by an implicit rivalry for regional leadership. China's neotraditional new order in East Asia has received more mixed reviews. The 1995 confrontation with Manila over Mischief Reef in the Spratlys, followed in 1995–6 by the use of coercive diplomacy to intimidate Taiwan, did not incur material losses or plunge the country into war, but incurred few gains and was in many respects counterproductive, leading *inter alia* to an expanded interpretation of the Japanese–American Mutual Security Treaty and to tentative plans to install Theater Missile Defense systems in Japan and Taiwan. This response to a more powerful China's diplomatic activism threatens, as in the classic security dilemma, to undermine the PRC's security even as its force projection capabilities increase.

Conclusions

Chinese foreign policy during reform and opening may in general be considered highly successful, in contrast with the more dramatic aspirations but meager results of the Maoist era. While striving for less, China has achieved more: a stable and peaceful environment in which to pursue modernization, the restoration (*huigui*) of Hong Kong and Macao, and an improved relationship with Taiwan. Albeit not entirely by dint of its own efforts, China has been absolved of national security threats and enjoys amicable relations with all powers capable of posing such a threat. Deng Xiaoping's foreign policy achievements seem to me particularly impressive, and hence warrant closer examination. His basic method was first to stabilize relations with the major powers (i.e., those potentially capable of threatening the PRC's survival) and then to make other gains around the margins. Inheriting a threatened and dependent position in the "strategic triangle," he succeeded in subtly readjusting China's triangular position in such a way that Beijing could "play" the triangle to its own advantage. Though this involved reconciliation with a power to whom Mao had sworn eternal enmity on ideological grounds (and to whom Deng himself did not have warm feelings), Deng did so upon exacting what he deemed an appropriate and necessary price. This made possible China's steady reduction of military expenditures in a no longer threatening international environment. Having thus stabilized China's relationship with the superpowers, he reoriented China's international position from exclusive identification with the Third World to an all-azimuth diplomacy, finding First World countries to be far more economically useful than "old friends" in the Third. To resolve the Hong Kong and Taiwan dilemmas he made parallel offers to both of unprecedented magnanimity, which Hong Kong accepted, while Taiwan, in an inherently stronger position, equivocated. Finally, while Deng admittedly dropped the stone on his own foot at Tiananmen (to use a Maoist expression), he showed extraordinary skill in removing it.

Jiang Zemin, from an inauspicious and frequently scorned beginning, has been able to consolidate his leadership and to put his own mark on Chinese foreign policy within an amazingly short time. He has contributed to the institutionalization and professionalization of the foreign policy apparatus, while providing vigorous high-profile personal leadership to the continuation and furtherance of Deng's basic policy line. At the same time, we argue that he has also introduced certain innovations. With the notion of a "partnership," China has been able to build a series of relationships with the other major powers that enhance its attractiveness as a partner while maximizing its own leverage and flexibility by not firmly aligning with any particular state or group of states. Rather than explicitly identifying China's international friends and foes (as Mao might have done), Jiang's strategy seeks to establish partnerships with each as a way of binding their interests to China's and reducing the likelihood that any will be able to cobble together a hostile coalition. Though one may argue that such partnerships have amounted to mere window-dressing for existing links that make no commitments but elicit few tangible advantages, they project a vision of multipolarity that exerts a certain appeal in the post-Cold War strategic vacuum, and may have enhanced China's incipient Great Power status. China's relationships with smaller powers in the Asian region and the Third World have on the whole also been positive, thanks in part to the diplomatic competition with Taiwan at this tier. The problem for Jiang, to judge from the admittedly anecdotal evidence imparted by some of his keenest critics among Beijing's policy intellectuals, is that he combines a love for grandiloquent rhetoric and Mao-size achievements with a tendency to try to please everyone in his expanded decision-making arena, with the paradoxical result that he has been put down as "soft" (*ruan*) for policies no less harsh than those of his predecessor.

Notes

1   Viz., the "joint declaration" of 1972 on the occasion of formally normalizing Sino-Japanese relations, the "Sino-Japanese peace and friendship agreement" negotiated in 1978, and the "Five Principles for the Future Course of Bilateral Relations" negotiated by Li Peng on the occasion of the twenty-fifth anniversary of diplomatic normalization in November 1997.

2   For an excellent overview of the structure of the Chinese foreign-policy-making establishment, see Robert G. Sutter, *Shaping China's Future in World Affairs* (Boulder: Westview, 1996).

3   See Lu Ning's outstanding study, *The Dynamics of Foreign-Policy Decisionmaking in China* (Boulder: Westview, 1997), pp. 21–31 *et passim*.

4   Especially in 1994, Qian Qichen was reproached in a public letter from the National Defense University of "right deviationism," specifically for being too conciliatory toward the United States and in the negotiations with the United Kingdom over the retrocession of Hong Kong. See *Zheng Ming*, 1 May 1994, pp. 10–12. To thus proceed against a Politburo member and one of China's four vice-ministers indicates that his critics must have had a base at least as high as the Central Committee. Since 1995 Qian's public foreign policy pronouncements have been harder line, particularly on Taiwan.

5   Ning, *Dynamics*, pp. 20–40.

6   By late 1998, the ILD had established party-to-party relations with some 300 political parties and organizations from 130 countries and regions on five continents; following the June 1998 Clinton visit, overtures were even made to the American Democratic and Republican parties.

7   Willy Wo-Lap Lam, *The Era of Jiang Zemin* (New York: Prentice Hall, 1999), pp. 164–5.

8   Thus for the first time in more than twenty years, the military has no representation on the Standing Committee of the Politburo (though Generals Chi Haotian and Zhang Wannian have full Politburo membership). Military intervention in the economy is a different matter, as indicated by widespread popular support for the PLA's yeoman service during the disastrous floods of the 1998s.

9   Personal communication from Professor Murray Scot Tanner, based on his research on public security.

10 Ning, *Dynamics*, pp. 107–43.

11 For example, see Paul A. Papayoanou and Scott Kastner, "Assessing the Policy of Engagement with China," University of California Institute of Global Conflict and Cooperation, San Diego, CA, Policy Paper No. 40, July 1998.

12 As quoted in Peter J. Opitz, *Zeitenwechsel in China: Die Modernisierung der chinesischen Aussenpolitik* (Zurich: Interfrom, 1991), p. 25.

13 See Sanqiang Jian, *Foreign Policy Restructuring as Adaptive Behavior: China's Independent Foreign Policy, 1982–1989* (Lanham, MD: University Press of America, 1996).

14 From 1980 to 1989, China's military spending dropped from 16.9 percent of GDP to 8.34 percent. Jian, *Restructuring*, p. 147.

15 For example, China's defense budget according to official figures amounted to RMB 28.97 billion in 1990, compared to 25.10 billion in 1989; this grew by 15.2 percent in 1990, 12 percent in 1991, 12 percent in 1992, 13.5 percent in 1993, 20 percent in 1994, 21.25 percent in 1995, 11.3 percent in 1996, 14.7 percent in 1997, and 12.8 percent in 1998. Lam, *Era of Jiang Zemin*, p. 169.

16 Samuel S. Kim, "Chinese Foreign Policy in Theory and Practice," in Samuel S. Kim (ed.), *China and the World: Chinese Foreign Policy Faces the New Millennium* (Boulder: Westview, 1998).

17 *Foreign Broadcast Information Service – China*, 3 October 1989, p. 3.

18 As quoted in *Zheng Ming*, August 1990, p. 15.

19 Samuel S. Kim, "International Organizational Behavior," in Thomas Robinson and David Shambaugh (eds.), *Ideas and Interpretations in Chinese Foreign Policy* (New York: Oxford University Press, 1993), p. 9.

20 For example, China's trade dependency ratio had by 1997 reached 40 percent, which is quite high for a large continental power with its own domestic market. By 1994 China had become the largest creditor of the World Bank.

21 For example, cf. Richard A. Bitzinger and Chong-Pin Lin, *The Defense Budget of the People's Republic of China* (Washington, DC: Defense Budget Project, 1994); and Shaoguang Wang, "Estimating China's Defence Expenditure: Some Evidence from Chinese Sources," *China Quarterly*, no. 147 (September 1996), pp. 889–911.

8 Twenty years of Chinese reform

The case of non-proliferation policy

Bates Gill

Introduction

Over the past twenty years, and especially in the 1990s, Chinese non-proliferation policy – like much of China's foreign and security policy – has undergone dramatic change and reform. In a few words, this process has been marked by:

- more open and active Chinese participation in international organizations and regimes concerned with non-proliferation;
- more constructive Chinese positions contributing to widespread international norms on these issues, including reaching accords for the benefit of improved relations with the United States;
- a greater degree of pluralization and institution building within the Chinese decision-making structure on these issues; and
- an effort within the bureaucratic structure to implement Chinese non-proliferation commitments.

In spite of these encouraging developments, however, there remain a number of concerns about China's willingness and ability to further strengthen its commitments to other non-proliferation regimes and agreements. Moreover, given recent controversies in the United States – including assistance of US companies in support of Chinese missile development, Chinese assistance to North Korean, Iranian, and Pakistani missile development, the Chinese missile buildup opposite Taiwan, and Chinese nuclear weapons espionage – it is both timely and important for policy development that we carefully interpret past and likely future Chinese activities with regard to non-proliferation. As we will see, the difficulties of reform not only encourage stricter non-proliferation policies, but also contribute to proliferation problems.

To frame this discussion, this brief study first offers a thumbnail sketch of positive developments and continuing concerns related to China and non-proliferation. Second, the study considers two cases of the impact of reform – one positive, the other potentially negative – on Chinese proliferation activities. Drawing on these developments and cases, the study then reaches some basic conclusions about how the reform process has affected Chinese non-proliferation policy, and the implications of these findings for the international community.

Background: positive developments, continuing concerns

It is important to recognize an overall positive set of developments related to Chinese proliferation activity, and that this process has largely paralleled and is closely related to China's opening and reform process. It is encouraging, for example, that the greatest concerns about Chinese proliferation activity relate largely to two countries: Iran and Pakistan. Even in these two cases, China has taken steps to constrain or halt activities of proliferation concern. In particular, given China's long-standing and close political relationship with Pakistan, such steps are especially noteworthy. Without going into detail, a review of positive Chinese non-proliferation activities in the 1980s and 1990s is provided below. It is encouraging to note that Chinese activities in this regard have especially accelerated since the early 1990s.

China began its most positive steps toward non-proliferation in the early 1980s. For example, China joined the International Atomic Energy Agency (IAEA) in January 1984 and in November 1984 acceded to the Biological Weapons Convention. In the same year, China announced it would require IAEA safeguards on its nuclear exports. (However, this announcement did not require full-scope safeguards which should be a continuing goal in non-proliferation efforts with China.) Later in the decade, in January 1989, China acceded to the Convention on the Physical Protection of Nuclear Material.

Beijing's positive approach to non-proliferation gained considerable pace in the 1990s, in part a response to the post-Cold War security environment and in part an aspect of its multilateral diplomatic breakout strategy in the wake of the Tiananmen crisis of 1989. China declared in November 1991 that it would report to the IAEA on the export or import of nuclear materials exceeding 1 kilogram for peaceful purposes to non-nuclear-weapon states. In February 1992, China pledged to abide by the original 1987 Missile Technology Control Regime guidelines, and a month later took a big step forward by acceding to the Nuclear Non-Proliferation Treaty (NPT). China signed the Chemical Weapons Convention in January 1993, formally submitted its instruments of ratification in April 1997, and joined the Organization for the Prohibition of Chemical Weapons as a founding member as of May 1997.

Beginning in 1993, China has fully participated in the United Nations Register of Conventional Arms (but has not provided a submission since 1998 in protest over the US listing its arms sales to Taiwan). Over the course of 1993 and 1994, China contributed to gaining North Korean acceptance of the October 1994 US–North Korea Agreed Framework, which has led to a freeze of the North Korean nuclear weapons program; since that time, China has been generally supportive of the efforts by the United States and others to moderate North Korean missile testing and exports. China supported the May 1995 indefinite extension of the NPT. In another set of important steps, China halted nuclear testing in July 1996, and announced a unilateral moratorium on further testing, and then signed the Comprehensive Test Ban Treaty in September 1996.

In a number of cases, China's support for non-proliferation was closely associated with US diplomatic pressures, or as part of the package of "deliverables" accompanying the two US–China summits in 1997 and 1998. For example, under considerable US pressure, China suspended plans to provide Iran with two 300 megawatt Qinshan-type nuclear power reactors in September 1995. Following revelations by the United States that China had provided ring magnets to unsafeguarded nuclear facilities in Pakistan, Beijing pledged in May 1996 not to provide assistance to unsafeguarded nuclear facilities. In preparation for the October 1997 summit, China attended the Zangger Committee meeting in May 1997 as an observer, and joined the committee as a full member in mid-October 1997. Also in preparation for the summit, in August 1997 China reportedly cancelled plans to construct a uranium conversion facility in Iran, and as part of the actual summit package, agreed to halt all new nuclear-related assistance to Iran. Also during the summit, China agreed to halt further anti-ship cruise missile sales to Iran. As part of the June 1998 summit, China announced an expanded chemical export control list, and agreed in an official statement with the United States that "our respective policies are to prevent the export of equipment, materials or technology that could in any way assist programs in India or Pakistan for nuclear weapons or for ballistic missiles capable of delivering such weapons."

In some cases, China took unilateral action to strengthen its commitments to non-proliferation. In November 1996, for example, China agreed to establish comprehensive nationwide regulations on nuclear export controls. In the fall of 1997 China formally established a new Arms Control and Disarmament Department (equivalent to US State Department bureau level) within the Chinese Ministry of Foreign Affairs. This department of approximately thirty persons is divided into four divisions, nuclear, chemical/biological, conventional, and research, marking a significant government commitment to address arms control and non-proliferation issues. In September 1997 China issued new nuclear export control regulations and an attached list of items to be controlled. This document formally acknowledges China's adherence to its "Three Principles for Nuclear Exports" and mandates its acceptance not to export nuclear materials to unsafeguarded facilities.

On the other hand, concerns about China's proliferation activity continue. There are some limited signs that proliferation concerns are now clearly understood by China's top leadership as a critical impediment to improved US–China relations, and that China's "image" is often at stake internationally on non-proliferation issues. But much work needs to be done to encourage and lock in improved Chinese non-proliferation policies. In spite of reform efforts (and, in some cases, *because* of reform efforts), persistent concerns continue. For example, China lacks a comprehensive and effective national export control system to implement and properly monitor transfers of nuclear, biological, chemical, missile, conventional, and dual-use exports. In spite of some encouraging developments for their export control system, the Chinese do not require full-scope safeguards for their nuclear exports. This is of particular concern for Chinese nuclear exports to Pakistan, which have facilities not under a safeguards agreement with the IAEA. There is also concern that Iran, which has a full-scope safeguards agreement, may have a clandestine nuclear program. This raises the possibility for diversion of nuclear imports to clandestine nuclear weapons programs even if China adheres to its stated commitment not to provide nuclear assistance to unsafeguarded facilities.

In addition, the Chinese have thus far remained outside a number of important multilateral export control regimes such as the Nuclear Suppliers Group, the Missile Technology Control Regime, the Australia Group, and the Wassenaar Arrangement. In China's view, these organizations are "supply-side cartels" made up of mostly Western states which discriminate against developing nations and their legitimate requirements for high-technology imports. At the multilateral level, China has obstructed progress in the United Nations Conference on Disarmament by demanding that any progress on a Fissile Material Cut-off Treaty be linked to progress on preventing an arms race in outer space (in this way, China wishes to pressure the United States to forgo its plans to deploy a national missile defense system).

As a result, a number of questions arise about China's non-proliferation commitments. Continued suspicions persist of the existence of Chinese offensive chemical and biological weapons programs, in violation of China's commitments to the Biological Weapons Convention and the Chemical Weapons Convention. Reports continue of China's non-compliance with its 1992 pledge to the United States to abide by the original 1987 Missile Technology Control Regime (MTCR) guidelines, and its 1994 bilateral statement with the United States to accept the "inherent capability" concept associated with the MTCR. Examples of these allegations include the export of equipment and technology for missile guidance, testing, and production to Iran, and the provision of missiles and missile components to Pakistan, as well as a missile production complex at Fatehgarh, near Rawalpindi. China apparently continues a number of nuclear-related assistance programs with Iran. Reports of this activity include the export of an electromagnetic isotope separation system and possible assistance in the construction of a uranium hexaflouride conversion facility. Concerns also persist related to Chinese chemical-weapons-related sales to Iran. As a result, in May 1997 the United States imposed sanctions on two Chinese companies, a Hong Kong company, and five Chinese citizens for chemical-weapons-related exports to Iran. These sanctions remain in place today as the only proliferation-related sanctions between the United States and China. Concerns continue as well regarding China's nuclear-related exports and assistance to Pakistan. As noted above, these concerns include the provision of 5,000 ring magnets to the unsafeguarded A. Q. Khan facility in Kahuta and assistance to the unsafeguarded Khushab heavy-water reactor. There are even concerns about illicit transfers inside of China: Chinese diversion to military-related facilities of US dual-use exports intended for peaceful purposes, including machine tools and supercomputers, highlights unease about China's acceptance of non-proliferation norms and its ability to properly monitor the end-use of militarily-relevant technologies within its own borders.

These positive and negative developments suggest a steady, if uneven, set of encouraging breakthroughs in Chinese non-proliferation activity. By looking at two specific cases – China's decision to sign the Comprehensive Test Ban Treaty (CTBT), and potential missile proliferation problems – we can see more clearly how external and internal reform pressures have shaped this back-and-forth dynamic of positive and negative developments.

External forces and the CTBT decision

China's decision to go along with the CTBT is particularly intriguing because, along with the Chemical Weapons Convention, it marked the first time China agreed multilaterally to place effective limits on its own weapons capabilities. Placed in the uncomfortable position of opposing an achievement which had near universal support in the developing world and among the other nuclear powers, China was compelled to "go along" with the international community – in spite of deep reservations on the part of its military–scientific community – and live up to its decades of disarmament rhetoric. This critical Chinese decision was driven in large measure by international pressures and a fractious internal debate which in the end favored – for the sake of China's international image, and some possible relative gains in Chinese security – a decision to sign on to the treaty. Here we see how the reform era's opening to the outside world had an important role in shaping Chinese non-proliferation decisions.

The negotiations over the CTBT from January 1994 to August 1996 took place in the context of growing international opposition to nuclear proliferation and nuclear testing which increasingly came to bear on China. Normative pressure not to test had built up both in the developing world and, importantly, among several nuclear weapon states. An informal testing moratorium among four of the nuclear weapon states – the Soviet Union/Russia, the United States, France, and the United Kingdom – had already been in place for several years.[1] The United States was particularly vocal in urging the Chinese to join in a testing moratorium during this period. By the end of 1995, China made the difficult choice to oppose a UN General Assembly resolution on disarmament urging the halt of nuclear testing.[2] Following France's last test in January 1996, China was left alone as the only country testing even as the CTBT reached its final stages.

China was also pressured by several of its neighbors in Asia. Following the Chinese test of May 1995, Japan suspended the grant portion of its foreign aid program to China in protest against China's continued nuclear weapon testing. Later, in August 1995, the Japanese legislature passed a resolution protesting China's testing and later that month, Japan froze government grants for the remainder of 1995. Some analysts suggested that China actually called off a planned test in fall 1995 to avoid a further cut-off in Japanese aid and to quell the rising tide of concern among China's neighbors over Chinese testing; concern over testing especially gathered momentum in the Asia–Pacific with the resumption of French testing in September 1995.[3] After China's July 1996 test, Japan considered extending the ban to include official soft loans (the majority of Japan's official funding for China), but in the end took no action. Instead, once China announced its testing moratorium and signed the CTBT, the two sides began negotiations on the fourth yen loan package to China for 1996–8 in late 1996. In March 1997, Japan's foreign minister stated that Japan would restore grant aid to China.

To China's west, countries near China's Lop Nor test site – Kazakhstan, Kyrgyzstan, and Uzbekistan – sternly criticized Chinese testing in 1994–6, both at official and unofficial levels. Numerous protests were staged at Chinese embassies in the capitals of these Central Asian republics, and officials from the three countries lodged formal diplomatic protests and raised concerns over the environmental damage caused by testing at the Lop Nor site. The protests were enough to have Chinese President Jiang Zemin acknowledge these problems, stating that "China fully understands the concerns of Central Asian states over the possible negative impact of atomic testing on the environment," but added that there was no evidence that there were negative effects.[4]

Persons and institutions associated with the Ministry of Foreign Affairs – who in a more open China are most directly involved in the country's image building abroad – appeared to take the lead in arguing, in the end, for signing on to the CTBT, in spite of the problems it poses to China's nuclear deterrent. China's lead negotiator on the CTBT and chief arms controller in the Ministry of Foreign Affairs (MFA) went directly to military leaders to discuss the CTBT, and made the case for Chinese adherence.

The MFA argued that China's international stature and image as a responsible Great Power were at stake, and that China's political and diplomatic maneuverability and progress required a constructive position on the CTBT. In addition, it was argued that China would gain certain concrete benefits from signing the treaty. Specifically, it was argued that supporting the CTBT would not only be beneficial to China's Great Power image, but promote the goals of the non-proliferation regime by demonstrating good faith in Article VI of the NPT (that the nuclear powers would work toward general and complete disarmament), create more favorable and peaceful international conditions for Chinese economic development, and would contribute to further disarmament on the part of the major nuclear powers, the United States and Russia.

But not only MFA officials held this view. Indeed, from the outset of CTBT negotiations in early 1994, top Chinese leaders and officials consistently maintained their desire to conclude a treaty by the end of 1996, which suggests that a political decision to sign the treaty in principle had been made by 1993 or earlier. This may suggest in part that Chinese leaders recognized early on the importance of adhering to international opinion. In any event, it is clear that as a result of China's opening and reform program, the country's leadership was far more sensitive to international pressures.

Internal reforms and potential for missile proliferation

But just as China's reforms and opening have a positive effect on the country's non-proliferation policy, so too it can have unintended negative effects. For example, far-reaching domestic reforms and government restructuring launched in early 1998 may have an effect on Chinese missile proliferation (as well as other types of proliferation). These effects will most likely occur as a result of defense-industrial restructuring in the state-owned sector, reforms within the PLA, and reorganization of the export control bureaucracy.

Two general points can summarize the implications for proliferation of these developments. First, these restructuring efforts are still in their earliest stages, and lines of authority and responsibility remain unclear even some years after their initiation; this strains an already weak system of export control implementation and monitoring. Second, and exacerbating the first point, the restructuring, downsizing, and elimination of defense-industrial firms and PLA-related businesses may prompt some entities to traffic in sensitive exports in return for hard currency and other economic incentives.

State-owned enterprise reform

In September 1997, at the 15th Congress of the Chinese Communist Party, the Chinese leadership announced its intention to radically downsize the burdensome state-owned enterprise (SOE) sector. Chinese defense-industrial firms and factories, representing perhaps as much as 30 percent of SOEs, were among the primary targets for reform, downsizing, mergers, sell-offs, and elimination. Hulking, backward, faced with declining procurement orders, and long isolated from the dynamism of China's economic reforms, the defense-industrial sector had long been awash in red ink and an increasing burden on state coffers as a larger and larger recipient of subsidies.[5] Estimates as to the size of the entire defense-industrial base – perhaps as many as 3 million employees working at some 2,000 enterprises – suggest the scale and importance of the sector. The ongoing process of restructuring this massive industrial sector will affect the ability of the central government to monitor its potentially sensitive exports, transfers potentially driven by the bottom-line pressures of the reform program itself.

At least two important developments related to SOE reform should be considered as having a potential impact on Chinese proliferation activities. First, an important and pervasive part of the reform effort within the defense-industrial base has been the steady "corporatization" of the sector over time. By the March 1998 reform, the former "big five" defense-industrial sectors (nuclear, aviation, ordnance, naval vessels, space and missiles) had shifted from state ministries to become ministry-level corporations, with the expectation that they would eventually become full-fledged corporations with nominal state control. Under the State Council, the former defense-industrial ministries are now known as the China National Nuclear Corporation (CNNC), Aviation Industries of China (AVIC), China North Industries Group (NORINCO), the China State Shipbuilding Corporation (CSSC), and the China Aerospace Corporation (CAsC); the former electronics ministry was merged into the new Ministry of Information Industry, though the former ministry has a number of corporate spin-offs now operating in the marketplace. Furthermore, the "big five" corporations have each been divided into two conglomerates in order – ostensibly – to foster greater intra-sector competition.

For example, reports suggest that CNNC will be split into two groups in the future, with one part focusing on nuclear power plant construction and the other, larger part handling a range of activities from "mining of uranium to nuclear fuels, isotopes, nuclear manufacturing for both military and civilian use, nuclear waste treatment, and nuclear safety."[6]

This corporatization dynamic – at least the fourth major defense-industrial reorganization in China since the early 1980s – has at least two facets relevant to proliferation concerns. First, the dynamic has built into it an ever-greater urge toward profit-making, an issue especially poignant at a time of shrinking state subsidies, increased competition, and pressures to downsize. As a result, these companies, as manufacturers of military- and dual-use goods, have added incentives to seek profits for their potentially sensitive exports. Second, the dynamic entails significant decentralization from state control, which allows the corporatized entities to operate with less government oversight, raising concerns about export control implementation and monitoring.

A second important proliferation-related aspect of state-owned enterprise reform concerns restructuring of the high-level oversight body for the Chinese defense-industrial base. COSTIND, the body under the Central Military Commission and the State Council charged with overseeing China's defense production, was formally abolished and then reconstituted as part of the government organizational reforms announced at the National People's Congress in March 1998. COSTIND, which was headed by military personnel, was "civilianized" under the reforms; the "new" COSTIND is headed by civilian leaders, and appears to be tasked largely with coordinating and regulating the civilian side of China's defense-industrial production. With this reorganization, the new COSTIND lost its formerly prominent role in arms control and non-proliferation policy making. The Arms Control Division within the former COSTIND's Foreign Affairs Office and COSTIND's arms control research staff at its China Defense Science and Technology Information Center were transferred to the newly established General Armaments Department under the military (see below).

At present, COSTIND's role in non-proliferation appears to be limited to the realm of assisting the export control process. As part of the reforms announced in March 1998, in addition to the defense production units noted above

(CNNC, AVIC, CASC, CSSC, NORINCO), COSTIND also oversees two subsidiary bureaus, the State Aerospace Bureau and the China Atomic Energy Agency, whose principal role is to regulate the aerospace and nuclear industries, respectively. These organizations were formerly part of the larger corporate ministries CASC and CNNC, respectively. As part of their responsibilities, these bureaus are expected to vet applications for export licenses, especially those associated with nuclear and missile-related technologies. This development is probably a plus for non-proliferation as the placement of these regulatory bodies within the new COSTIND has separated them from corporate interests whose goals include exportation of aerospace- and nuclear-related goods and services.

PLA reform

The PLA and bodies associated with it would be key players in decisions related to sensitive exports such as missile technologies and systems. The precise scope of that influence is not well understood but appears to derive from the military's technical expertise, its traditionally powerful political position within the Chinese decision-making structure, the influence of certain high-ranking officers, and its past record as an exporter of surplus weaponry (such as the DF-3 ballistic missile sales to Saudi Arabia in the mid-1980s). However, country-wide reform measures have not left the PLA untouched, and, moreover, these PLA-related reforms could result in an increase in Chinese proliferation activities under certain conditions. Reform efforts of greatest proliferation concern fall under two main headings: the establishment of the PLA General Armaments Department (GAD) and the decision in July 1998 to separate the PLA from its business enterprises.

Formed in April 1998 as part of a range of economic and industrial reform measures announced that spring, the GAD draws together the uniformed military from the former COSTIND with the General Staff Department's Equipment Directorate, as well as with other military-equipment-related offices from other parts of the General Staff system. The GAD's responsibilities include determining the arms procurement needs of the PLA, reviewing certain military-related exports, as well having a voice in arms control negotiations affecting Chinese military capability. Specifically, the GAD's role in arms control and non-proliferation policy making results from three main activities.

First, as mentioned above, the GAD now controls the "old" COSTIND's arms control division which conducts research on the full spectrum of arms control and non-proliferation issues including nuclear, chemical, and biological weapons proliferation, exports controls, and nuclear testing issues. Presumably, the results of this research are furnished to the office of the Chief of the General Staff for use in interagency discussions. Second, the GAD plays a limited role in the export control review process. In the nuclear realm, for example, the GAD is responsible for controlling exports of nuclear materials; the GAD is also expected to have a hand in vetting exports of certain missile systems along with other agencies such as the Ministry of Foreign Trade and Economic Cooperation (MOFTEC), the State Administrative Commission on Military Products Trade (SACMPT), and the State Aerospace Bureau.

Lastly, the GAD will have key inputs into Chinese non-proliferation policies owing to the influence of certain individuals. The GAD is headed by General Cao Gangchuan, who was the head of the former COSTIND until its "civilianization" in March 1998. Cao was previously Deputy Chief of the General Staff, and has played an important role in some of China's more well-known arms export cases, such as the transfer of DF-3 intermediate-range ballistic missiles to Saudi Arabia. He was also appointed ex officio to the Central Military Commission in October 1998, the military's highest policy-making body. Zhu Guangya, an influential physicist closely associated with China's nuclear and missile programs, continues to head the Science and Technology Committee which formerly served as the chief advisory body to COSTIND, but which has now been transferred to advise the GAD; General Qian Shaojun, another physicist and also a member of the GAD's Science and Technology Committee, is the military's leading voice on arms control issues. Lieutenant-General Shen Rongjun, formerly a deputy director of the old COSTIND, now serves as Deputy Director of GAD, and has a long association with China's missile and aerospace development programs.

A second important area of PLA reform relevant to proliferation concerns is the decision announced by Jiang Zemin in July 1998 to separate the military from direct involvement in business activities. This decision, taken to eliminate corruptive and unprofessional influences eroding PLA effectiveness and social standing, will most directly affect individual units throughout the army which benefited from additional earnings to supplement meager rations and poor living conditions (those individuals who profited from PLA-related businesses can retire from the military and carry on their business activities). Because the business activities were originally intended to support on-the-ground, unit-level expenses, the central government has pledged to make up for the expected loss in income through an annual supplement to the officially announced PLA budget, to amount to some RMB 3.2 billion (approximately US$ 400 million, less than 5 percent of the official budget) each year.[7] This amount is likely to be well short of the annual net earnings of PLA enterprises, earnings the military was likely reluctant to fully reveal.

Having been officially cut off from these earnings, and finding the government supplement too little, some military leaders may see arms exports as a viable means to infuse the PLA with hard currency. As Lewis *et al.* have shown, the military employed precisely this argument in selling off its surplus inventory in the mid- to late 1980s – even new weapons it had acquired at highly subsidized prices from Chinese defense factories – including the aging DF-3 (CSS-2) missiles sold to Saudi Arabia. The decision-making structure in China for such exports appears more pluralized and restrained today, and the global marketplace for Chinese weapons has reached new lows, factors which weigh against the "PLA as proliferator" scenario. But degenerating relations with the United States, an economic downturn in China, and a perceived need by the PLA to rapidly augment access to foreign exchange (in order to purchase foreign weapons systems, for example) could spur the Chinese military to enter the arms trade business once again.

Export control reform

As noted above, in March 1998, after meetings of the 9th National People's Congress, the Chinese government initiated a major restructuring of its bureaucracy and especially its military–industrial complex. These reform and restructuring activities continue and are likely to have profound effects on China's export control system, including export controls for missiles. The reorganization effort has involved the abolition of entire government organs such as the Ministry of Chemical Industry and, in other cases, has involved the transfer of authority among agencies and commissions, such as the State Aeronautics Bureau, whose authority may include export control issues, now exercised under the newly formed COSTIND. These changes, in turn, have shifted the responsibility for export controls among various agencies in the Chinese bureaucracy.

On the specific issue of export controls – formulating, implementing, and enforcing control over the export of sensitive materials – the situation in China is also in flux, resulting in greater diffusion of decision-making authority. According to a Chinese arms control official, under the planned economy, a centralized system of "executive decrees" sufficed to effectively implement export controls. However, under the conditions of "reform and opening to the outside world and the rapid development of the socialist market economy," the Chinese government has had to implement a new system which is more authoritative, comprehensive, and consistent with international practice (including licensing procedures and export control lists).

These steps involve the delegation of authority to various government ministries. According to past regulations (and depending on the export), the various responsibilities for licensing the export of sensitive materials and military products fell to such organizations as the Chinese Atomic Energy Authority (CAEA), COSTIND, the Ministry of Foreign Trade and Economic Cooperation (MOFTEC), the State Administration of Military Products Trade, the Ministry of Chemical Industry, and the State Customs Administration. Effectively implementing these export controls was made even more complex with the March 1998 restructuring of China's defense industry. This decision, which aimed in part to draw clearer lines between the military and civilian production activities, abolished some of the main entities involved in administering export controls. In other cases where complete organizations were not abolished and responsibilities shifted, the lines of authority among various organizations are murky, possibly complicating their ability to coordinate on export control decisions.[8]

Adding to concerns, there is no known public document or control list to regulate missile exports. This contrasts with published laws regulating the exports of other sensitive materials such as chemicals, nuclear materials, dual-use goods, and a catch-all category, "military products"; the Chinese claim that missile exports fall under the latter category. However, with the restructuring of the government beginning in 1998, some of the lines of authority set out in those regulations are not clear. Recent inquiries with authoritative Chinese officials as to the existence of specific missile export controls and how the shakeup in the defense industry affects missile export controls resulted in silence, or the response that the Chinese are "actively studying" the issue; some Chinese aerospace officials state that there is a missile control list, and adherence to that list is assured by the government which is "in control" of missile-related factories.

It is possible that the Chinese, as an interim measure, might publicly issue export control regulations based on the MTCR guidelines and control lists. That would be seen as a step toward eventual membership in the regime at a later date. But to date, owing in significant part to the apparent absence of explicit regulations as well as continued uncertainties within the defense-industrial and export control bureaucracies, missile-related proliferation is a likely possibility for the near future.

Economic downturn?

All of these potential proliferation drivers related to reform – defense-industrial downsizing, PLA reform, and export control reorganization – would be exacerbated proportionally by an economic downturn in China, which itself could result in part from fast-moving reform plans there. Severely diminished resources would strain the already weakened state-owned sector, and would fall hardest on the least reformed SOEs, those in the defense-industrial sector. For some, exports of sensitive technologies would be a likely outlet to relieve economic hardship, and under difficult conditions might be acceptable actions in the view of the Chinese leadership. Should an economic crisis squeeze PLA R&D and acquisition budgets, its leadership too would likely support arms exports as a means to bring in hard currency. Finally, an economic downturn would also reduce resources available to strengthen the country's fledgling export control infrastructure, which might in any event be circumvented or set aside in worsening economic conditions.

Conclusions

The developments and cases discussed in the previous pages lead to several basic conclusions and recommendations about Chinese reform-era non-proliferation policy and the role of the international community in its non-proliferation policy vis-à-vis China.

First, China's reform and opening up have critically affected China's non-proliferation and arms control policy. As is the case with other foreign policy areas, the decision-making system in non-proliferation and arms control has opened up to, and is buffeted by, far more pluralization and omnidirectional influences, both abroad and at home. Second, and on a related note, Chinese policy choices in non-proliferation and arms control which most closely track with widely accepted international norms and practices coincide with the post-Tiananmen, post-Cold War diplomatic offensive of the early to mid-1990s indicating the strong influence of external, usually multilateral, consensus as a factor influencing China's more open decision-making structure. To a lesser degree, the influence of certain bilateral relations – especially with the United States – is a key factor in shaping Chinese decisions in some cases. Third, the reform-oriented, more open policy-making structure in China allows for more pluralized discussion, but also results in a more open degree of bureaucratic in-fighting and disagreements, a devolution of authority, difficulties in implementing and monitoring decisions, and some policy paralysis and disarray.

Finally, a "realpolitik" and "adaptive" approach to non-proliferation and arms control appears to dominate Chinese decision making in this policy area. But the relative independence and unilateralism which this understanding implies cannot be overestimated. Rather, China's policy making is increasingly constrained by the intricate web of international dependencies, commitments, status relationships, and security realities it faces. Chinese positions in line with international norms and practices often result from "realpolitik" calculations, but are hemmed in by the very benefits of international integration and acceptance that the decisions hope to preserve and enhance. However, given the internal debates over China's future course in this policy area, the process will not be smooth, and will involve bumps, stops, and backtracking.

Given these conclusions, what approaches might be developed within the international community to foster movement by China toward a greater acceptance and implementation of non-proliferation norms and policies? As the world's leading advocate for non proliferation, and with a particular stake in this issue for US–China relations, the United States has a particularly important role in this process.

As a first step, we should note that, in general, targeted and limited penalties – such as sanctions – have had some positive impact, but only when combined with other policies. Thus, while sanctions and other penalties have an important role in achieving non-proliferation goals, they are likely to be less effective if imposed in the absence of other activities and incentives. For example, China takes a more positive approach toward non-proliferation goals when faced with a clear international consensus on non-proliferation. The Chinese have demonstrated their sensitivity to international concerns; when confronted with such an international consensus, Chinese policy makers wish to be seen as taking part and supporting its goals. The international community should not overlook this often powerful lever to gain Chinese acceptance and adherence to non-proliferation norms and procedures.

The slow but steady process over the past decade of introducing international norms and procedures into the Chinese arms control and non-proliferation community has had a useful impact on the development of more positive non-proliferation behavior on the part of the Chinese. However, this type of communication and dialogue should not be conducted for dialogue's sake alone. Rather, such communication and exchange should be effectively implemented to strongly and clearly convey both incentives and disincentives for certain desired Chinese behavior. Such dialogue can take place in programs of research and training at the unofficial level, as well as through offers of assistance and expertise at the official level. These types of programs and incentives have supported the establishment and growth of a nascent official and unofficial non-proliferation community and culture in China. This process should be encouraged to continue.

More positive Chinese policies on non-proliferation have resulted when the international community makes a serious effort to analyze Chinese motivations and disincentives more carefully, and devotes greater resources to understanding the complexities of China's emergent influence in the international community. This seems particularly true in the case of US relations with China. As China continues to reform and open up, this process should be increasingly smooth – though not without its difficulties – and should result in a Chinese non-proliferation policy more convergent with widely accepted international norms.

Notes

1　The Soviet Union's last test was in October 1990; the newly independent state of Russia has not since tested; the last US test was in September 1992; the last UK test was in November 1991. France had participated in the moratorium for nearly four years, from late 1991 until late 1995, when it resumed its final series of six tests which ran from September 1995 to January 1996. Also during this period, the international community reached the decision to indefinitely extend the Nuclear Non-proliferation Treaty (in May 1995), which was achieved in large measure by a commitment on the part of the nuclear powers to engage earnestly in meaningful disarmament efforts, such as the CTBT.

2　M. Littlejohns, "U.N. Votes Against N-Testing," *Financial Times*, 14 December 1995, p. 6.

3　"Sources Indicate Plans for Nuclear Test Halted," *Itar-Tass*, 30 October 1995, in foreign Broadcast Information Service (FBIS), *Daily Report: China*, 31 October 1995; "Intention to Grant Yen Loans to PRC Firms Up," *Yomiuri Shimbun*, 25 October 1995, in FBIS, *Daily Report: East Asia*, FBIS-EAS-95–208, 26 October 1995.

4　D. Busvine, "China's Jiang Calls For Nuclear Test Ban Treaty," *Reuters*, 5 July 1996.

5　Greater detail on the problems of the Chinese defense-industrial base appears in J. Frankenstein and B. Gill, "Current and Future Challenges Facing Chinese Defense Industries," *China Quarterly*, no. 146 (1996), pp. 394–427.

6　"Nuke Sector Reform Underway," *China Daily*, 5 February 1999, p. A5.

7　Discussions with senior members of the PLA General Logistics Department, December 1998, Beijing, China.

8　Interviews with Chinese arms control officials, April and May 1998, Beijing, China.

9 Soldiers of fortune, soldiers of misfortune

Commercialization and divestiture of the Chinese military–business complex, 1978–99

James Mulvenon

Introduction

On July 22, 1998, PRC President Jiang Zemin publicly announced the dissolution of the Chinese People's Liberation Army's business empire, bringing an end to almost twenty years of government-sanctioned military commercialism. Five months later, the government declared that the PLA had been formally separated from its enterprises, which were henceforth being controlled by a government holding company pending asset valuation and sale. Beneath the veneer, however, has been a process marked by both common interests and acrimonious dispute. While the full details of the story cannot be known at present, enough information has been revealed to warrant a preliminary examination of the subject. This essay will attempt to explicate the extent of our knowledge thus far, examining the origins, course, structure, and important compromises of divestiture.

This chapter is divided into two principal sections. The first section briefly outlines the fiscal and civil–military origins of military commercialization, beginning with the early and primitive responses to defense budget cutbacks in the late 1970s that eventually grew into a multi-billion-dollar international business empire. The heart of the chapter is the second section, which tells the story of divestiture, assesses its successes and failures, and forecasts the future course of PLA separation from business.

Commercialization (1978–98)

Between 1978 and 1998, the PLA underwent a dramatic transformation. Faced with the contradictory forces of a declining military budget and pressures to modernize at the end of the Maoist era, the army reluctantly agreed to join the Chinese economic reform drive, converting and expanding its existing internal military economy to market-oriented civilian production. Both the civilian and military leadership hoped that the resulting profits could replace lost defense expenditures and help finance the army's long-needed modernization of weaponry and forces. In the two decades since those decisions were taken, the

PLA became one of the most important actors in the Chinese economy, controlling a multi-billion-dollar international business empire that ran the gamut from large farms to world-class hotels and transnational corporations.

To understand the reasons behind commercialization of the PLA after 1978, it is first necessary to understand the fiscal relationship between the state and military. There is strong evidence to suggest that the PLA during the Maoist era enjoyed virtually unlimited access to funds from the national budget. According to Jonathan Pollack, "few within the leadership ever challenged the army's entitlements," and, as a consequence, "the army grew by accretion and inertia."[1] The best example of the high budgetary priority placed on defense during this period was the Third Front industrialization campaign of the early 1960s, which was personally directed by Deng Xiaoping.[2] Predicated on Mao Zedong's fear of foreign invasion, one-fourth of the entire national defense-industrial complex was rebuilt in the mountainous regions of ten provinces. Chinese officials estimate that the financial cost of these enterprises was RMB 200 billion over a twenty-year period ending in 1984, equivalent to two-thirds of the defense budget over the same period.[3]

For Deng Xiaoping and the reformers in the late 1970s, however, the stagnation of the Chinese economy from the Great Leap Forward (1958–61) through the Cultural Revolution (1966–76) meant that the civilian government could not meet the budgetary needs of the PLA *and* provide the large capital investments necessary for an ambitious and costly program of post-Mao economic reforms.[4] At an enlarged meeting of the Standing Committee of the Central Military Commission on March 12, 1980, Deng Xiaoping drew a direct link between reducing the defense budget and strengthening economic reform, stating:

> our current military expenditures are rather high, to the detriment of national construction. … During this time, we should try our best to cut down military spending so as to strengthen national construction. In short, it is necessary to reduce "bloatedness" [in the army] if we want to carry out the Four Modernizations.[5]

Soon afterwards, appropriations for other parts of the state budget, including the defense budget, were slashed to pay for increased investment in civilian economic projects. Between 1979 and 1981, the official defense budget was cut by 24.6 percent, from RMB 22.27 billion to RMB 16.8 billion.

While the military was told that its defense budgets would eventually increase as China's economy became more developed, short-term measures were taken to supplement defense revenue. The most important of these involved the exploitation of the PLA's latent economic capacity, which derived from three sources: (1) fifty years of PLA experience with various types of economic production, (2) a well-developed and exploitable military logistics infrastructure, ranging from transportation to factories and farms, and (3) the deeply ingrained socialization among the ranks and the top-level civilian leadership that production was an acceptable military task. From later Chinese writings, it is clear that this internal military economy was expected to generate sufficient revenue to "make up for insufficient spending."[6]

Historically, there was an important precedent for military participation in economic activities. During the pre-Liberation period in the base area at Yan'an, the Red Army was ordered to engage in production and limited commerce in lieu of fiscal support from the government. After Liberation in 1949, the military, unlike other government organs, was permitted to continue and eventually expand these activities in order to reduce their fiscal burden on the state, though military economic work remained focused on "self-sustaining," subsistence farming and limited industrial production.

In the post-Mao era, by contrast, the PLA was permitted to gradually externalize and commercialize these previously internal activities, in order to make up for lost budget revenue. At the beginning of the commercialization process, the PLA first leveraged its internal assets and infrastructural privileges in limited ways. Military farms were encouraged to sell in the new local markets and the PLA began to "civilianize" some of its underused ports, wharves, airfields, trucks, and rail space.[7] Over time, the military moved into new areas of the economy, such as light industrial production for the civilian market, international trade, property development, transportation, vehicle production, medical care, pharmaceuticals, hotels, mining, telecommunications, and even securities exchange. By the late 1980s, the PLA economy had grown to over 20,000 enterprises, employing several million workers and generating profits of nearly RMB 5 billion in 1992.

Much to the chagrin of the military, the importance of the PLA's internal economy as supplement to the defense budget only grew over time, as declining defense budgets forced the military to become increasingly dependent on the rising extra-budgetary revenue from its enterprises. In terms of budgets, for example, there is a consensus among Chinese and Western analysts that, as a consequence of redirected fiscal priorities and the regime's diminishing capacity to extract rents from the economy,[8] the official defense budget between 1979 and 1989 declined considerably in real terms, while only increasing marginally in nominal terms (see Figure 9.1).

Even the double-digit budget increases since 1989, which averaged a rate of 14 percent per year, were largely absorbed by a 13 percent average rate of inflation. Any attempts by the government to arrest this decline in real defense budgets were offset by rapidly increasing budget deficits, reaching almost RMB 60 billion in 1996.

At the same time, the profits from the military's enterprises by the late 1980s and early 1990s were providing a significant percentage of local unit operating funds, especially subsidies for wages, food, and facilities. Furthermore, these enterprises employed soldiers' dependents and demobilized soldiers, supplementing the meager wages of active-duty personnel. Over time, the profits and revenue from these military enterprises became essential components of military financial management.

These two trends (the combination of decreasing government capacity to fund

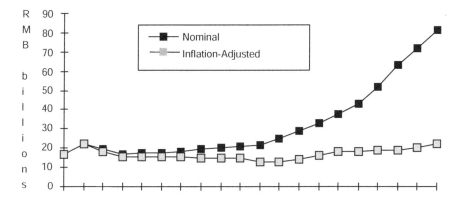

Figure 9.1 Nominal and inflation-adjusted defense budget, 1978–97

the military from central coffers and the increasing dependence of military units on profits from military enterprises) combined to create a sense of bureaucratic "lock-in" for the military–business complex. As a result, the military leadership found it increasingly difficult to contemplate an end to the military–business complex, despite the troubling rise in rampant corruption within the ranks. The PLA's level of dependency also made it impossible for the civilian leadership to wean the military away from commercial activity. The political leadership, ever cognizant of the central role of the PLA in the post-Deng transition, was understandably reluctant to separate the PLA from its businesses, unless it could replace the lost funds with increased budgetary allocation.[9]

For nearly twenty years, therefore, the PLA was trapped in a catch-22: it could not fully professionalize without abandoning its economic enterprises, nor could it sustain the current professionalization and modernization process without them. Even Jiang Zemin allegedly said: "if we were given an additional RMB 30 billion in a short time, there would be no need for the armed forces to engage in trade."[10] Since he did not have the extra funds, however, he publicly maintained the position that "the Army can play an active role in reducing the burdens on the state … when it engages in production." As the PLA approached the twenty-first century, most observers seemed convinced that the civilian leadership and the PLA would be forced to maintain this uncomfortable arrangement for the foreseeable future.

Divestiture (1998)

On July 22, 1998, at an enlarged session of the Central Military Commission, CMC Chairman Jiang Zemin gave a speech in which he called for the dissolution of the military–business complex, asserting:

> To make concerted efforts to properly develop the army in an all-around manner, the central authorities decided: The army and the armed police

[*wu jing*] should earnestly screen and rectify [*qingli*] various commercial companies operated by their subordinate units, and shall not carry out any commercial activities in the future. ... Military and armed police units should resolutely implement the central authorities' resolution and fulfill as soon as possible the requirements that their subordinate units shall not carry out any commercial activities in the future.[11]

Jiang then sought to consolidate the decree by publicly releasing the announcement through the party's extensive propaganda apparatus. That night, Jiang's speech at the meeting was broadcast on the CCTV Evening News, which has the highest rating in China and is closely watched by other Chinese media for cues about important stories. Observers took special note of the fact that the Chinese leader was shown flanked by the top brass of the PLA, implying at least tacit consent to the decision by the military. The next day, the party's official newspaper, *People's Daily*, ran a banner headline, declaring "PLA Four General Departments Convened in Beijing to Carry Out the Decision of the Anti-Smuggling Meeting," with the subtitle "Chairman Jiang Talked Seriously About Divestiture."[12] The announcement was then publicly seconded in subsequent days by key members of the military and civilian leadership, including the *de facto* head of the PLA, General Zhang Wannian, Chief of the General Staff General Fu Quanyou (23 July),[13] General Logistics Department Director Wang Ke (24 July),[14] General Political Department Director General Yu Yongbo (25 July),[15] and General Armament Department Director General Cao Gangchuan (26 July),[16] as well as Politburo Standing Committee member Hu Jintao.[17] From the media barrage, it appeared that the decision might actually have the political momentum to dislodge the Chinese military from its difficult catch-22.

While the divestiture announcement was immediately picked up by Western and Chinese media and portrayed as a dramatic reversal of policy, the reality of the situation was much more complicated. Divestiture was not a sudden decision at all. Jiang Zemin reportedly first floated the idea of the military "eating imperial grain" (*chi huangliang*, i.e., being funded solely by the government) in 1990, but it was judged to be impractical. In the absence of divestiture, the PLA underwent more than six years of rectification and consolidation campaigns in the military enterprise system, and divestiture should in many ways be seen as the logical culmination of that effort. Moreover, the July 1998 meeting was not even the first divestiture announcement. A decision to divest had actually been made over a year earlier in May 1997, although the major transfers were not set to begin until three years later in May 2000. One important preparatory move, the withdrawal of the preferential tax rates enjoyed by PLA enterprises (civilian companies previously paid 33 percent while PLA enterprises only paid 9.9 percent), had been implemented in early 1998, and the PLA had reportedly drawn up a plan for divestiture at least six months in advance of the July 1998 announcement.[18]

Thus, Jiang's order represented only an acceleration of the divestiture timetable. The complete reasons are not entirely known, but there are at least two competing stories. One rumor claims that divestiture was initiated by an angry Jiang Zemin upon receiving an account of the excessively corrupt activities of six PLA and People's Armed Police (PAP) companies, the most egregious of which involved oil smuggling that was bankrupting the country's two geographical oil monopolies.[19] Indeed, there were widespread reports that rampant smuggling by the military during the Asian economic turmoil in early 1998 allegedly deprived the government of hundreds of billions of *renminbi* of customs revenue and caused worsening deflation.[20]

A second version of the story actually begins with Zhu Rongji.[21] According to cited US intelligence sources, at the July 17, 1998 meeting of the anti-smuggling work conference Zhu Rongji angered the PLA by accusing the General Political Department's Tiancheng Group of rampant corruption.[22] In particular, he singled out a case in which the company had avoided paying RMB 50 million in import and sales taxes after purchasing a shipment of partially processed iron ore from Australia. "Every time our customs officials tried to snare these bastards, some powerful military person appeared to speak on their behalf," Zhu allegedly charged at the closed-door meeting. As anger and resentment spread through the PLA leadership, Jiang Zemin allegedly appeared at the conference four days later to lend his support to Zhu, confirming that "some units and individuals" in the PLA were involved in smuggling. According to this account, Jiang thereupon announced the divestiture order.

These accounts of the decision to divest the PLA of its enterprises raise a fundamental analytical question: How did the PLA and the CCP work their way out of what could only be described as the fiscal and political catch-22 of military commercialism? Contrary to the conflictual civil–military scenario put forward by many observers in the Hong Kong media, the evidence instead suggests that the divestiture in principle was largely supported by a corruption-weary military leadership. They generally agreed with the political, military, and economic rationales for divestiture. On the political front, divestiture was aimed at curtailing corruption within the ranks. The civilian leadership argued that as long as the military operated in the commercial economy, it was subject to "negative influences." Jiang Zemin reportedly spoke of preventing the military from "changing color" and of keeping the military "pure." At a military level, divestiture was designed to return the PLA to its primary professional mission: preparing for war. Finally, from an economic perspective, there was recognition that the military was not adept at running commercial operations.

A key condition for military acquiescence to divestiture, however, was an assurance from the civilians that the PLA would receive a sufficiently generous compensation package for handing over its businesses. Indeed, sources in Beijing confirmed that the faultlines in the divestiture process could be drawn between supporters, including the senior military leadership and the combat units, and those who resisted the ban, especially members of the logistics and enterprise management structure, military region commands, and military district commands that stood to lose their primary source of legal and illegal income.[23]

The heart of the bargain between the PLA and the civilian leadership therefore centered on financial compensation, in this case two separate financial deals. The first was the one-time transfer of the PLA's divested enterprises. Reportedly, the financial burden of these enterprises, including their weighty social welfare costs and debts, was to be placed upon local and provincial governments rather than the central government, though no money was to change hands. This devolution of responsibility from the center to the localities was seen by many as yet another attempt by Zhu Rongji to restore some measure of macro-level economic authority in China by forcing the lower levels of the system to assume greater financial responsibility for the economic units in their area.

The second negotiation focused on the annual budget increases to make up for lost enterprise revenues, with the goal of consolidating Jiang's earlier decree to the military to "eat imperial grain" rather than rely on business for revenue. Before the divestiture was completed, Hong Kong sources reported that the PLA would receive between RMB 15 and 30 billion per year, with the exact time frame subject to negotiation.[24] Two months later, the same author reported that the PLA would receive RMB 50 billion as compensation for its lost enterprises.[25] The *Wall Street Journal* quoted US diplomats as saying that the government offered about US\$ 1.2 billion, but the military demanded US\$ 24 billion. Sources at the General Logistics Department (GLD) claimed in December 1998 that the PLA would receive between RMB 4 and 5 billion in additional annual compensation, complementing continued double-digit budget increases.[26]

For local military units, however, the prospects of a lucrative budget deal must have been bittersweet, as it required that they buy into what might be called "the trickle-down theory of PLA economics." Whereas units previously had relatively direct control over enterprise finances, they now had to place their faith in the notion that the budget funds would trickle down through the system from Beijing to their level. Previous experience with the Chinese military bureaucracy did not inspire confidence that this would come to pass. To ameliorate these concerns, the military leadership took steps in the fall of 1998 to improve the standard of living for the rank and file. The principal measure was an increase in the salaries of servicemen by an average of 10–25 percent, depending on rank and location.[27] One lieutenant-general in Beijing reportedly received a raise of RMB 400 per month, while two senior colonels claimed increases of 20 percent from RMB 1700 to 2040.[28] Overall, the average soldier in the PLA reportedly expected to receive an additional RMB 100 per month.[29]

Phase 1: organization and strategy

Organization of the divestiture effort actually preceded Jiang's July 22 speech. On July 20, 1998, Jiang chaired a meeting of the Politburo, declaring that "the military cannot run businesses any more or the tool for the proletariat dictatorship would be lost and the red color of the socialist land would change." General Zhang Wannian chaired a CMC work meeting the next day to set up a military leading group, and established two clear milestones for the group's work: (1) by the end of 1998, all businesses must sever their link with the military, and (2) starting from 1999, the military should fully rely on the central budget.

Immediately after Jiang's July 22 speech, the four General Departments convened a meeting to implement the decision, discussing the issue from July 23 to 26.[30] The four directors and political commissar Li Jinai attended the meeting, which established a special task force to oversee divestiture. Later, thirty cadres from the four General Departments were chosen to staff the new office. The participants also drafted a preliminary plan, and began to lay out policies for dealing with issues such as displaced workers, debts and credits, and real estate.

At the same time, a top-level civilian leading group was reportedly established, with Jiang Zemin's chosen successor Hu Jintao as the head, and with other party, government, and military leaders, including Zhang Wannian, and Luo Gan, as members.[31] Hu's appointment served as an important prelude to his official appointment as Vice-Chairman of the CMC at the end of October 1999.[32] Despite Hong Kong media stories to the contrary, there do not appear to have been any major cleavages among the top civilian leadership over divestiture.[33] One well-informed observer relates that Jiang and Zhu were closely united on the issue, with Jiang providing the political clout and Zhu providing economic instructions to his subordinates at the State Economic and Trade Commission as to the specifics of the separation.[34] Over the next few weeks, corresponding leadership small groups at lower levels of the system, including military units and State Economic and Trade Commission branches, were also established.

During the summer, the divestiture process was delayed significantly by massive flooding, in which the military played a heroic role. By October 6 or 7, the situation had sufficiently stabilized for the Central Committee, State Council, and CMC to convene the "Divestiture of Military, People's Armed Police, and Law Enforcement Organs Work Meeting," aimed at producing a detailed plan for the separation of enterprises from units.[35] At that meeting, a new, temporary organization was created, known as the "National Office for the Handover of Enterprises Under the Army, People's Armed Police, and Law Enforcement Organs."[36] The office of this leading group was staffed primarily by personnel from the State Economic and Trade Commission. The following organizations were also involved: the four General Departments; the People's Armed Police Headquarters; officials from the Politics and Law Department of the State Development and Planning Commission; the Commission on Science, Technology and Industry for National Defense (COSTIND); the Ministry of Public Security; the State Planning Commission; the Ministry of Inspection; the Ministry of Civil Affairs; the Ministry of the Treasury; the Ministry of Personnel; the Ministry of Labor and Social Security; the Ministry of Foreign Trade and Economics; the People's Bank; the General Tax Bureau; the Industrial and Commercial Bureau; and the Ministry of State Security. The Handover Office was given the task of promulgating the detailed regulations governing the handover and takeover of the military enterprises, the organization and coordination of divestiture, and the oversight of lower level offices. The national office was also given responsibility for the divestiture of ministry-level enterprises.[37] Similar offices were also set up by the State Economic and Trade Commissions of provinces and autonomous regions to take charge of the takeover of enterprises based within their geographic purview.

On October 9, after a series of work conferences, the four General Departments of the PLA convened another meeting, entitled the "Divestiture of Military and People's Armed Police Work Conference."[38] Also in attendance were representatives of the CMC General Office, military region headquarters, and military district headquarters. At this meeting, detailed plans regarding the handover of military firms were prepared. The guiding principle of this effort, as defined by the Central Committee, was: "turning over enterprises first, consolidating them later."[39] Accordingly, work teams were sent to military units to get a proper accounting of the units' legal and illegal commercial activities. Information on illegal activities was used to prepare cases for the military's discipline inspection commission, while data on the legal enterprises were used to give the military leadership a clear picture of the extent and financial viability of the military–business complex. Specifically, the work teams sought to assess the number of enterprises that required transfer, the number of enterprise employees involved in the process, and the asset and debt values of the enterprises. This first phase was completed by mid-October 1998. One official government assessment of the asset value of enterprises owned by the military was roughly RMB 50 billion (US$ 6.02 billion).[40]

Phase 2: formal registration and asset valuation

The second phase of the divestiture, begun in late October 1998, involved the formal registration and assessment of assets of the enterprises, followed by the expected official transfer of these enterprises to Handover Offices at the state, provincial, autonomous district, and municipality level.[41] The sixteen-character slogan for this phase was "comprehensive evaluation, good planning, discretionary treatment, and step-by-step implementation."[42] In general, stable enterprises were to be transferred to the governments, while profitable companies were to be placed under the SETC offices. In addition, a considerable number of banking, security, and trading companies that were poorly managed and operated, together with those industrial enterprises that had suffered serious losses were expected to be reorganized or closed down altogether.[43]

More specifically, divestiture affected each of the six parts of the PLA's business empire in different ways. The original divestiture order explicitly targeted commercial enterprises (*jingying xing qiye*), mandating that all of these businesses should be either handed over to civilian authorities or closed down. For the other five parts of the system, the party center was forced to adopt a series of gradual policies:

- "Units providing logistics needs" ("*baozhang xing qiye*" providing "*houqin fuwu*"), including repair shops, munitions factories, and uniform factories, were partially divested, with some businesses handed over to civilian authorities and others retained by the military. The guiding rationale is that the military does not need to make all of these things itself and should be able to outsource some of this production.

- Farms (*nongchang*), covering several million *mu* of land, have been completely retained.
- Fee-for-service businesses (*youchang fuwu*), such as hospitals and research facilities (*keyan danwei*), were retained because the facilities have excess capacity and highly advanced equipment not generally found in the civilian sector. In the case of hospitals, the military alone cannot provide enough patients to make efficient use of these resources. By serving the public, they can raise their level of expertise and earn a relatively insignificant amount of money for the military at the same time.
- Welfare businesses (*fuli xing qiye*), including factories set up to provide employment to military dependents (also known as *jiasu gongchang*), were partially divested, with some closed and others, particularly those in remote areas where relatives have no other options for employment, retained.
- Cover operations (*yanhu qiye*), including enterprises providing cover for intelligence gathering, national security, foreign affairs, and united front operations, were partially divested.

The center decreed that all military enterprises should be dealt with in one of three ways. The first option was "handover" (*yi jiao*) to civilian authorities. This applied to commercial operations and hotels, though not to guesthouses (*zhaodaisuo*). Most enterprises were to be handed over to local authorities. Some were handed over to the central government, specifically to the SETC (*Jingmaowei*). Local authorities were not to provide any compensation, which was supposed to come from the central government in the form of a lump-sum. Military employees of these enterprises could choose to return to the military or to stay with the enterprise. Not surprisingly, lower ranking military employees tended to stay with the enterprise, while higher ranking employees tended to return to the perquisites of the military. The second option was closure (*chexiao*) of the enterprise. There were many reasons for closure, including commercial inviability, heavy debts, or the location of the enterprise within the perimeter of a military installation, which meant that the business could not be handed over to the civilian authorities without creating a security problem. The third and final option was retention (*baoliu*), which was generally applied to those enterprises meeting specific military needs (*baozhang xing qiye*).

Not surprisingly, the divestiture encountered some resistance among military units reluctant to part with their enterprises during this second phase. Some departments reportedly attempted to fold their enterprises under subordinate institutions that were not being screened by the central authorities.[44] Others tried to shield their profitable enterprises while willingly sacrificing their bankrupt enterprises. In cases where the enterprise was using the label of "military enterprise" (*jundui qiye*) as a convenient cover for tax reductions and privileged access to transport or raw materials, individuals or units tried to have the enterprises reclassified as non-military enterprises. The situation was so serious that the office of the military leading small group in the first half of December 1998 was forced to dispatch four work groups of thirty members each to inspect the larger units.

Even some of the divestiture transfers themselves involved elements of illegality. One of the military's highest profile enterprises, the five-star Palace Hotel in Beijing, attracted interest from numerous civilian companies.[45] Eventually, the General Staff Department sold its joint venture stake in the hotel to a state enterprise, China Everbright Group, Ltd., which was looking to expand its hotel assets. According to the PRC Joint Venture Law, however, the remaining co-owners, Hong Kong's Peninsula Group (which managed the hotel) and the Japanese construction company Kumagai Gumi, should have enjoyed the right of first refusal of the army's shares. Instead, Peninsula got to approve the transfer only after it was arranged. Ironically, therefore, a movement designed to reduce the incidence of illegality among the armed forces was itself provoking illegal behavior. Moreover, the deal may prove to be detrimental to Peninsula Group. In 1997, China Everbright set up its own hotel management firm and may take over from Peninsula when the latter's management contract comes up for re-extension in 2002.

The emerging details of the second phase also aroused resentment among the central, provincial, and municipal bureaucrats, who were being "forced" to take over the PLA's many large and bankrupt enterprises.[46] The transfer of these enterprises to government offices was seen by many as another component of Zhu Rongji's strategy to recentralize macro-level decision-making authority and extract more resources from the provinces, many of which were perceived to have benefited disproportionately from reform at the expense of central coffers. For the local governments, however, these enterprises were simply another burden. The factories were particularly unattractive to the civilian governments, who would be saddled with the fiscal costs of free social services (education, housing, health care, etc.) for thousands of unemployed or underemployed workers. Furthermore, local officials would have to assume responsibility for finding new jobs for these workers, adding to the officials' already weighty burden in this area. Some of these problems were addressed at a critical "transfer work meeting" convened on November 29, 1998.

Phase 3: the real bargaining begins

By December 15, 1998, the government officially announced the end of the second phase. Reportedly, 2,937 PLA or PAP firms were transferred to local governments and 3,928 enterprises were closed, with one-third at the central level and two-thirds at the local level.[47] The big loser was the GLD, which saw more than 82 percent of its enterprises transferred or closed. A partial list of the divested enterprises can be found in Table 9.1.

One-third of the companies and their subsidiaries were retained by divestiture offices at the central level, while the remaining two-thirds were transferred

Table 9.1   Partial list of divested PLA and PAP enterprises

Province	Units divested	Workers	Output value	Profits	Asset values	Debt values
Hebei[48]	122				1.47b	1.07b
Guangdong[49]	390	6,700			2.0b	
Jiangsu[50]	64				1.4b	830m
Beijing[51]	68	2,300			1.4b	
Shenyang[52]	47	762	534m			
Hainan[53]	29					
Shanghai[54]	9	600		30m	300m	
Tianjin[55]	67					
Jiangxi[56]	8	687			45.75m	
Lanzhou[57]	68					

to divestiture offices at the local level. Profitable regional military conglomerates, such as the Jinling Pharmaceuticals Group in the Nanjing Military Region, were placed directly under the direction of the regional commission.[58] By contrast, the ten medium-sized firms and forty small-sized firms of the Strategic Rocket Forces, whose businesses had not been notably profitable, were given to their local governments.[59]

The commercial elements of China's most profitable military conglomerates, such as Xinxing, Songliao, and Sanjiu (999), were not handed over to local governments for reorganization, but were instead placed directly under the control of the SETC in Beijing.[60] Eventually, it was thought that these large companies would be independent, state-owned conglomerates. As an example, the experiences of Xinxing in this process are representative of the fate of these big firms.[61] Because Xinxing contained enterprises engaged in both military and non-production, its handover was very complicated. In the end, fifty-six chemical firms, which produced machines, logistics materials, clothes, and hats for the PLA, were kept under military control, but the trade group was transferred to the SETC. The ten specialized firms owned by Xinxing were reduced to seven after divestiture, with Xinxing Foundry retained by the military and two other firms transferred to chemical groups. At the same time, three new firms, including the General Logistics Construction Company that built the Military Museum, the new CMC Building, and the Beijing 301 Hospital, were added to Xinxing, restoring the number of firms to ten.

All of the large-size firms were be subject to a broad set of rules. The central government would still control the nomination of the leadership of large-sized firms, groups, and major enterprises of important industries. In terms of accounting and budget, the Ministry of Treasury would manage the financial affairs of those firms managed by the central government. All firms were required to participate in local social insurance plans according to geographic divisions.

The remaining 8,000–10,000 enterprises, most of which were the smaller, subsistence-oriented enterprises at the local unit level, remained in the military.[62]

The reforms were also "suspended" in some sectors, especially civil aviation, railway, and posts and telecommunications, because of the "special nature" of these industries.[63] For example, the Air Force's China United Airlines was permitted to continue operating.[64] Other notable exceptions included the fifty-five or so numbered factories previously under the control of the GLD's Xinxing Group, which remained under the administrative control of the GLD's pared down Factory Management Department (formerly the larger Production Management Department), and Poly Group, which was divided between the General Equipment Department (arms trading elements like Poly-Technologies), and COSTIND.

Exempted from divestiture: PLA telecoms

Military commercial telecommunications ventures were one sector singled out for special exemptions. Interviews in Beijing strongly suggest that PLA telecoms in general were given a "get-out-of-jail-free" card from the central leadership, because the resulting information technology acquisition was seen as an essential contributor to the C4I (command, control, communications, computer, and intelligence) revolution currently underway within the PLA. To manage the post-divestiture operations, the PLA created two communications groups. Reportedly, the first is dedicated exclusively to internal military traffic at high levels of security. The second leases some of the capacity of existing networks to civilian operators. In the latter case, the PLA was considered to be de-linked if it did not directly enroll individual subscribers (i.e., deal directly with the public), yet it could lease to operators who did enroll customers (i.e., cable companies). While radio paging was abandoned (e.g., CITIC/Pacific bought the Bayi radio paging business in Guangzhou) and many companies had to break their high-profile links with foreign companies, the China Electronic Systems Engineering Company (CESEC) in particular was allowed not only to stay in business but in some cases to expand its operations.

One illustrative case of the new ambiguous status of PLA telecoms, however, involves a fiber-optic network previously managed by the Guangzhou Military Region. At the end of 1998, the network's managing unit, the Office of Telecom Support for Economic Construction (OTSEC), was nominally transferred over to the Guangdong provincial government as part of the divestiture process. By all accounts, the transfer appears to have been a legal ruse to allow the PLA to continue to be engaged in commercial telecom activities. The office remains essentially military and it still oversees much of the military telecom network in the Guangzhou MR, as well as the optical fiber network. OTSEC is still actively negotiating with a large number of Chinese and foreign companies to lease surplus PLA telecoms networks and to build an updated high-speed data and voice transmission network. In February 2000, Hong Kong-based CITIC/Pacific purchased the fiber network itself from the PLA to be the corner-stone of its new network rollout. It is said that CITIC spent over RMB 2 billion buying unused fiber from the military. A US$ 80 million purchase of optical equipment from Lucent will expand the capacity of the existing 16,000 km of fiber and extend it to over 30,000 km nationwide.

Perhaps the most salient example of the uncertain legal and regulatory status of continuing PLA telecoms ventures involves the "Great Wall" CDMA (Code Division Multiple Access) cellular project owned by the General Staff Department Fourth Sub-Department's commercial arm, CESEC. In accordance with divestiture, CESEC sold its 20 percent share in the Nanjing-based satellite joint venture holding company with KPN Royal Dutch Telecom, but retained initial control of the four trial CDMA networks in Beijing, Tianjin, Xi'an, and Shanghai.

In 1999, CESEC's civilian partner in the deals, China Telecom, was ordered out of the projects, so that the networks could be prepared for handover to China Unicom, the weak number two telecom player, which was betting on CDMA to help it gain a respectable market share against the larger General Staff Department (GSD) networks run by China Telecom. As quickly as this arrangement was offered, however, the central authorities reversed themselves, and announced that the PLA would be retaining ownership of the networks. There are many competing reasons why the transfer fell through. China Telecom did not want Unicom to get Great Wall's CDMA networks, since the combined CDMA assets of the two players posed a greater threat to the dominant market share enjoyed by China Telecom's GSM (Global System for Mobile Communications) networks. Unicom did not want to be bothered with Great Wall's debt and overhead, which included significant personnel, housing, pension, and other social welfare costs. Moreover, the Great Wall system is a narrow-band second-generation CDMA standard, and Unicom wanted to wait for the upcoming broadband third-generation standard. More important, Unicom had been waiting so long for approval of CDMA that it had begun to build its own GSM networks to compete with China Telecom's GSM networks, and did not want to threaten its upcoming IPO (Initial Public Offering) by investing in "redundant" networks.

Before resuming its CDMA business, however, CESEC had to solve a big problem. Divestiture explicitly prohibited the PLA from dealing directly with customers, so they needed a new partner that could serve as an "interface." Eventually, CESEC appeared to partner with ChinaSat, the satellite communications company spun off from China Telecom. Since Great Wall was the name of the now defunct joint venture project between CESEC and China Telecom, the Great Wall joint venture was formally superseded by a company called China Century Mobile Communications Company, whose investors reportedly included CESEC, ChinaSat, the Beijing Municipal Government, Datang Group, and Beijing Zhongguancun Technology Development Ltd. The last company, which planned to invest US$ 6 million in Century Mobile once it was approved by the central government, was itself owned in part by two of China's best known companies, Founder Group and Legend Group Holdings, the country's biggest computer maker. Additional technical support (and perhaps a small share of equity investment) was to be provided by the Chinese Academy of

Telecommunications Technology, a research institute under the Ministry of Information Industry. CESEC's role in Century Mobile was also expected to be multi-faceted, undercutting earlier reports that ChinaSat would be the *de facto* operator of the networks with CESEC as a passive investor. Instead, it appears that CESEC hoped to retain its primary role as the designer, builder, and integrator of communications networks. As stated by one official from Shenzhou Great Wall Communications Development Center, the PLA company overseeing the trial CDMA network in Beijing: "Other companies will invest in the network, and we will build it."

The first hint of these new developments appeared in late December 1999, when Samsung and a company named Hebei Century Mobile Communications began construction of a new CDMA network serving eleven cities in Hebei Province. In a press release only circulated in Korea, Samsung heralded the opening of the Hebei 133 CDMA mobile telephone network. The Korean company reportedly supplied US$ 31 million of mobile systems equipment, including 11 mobile switching centers (capable of servicing 200,000 subscribers) and 165 base stations, and expected more than US$ 200 million in follow-up orders. By February 2000, this network reportedly had attracted 15,000 subscribers.[65]

The Great Wall/Century Mobile case was a striking illustration of the continuing role of the PLA in commercial telecommunications operations, and certainly suggested at the time that telecommunications were exempted from divestiture. At the very least, it suggested that the civilian leadership was willing to turn a blind eye to the activities, because of the side benefits for the military's own communications system. Divestiture, therefore, was not a blanket condemnation of the military's participation in business, but instead was a process capable of making logical exceptions, especially when it threatened to throw the baby out with the bathwater. At the same time, the PLA telecoms networks continue to operate in a hazy, inchoate gray area. At a July 18, 2000 cabinet meeting, for instance, State Council "Document No. 40" was reportedly issued, ordering the military once again to turn the Great Wall networks over to China Unicom as well as the 10 MHz of frequency in the 800 MHz band that the military was using for its CDMA systems. For more than a month, the military allegedly resisted the command, hoping to retain some or all of the networks and frequencies for its own secure communications. Given past reversals of similar policies, there is legitimate reason to question whether the transfer will ever take place.

Ending the second phase: a difficult transition

To close the second phase of the process, a Handover Office Work Meeting was held on December 28, 1998 at the Jingfeng Hotel in Beijing.[66] The meeting, chaired by Handover Office Director Sheng Huaren, was attended by the CEOs of the 148 large-sized PLA and PAP enterprises handed over to the SETC Handover Office. According to Sheng, these 148 enterprises and groups included 903 factories and subsidiaries, all of which had also been relinquished to the national office, and other military enterprises, which had been given to local handover offices. While these moves were significant in their scale and scope, the Central Committee's guidance cited above also suggested that the opening two phases of the divestiture were only the beginning of a much longer and more protracted process of allocating and restructuring thousands of troubled enterprises. This next phase of divestiture would include the difficult task of restructuring and consolidating the former military enterprises. According to Qin Chaozheng, the director of the Economic and Trade Commission of the Hebei Provincial Government:

> It will be an arduous task to turn these enterprises over to proper units for their management and to standardize their operation. More than half of these enterprises are poorly managed. It is necessary to further improve their management mechanisms and turn them into legal and competitive entities that are suitable for the market economy and that are able to conduct management independently.[67]

The first task for the divestiture offices in the third phase, which began after the December 15 transfers, involves going through the accounts of all PLA enterprises. These accounts must be squared before these enterprises are allowed to become fully civilianized or merged with civilian firms. It is expected that this process will take at least two to three years, depending on the number of major corruption cases that are generated. The asset evaluation was to be performed by accounting agencies designated by the SETC.[68] Some initial results of the third phase have already been publicized. Among many examples, the PLA's 9791 Cement Factory was turned over to local authorities in Tongchuan City on March 30, 1999 and renamed the "Shaanxi Provincial Lishan Cement Plant."[69] In March 1999, it was also announced that 150 large enterprises formerly owned by the military and the armed police were being transformed into state-owned corporate groups.[70] Xinxing, for example, remains as an independent, non-military entity, controlling one of the GLD's largest construction units. The top-level management of the large enterprises is being selected and appointed by the central government, especially the Ministry of Finance, which was placed in charge of supervising the assets of these enterprises. By contrast, nearly all of the smaller enterprises have been handed over to local authorities. Regardless of size, however, all enterprises are being required to transfer their credit liabilities as well as participate in the medicare insurance programs on behalf of their employees. Those that failed to offset their debts would be overhauled, shut down, or acquired by other, viable companies.

Divestiture problems: resource allocation and discipline

As the divestiture entered 1999, however, some serious bureaucratic and political conflicts began to surface. Overall, they can be divided into two categories:

resource allocation and discipline. Each of these disputes has important implications for our assessment of the final success or failure of the divestiture process.

In terms of resource allocation, recent trends suggest that the PLA's compensation, especially in the area of the official budget, is going to be far less than the military expected. In March 1999, the Minister of Finance Xiang Huaicheng announced the military budget for the new fiscal year in his annual work report:

> In line with the CPC Central Committee request, central finances will provide appropriate subsidies to the army, armed police force, and political and law organs after their severance of ties with enterprises. In this connection, this year's defense expense will be 104.65 billion yuan, up 12.7 percent from the previous year *because of the provision of subsidies to the army and of regular increases* [emphasis added].[71]

Outside observers immediately noticed the meagerness of the figure, both in relative and absolute terms. At a relative level, the 12.7 percent increase was not significantly higher than the 12 percent increase of the previous year, calling into question the notion that the fiscal priority of the PLA had been augmented. Even in absolute terms, the increase of RMB 13.65 billion between 1998 and 1999 was not that much larger than the RMB 10.43 billion increase between 1997 and 1998, and reportedly it included only a RMB 3 billion compensation for the loss of business income. Where was the additional RMB 15–50 billion reported in the Hong Kong media? Why did the military receive only RMB 3 billion extra when even the official *China Daily* newspaper pegged the estimated annual profits and taxes of the enterprises at RMB 5 billion (US$ 602 million)?[72]

There are several plausible explanations for this budgeting outcome. The first, and most difficult to prove, is that that PLA was sufficiently compensated with off-budget funds that are not calculated into the official budget. Given the Byzantine nature of the Chinese budgeting process, we may never have a definite estimate of any off-budget compensation. The second explanation is that the PLA did not have as much as leverage in the divestiture process as it or outsiders thought, allowing the civilian leadership to get the military out of business "on the cheap." The third possibility, supported by a loud chorus of PLA grumbling and complaining, is that the military was "duped" by the civilian leadership, who had implicitly promised a higher level of compensation. Indeed, there is some evidence to suggest that the RMB 3 billion of compensation is based on the conservative profit estimate of RMB 3.5 billion (on total revenue of RMB 150 billion) that the PLA gave to Zhu Rongji before the divestiture announcement in July. This low estimate was very much in line with previous PLA estimates by the GLD, which consistently undervalued the profit of the military enterprise system in order to lessen the central tax burden of the commercial units. If this story is true, then the major source of the PLA's animus may be that it was hoisted by its own petard. At the time of writing, however, it is difficult to judge which of these three explanations is correct, but the fact remains that vocal elements within the PLA appear to be significantly dissatisfied with the compensation package, above and beyond the usual bureaucratic rapaciousness for ever greater resources.

Apart from budgets, additional resource allocation disputes have arisen over distribution of enterprise assets in the post-divestiture environment. According to one well-informed observer, there have been some serious differences over levels of asset compensation because of the escalating costs of debts and liabilities incurred by enterprises.[73] Many firms were poorly managed, kept incomplete accounting records, and borrowed from multiple creditors. The firms' relationships with banks needed to be clarified, and their licenses needed to be re-registered. Another problem involved personnel. When military officers and workers were transferred to the localities, their health care and insurance had to be transferred as well, created unwanted social welfare burdens for the new owners.

In other cases, there is intra-military bargaining over the fate of individual assets. One of the most public examples of this was the dispute between the Beijing Military Region and the General Armaments Department (GAD) over the fate of the Huabei Hotel in central Beijing.[74] Under the rules of the handover, military units at the bureaucratic rank of military region, which also covers the new GAD, are allowed to keep only one three-star hotel. Before divestiture, the Beijing Military Region controlled two three-star hotels, including the Huabei, which it agreed to hand over to the SETC Handover Office. Since the GAD is a new organization and therefore had no hotels, it reportedly coveted the Beijing command's extra hotel. Thus far, however, the military region headquarters has declined to transfer the hotel to the GAD, igniting an unresolved bureaucratic struggle within the top military and civilian leaderships.

The second major set of problems resulting from divestiture involved discipline issues, mainly corruption and profiteering. While the data in this area remain anecdotal, there is some evidence to suggest that the civilian leadership has aggressively pursued discipline investigations involving corruption in PLA enterprises, much to the chagrin of PLA officers who feel that the effort is gratuitous and harmful to the public reputation of the military.[75] Susan Lawrence of the *Far Eastern Economic Review* reports from well-placed Chinese sources that the SETC Receiving Office has a list of twenty-three company executives at the rank of major-general or above who have fled the country since the divestiture was announced.[76] Seven of these officers are from the Guangzhou Military Region, which handed over more than 300 enterprises, and another five are from PLA headquarters. Among the latter is Lu Bin, former head of the General Political Department's Tiancheng Group, who was arrested overseas and extradited in January. Other arrestees include a senior colonel who was the head of one of the PLA's top hotels, the Huatian, which is located in Changsha. As the various receiving offices continue to process the assets and books of some of the shadier PLA enterprises, one can only expect the numbers of disciplinary investigations to increase.

Conclusion

In a sense, divestiture brings the PLA full circle. The pattern of the campaign, ranging from the transfers of its high-profile commercial enterprises to the retention of its lower level farms and industrial units, suggests that the military has essentially returned to the pre-1978 "self-sustaining" economy. Thus, the widespread conclusion that the PLA has been "banned" from business is far too simplistic. The military will continue to operate a wide variety of small-scale enterprises and agricultural units, with the goal of supplementing the incomes and standards of living for active-duty personnel and their dependents at the unit level. No longer, however, will profit and international trade be critical features of the system. Moreover, the military leadership hopes that the divestiture of profitable companies will greatly reduce the incidence of corruption and profiteering in the ranks, and thereby refocus the PLA on its important professionalization tasks.

At this point, of course, it is too soon to judge the long-term impact of this divestiture on the PLA. While participation in business had spawned endemic levels of corruption, an honest assessment would also admit that the military–business complex made positive contributions by subsidizing an underfunded military, improving the material life of the rank-and-file, and creating jobs for cadre relatives. Despite these benefits, however, the military and civilian leadership in the end decided that the disadvantages of commercialism outweighed the advantages, particularly with the prospect of professional tasks like the liberation of Taiwan and potential military conflict with the United States on the horizon.

What will the short- to medium-term future hold for the divestiture process? Most likely, the next few years will witnesses repeated "mop-up" campaigns on the part of the central leadership and significant resistance and foot-dragging on the part of local military officials, repeating the pattern of earlier rectifications. An audit in early 1999 revealed that the military had kept back some 15 percent of its businesses, necessitating the extension of some deadlines until August 1999. As late as May 2000, a top-level meeting on divestiture all but admitted that the military continues to shield some assets from the process, stating that the withdrawal of the military from business activities had only been "*basically* completed" (emphasis added).[77] None the less, it is important not to downplay the importance of what has already occurred. China's paramount leader has, for the first time, publicly called for the ending of the system altogether, perhaps closing one of most unique and interesting chapters of the post-Mao revolution.

Divestiture chronology

July 21–22, 1998 The four General Departments of the PLA meet in Beijing to transmit and implement the spirit of the "National Work Meeting to Combat Smuggling." CCP General Secretary, President, and CMC Chairman Jiang Zemin was present at the meeting, where a decision was announced that called for military units, PAP units, and security departments to no longer engage in business (*buzai jingshang*).

July 23, 1998   CMC Member and GSD Director Fu Quanyou, speaking at an enlarged GSD party committee meeting, indicated that the GSD party committee would resolutely implement the important decisions of the CCP and CMC regarding the anti-smuggling struggle and the removal of the military from business activities. He called for resolute completion of the tasks entrusted to the military by the CCP and CMC.

July 24, 1998   CMC Member and GLD Director Wang Ke, speaking at a GLD Work Meeting to combat smuggling, called upon logistics units to implement the spirit of the All-PRC, All-Army Work Meeting to Combat Smuggling, and implement the important central decision on removing military units from commercial activities.

July 25, 1998   CMC Member and GPD Director Yu Yongbo, speaking at an official GPD meeting, pointed out that the center had decided that military and PAP units henceforth and without exception must no longer be engaged in commercial activities. He described this decision as brilliant and correct. He called upon the GPD to safeguard the overall situation of reform, development, and stability, and to implement the decision to the letter.

July 26, 1998   At a GAD teleconference, GAD Director Cao Gangchuan and GAD Political Commissar Li Jinai made remarks, expressing their determination to implement the center's decision to oppose smuggling and remove military units from commercial activities.

July 28, 1998   A joint videoconference meeting of the Central Discipline Commission and Central Politics and Law Commission was convened to implement the center's decision regarding the removal of military, PAP, and politics and law organizations from commercial activities. At this meeting, Hu Jintao delivered an important speech, and Wei Jianxing insisted that the implementation of the center's decision by political organizations include *all* organizations affiliated with the ministries. The head of the Supreme People's Court Xiao Yang, the head of the Supreme People's Procurate Chao Zhubing, the Minister of Public Security Jia Chunwang, the Minister of State Security Xu Yongyue, and the Minster of Justice Gao Changli successively articulated their positions at the meeting.

Oct 6, 1998   The CCP, State Council, and CMC convene the "Removal of the Military, PAP, and Political-Legal Units From Commercial Activities Work Meeting" to discuss the work being carried out by specific organizations affiliated with the ministries. In order to ensure the proper execution of this work, the center decides to establish the "National PLA, PAP, and Political-Legal Unit Enterprise Handover Work Office." This office, which is headed by the SETC, also includes the State Development and Planning Commission, COSTIND, and sixteen other ministry-level units. These specific organizations will coordinate the handover of the PLA, PAP, and political–legal unit enterprises, which includes taking stock of the enterprises and standardizing them.

Oct 9, 1998   The "Removal of the Military, PAP, and Political-Legal Units From Commercial Activities Work Meeting" convenes in Beijing. The meeting's primary focus is the transfer, withdrawal, and retention work directed toward PLA, PAP, and political–legal unit enterprises. CMC Member and GPD Director Yu Yongbo, CMC Member and GLD Director Wang Ke, and others, attend the meeting and make remarks. Also attending the meeting are members of the "Divestiture of the PLA and PAP From Commercial Activities Leading Small Group," as well as representatives of the four General Departments, the leaders of the CMC General Office, representatives from the relevant sub-departments of the four General Departments, and leaders from each of military regions, provincial military districts, and PAP units.

Nov 26, 1998   Jiangxi military units hand over eight enterprises, with an asset value of RMB 45.7499 million, to the Jiangxi provincial government. On the same day, the Tianjin PLA and PAP hands over sixty-seven enterprises.

Nov 29, 1998   Hainan Military District PLA and PAP representatives hand over twenty-nine enterprises to the Hainan provincial government.

Nov 30, 1998   The Guangdong provincial government receives 390 military enterprises, with a net asset value of more than RMB 2 billion.

Dec 4, 1998   Sixty-eight Beijing-based PLA and PAP enterprises are handed over to the Beijing municipal government. These enterprises, which have an asset value of RMB 1.4 billion, employ 2,300 workers and have net assets of RMB 350 million.

Dec 15, 1998   All enterprises belonging to PLA and PAP units are handed over to the National Handover Work Office.

Dec 28, 1998   The National Handover Work Office convenes an enterprise work meeting in Beijing. The purpose is to discuss the implementation of management as well as the assessment and standards work during the transition period. Speeches are given by National Handover Work Office Director and SETC Chairman Sheng Huaren and National Handover Work Office Vice-Director and GLD Vice-Director Wang Tailan.

Notes

1 Jonathan Pollack, "Structure and Process in the Chinese Military System," in David Lampton and Kenneth Lieberthal (eds.), *Bureaucratic and Elite Decision-making in China* (Berkeley: University of California Press, 1991), p.154.
2 Barry Naughton, "The Third Front: Defense Industrialization in the Chinese Interior," *China Quarterly*, vol. 115 (September 1988), pp. 351–86.
3 Zhou Changqing, Deputy Director of the Third Front Office of the State Council, "Yi ge judadi jingji wutai" (A giant economic stage), *Renmin ribao* (People's Daily), 8 June 1987, p. 3.
4 As an example of the economic stagnation of the Maoist period, it is estimated that wages in China were frozen for nearly twenty years from 1958 to 1978.
5 See Deng Xiaoping, "Streamline the Army to Increase its Combat Effectiveness (12 March 1980)," *Deng Xiaoping wenxuan* (Collected works of Deng Xiaoping), p. 269.
6 Lu Tianyi, "Liu Mingpu Spoke on Reasons for Tight Military Spending at a Plenary Meeting of the PLA Delegation," *Jiefangjun bao* (Liberation Army Daily), p. 1, in *FBIS*, 3 April 1989, p. 52.
7 For example, see Liu Huinian and Xu Jingyao, "PLA Releases Airfields, Ports for Civilian Use," *Xinhua Domestic Service*, 17 February 1985, in *JPRS-CPS-85–020*, 13 March 1985.
8 Huang Yasheng, *Inflation and Investment Controls in China: The Political Economy of Central–Local Relations During the Reform Era* (Cambridge, Cambridge University Press, 1996); Christine Wong, *Central–Local Relations in an Era of Fiscal Decline: The Paradox of Fiscal Decentralization in Post-Mao China* (Santa Cruz, CA: Group for International and Comparative Economic Studies, Dept. of Economics, University of California 1990); and Jia Hao and Lin Zhimin (eds.), *Changing Central–Local Relations in China: Reform and State Capacity* (Boulder: Westview, 1994).
9 The Hong Kong press has published reports in which Jiang Zemin laments the situation, claiming that if he had an additional US$ 5 billion, he would give it to the PLA in exchange for a clean break from the economy.
10 "Central Military Commission Holds an Enlarged Meeting Before the Spring Festival to Discuss the Key Issues of Unity and Anti-Corruption in the Army," *Ming pao*, 3 February 1993.
11 "Jiang Orders PLA-Owned Firms to Close," *Xinhua Domestic Service*, 22 July 1998, in FBIS-CHI-98–204, 23 July 1998.
12 See *People's Daily*, 23 July 1998, p. 1.
13 "Fu Quanyou on Supporting Jiang's Anti-Smuggling Drive," *Xinhua Domestic Service*, 23 July 1998, in FBIS-CHI-98–206, 25 July 1998.
14 Cao Haili, "No More Business for the PLA," pp. 1–16.
15 "Yu Yongbo Calls on Army to Cease Business Operations," *Xinhua Domestic Service*, 26 July 1998, in FBIS-CHI-98–208, 27 July 1998.
16 "General Armament Department to Fight Smuggling," *Xinhua Domestic Service*, 26 July 1998, in FBIS-CHI-98–209, 28 July 1998.
17 Wu Hengquan, Liu Zhenying, and Wang Jinfu, "Hu Jintao Speaks on Banning PLA Businesses," *Xinhua Domestic Service*, 28 July 1998, in FBIS-CHI-98–209, 28 July 1998.
18 Cao Haili, p. 5.
19 Personal communication with Tai Ming Cheung, November 12, 1998.
20 Cao Haili, p. 3.
21 This account is taken from Susan Lawrence's excellent article "Bitter Harvest," which can be found in the 29 April 1999 issue of *Far Eastern Economic Review*, pp. 22–6.
22 Ibid.
23 Personal communication with Tai Ming Chueng, November 12, 1998.
24 The RMB 15 billion figure comes from Kuang Tung-chou, "Premier Promises to Increase Military Funding to Make Up For 'Losses' After Armed Forces Close Down All Its Businesses," *Sing tao jih pao*, 24 July 1998, p. A5, in FBIS-CHI-98–205, 24 July

1998. For the RMB 30 billion figure, see Willy Wo-Lap Lam, "PLA Chief Accepts HK47 Billion Payout," *South China Morning Post*, 9 October 1998.

25 Willy Lo-Lap Lam, "PLA to Get HK28 Billion for Businesses," *South China Morning Post*, 3 August 1998.

26 The author would like to thank Dennis Blasko for this information.

27 "Military Reportedly Raises Pay to Avoid Discontent," *Ming pao*, 23 January 1999, p. 15, in FBIS-CHI-99-023, 23 January 1999.

28 Interviews in Beijing, February 1999.

29 Kuang Tung-chou, "Beijing to Comprehensively Raise Servicemen's Remuneration," *Sing tao jih pao*, 25 November 1998, p. B14, in FBIS-CHI-98-349, 15 December 1998.

30 The account of this meeting can be found in Cao Haili, p. 7.

31 "Military Meets Resistance in Enforcing Ban on Business," *Ming pao*, 9 September 1998, p. A16, in FBIS-CHI-98-253, 10 September 1998.

32 "Hu Jintao Appointed CMC Vice-Chairman," *Xinhua*, 31 October 1999.

33 Willy Wo-Lap Lam, "Problems Between CCP, Army," *South China Morning Post*, 20 October 1999, p. 19.

34 Personal communication with Tai Ming Cheung, September 9, 1999.

35 Cao Haili, p. 11.

36 Han Zhenjun, "Military Business Said 'Disconnected' By 15 December," *Xinhua Domestic Service*, 28 December 1998, in FBIS-CHI-98-362, 28 December 1998.

37 "Work of Disengaging Armed Forces and Armed Police From Their Enterprises to Be Completed in Mid-December – Over Ten High Officials Absconded With Money," *Ming pao*, 7 December 1998, p. A12, in FBIS-CHI-98-353, 19 December 1998.

38 Cao Haili, p. 9.

39 Yang Xinhe, "Hebei Takes Over Military Enterprises," *Xinhua Hong Kong Service*, 12 December 1998, in FBIS-CHI-98-350, 16 December 1998.

40 "Separation of Army From Business Done," *China Daily*, 21 March 1999, p. 1.

41 Willy Wo-Lap Lam, "PLA Cashes In Its Assets," *South China Morning Post*, 29 July 1998.

42 Cao Haili, p. 3.

43 "Work of Disengaging Armed Forces," p. A12.

44 "Military Meets Resistance," p. A16.

45 This account is taken from Matt Forney, "A Chinese Puzzle: Unwinding Army Enterprises: Who Gets Them, And What to Pay?" *Wall Street Journal*, 15 December 1998; and Matt Forney, "Chinese Army's Exit from Businesses Leaves Partners Guessing at Next Move," *Wall Street Journal*, 21 May 1999, p. A9.

46 "Military Meets Resistance," p. A16.

47 Yang Yang, Fu Aiping, and Zhao Fenglin, "March Out of the Business Sea – PLA and Armed Police Carrying out the Decision of 'Divestiture,'" *People's Daily Shidai Chao*, 1 March 2000.

48 Yang Xinhe, "Hebei Takes Over Military Enterprises," *Xinhua Hong Kong Service*, 12 December 1998, in FBIS-CHI-98-350, 16 December 1998.

49 "Guangdong Military Hands Over Enterprises," *Zhongguo xinwen she*, 30 November 1998, in FBIS-CHI-98-337, 3 December 1998. A different source relates that 368 of these firms, located in Guangzhou, Shenzhen, Zhuhai, Shantou, Huizhou, and Shaoguang, belonged to the Guangzhou Military Region, the South Sea Fleet, the Guangzhou MR Air Force, the Guangdong Military District, and the Guangzhou People's Armed Police Headquarters. The other twenty-two enterprises located in Guangdong were owned by the Beijing, Jinan, Lanzhou, and Chengdu Military Regions, as well as firms owned by the Navy's Guangzhou Maritime Academy. See Cao Haili, p. 5.

50 Jiangsu units also dissolved 194 enterprises, with RMB 360 million in assets. Jin Weixin, "The Jiangsu Forces in the Nanjing Military Region Turn Over All Army-

Run Enterprises, Stressing Politics, Considering the Overall Order, and Acting in Line With High Standards and Strict Requirements," *Nanjing Xinhua Ribao*, 10 February 1999, pp. 1, 3, in FBIS-CHI-1999–0222, 10 February 1999. See also "Jiangsu Troops Hand Over Enterprises to Localities," *Xinhua Domestic Service*, 27 November 1998, in FBIS-CHI-98–337, 3 December 1998.

51 Cao Haili, p. 12.

52 "Shenyang 'Theater of Operations' Transfers Enterprises," *Beijing Central People's Radio Network*, 25 November 1998, in FBIS-CHI-98–337, 3 December 1998.

53 Bu Yuntong, "Hainan Armed Forces Hand Over Enterprises," *Xinhua Domestic Service*, 29 November 1998, in FBIS-CHI-98–337, 3 December 1998.

54 This number refers only to the divestiture of Yunfeng Industries. See "PLA Garrison Turns Major Business Over to Shanghai," *Xinhua*, 21 November 98.

55 "Tianjin Hands Over All Military-Run Businesses," *Xinhua*, 8 December 1998, in FBIS-CHI-98–342, 8 December 1998.

56 Liu Yi, "Jiangxi Military Hands Over Commercial Firms," *Xinhua Domestic Service*, 26 November 1998, in FBIS-CHI-980337, 3 December 1998.

57 This number refers only to Lanzhou MR AF enterprises. See *Lanzhou wanbao*, 20 January 1999.

58 Jin Weixin, "The Jiangsu Forces in the Nanjing Military Region Turn Over All Army-Run Enterprises, Stressing Politics, Considering the Overall Order, and Acting in Line With High Standards and Strict Requirements," *Nanjing Xinhua Ribao*, 10 February 1999, pp. 1, 3, in FBIS-CHI-1999–0222, 10 February 1999.

59 Cao Haili, p. 13.

60 First rumors of Songliao's transfer began to appear in late July. See Christine Chan and Foo Choy Peng, "Jiang Demand Threatens PLA Business Empire," *South China Morning Post*, 24 July 1998.

61 This account is taken from Cao Haili, p. 14.

62 Personal communication with Tai Ming Cheung, January 24, 1999.

63 "Separation of Army From Business Done," p. 1.

64 China United Airlines survived divestiture because many remote towns protested that the shutdown on the airline would cut them off from the rest of the country.

65 Matt Pottinger, "China's Military Building Mobile Phone Empire," *Reuters*, 15 February 2000.

66 The account of this meeting is taken from Cao Haili, p. 15.

67 "Hebei Takes Over Military Enterprises," *Xinhua*, 12 December 1998.

68 Cao Haili, p. 16.

69 *Shaanxi Daily*, 12 April 1999.

70 "Separation of Army From Business Done," p. 1.

71 PRC Finance Minister Xiang Huaicheng, "Report on the Execution of the Central and Local Budgets for 1998 and on the Draft Central and Local Budgets for 1999," *Xinhua Domestic Service*, 18 March 1999, in FBIS-CHI-1999–0320, 18 March 1999.

72 "Separation of Army From Business Done," p. 1.

73 Personal communication with Tai Ming Cheung, September 9, 1999.

74 Susan Lawrence, "Bitter Harvest," *Far Eastern Economic Review*, 29 April 1999, p. 24.

75 Ibid.

76 Ibid.

77 Wang Yantian and Yin Hongzhu, "CPC Central Committee, State Council, Central Military Commission Hold TV, Telephone Meeting on Work of Withdrawing Military, Armed Police, and Political and Legal Organs from Business Activities," *Xinhua Domestic Service*, 25 May 2000.

10 Confidence-building measures and the People's Liberation Army

Kenneth W. Allen

Introduction

The purpose of this essay is to discuss military-related confidence-building measures (CBMs) that Beijing has utilized over the past decade, and to see if they could be extended to relations with Taipei over a period of several years to reduce tensions (see Appendix 1). These CBMs involve the People's Republic of China's (PRC's) People's Liberation Army (PLA) and the Republic of China's (ROC's) military on Taiwan.[1]

During the 1990s, Beijing began negotiating military-related CBMs with its neighbors in order to reduce tensions and promote regional stability and economic development. Although Taiwan is fairly isolated diplomatically, the ROC military does interact with other militaries through its weapons system procurement program and through informal information exchange channels. There have also been opportunities for direct and indirect interaction between the two militaries. Although military CBMs between the two sides will not be carried out in a vacuum and will most likely be implemented in conjunction with, or be subservient to, political and economic CBMs, other contributors will address those issues.

Interviews with military and civilian analysts from the PRC and ROC elicited two general reactions. The first reaction, which came from everyone interviewed, was that there must be movement on political issues before there is any movement on military CBMs. The second reaction, which came from the PRC side, was that CBMs are designed to be used between states. Therefore, since Taiwan is a province of China and is not a state, how can CBMs be used between Beijing and Taipei? Both of these reactions have merit.

The resumption of the Koo-Wang talks in October 1998 and the plans for Wang Daohan to pay a reciprocal visit to Taiwan in 1999 appeared to provide a good opportunity to establish some military CBMs.[2] However, Wang Daohan's visit was put on indefinite hold after President Lee Teng-hui made his "state-to-state relations" comments in July 1999. Lee's comments resulted in an immediate increase in military tensions across the Strait. Issues concerning Taiwan's independence that were raised during the campaign prior to Chen Shui-bian's election as president in March 2000 led to further strained relations between Beijing and Taipei. Although these events precluded any near term discussion of military CBMs, the concept should not be dismissed.

The first section provides a brief historical overview of the military confrontation between the PRC and ROC. The next section covers the ROC military's and PLA's foreign military relations. The third section provides a comparison of current military CBM agreements between China, India, Russia, and the Central Asian Republics with CBMs established by the Organization for Security and Cooperation in Europe. The fourth section provides a brief review of general military-related CBMs that could be used as a framework for cross-Strait military CBMs. The conclusion lays out a set of CBMs that Beijing and Taipei could implement over a long period of time under the right set of circumstances.

Historical overview

One of the primary purposes of CBMs is to develop trust between adversaries. Mistrust between the ROC military and the PLA stems from the early 1920s. Under Soviet guidance, the first rapprochement between the Chinese Nationalist Party (Kuomintang/KMT) and the Chinese Communist Party (CCP) brought communists into the newly established Whampoa Military Academy, with Chiang Kai-shek as the Commandant and Zhou Enlai as the Director of the Political Department.[3] This uneasy united front between the nationalists and communists lasted until 1927, when Chiang purged the communists and established a nationalist government in Nanjing.

Following several nationalist military campaigns to try to oust the communists from their mountain stronghold in southern China, the communists began their epic 6,000 mile Long March in October 1934, which took them to Yan'an. A second united front was established in July 1937 following the Marco Polo Bridge incident with Japan, but broke down again in late 1938. It effectively ceased following a clash between communist and nationalist forces in 1941. The last large-scale military clash came in 1958 over the Taiwan Strait.[4] Although economic links have increased and political tensions have subsided somewhat, the two militaries are still at a standoff across the Taiwan Strait.

Since China's economic opening to the outside world, including Taiwan, began in the late 1970s, the PLA has embarked on a campaign to improve its military relations with countries around the world. This program has seen a surge in activity during the 1990s as Beijing has tried to assuage fears of a "China Threat" and to lessen tensions along China's border to help promote economic development. It is the premise of this chapter that the time may be ripe for Beijing and Taipei to begin looking at military CBMs to lessen tensions across the Taiwan Strait. Before proposing specific CBMs, let us first examine the ROC military's and the PLA's relations with other countries since the 1950s.

Taiwan's foreign military relations

Prior to the PRC replacing the ROC in the United Nations in November 1971, the ROC military had an active foreign relations program, especially with the United States, Israel, South Africa, and other Asian countries, such as South Korea and Singapore. For example, from 1950 until the United States changed its diplomatic recognition from the ROC to the PRC in 1979, thousands of ROC military personnel received training at all levels in the United States. Beginning with UN recognition of the PRC in 1971, most countries began changing their recognition from Taipei to Beijing, so that today only about twenty-five countries still formally recognize the ROC. However, many countries still have strong relations with Taipei through reciprocal trade offices that function as consulates. Many of the ROC's trade offices overseas include active-duty military officers who perform the same functions as military attachés or military assistance and procurement officers.

While the PLA has opted for a visible foreign relations program since the early 1980s, the ROC military has opted for a low profile, but active program. For example, since 1979, US–ROC military-to-military relations have mostly been limited to discussions and training associated with acquisition and mainte-nance of US weapons systems. The ROC has also maintained continuous military-to-military relations and exchanges with several Asian, Latin American, and African countries, and established a European-wide weapons procurement office in Paris in the early 1990s. The ROC military's Political Warfare College provides a Foreign Officers Course for select officers from Africa, Latin America, and Southeast Asia. In addition, the ROC Naval Academy has special courses for foreign officers.

Active-duty ROC military officers are also involved in visiting fellow and graduate programs abroad, including the United States, the United Kingdon, Canada, and Germany. For example, there were sixteen officers involved in strategic studies, command and staff education, masters degree programs, and Ph.D. programs in foreign military and civilian universities in 1997. In addition, the Ministry of National Defense holds seminars and entrusts private academic institutes to hold seminars on national defense and special topics.[5]

Finally, the ROC military hosts numerous foreign retired senior officers and defense officials, who were not able to visit Taiwan when they were on active duty or serving in an official capacity. Taipei takes these opportunities to "educate" them on what is going on in Taiwan and to elicit their support when they return home.

PLA military relations: 1949–1989

The PLA's military relations with other countries began in the 1950s, but were limited to the Soviet Union, North Korea, and Albania, plus support for commu-nist insurgencies in Southeast Asia.[6] The PLA started developing military ties with Third World nations in Asia and Africa in the 1960s in an attempt to extend Chinese influence and counteract Soviet and US influence.

In the late 1970s and early 1980s, a major change in the PLA's foreign mili-tary cooperation occurred when China began developing military contacts with

West European nations and the United States, as well as providing considerable military assistance to countries such as Sri Lanka, Egypt, Tanzania, Sudan, Somalia, Zaire, and Zambia. At the same time, as Beijing began establishing diplomatic relations with countries in Southeast Asia and its relations with Vietnam cooled, Chinese military assistance to communist insurgents in Southeast Asia – with the exception of the Khmer Rouge and non-communist Cambodian resistance groups – tapered off. China continued to have close military ties and to sell military hardware under generous terms to traditionally friendly states in South Asia – Pakistan, Bangladesh, and Burma. Meanwhile, Sino-Albanian relations deteriorated in the 1970s, and Beijing terminated all assistance in 1978. However, China began to exchange military delegations with two other East European countries – Yugoslavia and Romania. Chinese military relations with these two countries were limited and, especially in the case of Romania (a Warsaw Pact member), served to irritate the Soviet Union.

These changes reflected China's desire to counter Soviet influence, especially in Europe and Africa, as well as to develop relations with modern armed forces. China needed advanced hardware and technology, as well as organizational, training, personnel, logistics, and doctrinal concepts for modernizing the PLA. Chinese military ties with West European countries were strongest with the United Kingdon, France, and Italy. Chinese military relations with the United States developed rapidly in the 1980s and included exchanges of high-level military officials and working-level delegations in training, logistics, and education. Washington also concluded four foreign military sales (FMS) programs with Beijing to help modernize the PLA. However, these programs ceased following the June 1989 Tiananmen incident.

To put this in perspective, the PLA hosted over 500 military delegations from 1979 to 1989 and sent thousands of military officials abroad for visits, study, and lectures. China received port calls from thirty-three foreign warships, including the United States, the United Kingdom, France, and Australia, and the PLA Navy sent ships to visit Pakistan, Bangladesh, and Sri Lanka in 1985. PLA departments, academies, and research institutes opened their doors to foreign military visitors. In 1989 China had ties with eighty-five foreign armies, posted Chinese military attaché offices in sixty countries, and hosted forty military attaché offices in Beijing.

Events leading to PRC military-related CBMs in the 1990s

It was not until China's economic opening to the West in the early 1980s and China's 1985 reassessment of its strategic defense policy that Beijing began to take notice of existing military-related CBM concepts. In 1985, the Chinese Communist Party's Central Military Commission (CMC) radically revised China's strategic defense policy by directing the armed forces to change from preparation for an "early, major, and nuclear war" to preparing for "local limited wars around China's borders, including its maritime territories and claims."[7]

Following the Gulf War, this was amended to "fight local wars under modern, high technology conditions." As a result of the economic opening and the strategic reassessment, Chinese leaders began to view the use of CBMs primarily as tools to maintain a peaceful regional environment beneficial to economic development. Therefore, over the next few years, Beijing began to look more favorably at using military-related CBMs to reduce tensions along its borders.

PLA military relations: 1990–present

In July 1998, China issued its first *Defense White Paper on National Defense*, which stated that China has been active in developing an omnidirectional and multi-level form of military diplomacy.[8] According to the paper, the PLA has established relations with the armed forces of more than 100 other countries. China has set up military attaché offices in more than ninety Chinese embassies abroad, and over sixty countries have set up their military attaché offices in China. In the last twenty years, more than 1,300 Chinese military delegations, of which some 180 were headed by senior officers, have visited over 80 countries. In the meantime, about 2,100 foreign military delegations involving several tens of thousands of persons have visited China, more than half of which were high-ranking delegations headed by defense ministers, commanders-in-chief of the armed forces or chiefs of the general staff. Since 1973, the PLA has trained nearly 10,000 officers at all levels as well as military technicians for developing countries, and sent over 8,000 experts to those countries.

During the 1990s, representatives from virtually every organization within the PLA, from the CMC to academic institutions, have been involved in the foreign relations program. They include vice chairmen of the CMC, the Minister of National Defense, heads of the four General Departments (General Staff/GSD, General Political/GPD, General Logistics/GLD, and General Armament/GAD), commanders and political commissars of the navy and air force, commanders and political commissars of the seven military regions and three naval fleets, members of the Commission for Science, Technology, and Industry for National Defense (COSTIND), the Academy of Military Science (AMS), the National Defense University (NDU), and service academies and schools. The only organization that is not commonly represented is the strategic rocket forces, known as the Second Artillery. However, some Second Artillery representatives have worked in Saudi Arabia since Riyadh purchased several DF-3/CSS-2 medium-range ballistic missiles (MRBMs) in the mid-1980s. Specific examples of visits that took place between 1995 and 1998 including the following:

- During 1995, the PLA hosted 125 military delegations from 55 countries, of which 47 delegations were led by either defense ministers, chiefs of staff, or commanders of various services. Visitors came from Australia, Austria, Belarus, Canada, Chile, Egypt, Ethiopia, Finland, France, Germany, Hungary, Israel, Kuwait, Kyrgyzstan, Namibia, the Netherlands, Nigeria,

Peru, Portugal, Switzerland, Syria, Turkey, the United Kingdom, Ukraine, and Zimbabwe.[9]

- During 1996 the PLA hosted more than 140 military delegations from over 60 countries, including Belgium, Bolivia, Finland, France, Hungary, Iran, Israel, Italy, Mozambique, Poland, Portugal, Romania, Spain, Tanzania, Uganda, the United Kingdom, the United States, Zambia, and Zimbabwe. They also included visits by US, UK, and Italian warships.[10]

- During 1997, the PLA hosted visits from over 150 delegations from 67 countries across five continents. Visitors included high-ranking military leaders from Russia, Kazakhstan, Singapore, Indonesia, Thailand, Bangladesh, Japan, South Korea, Nepal, North Korea, Thailand, India, Myanmar, Pakistan, Vietnam, and Laos. Among them, 23 were vice-premiers and defense ministers, a 64 percent increase from 1996. Fifty delegations were at the level of general commander or chief of staff of foreign armed forces, vice defense minister and commander of different military units. Commanders from the Shenyang, Beijing, Lanzhou, Guangzhou, and Chengdu Military Regions also increased visits and exchanges with their counterparts in bordering nations.[11]

- During 1998, the PLA hosted visits by 75 groups of high-ranking leaders of foreign militaries from more than 50 countries on five continents, including Australia, Belarus, Bolivia, Canada, Croatia, Egypt, Finland, Ghana, Indonesia, Israel, Japan, Kazakhstan, Mauritania, North Korea, Pakistan, Peru, Poland, Russia, and the United States. Leaders of the CMC, PLA General Departments, and various major military units led more than 30 high-level groups to visit more than 60 countries. In addition, 180 mutual exchanges between specialized technology, cultural, and sports groups were carried out between the militaries of China and more than 50 countries.

- During 1999, 33 senior-level delegations from the PLA visited nearly 50 countries, while the PLA hosted 89 military leaders.[12] The PLA also participated in 15 multilateral and regional forums on security cooperation and joint research on defense policy, army building, and regional security. China's military diplomacy with neighboring countries constituted a significant element of overall military diplomacy, which began when Defense Minister Chi Haotian and Chief of the General Staff Fu Quanyou chose bordering countries for their first annual visits. Foreign military leaders visiting China included defense ministers from Cambodia, Thailand, Laos, South Korea, and Australia, as well as army chiefs from Bangladesh, Pakistan, Mongolia, and Nepal, not to mention numerous other lower level groups. Besides South Korea, China's military had meetings with North Korea and conducted vice-ministerial-level security consultations with Japan. Vice-Chairman of the CMC Zhang Wannian visited Russia in June, followed by several other PLA delegations. While China developed close military exchanges with neighboring regions, it also further promoted ties with African and Latin American countries, and opened up new fields for military exchange.

PLA Navy port calls abroad

One of the most visible signs of PLA military cooperation is port calls abroad. In contrast to the coast-hugging visit to Sri Lanka and Pakistan in 1985 by two PLA Navy ships, a small Chinese naval task force sailed to North and South America in March 1997, stopping in Honolulu and San Diego before going on to ports in Mexico, Chile, and Peru. The vessels included one of China's few, relatively modern, surface combatants, a Luhu-class guided-missile destroyer. It was accompanied by a modernized Luda III destroyer and the largest ship in the Chinese navy, the *Nanchang*, a supply ship. The last time Chinese warships made a journey of comparable distance was in 1433, when the Ming dynasty admiral Zheng He sent a fleet of four-decked war junks and 27,500 troops through Southeast Asia to the Middle East and Africa.[13]

In addition, in 1996, the PLA Navy conducted its first port call in North Korea to celebrate the thirty-fifth anniversary of the Sino-North Korean Friendship Treaty. Another North Sea Fleet ship also visited Vladivostok. At roughly the same time as the 1997 historic visit to the Americas, two ships of China's East Sea Fleet sailed to Malaysia, Singapore, and the Philippines. These ships comprised the PLA's only other modern guided-missile destroyer (a Luhu launched in 1996) and one of the recently completed Jiangwei-class frigates. This was the first-ever visit to these three ASEAN countries by PLA warships. In the case of the Philippines, the only previous encounter with the PLA Navy's emerging naval power was in the South China Sea in March 1994, when Chinese ships supported the occupation of the Philippine-claimed Mischief Reef.

In May 1998, the navy headed south to Australia and New Zealand. A Luhu destroyer, supply ship, and training ship visited Auckland and Sydney, the most southerly point reached by the Chinese navy since Zheng He's historic voyage. While Japan and Russia have recently had exchange ship visits, China and Japan have not yet reached agreement on ship visit exchanges.

In an unprecedented 1998 move, Beijing accepted an invitation from Washington to send PLA Navy officers to observe RimPac, the major multinational Pacific Ocean naval exercise.[14] Similar previous invitations had been rejected, due to China's concerns about the appearance of any type of military alliance. Two Chinese representatives, the commanding officer of a PLAN destroyer and an associate professor at the Naval Command Academy, were sent to observe. The carrier USS *Nimitz*, an Aegis destroyer and cruiser, and a fleet command ship were among the ships they boarded during the exercise.

In 1999, the Singaporean Navy landing craft, RSS *Excellence* visited Qingdao, and the Royal Navy frigate HMS *Boxer* and two Russian warships – the *Varyag* (flagship of the Pacific Fleet) and the destroyer *Bungy* – visited Shanghai.[15] During July–August 2000, two PLA Navy ships – the guided-missile destroyer *Shenzhen* and support vessel *Nancang* – visited Malaysia, Tanzania, and South Africa.[16] The US Navy's guided-missile cruiser *Chancellorsville*, based in Yokosuka, Japan, visited Qingdao from July 31 to August 5, 2000, in conjunction with a visit to China by Admiral Thomas Fargo, Commander of the US Pacific Fleet.[17] The PLA Navy will pay a reciprocal visit to Hawaii and Seattle in the future.

PRC high-level visits and border talks promote CBMs

Breakthroughs in establishing CBMs have come most often as a result of high-level visits to or from China by heads of state or ministers responsible for foreign affairs and defense. The most prominent examples of China's high-level diplomacy in Asia that have resulted in military-related CBMs have been with Russia, the Central Asian Republics (Kazakhstan, Kyrgyzstan, and Tajikistan), India, and the ASEAN states. These discussions have resulted in programs for military exchanges and various border agreements, including the establishment of hotlines, border demarcation negotiations, prior notification and restriction of military maneuvers and troop movements along borders. Specific examples of these programs are described next.

China–Russia/Central Asian Republics relations

China's relationship with the Soviet Union was forged in historical distrust and disagreements between the two communist giants. In July 1986, Soviet President Mikhail Gorbachev opened the door to better relations with a speech at Vladivostok, saying the Soviet Union was prepared to enter into discussion with China "at any time and at any level" on the border dispute and on troop reductions along the border. During Gorbachev's visit to China in May 1989, he unilaterally announced a series of cutbacks in Soviet troop deployments near the Chinese border, which led to a series of talks on the mutual reduction of forces and negotiations on boundary disputes. During 1994, President Jiang Zemin visited Russia and signed a joint declaration with President Boris Yeltsin, including an agreement on detargeting missiles.[18]

In April 1996, the Presidents of China, Russia, and the Central Asian Republics of Kazakhstan, Kyrgyzstan, and Tajikistan signed the "Agreement on Confidence Building in the Military Field in the Border Area," which called for mutual non-use of force and renunciation of military superiority. It encouraged information exchanges on agreed components of military forces and border guard troops, restriction in the scale, geographic limits, and the number of troop exercises, and notification of large-scale military activities. The parties were encouraged to invite observers to troop exercises on a mutual basis and to strengthen friendly contact between military personnel. In addition, the presidents signed a series of separate agreements to increase economic, trade, scientific, technological, and cultural exchanges.

In June 1990, Rear Admiral Vladimir Khuzhokov, Head of the Soviet Ministry of Defense's Foreign Relations Department, led the first Soviet military delegation to China in over thirty years. During the visit, he stated:

> Military contacts have become a major instrument of the foreign policy of the countries. Without them it is hard to speak about normalizing relations between countries and establishing mutual trust. Exchange of official military delegations should be followed by regular contacts between the armed forces of the two countries.[19]

The senior military officer and Vice-Chairman of China's CMC, Liu Huaqing, followed this up with a trip to Moscow in July 1990 to begin discussions about purchasing Soviet military equipment and expanding military exchanges. Since then, Liu visited Russia three more times (1993, 1995, and 1997), and his successor Zhang Wannian visited Russia in June 1999. In addition, there have been almost annual exchanges between the ministers of defense. China's Qin Jiwei visited Russia in 1991 and Chi Haotian visited in 1994, 1997, and 2000. Russia's ministers of defense traveled to China in 1992, 1993, 1995, 1998, and 2000. Successive Chiefs of the General Staff – Chi Haotian, Zhang Wannian, and Fu Quanyou – also visited Russia in 1992, 1993, and 1998, respectively. Aside from these trips, GPD Director Yu Yongbo and GLD Director Wang Ke traveled to Russia on separate occasions in 1997.

During several of the trips to China by Russian ministers of defense, various agreements were signed for military cooperation. During a visit in November 1993, the ministers of defense signed an agreement on cooperation to cover the next five years. During the May 1995 visit, they held a series of talks aimed at formulating general provisions of an agreement on cooperation in the field of defense technologies. Following the December 1996 visit, a protocol on military and technical cooperation was signed, agreeing that Russia would sell China a consignment of Russian Sovremennyy-class destroyers, and that armament and navigation systems of Chinese naval ships of this type would be modernized.

Whereas many trips to other countries by senior PLA officials are more symbolic than substantive, the fact that Russia is willing to sell weapons systems and technology to China tends to lead to substantive discussions on everything from the systems themselves to the doctrine, strategy, training, logistics, and maintenance to support those systems. High-level delegations have visited numerous Russian cities, including Moscow, St Petersburg, Volgograd, Novosibirsk, Irkutsk, and Vladivostok, where they were given tours of military and defense-industrial sites such as the Mikoyan aircraft production plant. They also visited several unspecified industrial enterprises, research institutes, military academies, and military units.[20]

While these visits indicate a broad-based relationship, they have focused primarily on Chinese acquisition of Russian arms, equipment, and technology. Major purchases and contracts have been concluded on Ka-27 and Mi-17 helicopters, Su-27 and Su-30 fighters, T-72 tanks, S-300 surface-to-air missiles, IL-76 transports, Kilo-class diesel-electric submarines, and Sovremennyy-class destroyers, as well as various subsystems such as engines, air-to-air missiles, and anti-ship missiles (SS-N-22).[21] Of these weapons systems, China has also concluded agreements with Russia to co-produce the Su-27 and possibly the Su-30. With the exception of the Su-27s and Su-30s, China has merely purchased a set number of these systems and still relies on Russian support as a long-term supplier of spare parts. Even the Su-27 co-production contract limits China to domestically producing only about 70 percent of the aircraft. Russia will continue to supply the remaining 30 percent, including the engines and certain avionics subsystems.[22] Of equal concern to some countries are reports about

Russian scientists helping China build its own weapons. These Russian experts are primarily working with China's defense industries and not the PLA itself, although the PLA will benefit from their assistance in weapons programs.

The third part of China's military relations with Russia involves functional exchanges between military region and military district officers, academic institutes, and PLA delegations led by other than high-level officers discussed above. Although media reporting normally does not cover these types of visits, the reporting that is available gives a fairly good idea of the types and scope of visits that have taken place.[23]

The PLA has been an active participant since the beginning of the border negotiations. For instance, during the second round of talks in February 1990, both sides upgraded the military representatives on the negotiating teams, when a PLA major general replaced a senior colonel as the deputy head of the delegation in Moscow.[24] Once the border agreement was signed, the PLA's military districts within the Shenyang Military Region, under the auspices of the Ministry of Defense, were given the authority to implement the agreement and to help negotiate sub-agreements and protocols with Russia's border guards.

The current trends in Chinese–Russian military relations represent a textbook case of the imperatives that drive Chinese military relations in general.[25] First, the military relationship reflects the overall state of bilateral relations. As the political relationship has improved over the past few years, so too has the military relationship and the overall security relationship. Without greatly improved bilateral relations the current military relationship would not be possible.

Second, Beijing's military relationship with Moscow is based upon the pragmatic pursuit of Chinese national security objectives, not ideological affinities as in some points in the past. Circumstances have once again aligned major Chinese and Russian national security interests, especially vis-à-vis the United States. Thus, there is a common positive context against which the improvement in military relations has been possible. Both China and Russia are opposed to the perceived expansion of US military influence in Europe and Asia. Both find themselves threatened or unsettled by the eastward expansion of NATO and Partnership for Peace (PFP), plus the strengthened US–Japan military alliance.[26] Both China and Russia take exception to US plans to develop and deploy national and theater missile defense systems, and both endorse the trends toward the rise of multipolarity as opposed to the potential "hegemony of a sole superpower."

Third, China's military relations with Russia are a key component in shaping the international security environment, especially China's peripheral security environment. The security threat posed to China by the massive deployment of Soviet troops along the Sino-Soviet border as well as the real potential for armed conflict over unresolved border disputes with the Russians during the Cold War (such as in 1969) cannot, from a Chinese perspective, be overstated. Indeed, this was a driving force behind China's rapprochement with the United States in the 1970s and 1980s, to include the original impetus for the US–China military relationship. If Beijing is going to be able to continue to focus on economic modernization and reform as its own self-declared central task, then China must have peaceful borders with Russia. The relative reversal of fortunes in China and Russia have created an incentive in both countries to resolve outstanding border and security issues. As noted earlier in this section, the PLA has played an important role in negotiating and implementing the border agreements with Russia. Moreover, China must deal with Russia if it is to be successful in securing its borders in Central Asia, an area of increasing security concern to Beijing.

Fourth, Beijing's current military relations with Russia are a classic case of military relations enhancing China's defense modernization. Russia is one of the few relatively advanced military powers that is willing to sell China major weapons systems and other military end items, production technologies for indigenous manufacture, support packages of technicians in-country, as well as training for PLA officers and technical personnel at state-of-the-art military schools and facilities in Russia.

China–India relations

China's relations with India continue to be overshadowed by their border war in 1962. During February 1979, India's Foreign Minister (and later Prime Minister) Atal Bihari Vajpayee visited Beijing, but the visit was marred by China's incursion into Vietnam. However, in June 1981, China's Foreign Minister Huang Hua visited India, which led to eight rounds of border talks that took place between 1981 and 1988. In December 1988, Prime Minister Rajiv Gandhi visited China, which led to the creation in 1989 of a Joint Working Group to discuss border issues. In July 1992, the first visit by an Indian defense minister, Sharad Pawar, took place and led to a 1993 agreement in principle to settle the border dispute, to reduce forces and armaments, to improve mutual relations over the long term, and not to use their armed forces against each other.

In November 1996, in the first visit by a Chinese head of state to India, President Jiang Zemin and Indian President Shankar Dayal Sharma signed four agreements, including "The Agreement on CBMs in the Military Field Along the Line of Actual Control (LAC) in India–China border areas."

In the November 1996 CBM agreement, each side pledged not to attack the other or cross the LAC, and to reduce troops and armaments along the common border. The twelve-article, ten-page agreement stipulated that "neither side shall use its military capability against the other side." It also said that

> no armed forces deployed by either side in the border areas along the LAC as part of their respective military strength shall be used to attack the other side or engage in military activities that threaten the other side or undermine peace, tranquility and stability in the India–China border areas.

Pending an ultimate solution of the boundary question, the two sides reaffirmed their commitment to respect strictly and observe the LAC. They also agreed to avoid holding large-scale military exercises involving more than one division (15,000 troops) in close proximity to the LAC and to refrain from flying combat aircraft within 10 kilometers of the LAC. Unarmed transport aircraft, survey aircraft, and helicopters are permitted to fly up to the LAC.

Another major decision reflected in the 1996 CBM agreement was the reduction of field army, border defense forces, and paramilitary forces to ceilings to be mutually agreed upon. They also agreed to speed up the process of clarification and confirmation of the LAC and to clarify the alignment in the segments where perceptions differ. In addition, they agreed to exchange maps indicating their respective perceptions of the entire alignment of the LAC. Scheduled meetings between border commanders at designated points, telecommunication links between border meeting points, and medium- and high-level contacts between border authorities were to be expanded beyond those agreed upon in 1993.

The two countries also outlined steps to prevent dangerous military activities along the LAC. They would not open fire, use hazardous chemicals, conduct blast operations, or hunt with guns or explosives within 2 kilometers of the line. This prohibition would not apply to routine firing activities in small-arms firing ranges. If the border personnel of the two sides were to find themselves in a face-to-face situation because of differences in the alignment of the LAC or for any other reason, they were to exercise self-restraint and take all necessary steps to avoid an escalation of the situation. The Sino-Indian agreement remains valid until either side decides to terminate it after giving six months' notice in writing.

In May 1998, China's Chief of the General Staff, General Fu Quanyou, became the highest military officer to visit India. However, India detonated several nuclear devices immediately following his departure, initially justifying their detonations because of a "China threat." Relations were strained and the Joint Working Group (JWG) meeting scheduled for the second half of 1998 was canceled.[27] The eleventh meeting finally took place in November 1999, and the twelfth meeting was conducted in April 2000.[28]

In May 2000, Indian President Narayanan visited Beijing to get the border talks back on track.[29] In July, Chinese Foreign Minister Tang Jiaxuan traveled to New Delhi to meet with External Affairs Minister Jaswant Singh, where they agreed the JWG would accelerate talks on the LAC. Furthermore the two sides announced the resumption of high-level military interaction. Indian naval ships visited Shanghai in September 2000 and exchange visits by military chiefs of staff are planned.

China–ASEAN

China uses its participation in the ASEAN Regional Forum (ARF) as a military-related CBM.[30] When China hosted the Inter-Sessional Support Group on CBMs in March 1997, Beijing made overtures to enhance understanding and confidence with other members of the ARF on security matters by inviting diplomatic and defense officials of the twenty-one ARF members to visit a PLA division. Over 100 representatives visited the barracks of the PLA division at Yangcun, located 70 kilometers southeast of Beijing near Tianjin. After a briefing on the division's history, the ARF guests watched live-ammunition drills and visited barracks. Although Yangcun is one of the PLA's few "show bases" that all foreign attachés and delegations visit, China placed great importance on this three-day meeting because it was the first meeting on multilateral dialogue and cooperation hosted by China.

During the July 2000 ARF meeting, China tabled requests to organize a seminar on defense conversion, to host an international meeting of leaders of defense colleges and universities, and to set up a regional maritime information center.[31] According to some observers, the Chinese are essentially trying to keep some ball in motion to indicate there is progress on CBMs, but they do not want the ARF to move into preventive diplomacy, and they do not want it getting into concrete discussions on domestic affairs. For example, the internal unrest in Indonesia is an issue China seeks to avoid discussing because it fears talk about the domestic situation in other countries might set a precedent for discussion on issues China considers its own affairs, such as Taiwan and Tibet. But China will not hesitate to use the ARF platform to criticize US and Japanese plans to construct a theater missile defense (TMD) system in Asia.

China and Vietnam have established their own series of CBMs. In September 1998, during the sixth round of talks aimed at delineating the land border and the demarcation of the Gulf of Tonkin, China and Vietnam, who fought a border war in 1979, agreed to resolve outstanding land and sea border disputes by around 2000.[32] In addition, Beijing agreed in 1997 to disclose the number of land mines remaining on the border. Since November 1997, PLA troops have cleared 42 mine fields, including 106,200 mines, from the Chinese side of the border. This represents 60 percent of the total number of mines disclosed.[33] In December 1999, Beijing and Hanoi signed an agreement on the 1,300 kilometer long border. Both sides have pledged to finish negotiations in 2001 on the demarcation of the South China Sea and the Gulf of Tonkin.[34]

Comparison of the Sino-Indian, Sino-Russian/Central Asian Republics, and Organization for Security and Cooperation in Europe CBMs

A comparison of the 1996 Sino-Indian Agreement on the Line of Actual Control (LAC), the 1996 Sino-Russian/Central Asian Republics Shanghai Agreement, and the 1994 Vienna Document of the Organization for Security and Cooperation in Europe (OSCE), as shown in Table 10.1, provides a useful framework for potential military CBMs between Beijing and Taipei.[35]

The author of the study, Yuan Jing-dong, has made a number of observations based on the information in Table 10.1. First, there is a difference in the scope of application. While the Vienna Document covers the entire OSCE (Europe) area, the Sino-Indian and Sino-Russian Agreements concern only the border regions

Table 10.1 Comparison of the Sino-Indian Agreement on LAC, Sino-Russian/Central Asian Republics Shanghai Agreement, and the OSCE Vienna Document

Issue area	Sino-Indian Agreement on LAC	Sino-Russian/CAR Shanghai Agreement	OSCE Vienna Document
Underlying principles	Transparency in the military field Mutual non-aggression Non-use of force Respect the LAC Peace and tranquillity Force reduction Non-interference in internal affairs	Transparency in the military field Mutual non-aggression Non-use of force Peace and stability Force reduction	Transparency in the military field Non-use of force or threat of use of force
Geographic area	10 km from the LAC	100 km from border line	Whole of Europe, adjoining sea air space
Military activities/ exercises parameters	No exercises larger than 1 division (approx. 15,000 troops)	Within 100 km: no exercises of more than 40,000 troops (Eastern Section); 4,000 troops and/or 50 tanks (Western Section)	Every 2 calendar years: no more than 1 military activity involving more than 40,000 troops or 900 tanks
	Exercises larger than 1 brigade group (approx. 5,000 troops) to be pre-notified	Within 15 km: no more than 1 regiment in live-fire exercise	Each year: no more than 3 military activities involving more than 25,000 troops or 400 tanks
	Prohibition of combat aircraft flights within 10 km of LAC except with prior notification Prohibition of firing, blasting, hunting within 2 km of LAC	Within 10 km: border guards only	Simultaneously: no more than 3 military activities involving more than 13,000 troops or 300 tanks
Equipment specifications	Combat tanks, infantry combat vehicles, guns (incl. howitzers) greater than 75 mm, mortar with 120 mm or bigger caliber, SSMs, SAMs, other weapons system as mutually agreed	Battle tanks, armored vehicles, artillery systems (greater than 122 mm), aircraft, helicopters, tactical missile launchers	Battle tanks, armored combat vehicles, APCs and armored infantry fighting vehicle look-alike, anti-tank guided missile launchers permanently/integrally mounted on armored vehicles, self-propelled and towed artillery, mortars, and MRLs (100 mm and above), armored-vehicle-launched bridges, combat aircraft, helicopters

Cont.

Issue area	*Sino-Indian Agreement on LAC*	*Sino-Russian/CAR Shanghai Agreement*	*OSCE Vienna Document*
Information exchanges	Data exchange on military forces and arms to be reduced or limited	Annual exchange on main categories of equipment	Annual exchanges on military organization, designation, and subordination of units, manpower, major categories of equipment, planned troop increase, purposes, and start/end dates of unit increase/activities, HQ locations, military budgets, planned notifiable military activities and plans for deploying major equipment systems
	Ceiling to be determined on principle of mutual and equal security	Personnel strength (incl. Ground forces, air force, air defense aviation, border guard troops)	
Notifications	10 days in advance Exercises exceeding 5,000 troops (1 brigade)	10 days in advance Exercises exceeding 25,000 troops	At least 42 days in advance Activities involving 9,000 or more troops or 250 or more tanks or 200 or more aircraft sorties
	Notification of exercise termination within 5 days	Exercises which include 9,000 troops and/or 250 tanks from outside the border area	Amphibious or parachute landings involving 3,000 or more troops.
		Exercises in the border area which include 9,000 reserves	Transfer into or to a point of concentration within the zone of application of 13,000 or more troops or 300 or more tanks or 3,500 or more paratroops/amphibious troops
		Voluntary notification of any exercise involving more than 9,000 troops or 250 tanks	Changes to information provided on an annual basis (by the time activation occurs)
			Activities carried out without advance notice to the troops involved
Consultations	Clarification of doubtful situations	Request and response about ambiguous situations within 7 days	Reporting and clarifying hazardous military incidents
	Timely clarification for exercises	Mutual visits of military commanders	Consult and cooperation within 48 h on unusual/unscheduled significant military activities occurring outside normal peacetime locations
	Expanded regime of scheduled and flag meetings	Study tours by expert groups	Annual implementation assessment meeting

Issue area	*Sino-Indian Agreement on LAC*	*Sino-Russian/CAR Shanghai Agreement*	*OSCE Vienna Document*
Consultations (cont.)	Expanded telecom links along LAC	Experts meetings to discuss implementation	Establishment of Conflict Prevention Center
	Establishment (step-by-step) of medium- and high-level contacts		Voluntary invitations on visits to dispel concerns
Exchange/ cooperation	(Not included)	Experience exchange (construction, training, etc.)	Exchanges/visits of senior military/defense representatives and military commanders
		Cooperation in logistics etc.	Contacts between military institutions
		Other forms of cooperation, e.g., mutual participation in national holidays, athletic, and cultural events	Attendance on courses of instruction
			Exchanges/contacts between academics/military experts Sporting/cultural events contacts
Observations	(Not included)	To exercises involving more than 35,000 troops	To all notifiable military activities
		Voluntary invitation to exercises involving more than 13,000 troops, 300 tanks	To demonstrations of new types of major equipment systems when first introduced into the zone of application
			States may conduct inspections (subject to quota limits) States to provide opportunities for visits to active formations/units to allow evaluation of information provided (subject to quota limits)

Source: After Amitav Acharya, *ASEAN Regional Forum: Confidence Building* (Ottawa: Department of Foreign Affairs and International Trade, February 1997), Table 5, pp. 20–23.

and the LAC. Second, the provisions and clauses in the Vienna Document are more elaborate, numerous, and more specific, while those in the Sino-Indian and Sino-Russian Accords are more general and in places rather vague. Third, implementation and verification have received scant mention in the Sino-Indian/Sino-Russian Agreements while the Vienna Document has detailed provisions. In the case of Sino-Indian Agreements, no timetable is specified for withdrawing troops from the border (LAC), nor is the number of troops to be pulled back spelled out.[36]

Potential military-related CBMs between the PLA and ROC military

The idea of military CBMs across the Taiwan Strait is beginning to receive greater attention, especially in Taiwan. According to a December 31, 1998 report in Taiwan's Central News Agency, Chang King-yuh, Chairman of Taiwan's Cabinet-level Mainland Affairs Council, made an appeal at his year-end news conference that mainland China should seriously consider the ROC's proposal that the two sides of the Taiwan Strait establish a "military mutual trust" mechanism to facilitate eventual reunification. Chang said that some tasks in this domain could be done unilaterally, such as keeping the military budget transparent and exempting each other from becoming the target of military exercises.[37]

On July 6, 2000, Taiwan's Ministry of National Defense sponsored a seminar on the proposed establishment of a mechanism for military exchanges across the Taiwan Strait.[38] The seminar, chaired by Vice-Chief of the General Staff Hou Shou-yeh, brought together government officials, industry executives, scholars, and experts and was designed "to forge a national consensus on establishing a cross-Strait military mutual trust mechanism to help maintain peace in the Taiwan Strait." Four papers on related topics, including prospects for establishing a cross-Strait military mutual trust mechanism, cross-Strait relations and the proposed military exchange mechanism, international confidence-building measures, and mainland China's stance and views on confidence-building measures, were discussed during the one-day seminar.

Members of Taiwan's Legislative Yuan have also expressed interest in establishing cross-Strait military CBMs.[39] On July 20, 2000, a legislative subgroup dominated by opposition Kuomintang lawmakers announced plans to establish a cross-Strait forum in the Legislative Yuan to promote exchanges between Taipei and Beijing. Ho Chih-hui, head of the Taiwan Union Club (TUC), said that the TUC would invite ARATS officials and members of China's National People's Congress to attend the forum. According to Ho, Chinese Vice-Premier Qian Qichen told him and his eighteen-member delegation during a June trip to China that as long as Taiwan acknowledges that there is only "one China," any topic is open to discussion – including cross-Strait military CBMs.

CBM tools

Military CBM "tools" can be of a declaratory nature, can have communication channels, impose constraints on military capabilities, require transparency for military activities, improve maritime safety, and assist in the verification of obligations reached. These tools are designed to make the behavior of states more predictable by facilitating communication between states and establishing rules or patterns of behavior for their military forces, as well as the means to discern and verify compliance with those patterns. This section will examine each of these tools to see how they could possibly be applied across the Taiwan Strait.

Declaratory measures

These state a country's position on a particular issue in ways that are reassuring. They can be unilateral or reciprocal and can be merely symbolic or have substance. Beijing's affinity for "declaratory" CBMs is most evident in the nuclear field, where Beijing supports, among other issues, an international convention on unconditional no-first-use of nuclear weapons. In addition, China and Russia pledged in 1994 not to use nuclear weapons against one another and not to target each other with nuclear weapons. A similar agreement not to target each other with nuclear weapons was signed between China and the United States in June 1998.

As for cross-Strait relations, Taipei and Beijing have each used declaratory statements to state their basic positions on military relations. In 1987, Taipei lifted martial law, and in 1991 terminated the "period of mobilization against communist rebellion" marking an end to the ROC's stated aim of retaking the mainland by force. These moves, though with marginal meaning in military terms, did indicate a fundamental shift in Taiwan's policy toward the PRC.[40] On the other hand, Beijing has included language on the "non-use of force" in its agreements with Russia, the Central Asian Republics, and India in order to promote CBMs. However, in Taiwan's case, Beijing has consistently declared that "China will not commit itself not to resort to force" to reunify Taiwan with the mainland.[41]

Communication measures

These measures, including military ties and hotlines, help keep channels of communication open between conflict-prone states or states with tense relations. Communication measures can be employed on a regular basis as consultative mechanisms designed to allow states to air grievances and ward off crises before they occur. They can also help defuse tensions during periods of crises.

Military-to-military communication can be fostered by visits of high-level delegations, ship visits, and functional exchanges.[42] They can also include participation in conferences, visiting fellow programs, and student/faculty exchanges. They can be bilateral as well as multilateral. While the PLA is involved in each of these categories, the ROC military is pretty much limited to visits directly related with arms purchases, plus participation in conferences, visiting fellow programs, and student/faculty exchanges. As noted above, the PLA has expanded its military relations world-wide since the late 1970s. These communication measures help the PLA and ROC military learn about other countries' militaries and other countries to learn about them.

Bilateral and multilateral conferences, whether Track I (governmental) or Track II (non-governmental), provide an opportunity for military personnel to meet each other and to exchange information. Both the PLA and ROC militaries are involved in conferences, but they rarely participate together. For example, China became a full member of the Council for Security Cooperation in the Asia Pacific (CSCAP) in 1996.[43] Membership is open to all countries and regions in the Asia–Pacific region. Although Taiwan has tried to become an associate member, Beijing has successfully blocked Taipei's participation. However, after lengthy negotiations, Beijing agreed to have Taiwan participate in working groups only (but not at steering committee meetings or general membership meetings), and only in their private capacities. There is a pre-approved list of names of Taiwan scholars who can come to working group meetings and procedures for clearing others. No Taiwan government officials or military officers are on the list or are likely to be approved in the near future.

Although Beijing has resisted allowing the ROC military to be involved in formal military and military-related international forums, the PLA, through its China Institute for International Strategic Studies (CIISS) and National Defense University (NDU), has invited national security academics and retired ROC military officers to Beijing for discussions on national security issues.[44]

There have also been opportunities over the past several years for active-duty officers from the PLA and ROC military to be visiting fellows or students at the same organization or school in the United States,[45] and opportunities for visiting fellows or students in different organizations or schools to be at the same meetings. Each of these situations has allowed interaction between them.

Hotlines, if used correctly, can provide direct channels of communication between government leaders to discuss specific issues and can be used during moments of crisis to reduce tensions. Hotlines can also be used at lower levels, including communications between military forces facing each other across a border and hotlines for maritime rescue. During the 1990s, Beijing has used each of these types of hotlines.

During 1998, Beijing established head-of-state hotlines with Russia and the United States. In April 1996, during Russian President Yeltsin's third summit meeting in Beijing (and the fifth overall summit with Chinese President Jiang), the two sides agreed to maintain regular dialogues at various levels and through multiple channels, including a governmental telephone hotline. On May 3, 1998, a hotline between Zhongnanhai and the Kremlin finally began operating. This is the first time Beijing has established a hotline with the head of a foreign state. In April 1998, China's Minister of Foreign Affairs Tang Jiaxuan and US Secretary of State Madeleine Albright signed an agreement to establish a hotline between the governments of the two countries. The hotline was activated during President Clinton's visit to China in June 1998.[46]

In February 1998, the Fujian Border Defense Corps, which is responsible for guarding the 3,300 kilometer coastline, disclosed that its major tasks for the year included investigating crimes in the Taiwan Strait. Because of the unique geographical and political background of the Taiwan Strait, there have always been areas where there are no patrols, thus causing security gaps in the Strait's maritime space. Criminal elements often take advantage of such gaps and endanger travelers passing through the Strait. Very often, their acts of smuggling and killings go unpunished. The Fujian Border Defense Corps also stated that it would explore channels with Taiwan for jointly maintaining cross-Strait security and cooperation. [47]

In January 1999, Sun Yafu, Vice President of China's Association for Relations Across the Taiwan Strait, lead a small delegation of scholars to several cities in the United States for discussions about China–Taiwan relations. During a meeting in New York, Wang Zaixi, a senior PLA officer and research fellow at the CIISS in Beijing, advocated that Beijing and Taipei should establish a military hotline.[48]

Maritime safety measures

These are closely linked to communication measures. They insure maritime safety, including maritime safety agreements and discussions about joint search and rescue exercises. For example, in January 1998, China and the United States signed the "Agreement Between the Department of Defense of the United States of America and the Ministry of National Defense of the People's Republic of China on Establishing a Consultation Mechanism to Strengthen Military Maritime Safety." According to the agreement, the agenda items of their maritime and air forces may include, among other items, such measures to promote safe maritime practices and establish mutual trust as search and rescue, communications procedures when ships encounter each other, interpretation of the Rules of the Nautical Road, and avoidance of accidents-at-sea. Beginning on December 3, 1998, the US Navy and the PLA Navy conducted a three-day joint search and rescue exercise (SAREX 98) south of Hong Kong.[49]

In addition, Beijing and Taipei have already implemented some maritime safety measures involving hotlines. Two significant maritime CBMs took place between the PRC and ROC in April 1997. First, direct shipping began on a trial basis. A year later, ten ships (six from the mainland and four from Taiwan) authorized to participate had completed 154 voyages. Second, a hotline telephone was set up to assist in maritime rescue. Previously, messages had to be transmitted through Hong Kong and it was impossible to have dialogue between the two sides when maritime rescue was needed.[50]

In November 1997, the Taipei-based China Rescue Association and its mainland counterpart, the China Marine Rescue Center, reached an agreement to set up a hotline to facilitate marine rescue work in the Taiwan Strait. Under the agreement, when accidents involving the ships of both Taiwan and the Chinese mainland happen in the Strait, the ships in distress and the rescuing ships may use the hotline to ask for help and request permission to enter the waters and harbors of the other side. The hotline will operate twenty-four hours a day.[51]

Constraint measures

These measures, including "thin-out zones," are designed to keep certain types and levels of states' military forces at a distance from one another, especially along borders. Constraint measures, in the form of requirements to provide advance notice (up to 1–2 years in some cases in Europe) of certain levels of troop movements, also aim to constrain states' abilities to move the troops and equipment needed to mount large-scale offensives.

Thin-out zones, or limited force deployment zones, restrict the type and number of military equipment or troops permitted in or near a certain territory or boundary. In China's 1996 border agreement with India, each side pledged not to attack each other or cross the LAC, and to reduce troops and armaments along the common border. They also agreed to avoid holding large-scale military exercises involving more than one division (15,000 troops) in close proximity of the LAC and to refrain from flying combat aircraft within 10 kilometers of the LAC. Unarmed transport aircraft, survey aircraft, and helicopters are permitted to fly up to the LAC.

In the Taiwan Strait, the ROC Air Force and PLA Air Force have established voluntary constraint measures. For example, according to a 29 November 1998 article in Taipei's *Tzu-Li Wan-Pao*,

> since the end of air battles over the Taiwan Strait in 1958, when carrying out patrol duties during ordinary times, our fighters have always kept a distance of 30 sea miles from the mainland's coast, while the Chinese Communist fighters usually carry out their duties close to their own coast line. Maintaining a tacit agreement on an invisible central line of the strait, neither side has conducted any provocative flights against each other, so as to prevent an air battle from breaking out due to misjudgments made by their pilots.[52]

Transparency measures

These are used by states to foster greater openness of their military capabilities and activities. The measures include publication of defense white papers, pre-notification requirements for exercises and troop movements, data exchanges, voluntary observations, and exchange of military attachés.

China lags behind other Asia–Pacific countries in providing military transparency through publication of defense white papers. As tensions mounted in the Taiwan Strait, Beijing published a *White Paper on Arms Control and Disarmament* in November 1995. The twenty-page paper, released during the negotiating end game of the Comprehensive Test Ban Treaty (CTBT) and while China was conducting nuclear tests, attempted to defuse concerns about a "China threat" and accusations that Beijing was supplying weapons of mass destruction to friendly neighbors. Beijing published its first *Defense White Paper* in July 1998, proposing a two-part strategy based on international security cooperation via the United Nations Security Council and on promoting mutual understanding through military exchanges. Meanwhile, Japan has published its *Defense of Japan* white paper annually for over two decades, South Korea began publishing an annual *Defense White Paper* in 1988, Taiwan has published its *National Defense Report* every two years since 1992, and Mongolia issued its first *Defense White Paper* in 1997. Other countries in Southeast Asia have also published their own white papers.

Pre-notification requirements of a certain time period for planned military exercises or troop movements of an agreed upon level also help make a state's military intent more transparent. Notification mechanisms can also be applied to missile tests. Near contentious borders, this type of transparency measure can help eliminate fears that an exercise may be part of preparations for war. Establishing and exchanging a regular schedule of military exercises can further build confidence between parties.

Data exchanges detailing existing military holdings, planned purchases, military personnel, and budgets can clarify a state's current and projected military capabilities and provide advance notice of destabilizing arms buildups. Data exchanges can take place bilaterally or multilaterally. An example is the United Nations Register of Conventional Arms established in December 1991, in which states are asked to report all imports and exports of weapons in seven categories.[53] Prior to November 1998, when Beijing withdrew to protest against US arms sales to Taiwan, China was one of ninety-two countries that reported in at least some areas.[54]

Voluntary observations on another state's military exercises provide first-hand access to that party's equipment and operating procedures. For example, in the 1996 Sino-Russian/Central Asian Republic Agreement, the parties were encouraged to invite observers to troop exercises on a mutual basis and to strengthen friendly contact between service personnel. As mentioned above, Beijing hosted the ASEAN Regional Forum's Inter-Sessional Support Group on CBMs in March 1997 and invited attendees to visit a PLA division to watch live-ammunition drills and visit the barracks. In addition, in July–August 1998, two PLA Navy officers became the first Chinese participants to observe the multinational Rim of the Pacific (RimPac) '98 naval exercises near Hawaii.

Exchanging military attachés is a valuable means of providing transparency, because it allows countries to have a direct link between their military organizations. As mentioned above, the PRC and ROC have military attachés in their embassies throughout the world. In 1988 the PRC had ties with eighty-five foreign armed forces, posted military attaché offices in sixty countries, and hosted forty military attaché offices in Beijing. Today, the PLA has established relations with the armed forces of more than a hundred countries, has set up military attaché offices in more than ninety countries, and hosts over sixty military attaché offices in China. The ROC has military attachés in many of its embassies and in its unofficial trade offices where it does not have an official embassy or consulate. All of these attaché offices help facilitate exchanges of high-ranking officials and functional delegations.

Beijing and Taipei already provide public notification through their respective Ministries of Defense or government spokesmen about pending military exercises. In order to establish a form of transparency CBMs, Beijing and Taipei could make formal notification to each other through organizations such as Taiwan's Strait Exchange Foundation (SEF) or the mainland's Association for Relations Across the Taiwan Strait (ARATS). As has been done in Europe, agreements could be made to specify the amount of lead time for announce-ments, and then gradually increase the lead time.

Verification measures

These are designed to collect data or provide first-hand access in order to confirm or verify a state's compliance with a particular treaty or agreement. Verification measures include aerial inspections, ground-based electronic sensoring, and on-site inspections. However, in order for any CBMs to be effec-tive, they have to be voluntary and the states have to have a commitment to implement them.

Aerial inspections enable parties to an agreement to monitor compliance with force deployment limitations in restricted zones, to confirm data exchanges on the disposition of military forces, and to provide early warning of potentially destabilizing activities. Third parties may carry out aerial inspections, or the parties themselves may jointly participate in overflights. Strict guidelines regulate the type of aircraft and surveillance technology allowed on board, as well as flight patterns permitted.

Ground-based electronic sensoring systems, whether manned or unmanned, can also verify states' compliance to agreed restrictions on equipment deploy-ment or troop movements.

On-site inspections, consisting of challenge and routine inspections, can help verify that states are complying with agreements. Inspections may be carried out by third parties, or jointly. For example, China has accepted on-site inspections as a signatory to the 1994 Chemical Weapons Convention.

Conclusions

Three conclusions follow from this analysis. First, China's movement on military CBMs has followed breakthroughs in high-level political visits. Following these visits, it has taken several years to work out details and begin implementing the military CBMs. Second, it is unlikely there will be any significant movement toward military CBMs across the Taiwan Strait until there is movement on polit-ical issues. Now that the ROC's March 2000 presidential election is over, the next major political event is the PRC's Communist Party Congress in 2002. Third, Beijing has moved forward on military-related CBMs with most of its neighbors during the 1990s, and Taipei and Beijing have established communi-cations on maritime rescue issues. In addition, there have been meetings between the PLA and national security-related organizations in Taiwan, as well as contact between active-duty PLA and ROC military officers in the United States. While Taipei appears to have addressed Beijing's concern about the term CBMs by using the term military mutual trust mechanisms, the PRC will most likely not allow the ROC military to participate in multilateral events in the near future. Taipei is, however, at least addressing the issue in an open forum.

Several types of CBMs could be established between the PLA and ROC military under the right set of circumstances. Although many of these CBMs would be symbolic in nature, they could eventually lead to substantive CBMs. A list of possible CBMs, without specifying any particular time frame, is as follows.

Two of the most important, and most difficult, measures involve declaratory statements concerning the use of force and Taiwan independence. Either side could break the logjam by making unilateral declarations. Beijing could renounce its policy to use force to reunify Taiwan with the mainland. Taipei could also renounce the possibility of declaring independence for Taiwan.[55] However, the probability of either of these two situations occurring is not high, at least in the near term.

Communication measures are the most likely, and easiest, measures that the PLA and ROC military could implement. To begin with, there could be a formalized program that begins by exchanging delegations composed of retired military officers, as well as national security experts, sponsored by organizations like the PLA's CIISS and NDU and Taiwan's Chinese Center for Advanced Policy Studies and the ROC military's Armed Forces University. Active-duty officers could gradually be added as the program evolved. Eventually, direct military relations could be enhanced by exchanging military liaison officers or attachés. These officers might then be allowed to observe exercises.

As this program matures, Beijing could be inclined to withdraw its objection to ROC military officers attending international forums such as CSCAP and the ARF. A formula similar to Taiwan's participation in the Asia–Pacific Economic Cooperation (APEC) and international sports events might be worked out.

Establishing hotlines, whether symbolic or substantive, could be an important step in reducing tensions between the two sides. These hotlines could be at senior levels or at lower levels, such as the maritime rescue hotline discussed above. The PLA and ROC military could also use these hotlines to provide formal notification to each other about pending military exercises.

Beijing and Taipei could agree upon various transparency and constraint measures, including requirements to provide advance notice of certain levels of troop movements and exercises. At some point in the future, they could begin discussions about troop movements in Taiwan and within the Nanjing and Guangzhou Military Regions opposite Taiwan, as well as naval vessel movements. They could also agree to avoid holding large-scale military exercises involving more than an agreed-upon number of troops and vessels, and to refrain from flying combat aircraft within a specified area over the Taiwan Strait.

Once both sides have agreed upon various constraint measures, they will have to agree upon the necessary verification measures designed to confirm compliance with the agreement. They could agree to joint aerial inspections, ground-based electronic sensing, and/or on-site inspections. Or they could involve a third party in these measures.

While it appears that the near-term probability of Beijing and Taipei establishing new military CBMs is not high, opportunities for military CBMs can grow over time. For example, who could have predicted twenty years ago that China would have broad military relations with Russia and the United States today, given their adversarial relations during the 1960s and 1970s? However, bold leadership provided the impetus for this to happen. Over the past decade, Taiwan has invested over $30 billion on the mainland. Although informal discussions between SEF and ARATS were put back on track in October 1998, they were put on indefinite hold following Lee Teng-hui's statement on state-to-state relations in July 1999. Bold leadership on both sides of the Strait could yet be the decisive factor in determining the future relationship.

Today, Beijing and Taipei have a choice of renewed confrontation, with potentially explosive results for the entire region, or a gradual accommodation and resolution of their differences. If they choose the latter, then CBMs will be an essential means for reconciliation.

Appendix 1: a brief history of CBMs

Beginning with the establishment of the "hotline" after the Cuban missile crisis, the East–West CBM toolbox grew to include agreed rules for superpower navies operating in close proximity, and data exchanges on military equipment and force deployments. The West made a concerted effort not just to negotiate CBMs in the military-security arena, but also to develop other "baskets" of measures to promote economic and cultural exchanges as well as respect for human rights.

One of the most important breakthroughs in US–Soviet relations – an agreement to accept mandatory on-site inspections – was first negotiated in the 1986 Stockholm accord to ease concerns arising from large-scale military exercises. Important new measures were added to the toolbox once the Cold War began to thaw, such as the acceptance of cooperative aerial inspections or "open skies," observations within military garrisons, and the creation of a crisis prevention center. Today there are literally dozens of CBMs to ease East–West security concerns that can be used to establish new patterns of cooperation between old adversaries.

None the less, nuclear arms control negotiations took center stage during the Cold War, as both sides invested these weapons with symbolic power to match their destructive potential. The strategic arms limitation and reduction talks paradoxically became a reflection of the strategic competition and a means to ameliorate it. In conflict-prone regions like South Asia and the Middle East, CBMs assume these dual roles. In the absence of political reconciliation in these tense regions, the negotiation and implementation of CBMs have been critical in maintaining the peace and preventing the use of weapons of mass destruction.

The East–West experience presents the most fully developed model for CBMs, notable for the 1975 Helsinki Final Act, which formally recognized the status quo in Europe and facilitated a process of interaction between East and West, including inviting observers to military exercises on a voluntary basis. The Stockholm Accord mandated such inspections, in addition to requiring an annual calendar of notifiable military activities. The 1990 Vienna Document considerably broadened data exchanges, including detailed information on force deployments, major weapons programs, and military budgets. The 1992 Vienna Agreement added another level of transparency by requiring demonstrations of new types of military equipment.

> *Source* Michael Krepon (ed.), *A Handbook of Confidence-Building Measures for Regional Security*, 2d ed. (Washington, DC: The Henry L. Stimson Center, January 1995).

Notes

1 A version of this essay was first presented at a conference sponsored by The Public Policy Institute at Southern Illinois University in December 1998. The author is not agreeing with or advocating a "two Chinas" or a "one China, one Taiwan" policy. The terms PRC and ROC are used to conform with the way each side of the Taiwan Strait refers to itself.

2 In 1987, the ROC renounced its goal of retaking the mainland and formed the state-funded, though technically private, Straits Exchange Foundation (SEF) under the Legislative Yuan's Mainland Affairs Council. Beijing established a similar non-governmental Association for Relations Across the Taiwan Straits (ARATS) in 1991. Bilateral talks between the chairmen of SEF, Koo Chen-fu, and ARATS, Wang Daohan, began in Singapore in 1993, which established mechanisms for regular contact between the two sides to be based on the "one China" principle. The semi-official talks, referred to as the Koo–Wang talks, were suspended in mid-1995 following Taiwan President Lee Teng-hui's private, but high-profile, visit to the United States. Following the visit and in the runup to the island's March 1996 presidential election, China held extensive military exercises opposite Taiwan, including missile launches into the ocean just off Taiwan's northern and southern coasts. Washington responded by deploying two carrier battle groups off Taiwan. A gradual warming in relations between Beijing and Taipei took place during 1998, resulting in Koo Chen-fu's visit to Beijing and Shanghai in October 1998.

3 Chiang Kai-shek attended several months of military and political training in Moscow in 1923 before returning to become the Whampoa commandant. The Chinese Communist Red Army was not formally established until 1927. Of particular note, the Soviet Union helped Sun Yat-sen's and Chiang Kai-shek's KMT and the CCP establish the same organizational structure during the 1920s. In response to Japanese actions in China, beginning with Japan's invasion of Manchuria in 1931, the Soviets supported the nationalists by providing arms and advisors. From late 1937 until Germany attacked the Soviet Union in June 1941, Stalin provided about $300 million in credits to Chiang Kai-shek's regime to finance Soviet aid, including hundreds of planes, pilots to fly them, and instructors to train Chinese pilots. Soviet advisors were also attached to nationalist army units.

4 From 1959 to 1967, the nationalists flew 100 U-2 sorties over the mainland and had five aircraft shot down. The first U-2 was shot down on November 1, 1963.

5 *Republic of China: 1998 National Defense Report* (Taipei: Li Ming Cultural Enterprise, 1998), pp. 184–5.

6 *China Country Study* (Washington, DC: Library of Congress, Foreign Research Division, 1987); plus numerous other periodicals and publications, including *White Paper on China's National Defense* (Beijing: Information Office of the State Council of the People's Republic of China, July 1998).

7 For a detailed analysis of this revised national military strategy, see Nan Li, "The PLA's Evolving Warfighting Doctrine, Strategy, and Tactics, 1985–95: A Chinese View," and Paul H. B. Godwin, "From Continent to Periphery: PLA Doctrine, Strategy, and Capabilities Toward 2000," both in David S. Shambaugh and Richard

H. Yang (eds.), *China's Military in Transition* (Oxford: Clarendon Press, 1997), pp. 284–312. See also James Harris et al., "Chinese Defense Policy and Military Strategy in the 1990s," *China's Economic Dilemmas in the 1990s: The Problems of Reforms, Modernization, and Interdependence* (Washington, DC: Joint Economic Committee, Congress of the United States, April 1991), pp. 648–9.

8 *White Paper on China's National Defense* (Beijing: Information Office of the State Council of the People's Republic of China, July 1998).

9 "Official Reviews 1995 Sino-Foreign Military Ties," *Xinhua*, 2 March 1996.

10 'Yearender; Active Military Exchanges Yield New Achievements," *Xinhua*, 19 December 1996.

11 "China: Report on Military Diplomacy in 1997," *Xinhua*, 12 January 1998.

12 "Good-Neighborly Ties Key to China's Military Diplomacy," *Xinhua*, 5 January 2000.

13 Gary Klintworth, "Expanded Horizons," *Free China Review*, October 1998, pp. 50–3.

14 Pacific Rim (RimPac) is a multinational, biennial naval exercise that has been held since 1971 during the summer months in the vicinity of Hawaii. Participants in RimPac '98 were 41 ships, 7 submarines, 250 aircraft, and over 30,000 personnel from the United States, Australia, Republic of Korea, Canada, Chile, and Japan. There were also eight observers: China, Ecuador, Indonesia, Mexico, Peru, Russia, Singapore, and Thailand. US Pacific Command website: http://www.pacom.mil/about/pacom.htm (accessed 1998).

15 "Singaporean Navy Ship Visits Qingdao," *Xinhua*, 23 March 1999. "British Navy Frigate Makes Friendly Visit to China Mainland," *The Desert News*, Salt Lake City, 14 March 1999. "Russian Navy Ships Visit Shanghai," *Xinhua*, 2 October 1999.

16 "Malaysian Navy Chief, Chinese Fleet Delegation Discuss Relations," *Nanyang Siang Pau, British Broadcasting Corporation*, 15 July 2000. "Chinese Naval Ships to Visit South Africa," *Xinhua*, 28 July 2000.

17 "US Navy Warship To Visit China," *Reuters*, 25 July 2000.

18 Altogether Jiang Zemin met with President Boris Yeltsin eight times, including meetings in each capital plus summits of the "Shanghai Five" (China, Kyrgyzstan, Russia, Kazakstan, and Tajikistan). By the end of 2001, Jiang will have met with Vladimir Putin five times since Putin became president in 2000.

19 "First Soviet Military Delegation Visiting China for 30 Years," *Radio Moscow, BBC*, 1 June 1990.

20 The information in this paragraph is a compilation of about fifty reports on PLA visitors to Russia. Some of the military installations visited include the 35th Airborne Brigade of the Kazakh Army, the cosmonauts' training center, the Academy of the General Staff of the Russian Armed Forces, the Moscow Air Force and Air Defense District command post, the motorized infantry brigade of the Moscow military area, the Kubinka Air Force garrison near Moscow, a Strategic Missile Troops command post near Novosibirsk, the Leningrad Military District headquarters, the Leningrad naval base, the Admiral Kuznetsov Naval Academy, and the Central Naval Museum.

21 Various reports have had the Chinese purchasing MiG-29 and MiG-31 fighters, Tu-22M/Backfire bombers, Su-24 fighter-bombers, SS-18 and SS-19 ICBMs, Typhoon-class nuclear submarines, but none of these alleged talks have come to fruition.

22 Nikolay Novichkov, "China To Begin Licensed Production of Su-27CK Fighters," *ITAR-TASS* (in English), 13 November 1997.

23 "Chinese Army Chief Meets Russian Military Delegation," *Xinhua*, 4 May 1993. Daniel Kwan, "Jiang Wins Backing of PLA Brass," *South China Morning Post*, 5 August 1994. "Military Delegation Visits Russia," *RIA News Agency, BBC*, 31 October 1995. "Military Delegation Visits Russia," *RIA News Agency, BBC*, 31 October 1995. "PLA Delegation Leaves for Visit to Finland, Russia," *Xinhua*, 5 October 1996. "China's Military Academy Delegation Back From Europe," *Xinhua*, 21 June 1997. "Chinese Military Delegation Arrives in St Petersburg," *St Petersburg Channel 5 TV, BBC* (in

Russian), 20 October 1997. "Chinese PLA Delegation Returns to Beijing," *Xinhua*, 25 November 1997. "Russian and Chinese Military Experts at One over Yugoslavia," *ITAR-TASS, BBC*, 23 April 1999.

24 Ann Scott Tyson, "Sino-Soviet Border Talks Look to Future Military Cooperation," *Christian Science Monitor*, 11 September 1990.

25 Information on China's relations with Russia come from Kenneth Allen and Eric McVadon, *China's Foreign Military Relations*, The Henry L. Stimson Center, October 1999, Section IV.

26 In 1994, NATO offered military cooperation and consultation to the states from the former Soviet bloc under the Partnership for Peace (PFP) program to make their military structures compatible with NATO.

27 K. K. Katyal, "China Claims 'Active Approach,'" *The Hindu*, New Delhi, 23 November 1998.

28 "India, China Resume Talks on Nagging Border Dispute," *Agence France Presse*, 24 November 1999. "President's China Visit Discussed at JWG," *The Hindu, FT Asia Intelligence Wire*, 29 April 2000.

29 "Sino-Indian JWG to Meet Often," *The Hindu, FT Asia Intelligence Wire*, 23 July 2000.

30 ARF is a governmental forum focusing on politics and security whose first session was held in Bangkok in July 1994. The ARF participants include the nine ASEAN member countries – Brunei, Indonesia, Laos, Malaysia, Burma, the Philippines, Singapore, Thailand, and Vietnam – the two observer countries Cambodia and Papua New Guinea, and the eleven dialogue partners – Australia, Canada, China, India, Japan, Mongolia, New Zealand, Russia, South Korea, the United States, and the European Union.

31 Michael Forsythe, "China Worried over N. Korean Role in ARF, Expert Says," *Kyodo News Service, Japan Economic Newswire*, 25 July 2000.

32 Reuters, "Beijing, Hanoi 'still committed' to Year 2000 Deadlines for Border Disputes," *South China Morning Post Internet Edition*, 30 September 1998.

33 "106,200 Mines Cleared Along China-Vietnam Border," *Hong Kong Zhongguo Tongxun She* (in Chinese), 2 October 1998.

34 "China Hails Border Agreement with Vietnam," *Agence France Presse*, 30 December 1999.

35 This is from a draft paper by Yuan Jing-dong "The Process of Sino-Indian Confidence-Building: A Preliminary Analysis," Institute of International Relations, University of British Columbia.

36 Damon Bristow, "Mutual Mistrust still Hampering Sino-Indian Rapprochement," *Jane's Intelligence Review* (August 1997), p. 370.

37 "Taipei Urges PRC To Build Up 'Military Trust Mechanism,'" *Taiwan Central News Agency*, 31 December 1998.

38 "Seminar Held on Military Exchanges with Mainland," *Taiwan Central News Agency*, 6 July 2000.

39 Fang Wen-hung, "Taiwan Union Club to Establish Cross-Strait Forum," *Taiwan Central News Agency*, 20 July 2000.

40 Alexander Chieh-cheng Huang, "Taiwan's View of Military Balance and the Challenge it Presents," *Crisis in the Taiwan Strait* (Washington, DC: NDU Press, 1997), pp. 282–3.

41 *White Paper on China's National Defense* (Beijing: Information Office of the State Council of the People's Republic of China, July 1998).

42 Another facet of military-to-military relations is arms sales and military assistance, but these do not necessarily fall into the category of CBMs.

43 CSCAP was established in June 1993 as a multilateral, non-governmental organization that links regional security-oriented research institutes and, through them, broad-based member committees composed of academics, business executives, security specialists, and former and current foreign ministry and defense officials.

44 CIISS is a think tank subordinate to the General Staff Department's Second (Intelligence) Department. The director is Deputy Chief of the General Staff Lieutenant-General Xiong Guangkai, who was a former military attaché to East Germany. Many of those who staff CIISS are former military attachés or people who have served overseas.

45 There have also been active-duty US military officer visiting fellows or students, as well as officers from other Asia–Pacific countries, at the same location.

46 Liao Xin, "New Relations Between China and Russia," FBIS-CHI-97–363, Beijing Review in English, December 1997, pp. 7–8. Grigoriy Arslanov, "Russia: Hotline for Russia's Yeltsin, PRC's Jiang Now Operational," FBIS-SOV-98–125, Moscow ITAR-TASS (in English), 5 May 98.

47 "Fujian Seeks Taiwan Cooperation on Fighting Crimes at Sea," FBIS-CHI-98–040, Beijing Zhongguo Xinwen She (in Chinese), 6 February 1998.

48 "Mainland Scholar Wang Zaixi Proposes Beijing and Taipei Establish a Military Hotline," *World Journal*, New York, January 19, 1999.

49 Brendan Delfino, "PLA Joins Forces with US in Historic Exercise," *South China Morning Post*, 3 December 1998.

50 "Cross-Strait Direct Shipping Test Goes Smoothly," FBIS-CHI-98–107, Hong Kong Zhongguo Tongxun She (in Chinese), 16 April 1998.

51 "Hotline To Facilitate Rescue Work in Taiwan Strait," FBIS-CHI-97–329, *Taiwan Central News Agency*, 25 November 1997.

52 "Mainland Fighters Said To Appear Above Taiwan Straits," *Tzu-Li Wan-Pao*, Taipei, 29 November 1998.

53 These seven categories include battle tanks, armored combat vehicles, large-caliber delivery systems, combat aircraft, attack helicopters, warships, and missiles or missile systems.

54 Thalif Deen, "China Pulls out of U.N. Arms Register over Taiwan," *Inter Press Service* (Internet), 11 November 1998.

55 During his inaugural speech on May 20, 1996, ROC President Lee Teng-hui stated:

> The Republic of China has always been a sovereign state. Disputes across the Straits center around system and lifestyle; they have nothing to do with ethnic or cultural identity. Here in this country it is totally unnecessary or impossible to adopt the so-called course of 'Taiwan independence.' For over 40 years, the two sides of the Straits have been two separate jurisdictions due to various historical factors, but it is also true that both sides pursue eventual national unification. Only when both sides face up to the facts and engage in dialogue with profound sincerity and patience will they be able to find the solution to the unification question and work for the common welfare of the Chinese people.

During a meeting with SEF Chairman Koo Chen-fu in October 1998, Qian Qichen, a member of the Political Bureau of the Central Committee Chinese Communist Party, urged early political talks between the Chinese mainland and Taiwan. Qian said cross-Strait political talks are only a matter of time should the reunification be achieved through peaceful means.

> Taiwan now practices a capitalist system and after the reunification, Taiwan may retain the capitalist system while the mainland of the motherland practices the socialist system. By reunification, we mean to safeguard the state territorial integrity and sovereignty, not to argue over systems.

He said the "one China" principle is the basis for maintaining stability and developing cross-Strait relations and is also recognized by various countries. "We are not in favor of all statements and actions about 'two Chinas' or 'one China, one Taiwan'. Nor will we tolerate Taiwan to be ceded."

11 The possibility of cross-Strait political negotiations

Chong-hai Shaw

The attitudes and positions of the two sides with respect to "cross-Strait negotiations"

The attitudes and positions of Beijing

Throughout the development of cross-Strait relations, the Beijing authorities have always placed entering negotiations, especially political negotiations, at the top of their priority list. This is readily apparent from the fact that the crucial documents issued by the PRC with respect to Taiwan policy have never failed to include this item.

The 1979 "Message to Compatriots on Taiwan" opens with the statement:

> There is still military confrontation between the two sides of the Taiwan Strait, which can only create tension. We believe that, first of all, talks between the government of the People's Republic of China and the Taiwan authorities should be used to end this state of military confrontation.

This theme was continued in the 1981 "Nine Points" plan announced by Marshall Ye Jianying:

> In order to bring an end to the unfortunate separation of the Chinese nation as early as possible, we propose that talks be held between the Communist Party of China [CCP] and the Kuomintang of China [KMT] on a reciprocal basis so that the two parties will cooperate for the third time to accomplish the great task of national reunification.

In 1983, Deng Xiaoping expressed his thinking on the peaceful unification of China and Taiwan in very similar terms to the Ye's "Nine Points Policy." He said: "To realize unification, we must have the proper method; therefore I suggest party-to-party talks, practicing the 'third cooperation'."

In order to respond to Taipei's termination of the "Period of National Mobilization for Suppression of the Communist Rebellion," in June 1991 Beijing delegated the head of the Central Office for Taiwan Affairs to pronounce the "June 7 Statement," of which the major element was to suggest to Taiwan: "Relevant agencies, delegated bodies, and individuals from both sides of the Strait should, as soon as possible, being discussions to solve the issues of the 'three links' and bilateral exchanges." In addition, it suggested that perhaps "the Communist Party of China and the Kuomintang of China should send representatives to engage in contacts, so as to create the conditions for the progress of negotiations for a formal end to hostilities and gradual peaceful unification."

In October of the following year, Jiang Zemin, in his political report to the 14th CCP Party Congress, reiterated:

> The CCP is willing to enter into contacts with the KMT at an early date so as to create the conditions for the progress of negotiations for a formal end to hostilities and gradual peaceful unification. In these talks, representative individuals from other parties and groups from both sides of the Strait could also participate. Under the 'one China' principle, any problem can be discussed with the Taiwan side, including the formal negotiating methods of both sides, to find a process acceptable to both sides.

"PRC's White Paper on Taiwan Unification" released in August of 1993 raised the basic idea of "peaceful negotiations." In concrete terms: "Achieving national unification through peaceful means via contacts and negotiations is the common wish of all Chinese people." Moreover, "in order to end the state of hostility and realize peaceful unification, the two sides should begin [such] contacts and negotiations as soon as possible." The white paper also reiterated that, under the "one China" principle, any problem could be discussed, including the format of negotiations, participation of political parties or other organizations, and all other issues of concern to the Taiwanese side.

Jiang Zemin's "Eight Points" of 1995 synthesized the suggestions of the previous Taiwan policy documents into the following formula:

> The first step is for the two sides to enter into negotiations and reach an agreement to, 'under the principle of one China, formally end the state of hostility between the two sides.' On this base, we can together shoulder our obligations, to defend the sovereignty and territorial integrity of China; moreover, we can begin to plan for the development of future cross-Strait relations. As for the name, place, and method of the negotiations, as long as discussions begin in good time, at any rate a solution acceptable to all can be found.

Directly addressing the formula in use since 1992 of "under the one China principle, any problem can be discussed," Jiang emphasized, "of course this includes all the problems the Taiwan authorities are concerned with." Even more important, in this major statement by Jiang, he stressed that "engaging in cross-Strait negotiations for peaceful unification has been our persistent position."

In his political report to the 15th CCP Party Congress in September 1997, Jiang placed special emphasis on the cross-Strait issue, in a section entitled "Promoting Peaceful Unification of the Motherland." Although the call for political negotiations did not deviate from the position set out in the "Eight Points," this re-emphasis further indicated the high level of concern of the Beijing authorities on the issue. His report read in part as follows:

> Now we should like to renew our solemn appeal: as the first step, the two sides of the Strait can hold negotiations and reach an agreement on, 'officially ending the state of hostility between the two sides … under the principle of one China.' On this base, we can together shoulder our obligations, to defend the sovereignty and territorial integrity of China; moreover, we can begin to plan for the development of future cross-Strait relations. We hope that the Taiwan authorities will earnestly respond to our suggestions and proposals, and enter into political negotiations with us at an early date. Under the one China principle, any problem can be discussed.[1]

In addition, since his New Year's Address of 1997 until today, Jiang has continued to seriously call on Taiwan to respond as soon as possible to the proposal for political negotiations under the "one China" principle. It is clear that the Beijing authorities have from the beginning established a very consistent position and attitude.[2]

Up to the time of writing, in March of 1999, we have not seen any alteration of this position. Whether in Zhu Rongji's report to the second session of the 9th National People's Congress, in the Chinese People's Political Consultative Conference, or in the closing ceremony of the NPC in mid-March, there is an unusual degree of unanimity, calling on Taiwan to speedily begin political negotiations, directly following Jiang's "Eight Points" formula.[3]

Taking these documents at face value, the Beijing authorities have demonstrated a strongly consistent position. For twenty years, the only significant change has been the shift in designation of the parties to the negotiations, from the two parties to "the two sides" or "both sides." Moreover, "political negotiations" have become a policy theme, while "ending the state of hostilities" and "realizing peaceful unification" have become the irreplaceable topics on the negotiation agenda.

The attitudes and positions of Taipei

When we turn to examine Taipei's position, we find that negotiation has always been a sensitive, even taboo, word. Before the early 1990s, the policy of the "three nos" (no contact, no negotiations, and no compromise) was an unbreakable policy premise. On the other hand, there was strong support felt by most citizens for cross-Strait negotiations.[4] This gap between public opinion and policy can be traced to the government's belief that any entry into negotiations would generate suspicion among the people that the government harbored the intention to surrender or "sell out" Taiwan. Thus no concrete progress was made during this period.

There were minor exceptions to this rule. For example, in May 1986, in order to resolve the dispute over the China Airlines cargo plane that had been flown into Guangzhou, China Airlines had engaged in what was known as the "airline negotiations" with the Civil Aviation Authority of China. There was also the 1990 "Kinmen Agreement" to ease the repatriation of illegal immigrants to China. None the less, the Taipei authorities never accepted that these constituted a precedent or a model for cross-Strait negotiations. Most international observers regarded the four agreements signed at the first round of the "Koo–Wang talks" in 1993 as the example of formal cross-Strait negotiations. However, the Taipei authorities gave a different definition to the event, avoiding the label "political negotiations." The official line was presented in a pamphlet entitled "Our View of the Koo-Wang Talks" published by the Mainland Affairs Council (MAC):

> The subjects discussed in the Koo-Wang talks were planned by the government in accord with the goals of the short-term phase in the Guidelines for National Unification. This phase stresses promotion of mutual understanding through people-to-people exchanges and elimination of hostility through reciprocity, in hopes that the order and rules for such exchanges can be established between the two sides. This was the highest authorized guiding principle for the SEF (Straits Exchange Foundation) in the talks with its mainland counterpart.

When SEF and the ARATS (Association for Relations Across the Taiwan Straits) held preparatory talks for the Koo–Wang meeting held in Beijing during early April of 1993, the two sides agreed that the talks would be non-governmental, practical, economic, and functional in nature. In the preparatory meetings, delegates from both sides scrupulously abided by their commitment to not touch upon any political subject, thus enabling the smooth completion of the preparatory meeting and laying a favorable foundation for the formal talks held later on in Singapore.

During the formal talks, the SEF delegates carefully stayed within the parameters set by MAC, and limited the discussion to the subjects agreed upon in the preparatory meetings, thus avoiding all political topics. Though the communist side brought up the political issue of "direct transport, mail and trade" (the "three links"), the SEF delegates ignored this and clung firmly to the authorized range of issues previously agreed upon.

As is apparent from the nature of the four agreements signed in the talks, the "Agreement on Document Authentication," the "Agreement on Tracing of and Compensation for Lost Registered Mail," the "Agreement on the Establishment of Systematic Liaison and Communication Channels Between the SEF and ARATS," and the "Koo–Wang Talks Joint Agreement," as well as from the SEF–ARATS decisions to give high priority in their future liaison to the dozen other issues emerging from exchanges across the Taiwan Strait, the Koo–Wang talks were obviously in no way political.

Although Koo Chen-fu is a member of the Kuomintang Central Standing Committee, he took part in the talks in his capacity as the Chairman of the SEF rather than as a KMT representative. Over the past years, in view of the gradually maturing development of a multi-party system in the ROC, the ROC government has either expressed its opposition to or ignored the repeated demands by the Chinese communists for party-to-party negotiations. This stance of the ROC government will never change.

According to the Guidelines for National Unification, exchange visits between high-level officials from both sides can only take place in the medium-term phase, and negotiations for unification are not to be held until the long-term phase. As the current cross-Strait relations are still in the short-term phase of private sector exchanges, the government will not recklessly hold any political negotiations with the Chinese communists.[5]

In this policy statement, the emphasis is clear that the Koo–Wang talks were not to be considered "cross-Strait negotiation," but only "meetings" to establish the procedures and rules for cross-Strait exchanges. Needless to say there was no talk at all of "political negotiations." The talks were carefully restricted to the four areas outlined in the preparatory talks: non-governmental, practical, economic, and functional. Even more obviously, the talks were not of the nature of "party-to-party negotiations."

In fact, ever since the "Guidelines on National Unification" were published in February 1991, in all the documents issued by the Taipei authorities, very careful efforts have been made in crafting the texts. The word "negotiation" is never used carelessly, and "political negotiations" even less so. Below are several examples from major documents.

First, in the "Guidelines on National Unification" themselves, each time that the text might have read "negotiation," that word was replaced or omitted. The effort to avoid its use was apparent. Many examples may be drawn, such as: "the two sides of the Straits should end the state of hostility and, under the principle of one China, solve all disputes through peaceful means"; "both sides of the Straits should establish official communication channels on equal footing"; "direct postal, transport and commercial links should be allowed"; "both sides of the Straits should work together and assist each other in taking part in international organizations and activities"; "mutual visits by high-ranking officials on both sides should be promoted"; and "a consultative organization for unification should be established through which both sides …. jointly discuss the grand task of unification." At no point did the word "negotiation" appear to describe the process or manner of these "concrete results."

Second, in the July 1994 MAC document "Relations Across the Taiwan Straits" we read: "The ROC government believes that both the current people-to-people exchanges and future government-to-government talks should be conducted according to the principle of mutual respect for each other's people and government." Although this statement did mention governmental channels, the word "negotiations" is replaced by "talks."

The only time that the word "negotiations" has appeared is in the speech by President Lee Teng-hui at the closing ceremony of the May 1995 meeting of the National Unification Council, which became known as the "Six Points" speech. President Lee broke with all previous official statements and boldly inserted the word, saying: "After the PRC announces that it renounces the use of force against Taiwan, Penghu, Kinmen, and Matsu, at the earliest suitable opportunity preparatory consultations for bilateral negotiations to end the state of hostility should begin." Note that although the word appeared, what President Lee actually suggested is "preparatory consultations" which must precede any formal negotiations; he did not directly agree to such negotiations.[6]

However, one year later in his inaugural speech, President Lee used the phrase "dialogue and communication" to pursue "reduction of differences"; he also hoped that "exchange of views" with the top leadership of the PRC could create a new turning point in national unification. The absence of any reference to "negotiations" is yet further evidence of the fact that all in Taipei had decided to discard the use of that word to describe communication with PRC officialdom.[7] In its place are the more flexible and vague usages "dialogue and communications," "exchange of views," or "constructive dialogue" to compete against the PRC's attempt to push "cross-Strait political negotiations" onto the agenda.

After the 1998 Koo–Wang meeting, "political dialogue" is taking the place of "political negotiations"

In October 1998, the Chairman of the SEF, Koo Chen-fu, and his mainland counterpart, ARATS Chairman Wang Daohan, meeting in Shanghai, resumed the cross-Strait contact that had been broken off for nearly twenty months. Although Koo's trip to the mainland was not considered to be a formal conference, but was labeled as a "visit" or "meeting" only, before he left Shanghai for Beijing, the SEF and ARATS, in dramatic fashion, did reach four points of consensus. From the press reports of the event, these included the following: strengthening cross-Strait dialogue; strengthening exchanges between the two organizations; more actively addressing the issue of personal security for those traveling between the two sides of the Strait; and issuing an invitation to Wang to visit Taiwan, which he promised he would do at the appropriate time.[8]

However, before this consensus was reached, the initial Shanghai meeting manifested a strong divergence of views, especially in the old issue of "negotiations." From ARATS, Wang re-emphasized the mainland side's hope that it could enter into political negotiations with the Taiwan side and its willingness to strengthen the contacts between ARATS and SEF. Wang further asserted that, in order to resolve the state of hostilities, realizing the "three links" would be the best starting point, and that discussions should be commenced, under the "one China" principle, on Taiwan's political status. For the SEF, Koo expressed that the most urgent task was to resume the institutionalized consultations, based on the consensus reached in Singapore, to address the less controversial issues that directly affect the people. Koo suggested that, in this process of practical consultations, political obstacles could be reduced, creating a more favorable environment for future cross-Strait talks.[9]

Of course the two organizations could not possibly have reached a consensus on this issue whether to proceed with practical discussions or political negotiations. Therefore, most predicted that the result of the meeting would be merely the restatement by both sides of their respective positions. The four points of consensus that in fact emerged came as something of a surprise, especially the first one, to strengthen mutual dialogue.

However, the "dialogue" that was mentioned was interpreted differently by both sides. In a press conference the day after the meeting, Tang Shubei rushed out one interpretation: "The political negotiations between the two sides have just commenced on the eighth floor." In Taipei, on the other hand, the dialogue was defined as "constructive dialogue." After Koo's meeting with General Secretary Jiang, he mentioned that he perceived the importance of constructive dialogue between the two sides, but he reserved comment on whether this "constructive dialogue" was equivalent to "political negotiations." He said that the two organizations had begun a dialogue, but that it was not possible to categorize it; in other words, "dialogue" could not be categorized as either political or functional. Then, using the example of fishing disputes, he explained that political issues would necessarily be touched upon, but that they could not be the only focus, leaving out the issues concerning people's rights to one side. Further, Koo warned: "If the dialogue is categorized, it will easily create unease or even a new conflict."[10]

Although the two sides continued to disagree on the name and definition of this "dialogue," the official organizations on both sides nevertheless all expressed support for its establishment. The Chairman of MAC, Chang King-yuh, upon receiving Koo's delegation back to Taipei, stated that the delegation's opening of this new constructive dialogue and the four points of consensus reached were achievements deserving a high level of support. A *United Daily News* opinion poll at the same time revealed that 69 percent of the people in Taiwan approved of the two sides' continuing the political dialogue begun by Koo.[11] In Beijing, the State Council's Taiwan Affairs Office Director Chen Yunlin on October 17, at the welcome dinner for Koo, stated that the four points of consensus reached in Shanghai, especially the fact that the two organizations had begun a multi-faceted political and economic dialogue, were "commended" by the Taiwan Affairs Group.[12]

International public opinion was similarly positive. For example, the *Washington Post*, in an editorial entitled "Return to Talks" on October 15, expressed the belief that the resumption of cross-Strait dialogue was extremely vital to the prosperity and stability of the whole Asian region. In Japan, the *Mainichi Shimbun* editorial on October 18 stated that, if the new dialogue could provide an effective channel for exchanging views, help increase mutual confidence, and ease the atmosphere across the Taiwan Strait, then Japan, as a neighbor, would warmly welcome this development. On October 19, the *New York Times*, in its report on the conclusion of Koo's visit, predicted that cross-Strait dialogue would continue, in order to avoid a ruinous conflict that no one hopes will take place.[13]

Of course, the US government maintained a similar attitude. In its evaluation of the Koo–Wang talks, the State Department stated: "We believe that mutual dialogue, contacts, and exchanges will provide an important channel for solving the differences between Taiwan and the PRC."[14] Despite the conventional wisdom as to the success of the "cross-Strait dialogue" established at the Koo–Wang talks, in fact deeper thought and analysis are needed as to the respective positions of Taipei and Beijing. There are two points that most easily raise questions among outside observers.

First, since the PRC has always insisted on the necessity of political negotiations, why did it at this point strongly push for "cross-Strait political dialogue"? In accepting this lower level and slower "dialogue," what is Beijing's strategic consideration?

The basic difficulty in answering this question is that, with the inability to collect information directly from the official authorities in Beijing, one must rely on the judgments of outside, academic sources. Only time will tell if these judgments are accurate.

In fact, Beijing has not completely abandoned its hope to establish political dialogue. On the eve of Koo's visit, the PRC Foreign Ministry spokesman Tang Guoqiang stated that the PRC hoped that his visit would improve cross-Strait relations and help promote the speedy opening of political negotiations. Tang further hoped that the visit would be able to resolve the procedural obstacles to political discussions.[15]

However, the PRC is perfectly clear that Taipei, at least in the short term, cannot accept Beijing's offer to come to the negotiating table, especially to discuss political issues. Thus, the strategy is to gradually lower Taipei's fear level and ease it to the table, which will require some time. On the other hand, there is the worry that the longer time passes, the less interested Taipei will be in any kind of negotiations. Therefore Beijing needed to come up with a policy that would keep Taipei from moving any farther away from the topic of negotiations but without unnecessarily increasing the pressure on Taipei. This is the apparent motive behind the formulation of "political dialogue."

In addition, concerning the international society, especially the United States, both sides hope to be seen to play a constructive role in establishing stability across the Strait. Therefore, creating any kind of channel, whether it is Beijing's "political dialogue" or Taipei's "constructive dialogue," as long as the result is not overly restrictive and enables communication on a certain number of divergent political issues, will come closer to the wish of both sides. If this kind of channel can be established, and if it is seen by the international community as equivalent to a kind of stability in the Strait, then in order for neither Beijing nor Taipei to be seen as a "troublemaker," the "dialogue will be more likely to have some success." In fact, the White House, just after the conclusion of the Shanghai meeting, issued a statement which contained language reflecting the high level of US attention and support to "political dialogue":

> Since the cross-Strait dialogue was broken off in 1995, Washington has urged the two sides to return to 'constructive dialogue.' Therefore, Koo Chen-fu's trip to the mainland and his meetings with the Beijing leadership and with Wang Daohan, are welcomed by the United States.

If we examine this statement from another angle, it seems that the two sides are willing to demonstrate that they have chosen the steps and decisions hoped for by the United States.[16]

However, what has made Beijing more eager to create a consensus around the idea of "political dialogue" has been the perception that it will be the prelude to a stage of "procedural consultations" leading to the true goal of "political negotiations." Obviously, any negotiations must be preceded by some such procedural or preparatory consultations; otherwise, at least for Beijing, such thorny preliminary questions as the "one China" principle or the political definition of the two sides might be muddled or even abandoned, to the possible detriment of the final conclusion of the negotiations. Therefore, to place political issues at the top of the agenda, including the inevitable preliminary procedural consultations, is Beijing's primary motivation in pushing for a strengthening of "political dialogue." Once there is dialogue, it will be impossible to avoid all topics with political content. Each time there is an exchange of views on a particular topic, it will be easier to agree to make it an "item for negotiation." For the PRC, such topics will certainly take on a political character, and for each topic that is agreed upon, procedural consultations will be the inevitable next step.

Based on this kind of strategic logic, Taiwan Affairs Office Director Chen has said:

> We hope that the two sides will continue [the dialogue] in earnest, to build agreement, to enlarge the consensus, to bring about procedural talks for cross-Strait political negotiations at an early date, and to create the conditions for resumption of economic and functional talks.

Xin Qi, researcher at the Beijing Peace and Development Center, expressed this idea even more clearly, stating that whether "constructive dialogue" or "political dialogue," this will be the prelude to discussions on political issues, a necessary step in the process of political negotiation.[17]

Second, although Taipei is not willing at present to begin political negotiations with Beijing, and does not fully accept Beijing's label and definition of "political dialogue," it has accepted the creation of a mechanism for "cross-Strait dialogue." It has simply changed its name to "constructive dialogue." What is the thinking behind this move?

The aforementioned need for both sides to take the "concern" of the United

States into account and to agree to engage in dialogue can also be used to partially explain Taipei's position. However, Taipei's need to pay attention to the views of the international community is greater than Beijing's, for the following three reasons:

1   In the cross-Strait relationship, Taipei is always the more reluctant to enter into negotiations, which has caused Taipei to be seen as a "troublemaker" creating tension across the Strait. A "dialogue" that is neither pressured nor binding, but that can dispel this mistaken impression is an opportunity that should not be missed.
2   "Dialogue" by its nature fits with the post-Cold War mainstream value preference for negotiations over opposition and communication over conflict.
3   "Dialogue" presents an opportunity for Taipei to make its views heard on equal footing, instead of allowing Beijing to continue to control the interpretation of events.

Moreover, for Taipei to accept the idea of dialogue but attach the label "constructive dialogue" to the process should be seen to stem from the following causes:

1   Although Taipei cannot in the short term accept political negotiations, it is extremely difficult for it to again reject the idea of "dialogue." Even more, whether or not Taipei agrees, the very existence of such high-level meetings, including both the Shanghai and Singapore talks, and no matter what types of topics Koo and Wang discuss, to insist that their exchanges do not even constitute "dialogue" strains logic. How can Taipei continue to paddle against this current?
2   The most politically sensitive issues are usually raised when each side is shouting at each other from a distance, and this is what causes unnecessary deterioration in the cross-Strait atmosphere. If there is an opportunity to meet and speak frankly, to give the other side a deeper impression of one's position, why shouldn't Taipei take it? For example, the SEF has been brave in raising topics such as the reality of the separate government of the two sides and the historical status of Taiwan. Shi Hwei-yow even put a turn on Koo Chen-fu's language, saying: "If we are not speaking directly, not speaking frankly, problems cannot be resolved."[18]
3   Although it is true that "dialogue" might risk touching on political issues, it also carries the prospect of resumption of functional consultations. Koo himself stated that he made his trip, and had his meetings with the top leaders of the PRC, in the hope that through honest communication and a free exchange of views, understanding could be promoted and unnecessary misunderstandings eliminated, and that this improvement in the working environment of the two organizations would enable them to renew the institutionalized consultations that had been broken off for more than three years.[19]

4 While in China, Koo strengthened Taiwan's trump card in cross-Strait relations, speaking about issues of democracy and advocating enlightened moves toward democracy in the mainland. This kind of goal can only be achieved through the opportunities provided by "dialogue." The signs of this possibility are evident in the amount of space Koo dedicated in his October 18 press conference to detailing how he exchanged views on democratization with the PRC leadership.

5 Using the label "constructive dialogue" reduces to a certain extent the political appearance of the process. It therefore reduces the controversy between unification and independence in the domestic political realm, enabling the dialogue to achieve broader support and approval from both ruling and opposition parties.

Therefore, since Koo's visit to the mainland in October 1998, one conclusion is visible: the dialogue that has been established is in fact a replacement for political negotiation. One needs only add a single qualification, that Beijing regards the dialogue as an expedient means to reach the final goal, which remains political negotiation.

The offensive and defensive strategies of the two sides regarding political negotiations

The PRC's strategy of "using threats to force talks"

After the Koo–Wang meeting, the beginning of "political dialogue" did not bring about the end of the PRC's call for and suggestions of political negotiations. In essence, the PRC's Taiwan policy has two facets. First, to strengthen political and economic dialogue, in order to build consensus on topics that could then be a basis for negotiations. Second, to use the strategy of "using threats to force talks" to achieve a commencement of negotiations on major political issues in the near term. In this usage, "threats" refer to the threatening language used to urge Taiwan to respond to the mainland's call to enter negotiations in an expeditious manner.

In the middle of February 1998, the Cross-Strait Relations Research Center of ARATS held a large-scale academic conference, including more than fifty scholars from both sides of the Strait. Among them was Jiang Dianming, the former head of the Institute of Taiwan Studies at the Chinese Academy of Social Sciences and the then head of the National Association of Taiwan Studies. Jiang delivered a paper entitled "The Taiwan Straits Situation Cannot be Stabilized." His view was indicative, representing the collective judgment of a large number of mainland Taiwan scholars. In fact, although Jiang's language was novel, the point of view was not especially advanced. Years earlier, the "patience" of China, as well as Taiwan's perceived willingness to cooperate with the process of unification, were identified as the keys to resolving the Taiwan question in a peaceful manner. Jiang Zemin, in his "Eight Points" address, stated: "An early completion to the unification of the motherland is the collective wish of all the peoples of China; an indefinite delay of unification is something that no patriotic citizen wishes to see."[20]

However, the first time that the PRC formally expressed its urgency on this question was probably in remarks made by Vice-Premier Qian Qichen on January 28, 1999, on the occasion of the fourth anniversary of the "Eight Points" address and the twentieth anniversary of the release of the " Taiwan Compatriots." Qian announced that, after the return of Hong Kong and Macao, "the Taiwan question cannot continue to be delayed indefinitely." Although the strongest of Qian's wording was omitted from the Xinhua reporting, it was recorded by China Central Television.[21]

While observers were still processing this statement, Jiang commented that after the return of Hong Kong, at the turn of the century, the PRC's desire for unification was undoubtedly "urgent." He continued, saying that the unification of China "cannot be something far off in the future." Because these remarks were made to the Hong Kong delegates to the NPC, they are likely to be politically indicative.[22]

Of course, in addition to expressing the urgency of unification, the meaning behind these statements might include the intent of Beijing to set down a "timetable" for resolving the Taiwan question. However, the most direct and concrete answer to this policy shift question is that "cross-Strait political negotiations" are already the first-priority method of resolving the issue for the Beijing authorities. Because it is expedient to proceed to political dialogue, this must be to lay the foundation for such negotiations. As soon as such negotiations have entered the substantive phase, the process of unification will have begun. Therefore, the PRC will naturally spare no effort to promote and engage in the necessary arrangements for "political negotiations."

The most representative example is Premier Zhu Rongji's call for quick progress on political negotiations, made two times in two months at major public events. The first time was on January 15, 1999 at the Party Central Committee and the State Council joint New Year's gathering; the second was during Zhu's work report to the second session of the 9th NPC. According to the analysis of the *United Daily News*, the January event marked the first time that Zhu had called for political negotiations since taking office as premier.[23] Furthermore, the unchoreographed echoing calls expressed by the NPC and the Chinese People's Political Consultative Conference add additional emphasis to the PRC's determination that political negotiations must be brought out onto the cross-Strait stage.

The PRC's strategy of "using external power to solve internal conflicts"

The second strategy that Beijing is using to force Taipei to the negotiation table is "using external power to solve internal conflicts." This consists of trying to make the international community, particularly the United States, view Taipei, with its long-term unwillingness to enter into negotiations, as the uncooperative side, and to emphasize that Taipei's refusal of Beijing's proposals is the main source of cross-Strait tensions.

Not long ago, on April 14, 1997, the *New York Times*, in an editorial entitled "The Taiwan Factor," insinuated that the tensions created by a series of Taiwan's diplomatic actions had caused cross-Strait conflict, such as the dangerous 1996 missile crisis, and generated serious concern in the United States. Thus, the editorial suggested, "encouraging the PRC and Taiwan to avoid conflict and in the hopes of that a more attractive solution may appear, is in the US interest."[24] This type of statement undoubtedly strengthened the US perception that Taiwan is the "troublemaker" and also prompted the Beijing authorities to consider that the road to Taipei leads through Washington. Only cross-Strait negotiations, especially those aimed at ending the state of hostilities, can bring definitive calm to the Taiwan Strait situation, and a stable Strait is squarely in the interest of the United States in the Pacific region. Therefore, Beijing decided that, to promote negotiations to end the state of hostility, not only to shout at Taipei, but also to notify the United States of its hope that US interest in a stable Pacific region could be turned to pressure Taipei to get Taipei to the negotiating table.

Of course, from the PRC's point of view, Taiwan is a purely domestic issue, and it is not only unnecessary but unacceptable for foreign powers to intervene; thus, in any public remarks, the Beijing authorities will never openly refer to the idea of "using the outside to force the inside." Even scholars on Taiwan from the mainland will not express their views on this strategy; they need to consider not only the suitableness of the strategy itself, but also strong feelings of national pride on the mainland that cannot allow foreigners to interfere in China's domestic affairs.

None the less, when we closely observe the subtle interaction between Beijing and Washington, we can perceive the existence of such a strategy. For example, the great stress placed by the United States on "maintaining peace and stability in the Taiwan Strait," based on its interests in the Pacific region, creates the need to engage in more communication and cooperation with the PRC. From another point of view, the PRC understands that if it can promote and guarantee such stability, it can immediately receive the support and backing of the United States. Therefore, when both governments are loudly proclaiming their determination to achieve "peace and stability in the Taiwan Strait," they are actually close to achieving another, hidden objective.

Purely from Beijing's point of view, it paid most attention to the statement made by then Secretary of State Warren Christopher on May 17, 1996, in which he commented on the "one China" policy: "America's 'one China' policy is predicated on the PRC's pursuit of a peaceful resolution of issues between Taipei and Beijing." This statement was quoted by the Shanghainese scholar Chen Qimao, always identified as part of Jiang Zemin's brains trust, in his article in *Asian Survey*, "The Taiwan Crisis." Chen went on to say that, although Beijing did not agree with Christopher on all of his points, his reaffirmation of the 'one China' policy as the basis of a resolution of the cross-Strait question was welcomed.[25] By welcoming US endorsement of the "one China" policy, the PRC thus agrees to be willing to settle the problem by peaceful means. However, when Beijing begins to seek political negotiations as the method of sitting down with Taipei, and Taipei continues to reject or refuse these overtures, Beijing makes a point of drawing US attention to this situation. The fact that this will inevitable result in a form of US "pressure" on Taipei goes without saying. As National Chengchi University Professor of Diplomacy David Chou recently wrote, the United States understands that "a stable situation in the Taiwan Strait is the most important condition for a harmonious relationship between the US and the PRC; therefore it seeks to promote a resumption of cross-Strait dialogue, to settle differences in a peaceful manner." Chou adds that, although Washington has indicated that it will not put pressure on either side, US officials have been urging dialogue: former high-ranking officials such as former Defense Secretary Perry travel to both sides of the Strait bearing US information and expectations, creating both concrete and intangible pressures on both sides.[26]

This is the explanation of the PRC's strategy of "using the outside to press the inside." It does not require announcing that the United States must make an unruly Taipei fall into line; it only requires catering to the US demand for a peaceful resolution of the Taiwan crisis to generate strong encouragement for cross-Strait political dialogue or negotiations. If Taipei at any turn slackens the pace, it will incur US "concern." For Beijing, compared to any method of directly applying pressure on Taipei, this is certainly much easier.

Taipei's strategy of "using the soft against the hard"

For Taipei, facing the closing in of Beijing's double strategies, "using threats to force talks" and "using external power to solve internal conflicts," the weight of the pressure can be readily understood. Taipei has not simply continued to respond to Beijing's proposal for negotiations with refusal or avoidance, but in its response has adopted the following more creative and flexible strategic steps:

1   Facing Beijing's call for negotiations, Taipei responds that one should "restart the process where it was left off," with the focus fixed at the level of discussions on functional issues. This strategy demonstrates that Taipei is not simply refusing any kind of negotiations, but merely disagreeing with Beijing over their content.

2   Facing the demand for political and economic negotiations, Taipei uses the term "constructive dialogue" to respond. For Taipei, as soon as political and economic dialogue is established, it will be easy to fall into an agenda-setting process dominated by Beijing. However, "constructive dialogue" can cover a broad spectrum, including economic and political topics, and it can also include what Taipei generally regards as priorities, the issues of the rights and interests of people of both sides of the Straits. Especially, if the latter topics can be set, cross-Strait discussions can proceed according to the format of the 1993 Singapore Koo–Wang talks, instead of creating from

scratch a new type of official negotiating channel to prepare the ground-work for political negotiations.

3   If political negotiations become inevitable, Taipei is in fact willing to take part. Some time ago, on August 8 and 15, 1997, then MAC Vice-Chairman Kao Koong-lian twice spelled out a way for the two sides to begin political negotiations at the current stage. He even suggested that "official-to-official" negotiations could begin. Kao's remarks were later supported by his successor Chang King-yuh. Chang said that Taipei viewed with favor Beijing's sending delegates to discuss the advance work for political negotia-tions.[27] However, the actual entry into formal political negotiations would not be so smooth, because MAC stated clearly that, if only Beijing did not place any initial conditions, and did preset its position, the two sides of the Strait could resume discussions at any time.[28] This formula denies Beijing's oft-repeated insistence that any talks must proceed "under the premise of the 'one China' principle." One should also add the additional precondition that negotiations cannot be conducted without the support of Taiwanese public opinion. As Koo Chen-fu has stated: "If we do not have the support of public opinion, even if we resume negotiations, there can be no substan-tive result."[29]According to these positions, it seems that a long period of time must elapse before the two sides can begin the substantive phase of negotiations; however, can outside observers really blame Taipei for contin-uing to refuse the offer of cross-Strait negotiations?

Therefore, from the steps that Taipei is taking to respond, we can see a full use of the traditional Chinese tactic of using the "soft" (deflection and evasion) to respond to the "hard"; we may see mutual encounter, but we are unlikely to see mutual common ground. This is why there have been no major breakthroughs in cross-Strait relations since they were frozen in 1997.

The possibility of cross-strait political negotiations

There are two levels at which one needs to analyze the possibility of cross-Strait political negotiations.

The pessimistic short-term sticking point

First, in the short term, at least until the year 2000, there will be no political negotiations of any sort. The reasons for this pessimistic outlook include the following:

1   *The time factor.* During the visit of the ARATS Deputy Secretary-General Li Yafei to Taipei at the end of March 1999, he agreed with the SEF that the visit of Wang Daohan would not take place before autumn of that year. From this scheduling agreement, it is apparent that there is essentially no chance of any political negotiations in that year. On the one hand, in order

to put any agenda on the table, a consensus will have to be reached by Koo and Wang at their Taipei political dialogue on any set of issues to be included. After that, there must be the so-called procedural or preparatory consultations to settle the relevant procedural issues, which might well take some time. On the other hand, to assume that Koo and Wang would in fact be able to reach such a consensus right away is probably overly optimistic. Perhaps only by the third or fourth dialogue meeting might we expect to see some conclusion. There is obviously not enough time to accomplish this before the year 2000. Koo, speaking in an interview on February 22, 1999, at one point replied that it was his feeling that a difficult and rather long road needed to be traveled before there would be any tangible results from negotiations. He said:

> Our side has never avoided political negotiations, if only the other side would stop demonstrating their military power, and stop trying to squeeze our diplomatic space, and recognize the reality that the two sides of the Strait are governed by separate and equal entities, we can return to the institutionalized discussions and, if both sides agree, any subject may be discussed.[30]

This wording almost exactly duplicated that of the Guidelines for National Unification; therefore, it is clear that if Taipei has continued to maintain this firm position, which it has held from 1991 without any breakthrough in the area of cross-Strait political negotiations, then this situation may well continue into the next century.

2   *Differing views as to the topics.* For Beijing, the possible topics for negotiations mentioned most frequently are ending the state of hostilities and direct air and shipping links. Vice-Premier Qian Qichen, at the end of January 1999, at the major gathering to celebrate the fourth anniversary of the announcement of Jiang's "Eight Points," emphasized his hope that negotiations with Taiwan could swiftly bring about the "three links," as well as, under the principle of "one China," the formal end of the state of hostilities.[31] This statement completely reflects the PRC leadership's views. Of course, Qian also mentioned economic, agricultural, and technological cooperation, etc., but these were clearly lesser priorities. In contrast, Taipei's position is that, if there are to be negotiations, they should be separated into "low political" and "high political" levels, and Taipei is not willing at the present stage to discuss the latter, which might involve questions of "sovereignty." Su Chi, having just taken office as MAC Chairman, has in numerous interviews since the beginning of the year spent considerable time explaining the choice of "negotiating topics." From these interviews, Su is obviously more willing to discuss agricultural cooperation, fishing disputes, protection of Taiwanese investment in the mainland, and other such "soft" issues. On the other hand, on "harder" diplomatic issues that involve "sovereignty," "one China," or "Taiwan is a part of China," his attitude and tone become stiffer, indicating that these are not the topics that the Taipei authorities are most pleased to see. In another interview, Su stated his belief that, in the

process of planning the topics for negotiations, one must work from the simple to the complex, from the easy to the difficult, in order to more easily reach consensus. If one insists on starting from the most difficult political issues, from the experience of interaction between the SEF and ARATS, it will probably not be possible to reach any conclusion, but only to hurt each side's feelings, creating a deep chasm between the two sides and in no way helping to solve any problems. Koo Chen-fu has also said that, if the two sides leapfrog up to the top-level political issues, this will only have negative results.[32] From the preceding description of the topics chosen by Beijing and Taipei, it is obvious that the common points are few and the differences many, and it is unlikely that any consensus can be reached in the short term.

3   *Political differences.* This factor is probably the most critical reason why it will not be possible to begin political negotiations in a timely and effective manner. For example, the PRC has repeatedly insisted that any issue can be discussed, as long as the premise of the "one China" principle is adhered to by both sides. However, the problem is precisely the difference of understanding of that premise itself; thus, Taipei will hesitate as to whether to agree to establish the "one China" principle in the cross-Strait political negotiations. If the two sides cannot reach agreement to establish the "one China" principle, how will it be possible to begin what the PRC calls the second stage, where "any problem can be discussed?" Even more important, without the "one China" principle as a premise, once the two sides get involved in political negotiations, what will the "political status" of each side be? In this area Beijing will obviously have reservations, but if there is that premise, the question of Taipei's political status in any cross-Strait negotiations will always be Taipei's insoluble nightmare. Therefore, before any political negotiations, if the issues around the "one China" principle and the equal political status of both sides are not thoroughly resolved, then these kinds of talks can never take place. Although the Executive Vice-President of ARATS, Tang Shubei, has said that the basic separation between the two sides is a political separation that should be gradually resolved by political negotiation, for Taipei political negotiations can only be held after this issue is resolved or shelved. Thus Taipei has repeated the suggestion either that each side define "one China" for itself or that the sovereignty issue be put to one side, but this idea was not accepted by Beijing. Thus, to address the political separation, Taipei played the card "if there are political negotiations, there must be mutual agreement on the topics," that is to say, if Taipei will not agree on the political separation or the high-level political topics, there will not be any consensus for cross-Strait political negotiations. As Vice-President Lien Chan has said: "In the process of cross-Strait reciprocity, all of a sudden we should talk about questions such as sovereignty, at the present time this has no meaning." This sentence in reality already indicates the bottom line of Taipei's refusal to discuss the issue of political separation.[33]

Of course, at this stage, if Taipei's National Assembly passes the constitutional amendment to allow referenda, or the Ministry of Defense opts to participate in the Theater Missile Defense (TMD) system, or if there are other major changes to the overall environment affecting the development of cross-Strait relations, the already low probability of cross-Strait political negotiations will disappear completely. A new Taiwan Strait crisis may well erupt. However, because the possibility of any of these changes occurring is unclear, we will not discuss them further at this point.

An evaluation of the long-term prospects

Second, in the long term, at least in the next five years, the possibility that the authorities of the two sides will reach a consensus on certain topics and take them to the negotiating table cannot be ruled out. The reasons for this optimistic outlook should include the following several developments:

1   The timing of the second Koo–Wang meeting was settled surprisingly smoothly. Starting from March 19, 1999, the ARATS Deputy Secretary-General Li Yafei visited Taipei for a hurried three-day visit to discuss with the SEF the dates for Wang Daohan's visit to Taiwan. Before these discussions, Taipei and Beijing had put forward differing proposals. Taipei hoped that Wang could come at or near April 29, because that would be the sixth anniversary of their first meeting in Singapore and thus have special significance. However, Beijing replied that Wang's schedule was full until May and requested a later date. Originally, the assumption was that the outlook for setting the date of the meeting was not good, and that the meeting might be postponed indefinitely; however, Li and SEF Deputy Secretary-General Jan Jyh-horng, in their first consultation, were able to agree in principle on Wang's itinerary for an autumn visit and other detailed matters, and agreed to stage further consultations on the question of the exact date.[34] Observers were impressed that the issue of the date was smoothly decided upon and that the visit will take place; furthermore, although both sides had differing considerations regarding the date, there was a strong consensus that the visit should proceed successfully. Therefore, if in the future similar situations arise, this case can provide a precedent for the two sides' paying attention to the substantive goal and abandoning some differences on lesser issues.

2   Regarding the TMD system, although the possibility of Taiwan's being included has incited a negative reaction from Beijing, former US Defense Secretary Perry on March 8, 1999, coming to Taipei after his visit to Beijing, revealed that he had discussed this matter with relevant PRC officials, among whom Wang Daohan expressed the idea that the two sides of the Strait could take arms reduction measures. Perry expressed his own view that if the PRC could reduce its military deployment, much of the mutual apprehension could be reduced. When Perry brought this issue before

President Lee, the latter replied clearly that, although the reasons for Taiwan's participation in the TMD systemare many, essentially, if the PRC would not treat Taiwan as an enemy, and would abandon most of its missile deployment along the coast and its hegemonic attitude, then Taiwan would have no need to set up the TMD system.[35] This way of using a reliable and friendly American as a channel to mutually explain friendly information and acquire reliable information naturally will help both sides to understand the situation accurately. Moreover, the observations of both Wang and Lee could easily form the basis for cross-Strait discussions leading toward ending the state of hostilities. In fact, a peaceful and stable environment across the Strait should be a point of consensus among Taipei and Beijing. If the two sides can have more dialogue at high levels on such topics, there will be an opportunity to increase the space for cross-Strait discussions.

Of course, the feasibility of both sides genuinely sitting down at the negotiating table to discuss political-related issues will rest on the following types of circumstance:

1   The Beijing authorities need to find an adjustment regarding certain "premises" or "conditions." For example, although it is not easy for Beijing to accept shelving the sovereignty argument, if it is necessary for Taipei to accommodate the "one China" principle, could Beijing not change "the present China" to "the united China that both sides are seeking?" If this kind of locution could be established, the political status of the two sides could be left expediently vague, but the necessary reciprocity and respect of both sides must remain clear.
2   The Taipei authorities must enunciate Taiwan's future direction more clearly. That is, to seek a unified China is to continue to follow the format of the Guidelines on National Unification, and not to seek Taiwan independence or two Chinas is an unchanging position. Regarding any factor that may influence the development of substantive cross-Strait relations, such as adding referenda into the constitution or joining the TMD system, Taipei must exercise self-restraint or handle the matter with prudence.
3   Finally, although it is not appropriate for the United States to be involved in cross-Strait affairs, it might need to play a more active role promoting cross-Strait dialogue and negotiations. The experience of history tells us that it is because of the use of the US role that the KMT and CCP have had several examples of negotiations. However, once the two sides are at the negotiating table, it would be best if the United States were not present, because over-involvement would make it impossible for the two sides to directly confront the reality of their situation.

The US Assistant Secretary of State for East Asian Affairs, Stanley Roth, speaking in a conference co-sponsored by the American Institute in Taiwan and the semi-official Wilson Center on March 24, 1999 in Washington, for the first time publicly stated that the cross-Strait dialogue to seek a peaceful resolution of differences may require a lengthy process. He continued that, in order to maintain the forward momentum, some kind of "interim agreement" ought perhaps to be considered. This "interim agreement," according to the Dean of George Washington University School of International Affairs, Harry Harding, might involve reaching a "temporary agreement" in which Taiwan renounced a unilateral declaration of independence and the PRC announced it will not use force against Taiwan; the United States could act as the guarantor of such an agreement.[36] If this idea can be confirmed as official US policy, then it will certainly have a positive impact on cross-Strait political negotiations.

Even if the final development of these circumstances is as outlined here, all we can say for sure is that the probability of cross-Strait political negotiations will increase. It does not mean that such negotiations will progress smoothly or that they will achieve a satisfactory result.

Notes

1 For the content of the 1991 "June 7 Statement," see Kuo Li-min, *The PRC's Taiwan Policy: Collected Materials*, vol. 2 (Taipei: Yungle, 1992), pp. 1204–6. For the content of the "Political Report of Jiang Zemin to the Fourteenth Party Congress," see *Mainland Work Reference Materials* (Taipei: Mainland Affairs Council, 1993), p. 268. Other important documents are collected in Chong-hai Shaw (ed.), *Cross-Strait Relations: The Differing Views on Cross-Strait Consensus*, 2nd ed. (Taipei: Wunan, 1998).

2 Regarding the 1998 and 1999 New Year's Address by Jiang Zemin, see *Mainland Work Reference Materials* (Taipei: Mainland Affairs Council, 1998), p. 281, and *United Daily News*, 1 January 1999, p. 1.

3 Regarding Zhu Rongji's work report, and the report to the closing ceremony of the Political Consultative Meeting and NPC, see *United Daily News*, 6 and 12 March 1999, p. 13 of each issue.

4 From October 1990 to February 1992, the MAC and other agencies carried out opinion surveys of Taiwan residents on the idea of both "party-to-party" negotiations and "government-to-government" negotiations. In most of these polls, the public expressed confidence for the latter proposition, with at least 50 percent support. This result was reported in the pamphlet edited by then MAC Chairman Huang Kun-huei, entitled "Mainland Policy and Cross-Strait Relations" (Taipei: Mainland Affairs Council, 1993). Its Table 13 contains all of the poll results.

5 Mainland Affairs Council, "Our View of the Koo-Wang Talks" (Taipei: Mainland Affairs Council, 1993), pp. 6–7.

6 For the content of Lee's "Six Points," see Shaw (ed.), *Cross-Strait Relations*.

7 Kuomintang Party Headquarters Department of Cultural Affairs, "The Complete Text of the Inaugural Address of the Ninth President of the Republic of China," Taipei (1996).

8 "The Second Koo-Wang Meeting: Four Points of Consensus Reached," *China Times*, 16 October 1998, p. 2.

9 For the position of ARATS, see "Wang: Promoting Political Negotiation," *China Times*, 15 October 1998, p. 2. For the SEF position, see "Koo: Returning to Institutionalized Discussions, Eliminating Political Obstacles," *China Times*, 15 October 1998, p. 2.

10 "Koo Chen-fu's Press Conference: Constructive Dialogue Further Raises the Importance of Priorities," *United Daily News*, 19 October 1998, p. 5.

11 For Chang King-yuh's remarks, see "Koo's Ice-Breaking Visit: All Government Agencies Approve," *China Times*, 20 October 1998, p. 1. For the content of opinion polling, see *United Daily News*, 18 October 1998, p. 4.

12 "Chen Yunlin: Revealing the Direction of Jiang's Eight Points," *United Daily News*, 18 October 1998, p. 4.

13 For the content of the *Washington Post* editorial, see *China Times*, 16 October 1998, p. 14. For the content of the *Mainichi Shimbun* editorial, see *China Times*, 19 October 1998, p. 4. For the content of the *New York Times* report, see *China Times*, 20 October 1998, p. 3.

14 "US State Department Welcomes the Positive Cross-Strait Development," *United Daily News*, 20 October 1998, p. 2.

15 "Tang Guoqiang: Hope for Help Promoting Political Negotiations," *China Times*, 14 October 1998, p. 2.

16 "The Koo's Mainland Trip, the White House Formally Welcome the Koo-Wang Meeting," *United Daily News*, 18 October 1998, p. 4.

17 For Chen Yunlin's remarks, see note 12. For Xin Qi's, see "The Four Points of Consensus at the Koo-Wang Talks are Helpful to the Development of Cross-Strait Relations," *China Times*, 22 October 1998, p. 14.

18 "Shi Hwei-yow: The Separate Governance of the Two Sides of the Strait Cannot be Denied," *China Times*, 15 October 1998, p. 2.

19 For Koo Chen-fu's remarks, see note 9.

20 For the Content of Jiang's "Eight Points," see note 1. Jiang Dianming's remarks were made in a workshop chaired by the author.

21 "Qian Qichen: The Taiwan Question Cannot be Extended Indefinitely," *United Daily News*, 29 January 1999, p. 1.

22 "Jiang Zemin: The Unification of Taiwan is an Urgent Desire," *China Times*, 8 March 1999, p. 1.

23 See "Zhu Rongji Calls for Early Cross-Strait Political Negotiations," *United Daily News*, 16 January 1999, p. 1, and "Zhu Rongji Calls on Taiwan to Begin Political Negotiations Soon," *China Times*, 6 March 1999, p. 14.

24 The Chinese translation of the *New York Times* editorial "The Taiwan Factor" appeared in the *Central Daily News*, 15 April 1997, p. 2.

25 For Christopher's comments, and Chen Qimao's own views, see Chen Qimao, "The Taiwan Straits Crisis," *Asian Survey*, vol. 36, no. 11 (November 1996), p. 1064.

26 David Chou, "The Clinton Administration's Policy of Engagement and Cross-Strait Relations," Paper presented at the conference "Twenty Years of the Taiwan Relations Act: Washington, Taipei, and Beijing," sponsored by the Professors World Peace Academy of the ROC, 13 March 1999.

27 For Kao Koong-lian's earliest political statement, see *United Daily News*, 9 August 1997, p. 1. For his later addition, see "I am Willing to Enter into Official Negotiations with the PRC," *China Times*, 16 August 1997, p. 1. For Chang King-yuh's view, see "Chang King-yuh Welcomes the Beginning of Official Negotiations Across the Strait," *United Daily News*, 17 August 1997, p. 1.

28 "Chang King-yuh: To Improve Cross-Strait Relations, Beijing Should Open the Door for Coordination," *China Times*, 17 August 1997, p. 2.

29 "Koo Chen-fu: Observing the Principle of Sincerity, in Order to Break the Mold of Cross-Strait Relations, Beijing Should Open the Door for Coordination," *China Times*, 23 August 1997, p. 9.

30 "Koo Chen-fu Indicates that any Cross-Strait Topics Need Both Sides to Agree that 'No Topic Cannot be Discussed,'" *United Daily News*, 23 February 1999, p. 4.

31 "Qian Qichen: Wang Daohan Will Visit Taiwan This Year to Proceed with Political and Economic Dialogue," *China Times*, 29 January 1999, p. 2.

32 These two interviews by Su Chi appeared in the following articles: "Su Chi: Sovereignty, Diplomacy, and National Defense Can Never be Compromised," *China*

Times, 22 February 1999, p. 4, and "Su Chi: A China with Separated Governance is the True Description of the Current Cross-Strait Situation," *China Times*, 29 January 1999, p. 2. On Koo's view, see "Koo Chen-fu: Willing to Discuss any Topic with Wang," *United Daily News*, 5 February 1999, p. 13.

33 Tang Shubei's remarks can be found in "Tang Shubei: Cross-Strait Political Negotiations Cannot be Avoided," *China Times*, 10 February 1999, p. 14. For Taipei's view that "political negotiations require mutual agreement on topics," see note 29. For Lien Chan's view, see "Lien Chan: Mutual Visits Across the Strait Are Better than Each Side Shouting in a Vacuum," *United Daily News*, 23 January 1999, p. 4.

34 "SEF and ARATS Agree in Principle that Wang Daohan Will Visit Taiwan in September or October," *United Daily News*, 19 March 1999, p. 1.

35 Regarding Wang Daohan's and President Lee's suggestions, see "President Lee: If the PRC does not Deploy Missiles along the Coast, We do not Need TMD," *United Daily News*, 9 March 1999, p. 1.

36 Regarding Stanley Roth's and Harding's remarks, see "The US Officially Proposes a Cross-Strait 'Interim Agreement' for the First Time," *United Daily News*, 26 March 1999, p. 1.

Index

*For Product Safety Concerns and Information please contact
our EU representative GPSR@taylorandfrancis.com Taylor & Francis
Verlag GmbH, Kaufingerstraße 24, 80331 München, Germany*

T - #0100 - 270225 - C0 - 234/156/16 - PB - 9780415260268 - Gloss Lamination